Beyond Cold Blood

Beyond Cold Blood

The KBI from
Ma Barker to BTK

Larry Welch

University Press of Kansas

© 2012 by the University Press of Kansas

Published by the University Press of Kansas (Lawrence, Kansas 66045), which was organized by the Kansas Board of Regents and is operated and funded by Emporia State University, Fort Hays State University, Kansas State University, Pittsburg State University, the University of Kansas, and Wichita State University

Library of Congress Cataloging-in-Publication Data

Welch, Larry.
Beyond cold blood : the KBI from Ma Barker to BTK / Larry Welch.
   p. cm.
Includes bibliographical references and index.
ISBN 978-0-7006-1885-9 (cloth : alk. paper)
  1. Kansas Bureau of Investigation—History. 2. Law enforcement—Kansas—History.
3. Criminals—Kansas—History. I. Title.
HV8145.K2W45 2012
363.2509781—dc23
2012016528

British Library Cataloguing in Publication Data is available.

Printed in the United States of America

10 9 8 7 6 5 4 3 2 1

The paper used in this publication is recycled and contains 30 percent postconsumer waste. It is acid free and meets the minimum requirements of the American National Standard for Permanence of Paper for Printed Library Materials Z39.48-1992.

The wicked flee when no man pursueth,
but the righteous are bold as a lion.
—Proverbs 28:1

To all the lions and Shirley

Contents

Photographs follow page 181.

Preface

The Kansas Bureau of Investigation (KBI) is a collection of fewer than 300 professional men and women positioned across the state of Kansas to serve the criminal justice systems of both the state and nation. They are assigned to nationally accredited forensic laboratories in Topeka, Kansas City, Pittsburg, and Great Bend; field offices in Overland Park, Great Bend, Wichita, and Pittsburg; or the headquarters in Topeka. They are ordinary men and women who do extraordinary things in pursuit of criminal justice, as others before them have done since 1939.

I have always believed that leadership is best defined as the privilege of directing the actions of others, with the emphasis on privilege. No better example of such privilege exists than the directorship of the KBI. From July 18, 1994, when I was appointed the tenth director of the KBI by Kansas Attorney General Robert Stephan, until June 1, 2007, when I retired as the second-longest-serving KBI director, four attorneys general and almost thirteen years later, that great privilege was mine.

Collectively, my nine predecessors and I served fourteen attorneys general. The KBI continues to be a unit of the office of the Kansas attorney general, as it was in 1939, and the director continues to serve at the pleasure of the attorney general, as he did in 1939. Attorney General John Anderson's only instruction to Logan Sanford, when in 1957 he asked the agent to step up to director and move to Topeka was, "You take over. You run it. If I have any objections, I'll let you know." That simple admonition has characterized the relationship between the attorney general of Kansas and the director of the KBI from 1939 to the present day. There has never been a signed contract between the two offices, and there has never been any guarantee of longevity for the director. There has always been a simple oath of office, a handshake, and subsequent confirmation by the Kansas senate.

Often understaffed, underfunded, undersized, and overassigned, the significant contributions of the KBI to the criminal justice system, state, and nation have always been disproportionate to the size of the agency. That was true in 1939 when the entire staff consisted of one director, nine special agents, and one secretary. It remains equally true today with the larger, but still insufficient, staff.

Despite a proud, scandal-free record of exceptional achievement in criminal justice and dedicated service to Kansas prosecutors, law enforcement, and crime victims and their families, no one has attempted to write a history of the KBI for public consumption. The closest effort was an internally prepared publication commemorating the agency's first fifty years, 1939–1989, printed in 1990 and distributed almost exclusively within the KBI family. *In Cold Blood*, Truman Capote's best seller, tells the story of one chapter in the KBI's history, an iconic chapter but nonetheless only one. The same can be said of KBI involvement in the infamous BTK case. Much has been written about the investigation to identify, apprehend, and prosecute Dennis Rader for the serial murders of ten citizens of Wichita from January 1974 to January 1991, and the KBI's proud participation in the Wichita Police Department's BTK Task Force, March 2004 to August 2005. Again, an essential chapter in KBI history, but merely one chapter in that story. Indeed, not a single KBI director preceding me wrote anything resembling a public memoir about his tenure. This book, then, is intended as an effort to reveal more of the history of a deserving agency.

The KBI has never been more important to the Kansas law enforcement community or the Kansas criminal justice system than it is today. The Kansas Law Enforcement Training Center, repository for Kansas law enforcement training records, reported on January 19, 2011, that 72 percent of all municipal and county law enforcement agencies in the state had ten or fewer full-time officers and that 50 percent had five or fewer full-time officers. Reliance on KBI resources, meager though they often are, necessarily follows.

Today's KBI employees are not dissimilar to their 1939 predecessors. They share a common mission: "Dedication, Service, Integrity," the motto that has always adorned the beautiful KBI seal. The KBI has always striven to provide service to the law enforcement community and the criminal justice system with dedication and integrity. Excellence has remained the goal, and justice, not just prosecution, the objective.

As noted, the KBI began with just ten men and that would remain the number of agents for several years. Why ten? Probably for budgetary reasons, as well as a reflection of the reluctance of the legislature to create the agency in the first place. Perhaps, too, it was because another law enforcement agency with which the KBI was compared frequently at the time of its creation and in the years since, the Texas Rangers, also began with ten men. That, however, was in 1835, and the targets in that time and place were of the Apache and Comanche variety, not the gangsters, bootleggers, bank robbers, motorized cattle rustlers, and general lawlessness of the 1930s. Indeed, the creation of the KBI followed nearly a decade of lobbying efforts by the Kansas Bankers' Association, the Kansas State Peace Officers' Association, and the Kansas Livestock Association. Prior to 1939, law enforcement juris-diction ended at the city limits and the county lines, and all responsibilities ended at the state line. The agency's creation changed that culture.

Born in that narrow corridor of time between the Great Depression and World War II, the bureau's earliest assignments reflected the interests of its original sponsors and the needs of the time: bank robberies, homicides, gangster activities, livestock theft, especially cattle rustling, and narcotics. Yes, narcotics, even then.

Over sixty years later, when I retired, the KBI's priorities, investigative and forensic, included narcotics, especially methamphetamine; violent crime, especially homicide and rape; and cyber-crime, especially child pornography and identity theft.

What follows is all true. These are stories of generations of crime fighters and criminals, heroes and villains, told in chapters that highlight crimes, criminals, crime victims, skilled and relentless investigators, dedicated and determined forensic scientists and crime analysts, and all those who labor and have labored on behalf of the KBI for the state and nation. Everything represented herein was inspired by real people and actual events. With such history, there is no need for fiction or imagination.

I owe a debt of gratitude to many people for their willingness to share gener-ously of their time, insight, counsel, experiences, memories, knowledge, and expertise in support of this effort.

First and foremost, I am especially grateful to Shirley, my high school sweetheart and wife of more than half a century, who, with love and patience, typed every word, and to Barbara Watkins, who read every word, edited ev-ery page, and was the first to encourage me to finish what I had started.

I will also be forever indebted to Bob Stephan, attorney general of Kansas for sixteen years, who twice presented the opportunity of KBI leadership to me, and who, with Bob Senecal, the retired dean of continuing education at the University of Kansas, and Dolph C. Simons Jr., editor of the *Lawrence Journal-World*, read much of this manuscript and offered early encourage-ment and endorsement.

Special thanks, too, to PJ Adair, my KBI executive secretary and admin-istrative assistant, who, from 1995 to 2007, helped collect and organize KBI archives of personal, official, unclassified, and nonconfidential correspon-dences, reports, notes, memoranda, and relevant news items from wire ser-vices and newspapers. Those sources of information were invaluable in tell-ing this KBI story and in describing the cases, events, and people selected from KBI history, from 1939 to 2007.

A few of the many others to whom I owe thanks for answering questions and/or sharing observations include Peggy Summerville, the niece of former KBI director Lou Richter and perhaps his only living relative, and her husband, Jack, who provided helpful insight through the years into Richter's life; Margaret Symns, Bonnie Jo Williamson, and Corine Christman, daughters of former KBI director Logan Sanford, for their contributions, including editing references to their father; Gene and Peggy Schmidt, parents of Stephanie, for their assistance; Jeanette Stauffer, mother of Shannon, for her gracious help; and Tammy Samuels, widow of Sheriff Matt Samuels, for her contributions. These individuals all graciously read the chapters that detail painful personal memories within their respective families. I also wish to thank Wichita Police Chief Norman Williams, Lt. Ken Landwehr, and their BTK Task Force, who invited the KBI to join them in pursuit of BTK, for the wonderful liaison they extended to me personally, from March 2004 to February 2005; and, lastly, Wichita Police Department alumni Bill Cornwell, Bobby Stout, Al Thimmesch, Clyde Bevis, Bob Bulla, and Bernie Drowatzky, among many others, for their willingness to share their memories of the original BTK investigation.

Lastly, my sincerest appreciation to Fred Woodward, director of the University Press of Kansas, for his decision, encouragement, and guidance in the publication of the book, and for the expertise, assistance, and patience of his staff, especially Kelly Chrisman Jacques and Susan Schott.

Clearly, with such stalwart sources and contributors, any errors herein are my responsibility alone.

Larry Welch
Lawrence, Kansas

CHAPTER ONE

Macksville: The Escape from Lansing and the Shootout on Main Street

The land on which it was to be built was purchased by the Kansas legislature in 1861, the same year Kansas became a state and the first year of the Civil War. It was built to hold the very worst of Kansas. It was opened in 1868 and it continues to hold some of the worst of Kansas today. In the beginning it was officially called the Kansas State Penitentiary at Lansing. Today it's officially called the Lansing Correctional Facility. But, to Kansans, it was and is simply "Lansing."

In 1941, among the worst in Kansas, and in Lansing, were George Raymond Hight, Kansas State Prison (KSP) number 9847; Frank Wetherick, KSP 3499; Lloyd Swain, KSP 9146; George Swift, KSP 2096; and John Eldridge, KSP 2559. All white males. All career criminals.

Hight, age forty-one, was a Kansas oil field worker from Dodge City serving ten to fifty years for a bank robbery in Byers, Kansas, in Pratt County. Imprisoned in Lansing since 1927, he was also a car thief and burglar. Wetherick, thirty-one years old, from Pottawatomie County, Kansas, had been sent to Lansing from Shawnee County in 1933 to serve ten to twenty-one years for a Topeka bank robbery. He had been a barber, but his heart had not been in it. Swain, age forty, a tall, thin chain-smoker, raped and murdered a woman in Marshall County in 1925 and was serving a life sentence. He appeared considerably older than his age. Swift, age thirty-six, was a habitual criminal from Rice County, Kansas, serving a life sentence, primarily due to multiple theft and robbery convictions. Eldridge, thirty-one years of age, an Oklahoma laborer, was serving ten to fifty years for having robbed the bank in Peru, Kansas, in Chautauqua County, in 1931, which took place while he was on parole after having robbed an Oklahoma bank in 1928. He was denied parole in 1936, 1939, and again on February 4, 1941, but with a parole violation detainer in his Lansing file he would be transported to Oklahoma to serve the remainder of his Oklahoma sentence when he completed his Kansas term. Like the others, he wasn't going anywhere very soon. At least they were not scheduled to go anywhere very soon.

The five had more in common than their criminal professions, their long tenures in Lansing, and the lengthy sentences still ahead of them. They also shared a common belief that they had served enough of their respective sentences and it was time to leave the ancient, gray, foreboding walls of Lansing, where they dug coal for the state of Kansas, as had Lansing inmates since a coal mine was opened beneath the prison in 1882. Accordingly, they had spent weeks, under Hight's leadership, tunneling out of the Lansing coal mine into a large drainpipe that ran under the prison yard wall to freedom.

During the early morning hours of May 27, 1941, Hight, Wetherick, Swain, Swift, and Eldridge crawled through the pipe and escaped into the countryside after stealing a guard's automobile in the prison parking lot. As they had planned, they soon separated. Swift and Eldridge headed to California together. Swain, a loner, perhaps not by his own choice, went south, and Hight, the escape ringleader, and Wetherick spent a few days in northeastern Kansas committing robberies and car thefts before heading west. Kansas Attorney General Jay Parker gave the assignment to capture and return the five escapees to Lansing to the Kansas Bureau of Investigation (KBI). The small, elite, fledgling bureau was not yet two years old.

Lloyd Swain, following the escape from Lansing, raped a young mother in Arkansas City and several women in Wichita before crossing the state line into Oklahoma. He was captured on August 9, 1941, near Bartlesville, Oklahoma, by Kansas Bureau of Investigation Director Lou Richter and three KBI special agents, Joe Anderson, Clarence Bulla, and Harry Neal, assisted by Oklahoma authorities. The capture followed weeks of tracking Swain out of Kansas into the Cookson Hills of Oklahoma and from one hideout to another. He was returned to Lansing by the KBI. This was the first apprehension of a major fugitive by the young agency.

Swift and Eldridge were eventually trailed by the KBI to San Diego, California. With the assistance of local law enforcement, they were quietly taken into custody by Director Richter and Special Agent Anderson on October 23, 1941, and returned to Lansing.

Hight and Wetherick, however, were a different story. They initially evaded forty officers and bloodhounds across two Kansas counties before stealing a car in Onaga. On June 24, following a bitter running gun battle with law enforcement officers on Highway 75 north of Topeka, they fled the northeastern part of Kansas and disappeared, due in large part to Wetherick's skillful driving and knowledge of that area, but mostly due to a complete absence of radio communication in the pursuing law enforcement officers' patrol cars.

Because of the successful escape of Hight and Wetherick from the pursuing officers, the *Topeka Daily Capital,* in a July 13, 1941, editorial, pleaded with the Kansas legislature to equip KBI and Kansas Highway Patrol cars with two-way radios.[1] Quoting Richter, the newspaper pointed out that the pursuing troopers, had their automobiles been properly equipped, could have summoned help and roadblocks could have been established, which surely would have resulted in the duo's capture. During the next legislative session, thanks to the notoriety of Hight and Wetherick, the purchase of two-way radios for state lawmen's cars commenced.

KBI interrogation of Swain and a series of car thefts and burglaries westward across Kansas indicated that Hight and Wetherick might be headed to Colorado.

In 1941, Director Lou Richter and the KBI had nine special agents, some of whom, like Richter, were former Kansas sheriffs. The KBI gave the capture of Hight and Wetherick its top priority, and most of the nine agents were assigned the task of finding and apprehending the two dangerous escapees. Rewards of $250—not a small amount for that day—were posted for each. Every informant the KBI had was contacted. Inmates at Lansing were interviewed. Swain was reinterviewed. Law enforcement agencies across the state of Kansas and in adjacent states, especially Oklahoma, Colorado, and Texas, were alerted. Every bit of evidence and intelligence, every scrap of information, every contact seemed to indicate the two might end up in the Oklahoma panhandle or eastern Colorado.

As the KBI search intensified and before they disappeared into the vastness of eastern Colorado, Hight and Wetherick stole another car in Satanta, Kansas, and burglarized a general store, taking cash, cases of canned goods, a crate of oranges, several milk cans (which they filled with gasoline), and several new pairs of coveralls.

George Raymond Hight immediately liked the Oklahoma oil field worker he and Frank Wetherick met in a bar at Pueblo, Colorado, during one of their many jaunts into town. He, like them, seemed to be on the run from law enforcement, maybe Oklahoma, but more than likely Kansas. He seemed to know a lot about Kansas.

He said his name was Joe; Hight had never pressed him for a last name. They liked him so much that when he admitted on one of their trips to Pueblo that he had run out of money for a motel and was going to be sleeping in his car, they invited him to spend a few days with them on the deserted sheep ranch twenty miles from Lamar where they had been staying the past three months.

Hight and Wetherick became so comfortable with Joe that they began to discuss openly in front of him their plans to rob a bank, maybe more than one. They told him that they were considering banks in Lamar, Colorado; Hugoton, Kansas; and Macksville, Kansas. Joe accompanied Hight and Wetherick on trips to Lamar and Hugoton to case those banks. He did not accompany them when they cased the Macksville bank. But he was still at the ranch when they returned from Kansas and announced it would be Macksville. Robbing the bank there, they told Joe, would be like taking candy from a baby.

Both had agreed Lamar was too close to their ranch hideout, and Wetherick had preferred Hugoton. But Macksville was in Stafford County, Kansas, immediately north of Pratt County, where Hight had robbed a bank years earlier. Hight also pointed out that Stafford County, a large county with few people, only had three law enforcement officers to cover the county: a sheriff, an undersheriff, and one deputy. With any luck at all the three would be at St. John, the county seat, thirteen miles east of Macksville, when they robbed the bank and headed west.

Joe agreed with them that it all made sense, so much that he wished he could go with them. He had to return to Oklahoma, however, for a few days on a family matter. Hight told him to be sure and return to the ranch pretty quick to help them count money, because he and Frank were going to go back to Macksville within the week, and he told Joe not to worry; there would be more trips to Kansas in the future.

As Joe drove toward Lamar, Colorado, he was troubled. Although Hight and Wetherick had not mentioned it, Joe knew there were two banks in Macksville. Which bank did they intend to hit? He had decided not to press his luck with Hight and Wetherick by attempting to identify which of the two banks in the small southwestern Kansas town they intended to rob. It was probably no big deal anyway. As Joe recalled, both banks were on the west side of the street and on the same block.

From Lamar, Joe telephoned Director Richter at KBI headquarters in Topeka, Kansas. Richter listened to Joe's report and then congratulated him on a job well done. Joe, or Special Agent Joe Anderson, as he was known to Director Richter and his eight fellow special agents, had spent almost three months in an undercover role in the Oklahoma-Texas panhandle and eastern Colorado tracking Hight and Wetherick. Through a Colorado woman he had learned where the escapees were hiding. At first he, other KBI agents, and Colorado officers had attempted to surveil the remote, deserted sheep ranch. But it had been impossible to get close to the pair's hideout, given the broad expanse of treeless prairie surrounding it. Hight and Wetherick could see miles in every direction. An assault on the ranch could take a deadly toll of law enforcement officers. No one doubted the joint vow of the two escapees to never return to prison.

Director Richter, however, thought that maybe a smooth talker like Joe Anderson could get close enough to the pair by himself to learn what they were planning. His confidence in Anderson had been well placed. Following his first visit to the ranch, Joe had confirmed Richter's worst fears. Hight and Wetherick had at least three shotguns, two rifles, two Colt .45 automatic pistols, a German Luger, and many boxes of ammunition. They had an arsenal at their disposal. He had also reported that Hight and Wetherick each kept a pistol at all times in their coveralls, of which they seemed to have an inexhaustible supply. Richter told Joe to meet him as soon as possible at the sheriff's office in St. John, Kansas.

Stafford County Sheriff Logan Sanford and the KBI staked out both Macksville banks for almost a week. It had been difficult maintaining concealment for seven officers in such a small town and especially difficult adequately covering both banks. Personnel at the banks had been informed. There was no other way to do it. The employees and their families had been sworn to secrecy by Director Richter and Sheriff Sanford. Others at certain businesses adjacent to the banks were also informed, reluctantly, by the lawmen. Director Richter and Sheriff Sanford were both beginning to suspect that, despite their best efforts, they had confided in too many people or had somehow tipped their hand to the would-be bank robbers.

For the first two days, officers were placed inside each bank behind newly erected false partitions. But Richter had become uncomfortable with that strategy. The officers would not be able to respond quickly from behind such obstructions. He and Sheriff Sanford each preferred to take Hight and Wetherick outside the bank, before entry, to minimize the risk to bank employees and customers. Therefore, they reduced the number of officers inside each bank to one and spread the others out within selected business establishments on both sides of the street. But with no communication available among the officers, other than the telephone in each business establishment, the arrangement was not ideal. Richter and Sanford were worried that the strategy relied on the individual alertness of each agent and the undersheriff, plus considerable luck. In any event, it was agreed that September 16 would be the last day. The stakeout would end at the close of business that day. They would then have to admit that Hight and Wetherick, for whatever reason, had changed their minds about Macksville.

Shortly after 9:00 A.M. on September 16, a new 1941 eight-cylinder Ford, occupied by two men, drove slowly up the main street of Macksville, Kansas, a town of approximately 800 people. Though the town itself was small, thanks to the area's agriculture and oil production economic base, the community supported two grocery stores, a movie theater, several churches and service stations, two drug stores, another combination drug store and pool hall, its own high school, two cafes, a Chevrolet automobile agency, a two-block business district, and two banks, the Macksville State Bank and the Farmers and Merchants State Bank.

The 1941 Ford, recently stolen from a dealer's showroom in Satanta, Kansas, was bearing a stolen Pottawatomie County, Kansas, license plate. The original license plate number, 39, had been painted over to read 89, and the car itself had obviously been painted by hand, from the original black to blue. The car headed north up the main street, made a U-turn at the end of the block, and cruised back south before turning slowly toward the curb in front of the Macksville State Bank.

There were seven Kansas lawmen on the scene—four KBI special agents (Joe Anderson, Clarence Bulla, Roy Dyer, and Harry Neal), Director Richter, Sheriff Sanford, and Undersheriff Wesley Wise. Some of them who saw George Raymond Hight's startled expression as he stepped from the passenger side of the Ford, later agreed that Hight had recognized Joe, or rather KBI Special Agent Joe Anderson, as one of the well-dressed men confronting him with guns drawn and demanding the pair's surrender. That might explain why Hight fired wildly when he fired the first shot. He was given no second opportunity to improve his marksmanship, however. Five of the seven officers returned his fire, killing him instantly and riddling the Ford as Wetherick attempted to drive south to Highway 50. Wetherick died within the next several seconds. The car, moving slowly, and with seven holes in the windshield in front of the lifeless Wetherick, continued down the street. Richter ran alongside the car, jumped onto the running board, and brought the driverless car to a stop.

In addition to the Colt .45 automatic pistol in Hight's hand, the KBI recovered two 12-gauge sawed-off shotguns, two Winchester rifles, a German Luger, two more Colt automatic pistols, and more than 200 rounds of ammunition from the car. The two most wanted criminals in Kansas were no longer threats to anyone.

Among the first of the Macksville citizens to gather in the street when the gunfire had subsided was Oscar Barnes, head mechanic at Elmore Chevrolet, half a block from the Macksville State Bank. As he and others stood by watching the KBI agents pull Wetherick from the bullet-riddled car and lay him alongside Hight's body in the street, Barnes suddenly saw his five-year-old daughter, Shirley, standing in the crowd near the bodies. He shooed her back home to her mother. Shirley Barnes later married her high school sweetheart, a St. John boy. He became an FBI special agent, thanks in part to his mentor, Logan Sanford, following graduation from the University of Kansas School of Law. Eventually, her husband became the tenth director of the KBI and author of this book.

The days following the Macksville shootout were heady times for the KBI. Praise poured into KBI headquarters from around the state and the nation. The KBI was the darling of the Kansas press and the citizens of the state. The politicians were thrilled and Kansas bankers in general and the Kansas Bankers' Association in particular were euphoric.

The *Stafford Courier*, in a story entitled "Good Work by KBI," reported that

> a lot of Kansas citizens had more or less overlooked the fact that Kansas has a Bureau of Investigation, modeled after the federal bureau, until Tuesday morning of last week, when the crime career of two escaped convicts came to an end at Macksville. Ably assisted by Sheriff Sanford and Deputy Wise, the KBI men did a good job. . . . The KBI had proved itself before last Tuesday morning to be a valuable arm of law enforcement, but this fact was not well known to citizens generally. Now people are aware that the state has an effective law enforcement group.[2]

A headline in the *Kansas City Star* later proclaimed "Bad Men of the Southwest Meet Their Masters in the K.B.I.," and the story lavished praise on the bureau and its director for a job well done in Macksville.[3]

An editorial in the *Wichita Beacon* on September 17, 1941, declared,

> Congratulations are due the Kansas Bureau of identification [*sic*] for its prompt and efficient manner in handling the attempted bank robbery at Macksville, Kas., on Tuesday. Two bandits, who recently escaped from the Kansas penitentiary, will no longer be a menace to their fellow men or an expense to the state. . . . The KBI . . . acquitted themselves with honor to themselves and glory to their organization. The entire state owes these brave men a vote of thanks, if not more material reward.[4]

The KBI was still in its infancy. If any case in the early years of the KBI left its mark and ensured the long life of the agency, it was the attempted robbery of the Macksville bank. From September 16, 1941, the KBI was forever ascendant.

CHAPTER TWO

Genesis: Director Lou Richter and the KBI's First Team

The Kansas Bureau of Investigation had a somewhat shaky start. Kansas Attorney General Jay Parker, later given much credit for the agency's inception, was initially a reluctant KBI sponsor. He would eventually become its most ardent supporter. Parker would also later become a justice and then chief justice of the Kansas Supreme Court. The fact that he had presided over the creation of the KBI would not impede his political progress.

The credit for the creation of the KBI belongs primarily to the Kansas Bankers' Association, the Kansas Livestock Association, and, in particular, the Kansas State Peace Officers' Association, today known as the Kansas Peace Officers' Association, which was the first group to lobby the state legislature for a state bureau and also the most persistent. In an impressive seven-page brochure, "How to Solve the Crime Problem," distributed to the legislature and throughout the state in 1931, the Kansas State Peace Officers' Association's legislative committee attempted to save the Kansas governor, attorney general, and state legislators considerable time and effort by writing for them proposed legislation entitled "An Act Relating to the Investigation, Detection, Apprehension, Identification and Prosecution of Criminals, and Making an Appropriation Therefor."

The proposed act began with the words "A Department of the State Government under the Attorney General is hereby created and established, and is designated as The State Department of Criminal Identification and Investigation." The act provided that the new department would have a director, an assistant director, and an unspecified number of investigators. The director would serve at the pleasure of the attorney general and would be appointed by the attorney general, "with the advice, consent and approval of a Council of three Advisors selected by the Kansas State Peace Officers' Association."[1] The director would have a minimum of five years' experience in law enforcement and would be appointed "without regard to political affiliation, but solely because of his practical experience in law enforcement and knowledge of the science of fingerprint identification."[2]

The proposed legislation, which would take effect July 1, 1931, contained twenty sections. Among the more interesting provisions was Section 8:

The Department shall co-operate with the respective Sheriffs, County Attorneys, Police Officers and all other law enforcement officers in the state in the investigation, detection, apprehension, identification and prosecution of criminals and shall maintain and index in standard manner all information relating to stolen property and shall, on the direction of the Attorney General, conduct such investigations and render such assistance as may be necessary to secure evidence essential to the conviction of alleged violators of the criminal laws of the state.[3]

The brochure was signed by the chairman of the Kansas State Peace Officers' Association's legislative committee, Coffey County Attorney Joe Rolston Jr., Burlington, Kansas, and the five members of his committee, including the undersheriff of Marion County, Kansas, L. P. Richter. The brochure didn't create the KBI, however. The idea, in 1931, instead fell on deaf ears. Nor would the agency that was eventually created eight years later exactly resemble the one advocated in the brochure, in name or organization. Even the proposal for the director's salary, $3,600, was changed to $3,000 when the KBI began—so much for inflation. But overall, the brochure's proposal was, at the least, a harbinger of things to come.

Over the next several years, the lobbying efforts by the Kansas Bankers' Association, the Kansas Livestock Association, and the Kansas State Peace Officers' Association to persuade the Kansas legislature to create the Kansas Bureau of Investigation continued and then intensified in 1938. A committee formed of bankers, ranchers, insurance people, sheriffs, and police chiefs visited Governor Payne Ratner in Topeka and pleaded with him to use his influence with the legislature and Attorney General Jay Parker to form a small, highly specialized group of investigators that could help combat the wave of armed robbery, homicide, cattle rustling, and theft ravaging Kansas.

All agreed they did not want a state police force. What they did want was a small group of investigators, something like the Texas Rangers or a small FBI, which could respond to requests for assistance from local police and local sheriffs, and which could transcend state lines, if required, to assist local Kansas law enforcement and to cooperate with other states' law enforcement authorities.

Governor Ratner agreed and turned to Representative Alfred H. Harkness to carry the flag in the legislature. Then he convinced his friend, Attorney General Parker, to lend his important support. He assured the less-than-enthusiastic Parker that the latter would be able to keep a close eye on the new organization because the bureau would be placed under the jurisdiction of the office of attorney general. The director of the new bureau would be appointed by and answer directly to the attorney general. They both agreed it was also vital that the new bureau avoid politics.

Governor Ratner pointed to the working relationship between the U.S. attorney general and Director J. Edgar Hoover of the FBI. Something like that was needed, he suggested. The Kansas bureau would operate independently, would not be subject to politics, would serve the Kansas law enforcement community, and would be directly responsible to the state attorney general. Subsequent legislative efforts by the eloquent and popular Parker and Harkness were eventually successful but not without considerable lobbying, persuasion, and arm bending.

On April 3, 1939, the Kansas legislature approved House Bill #427—"There is hereby established, under the jurisdiction of the attorney general, a division to be known as the bureau of investigation, which bureau shall not exceed ten persons who shall be trained in the detection and apprehension of criminals"—with considerable opposition, in the waning hours of the session, just before final adjournment. The KBI was born, but barely and not without legislative dissent.

On June 23, 1939, Attorney General Jay Parker announced that he had made his decision as to who would direct the new Kansas Bureau of Investigation. His choice was Lou P. Richter, the former sheriff of Marion County and a well-known Kansas lawman. The appointment would be effective July 1, 1939, the official establishment date for the KBI, and he noted that Director Richter would serve at the attorney general's pleasure. In making the announcement Parker said, "In selecting Mr. Richter as director of the new bureau I have endeavored to keep in mind two things—efficiency in the department and insured cooperation between it and peace officers of the state with whom its personnel must come in contact."[4]

Parker also announced that the Kansas legislature had limited the size of the new bureau to ten agents, including the director, and had budgeted $46,000 to "pay all salaries, buy all equipment and support the criminal investigations."[5] In addition to Richter's salary of $3,000 a year, his agents would be paid no less than $1,200 and no more than $2,000 annually. Richter, said Parker, would select the nine agents himself and would set his own hiring standards and agent qualifications.

Parker's choice of Richter proved to be wise. In an era in which police corruption was not rare, Richter had no blemish on his reputation. He was highly respected by his fellow Kansas sheriffs and had served as president of the Kansas State Peace Officers' Association in 1936. Richter, a large, dark-haired, handsome man, was a World War I veteran, a native Kansan, and highly regarded in Marion County, his home. He was already a career law enforcement officer when he accepted the reins of the new KBI. He had been undersheriff of Marion County and then a railroad special agent for Rock Island Railroad before serving four terms as sheriff of Marion County. He was forty-six years old and known as a God-fearing, strong family man, with little patience for criminals. He had attended Kansas State Agricultural College and graduated from a Topeka business college. He had served as secretary to Congressman Ed Rees in Washington, D.C., and later was a federal deputy marshal.

Richter's good reputation went back more than a decade. The 1926 issue of *The Peace Officer*, the official publication of the Kansas State Peace Officers' Association, featured in its nearly one hundred pages a wide array of articles, ranging from the legendary Kansas marshal "Wild Bill" Hickok to the creation of the Kansas State Peace Officers' Association in 1915 and the Kansas State Penitentiary in Lansing, but also a story about Marion County, "one of the cleanest counties in the State."

One of the reasons for the good state of affairs in Marion County, wrote the editor, was Sheriff L. P. (Lou) Richter. Another reason was Mrs. L. P. Richter.

> Sheriff Richter of Marion County, while being a comparatively young man, has had considerable experience as an officer in various capacities. Upon his discharge from the United States Army after the close of the World War he was appointed Undersheriff of Marion County serving two years. During this time an oil boom was in full swing in the county and he took an active hand in curbing the wave of crime and lawlessness that came with the boom.[6]

The story explained that Richter then spent a couple of years as U.S. Deputy Marshal and Rock Island Railroad special agent elsewhere in Kansas before being summoned back home to run for sheriff in 1924. He was

> elected by a large majority, being the youngest man to hold that office in the history of the county. . . . Mrs. L. P. Richter, wife of Sheriff L. P. Richter . . . has been an important factor in the success of her husband's administration. As the county does not furnish a jailer, Mrs. Richter was appointed a deputy sheriff and in that capacity has charge of the jail and feeding of the prisoners, and due to her vigilance two jail breaks were prevented, which speaks very well indeed for Mrs. Richter's ability as an officer.[7]

Parker's announcement of Richter as the first director of the KBI was greeted with approval across the state. Richter's hometown newspaper, the *Marion Record*, while perhaps prejudiced, was fairly typical of other Kansas newspapers in its response: "If he had been combing the state with a fine-tooth comb, Governor Ratner would not have found a better man to head the Kansas Bureau of Investigation than Lou Richter."[8] It mattered not that the choice had been Parker's, not Ratner's.

Richter was pleased that he had been given the latitude to select his own nine agents, but he saw this privilege as potentially a double-edged sword. Although it was good that he himself could determine the standards and qualifications for the new agency and its officers, he was also painfully aware that a wrong selection—the hiring of an agent who might yield to the temptation of graft, or who might confuse justice and politics—could result in the early demise of the agency. Many still feared the creation of a state police force, and the legislature that had created the KBI had been seriously divided on the issue of a state bureau of investigation. The state would be watching. The legislature, the governor, and certainly the attorney general would be following Richter closely as the agency developed. The KBI could be terminated as quickly as it was created.

Not only had the legislature strictly limited, by statute, the size of the new criminal investigation bureau to ten agents, including the director himself, but also it was clear that they had struggled with what authority to give it. They apparently decided the jurisdiction of the KBI would best lie somewhere between mandates of the attorney general and the authority of Kansas sheriffs. As the Kansas statute indicated, "It shall be the duty of the members of the bureau to make full and complete investigations at the direction of the attorney general. Each member of the bureau shall possess all powers and privileges which are now or may be hereafter given to the sheriffs of the state of Kansas."[9]

Perhaps that helps explain why so many of the first class of KBI agents were former sheriffs or deputy sheriffs. Who would better understand a sheriff's authority? And a Kansas sheriff's authority was no small thing. The original enabling statute (K.S.A. 19-813), entitled "Preservation of peace" and passed in 1868, read in part, "It shall be the duty of the sheriff and undersheriffs and deputies to keep and preserve the peace in their respective counties, and to quiet and suppress all affrays, riots and unlawful assemblies and insurrections."

Richter had already spent enough time in his consideration of agent candidates to know whom he wanted to join him when he took the oath of office on July 1, 1939, the first day in the life of the KBI. Joe Anderson, Herb Henderson, Robert A. "Jack" Huse, Harry Neal, and Glenn Morris were administered the KBI oath of office along with Richter that day. Clarence Bulla, Ron Fowkes, and Charles Maupin started in August and September 1939, and R. L. Griffith took his oath of office in October of the same year. Morris soon left the agency and was replaced in February 1941 by Roy Dyer.

Director Richter would later say of that original group of men, "There was not a dud in the bunch."[10] Herb Henderson, a native of Allen County, Kansas, had been an investigator and district manager with the Pinkerton Detective Agency in Cleveland and Indianapolis. Clarence Bulla, born and raised in Bourbon County, Kansas, had served as sheriff and undersheriff there. Ron Fowkes, born at Wamego, had worked for the Kansas Livestock Commission and served as deputy sheriff of Wabaunsee County. He was a cattle theft expert as well as a fingerprint and ballistics specialist. R. L. Griffith had been a deputy sheriff for the Wyandotte County sheriff's office and Harry Neal was a former police officer, private investigator, and chief deputy sheriff in Montgomery County. Jack Huse had been a deputy sheriff in Riley County as well as assistant chief of police in Manhattan. Charles Maupin, another cattle theft specialist, was former sheriff of Graham County. Not much was recorded about Glenn Morris, but Roy Dyer, born and raised in Chautauqua County, was a former sheriff of his home county.

It was, by any standard of the day, an outstanding group of experienced lawmen. Richter, in his selections, had placed heavy emphasis on Kansas natives and on men who had worked with Kansas sheriffs' offices or had been sheriffs. Each of these gentlemen received the starting monthly pay of $125. The big money, $160 monthly, was reserved for the highly regarded investigator who had the nickname "Manhunter" and who was generally considered the star of Richter's first class: Joe Anderson. A native of Baxter Springs, Anderson had previously served with the Kansas Highway Patrol and also had been a private investigator who had built a good reputation in Kansas, Missouri, and Oklahoma. Almost all the new special agents were also veterans of World War I, like the director.

In an interview with the *Kansas City Times* on June 27, 1939, Richter explained that the mission of the KBI would be, first and foremost, to serve local Kansas law enforcement. It would be a service organization and it would go and assist where it was invited. "It will not be the purpose of the bureau to interfere with or supersede local officers in any law enforcement problems. . . . We will be concerned only with major crime investigations, perhaps mostly upon request of local authorities."[11]

He acknowledged that it would take time to develop the agency as he envisioned it. He would require his agents to have a high school diploma and a minimum of five years of criminal investigation experience, and also to be physically fit and between the ages of twenty-four and forty-eight years. The reporter noted that Richter himself was six feet three inches tall, 240 pounds, and powerfully built.

In the beginning, KBI agents were required to furnish their own automobiles, and they were instructed to stay tuned to WIBW radio in Topeka for messages from KBI headquarters. Two-way radios were still years away for the KBI. Within a few months the agents were provided Chevrolet sedans, .30-caliber rifles, 12-gauge shotguns, tear gas, and fingerprint equipment. They would each provide their own revolver or pistol of at least .38-caliber.

The legislature would not relax its original ten-agent limit soon, with the result that no additional agent was hired until the end of World War II. The KBI was, however, given a "staff" to support the director and its agents. The "staff" was Mary Collins, who was the only non-agent employee for several years. She served as Richter's secretary and office manager, maintaining the case files and criminal history records and often traveling to assist the agents in recording interviews and confessions. She would serve the KBI more than twenty-two years and was instrumental in the development of the eventual clerical staff.

The first KBI office was in a 920-square-foot area on the first floor in the south wing of the state capitol building, the same building that housed every state representative and senator, the governor, and the attorney general. Politics might not be within the agency, but politics certainly encircled it.

While the KBI was not officially out of the starting gate until July 1, 1939, KBI archives reveal that Richter was up and running on the job a few days prior. In a letter on KBI stationery dated June 27, 1939, Richter referenced a letter earlier in June and informed the chief of police of Sioux Falls, South Dakota, that the KBI would be glad to conduct a local inquiry in Topeka in an effort to locate Sioux Falls fugitive Earl Gilbert, believed to be in that city. The Gilbert matter not only provided insight into the work ethic of the new KBI's director, but also represented the first official case in the agency's history. Records indicate that "case #1" resulted in the KBI capturing Gilbert for the South Dakota police. The arresting agent was Lou Richter.

Cases came rapidly after that and included a wide variety of criminal violations. The two violations exceeding all others in numbers in the earliest days were livestock theft, especially cattle rustling, and, surprisingly, narcotic violations, especially "marihuana weed." Those violations were followed closely in numbers by armed robberies, homicides, theft, forgery, and fraud.

Five of the first nine KBI investigations documented in the official *Kansas Bureau of Investigation Case Record,* a large, elegant, red leather and gold-trimmed book, refer to homicides in the counties of Cherokee, Crawford, Rice, Shawnee, and Montgomery.

The KBI's first case that involved a female subject was case #13, a murder investigation in Dickinson County that resulted in *State of Kansas vs. Mrs. J. W. Mitchell.* The disposition was not described.

Case #14, *State of Kansas vs. Meredith Hawkins Lynch,* also involving a female subject, resulted in a conviction in Barton County for forgery. Lynch received a sentence of one to ten years.

Richter's first statewide letter was headlined, "To All Sheriff's, Police Officers, County Attorneys and County Commissioners," dated July 27, 1939, imploring them to join the KBI in a unified effort to "eradicate Marihuana from our State."[12] The letter described the drug's threat to the young people of the state and provided detailed instructions on how to cut the "marihuana weed."

One could track the KBI's criminal investigative activities that first summer by simply following the front pages and/or the editorial pages of newspapers across the state. The *Kansas Stockman* and the Dodge City newspaper both described, with pleasure, inroads made by the KBI into cattle rustling. The *Topeka Capital* praised the KBI's arrest of investment swindlers in that city. The *Kansas City Star* applauded KBI arrests of illegal gamblers in Wyandotte County and the apprehensions of persons responsible for copper wire thefts in various Kansas counties.

In an editorial on November 10, 1939, the *Kansas City Star* concluded:

> The new Kansas bureau of investigation has made a place for itself, and a place which will have growing importance. . . . When the K.B.I. was established by the legislature, a good many of the state officials, as well as county law enforcement bodies, had their fingers crossed concerning it. It was stigmatized in some places as just another governmental gadget, with no real objective or need to give it an excuse for existence. . . . But, within four months Kansas has begun to realize that the creation of the bureau was a wise move. . . . The K.B.I. was well conceived and carried out.[13]

The only setback suffered by the KBI its first summer was a car wreck involving Director Richter. His right leg was broken and his hip shattered in the accident on an Iowa highway while away on business. He was forced to use crutches for several weeks. Unfortunately, a few months later, near Emporia, another agent and Richter were involved in yet another car wreck. While they were chasing a fugitive, they ran into a hayrack that a farmer had pulled in front of them. Richter was again injured, fracturing a rib and cutting a knee and his head. Some believe that the combined injuries of the two automobile accidents, during the summer of 1939 and the spring of 1940, respectively, plagued Richter's health the rest of his life and contributed to the eventual amputation of his right leg years later. Perhaps. But there was never any indication that his pace ever slowed until the twilight of his life and career.

On the evening of Monday, November 6, 1939, four months after the Kansas Bureau of Investigation was created, Attorney General Jay Parker addressed a large civic group in Kansas City. He confessed to the audience that he had, at first, not embraced enthusiastically the proposal to create the new bureau of investigation. He had feared any state police concept and he was not completely persuaded that the agency would be worth the effort it would take to give it life. Governor Ratner, however, was his friend and the governor was a believer and he had been quite persuasive.

That evening Parker made it quite clear to the large audience that he too was now a believer and ardent supporter of the new KBI. He boasted that, in four short months, Richter and his men had already opened ninety-two criminal investigations and obtained thirty-one convictions. And many more completed investigations were awaiting trial. Parker's original grudging support had given way to tremendous respect. In speaking of Richter and his special agents, Parker told the group, "They learn to differentiate between gossip and evidence. While much of our investigation deals with the more technical crimes from the investigation standpoint, our chief work is planned to cope with major crime, bank bandits or murder, or burglars who rob and then escape to another county." But, he admitted, it wasn't only bank robbery, murder, and burglary. "An early achievement was the breaking up of a Kansas racket which peddled coats of cheap rabbit fur as more expensive fur. Many Kansas housewives were victimized before the racketeers could be tracked down."[14] Murder or rabbits, they cared not. The Kansas City audience gave Parker, and the KBI in absentia, a standing ovation.

The Kansas news media also continued to applaud the young KBI, although some continued to confuse the new agency with its federal counterpart. The *Peabody Herald*, on December 7, 1939, for example, proclaimed, "F.B.I. Going Good under Lou Richter." They got it right in the story, however. "The Kansas Bureau of Investigation, offering a new service, is functioning efficiently under the supervision of Lou Richter, director, and calls for assistance are being received by his office from all parts of the state. The Bureau's latest important achievement was leading in the breaking up of a livestock rustling gang in Barber and other Southwestern counties. Sheriffs and their deputies joined in the investigation and three men were arrested and signed confessions."[15]

Speaking to the Riley County Republican Club in January 1940, Parker told the large audience that there was good news and bad news. The bad news, according to Parker, was that he personally was convinced President Roosevelt would seek an unprecedented third term. The good news was that he and Richter were so pleased with what the KBI had accomplished thus far, with no forensic weapons of its own, that they now had plans in the future to provide the agency with "a modern identification service, which would include ballistics, photography, fingerprinting and other mechanical devices." Parker said that "this service will be of use to sheriffs and police departments all over the state."[16]

In Parker's company that evening were Richter and his brother, E. W. Richter, the sheriff of Riley County. Director Richter, at Parker's insistence, modestly informed the audience that the KBI, after just six months of operation, had investigated 134 major crimes and obtained fifty-three convictions. He promised a complete report summarizing the KBI's first year in six more months.

On June 29, 1940, Parker announced with great pleasure that the KBI should receive a grade of "A" for its performance in its first year. The KBI had been called on to investigate more than three hundred major crimes. One hundred and fifty eight of those investigation requests had been completed and closed. The overwhelming majority of the cases had ended in successful prosecution. Cattle theft topped the list. Twenty-six cattle thieves, in forty different cases, had been put in prison by the KBI. Most had entered pleas of guilty, so overwhelming was the evidence developed against them by the KBI, reported the Kansas media. Parker boasted that, as a result of the KBI effort, livestock association officials estimated that cattle rustling had been reduced by 50 percent in the KBI's first year.[17]

A special esprit de corps, born of mutual respect, considerable self-confidence, and a growing reputation across the state, developed within the thin ranks of that first generation of KBI special agents. That same pride continues to this day and explains, at least in part, why generations of KBI employees have eschewed less stressful, less demanding, and more lucrative employment.

CHAPTER THREE

Transition: The Thirties, War, and New Leadership

Why the KBI was envisioned in the first place is as important as how it was envisioned. To understand why, one must understand the Kansas of the 1930s and the conditions that led to the creation of a new agency within the Kansas criminal justice system.

The KBI was born in the narrow corridor of time between the Great Depression and World War II, two of the most challenging crises to ever confront America and Kansas. Today it is difficult for Kansans to fully appreciate the poverty, unemployment, economic conditions, social circumstances, and crime that faced Kansans and their fellow Americans in the decade following the stock market crash of October 1929. There is no doubt that the Great Depression and its effects on Kansas played a major role in the establishment of the KBI.

Within months of "Black Tuesday," October 29, 1929, the day of the stock market crash, prices collapsed amid panic selling, and thousands of investors were financially ruined. Businesses quickly went bankrupt and almost 13 million people became unemployed, a rate of nearly 25 percent of the civilian labor force. That year, 235,000 were unemployed in Kansas. One hundred banks closed in the state in 1930 and 1931. Forty-two more closed in 1933. By 1940, there would be half as many Kansas banks as there had been in 1920.[1]

Given its vulnerable agriculture-based economy, Kansas would be spared none of the dire economic consequences of the Great Depression. The accompanying drought, which started in the plains states in 1933 and intensified in 1934, joined with higher-than-usual summer temperatures, below-average precipitation, never-ending wind, and an onslaught of cutworms, jackrabbits, and grasshoppers to create the Dust Bowl of the 1930s. Mother Nature was severely punishing Kansas, Oklahoma, and Texas.

One of the best descriptions of Kansas in the "Dirty Thirties" comes from David M. Kennedy, writing of the Dust Bowl and the Great Depression in his book *Freedom from Fear:* "The wind lifted the surface powder into the skies, creating towering eight-thousand-foot waves known as 'black blizzards'. . . . One dust storm so darkened Great Bend, Kansas, that a resident claimed, 'Lady Godiva could ride through the streets without even the horse seeing her.' The Kansas newspaperman William Allen White likened it to the ashes that had buried Pompeii."[2]

In July 1934, after many days of temperatures exceeding 100 degrees in Kansas, the mercury reached 112 in Independence. The years 1934 and 1935 saw frequent dust storms, which almost eliminated the Kansas wheat crop in both years. "Black blizzards" were especially prevalent in 1935. Wet towels and sheets were routinely placed over doors and windows of homes across western Kansas in unsuccessful attempts to keep out blowing dust and dirt. Sunday, April 14, 1935, was referred to as "Black Sunday" for many years for the intensity of the dust storms that struck Kansas and the Great Plains that day. The fifth year of the drought, 1936, was just as bad as those preceding it. Wichita's hottest recorded day ever was 114 degrees on August 12, 1936. The average temperature in Kansas for the month of July 1936 was an incredible 103.6 degrees. There were fifty days of 100-degree or higher temperatures. Thermometers in Fredonia reached 121 degrees on July 24, 1936. All before air conditioning.

The heat of the summer of 1937 was so oppressive that Kansas Amish Church leaders, to reduce the suffering of their farm horses, gave unprecedented permission for their farmers to use tractors. Few Amish, of course, could afford such modern technology, nor could many other Kansans.

In his second inaugural address, on January 20, 1937, President Roosevelt lamented, "I see one-third of a nation ill-housed, ill-clad, ill-nourished." Many Kansans could be counted in that suffering one-third. Not all "Okies" streaming west out of the plains en route to California were from Oklahoma. The population of Kansas decreased almost 100,000 between 1930 and 1940.[3] The state had 9,715 fewer farms in 1940 than it did in 1930. *The Grapes of Wrath,* John Steinbeck's best-selling novel of 1939, and the subsequent movie adaptation of 1940, could have as easily depicted a Kansas farm family as one from Oklahoma.

That generation also had to face the threats of polio (the March of Dimes campaign to combat polio was organized in 1938), tuberculosis, and dust pneumonia, to name a few of the more prevalent life-threatening afflictions of that day. And the threat of war loomed in Europe and Asia, with little but the Pacific and Atlantic Oceans protecting America.

President Roosevelt delivered the first of his popular radio "fireside chats" to Americans on March 12, 1933. More than 230,000 Kansans were still unemployed and many of those still working were laboring for reduced or nominal wages. That year Kansas passed its first state income tax, and FDR and Congress created the Civil Works Administration (CWA) as part of the New Deal, in an effort to create jobs for the unemployed. That was followed with the Works Progress Administration (WPA) in 1935. The CWA and WPA provided employment, albeit temporarily, to thousands of Americans. Kansans, grateful for the few jobs created by government, worked on everything from building and improving roads and constructing public buildings to anti-erosion measures such as the construction of shelter belts of trees across rural Kansas, many of which still stand today. More than 38,000 workers built dams and lakes across Kansas for the Civilian Conservation Corps (CCC), one of the New Deal's most successful programs.

Still, economic conditions in Kansas, as in the rest of the nation, remained dreadful. Destitute men drifted across the state seeking work or a handout. Farm foreclosures, failing businesses, unemployment, poverty, and a paucity of indoor plumbing and electricity were no strangers to Kansans of the 1930s. Neither was crime.

President Roosevelt, on one particularly discouraging occasion during his first term, is said to have asked rhetorically of his advisors why they thought Americans had not actually revolted, given the desperation of their lives during the Great Depression.

Some did revolt. They robbed banks. They kidnapped. They stole. And they killed.

The KBI was created as a result of the Great Depression and its social consequences. The idea of a state bureau of investigation was promoted by the Kansas Bankers' Association, the Kansas Livestock Association, and the Kansas State Peace Officers' Association to combat some of the criminal symptoms of that desperate economic environment: bank robberies, homicides, cattle theft, and burglaries, in particular. The miseries of the Great Depression had gripped Kansas as severely as any other state in the nation. One of those miseries was crime. Poverty and unemployment are, after all, frequent breeders of crime.

In an April 1966 article that ran as part of a series on the history of the KBI, the *Denver Post* noted that "Kansas in the late 1930s was plagued by a seemingly never-ending string of bank raids by packs of criminals led by Alvin Karpis, Jake Fleagle, Kate (Ma) Barker, Charles (Pretty Boy) Floyd and Wilbur Underhill."[4]

The story was accurate. Indeed, at the urging of Governor Alf Landon, the Kansas legislature in 1935 enacted a new capital punishment law because of an epidemic of bloody bank robberies across the state. *The Kansas Banker,* the official publication of the Kansas Bankers' Association, reported paying rewards totaling $51,835 for information leading to the apprehension of 184 "bandits" in the nine years from April 30, 1930, until April 29, 1939. The smallest reward paid for the arrest of a bank robber was $50 and the largest $500, a princely sum in those days.

As the October 1938 issue of *The Kansas Banker* lamented, "At present Kansas is without a properly set-up state investigating unit, the bill in the last legislative session providing such a unit having been vetoed by the Governor. A small Bureau of Investigation and Identification, set up either in the State Highway Patrol or in the office of the Attorney General, should be provided by the 1939 Legislature."[5]

Today, rewards for crime solution or captures of criminals cannot be paid to law enforcement officers. Ethics forbid it. Obviously, no such ethical restrictions existed in 1938. That same issue of *The Kansas Banker* described the successful conclusion of a Parsons, Kansas, bank robbery: "Officer Pat Dixon quickly met the situation by covering the bandit . . . and when the bandit threatened him Dixon shot twice and this particular criminal is no more. The Association's reward of $150, together with a similar reward which has been made up by the members of the Labette County Bankers Association, is being paid to Officer Dixon. Good work all around."[6]

With no KBI yet to do the work for free, the Kansas Bankers' Association was not above paying rewards to non-Kansas officers either. "A few weeks prior the Association authorized two rewards of $150 each to the members of the Missouri State Highway Patrol who captured the two bandits who had attacked a half dozen Kansas banks during the past year, and as many more in neighboring states."[7]

The April 1939 issue of *The Kansas Banker* hailed House Bill 427, introduced that month in the Kansas legislature, which would create the Kansas Bureau of Investigation:

> This measure probably provides the one most needed police facility in this state. In setting up a bureau of investigation of ten persons in the Attorney General's Office it will now be possible to report to that office for action, check artists, bandits and others defrauding banks and, of course, the bureau will be of service in the event of any form of major crime or in the solution of continuing minor criminal activities. In addition to investigation after the commitment of the crime the bureau will maintain finger prints and other criminal records which will be available for use of local officers in Kansas and elsewhere.[8]

And, with a sigh of relief, the story noted that the statute creating the KBI was passed, with considerable funding reluctance by the Kansas Senate, just before "final adjournment."

Some of the nation's best-known criminals were, in fact, coming and going across the state with relative impunity. None were more famous than the bank-robbing team of Bonnie Parker and Clyde Barrow, and their occasional associates. For more than two years the pair stole cars and robbed banks, gas stations, and jewelry stores in Texas, Louisiana, New Mexico, Oklahoma, Missouri, Illinois, Iowa, and Kansas. They were accused of at least twelve homicides, including several law enforcement officers. When the petite Bonnie Parker, less than five feet tall and ninety pounds, and Clyde Barrow, both still in their twenties, were shot to death by Louisiana and Texas law enforcement officers in a Louisiana ambush in 1934, they were driving a tan 1934 Ford they had stolen from a residential driveway in Topeka, Kansas, less than a month earlier. In the car, with more than one hundred bullet holes and the riddled bodies of Parker and Barrow, were a Thompson machine gun, twelve handguns, three rifles, two shotguns, and considerable ammunition.[9]

In a typical sign of the times, *Kansas Peace Officer* magazine in December 1934 carried routine wanted notices for twenty-five-year-old Alvin Karpis and the diminutive Fred Barker, one of four famous criminal sons of the famous criminal mother "Ma" Barker. Barker's physical stature, five feet five, 117 pounds, belied the size of his reputation. But he was still the tallest of all the Barkers and two inches taller than his youngest brother, Arthur "Doc" Barker. Both Karpis and Barker were, at that time, wanted by the Shawnee County sheriff's office in Topeka for bank robbery.

Alvin Karpis, named "Public Enemy No. 1" by the FBI in 1936, had grown up in Topeka as a petty thief and burglar. Called "Old Creepy" for obvious physical reasons, Karpis served prison sentences in the Kansas State Industrial Reformatory in Hutchinson, Kansas, and in Lansing, where he dug coal for the state for a few years and became friends with Fred Barker. Later he also served time at Leavenworth before graduating to Alcatraz, where he relived old times with another Barker, "Doc."

Karpis, at five feet ten, was one of the tallest of the famous Depression-era "bandits," and he and the Barkers robbed banks in Kansas, as did Jake Fleagle, Wilbur Underhill, "Pretty Boy" Floyd, of Akins, Oklahoma, and Bonnie and Clyde. John Dillinger, shot dead by FBI agents outside the Biograph Theater in Chicago on July 22, 1934, had robbed banks in at least five states and was a strong suspect in some Kansas bank robberies, as were Lester Gillis, aka George "Baby Face" Nelson, and Homer Van Meter, all of national reputation.

The vicious, cold-blooded "Baby Face" Nelson, a mere five feet four in height himself, would later die of seventeen bullet wounds as a result of a running gun battle on November 27, 1934, with two FBI agents near Barrington, Illinois. Sadly, the two agents who inflicted Nelson's wounds also died as a result of the gunfight.

"Ma" Barker, one of the worst of the criminal threats to Depression-era Kansas and the Midwest, had raised her four undisciplined sons just across the Kansas line in Webb City, Missouri. The genetically challenged Barker boys graduated from truancy and juvenile delinquency to homicide and bank robbery under their mother's devoted tutelage. Herman, the oldest son, after killing a deputy sheriff near Wichita, Kansas, and while surrounded by officers, shot himself rather than be captured. "Ma" and Fred were killed by FBI agents at Lake Weir, Florida, in 1935, during a thirty-minute gunfight. Both died with machine guns in their hands. Arthur "Doc" Barker, the youngest son, a morphine addict with an IQ of 80, was killed in 1939, attempting an escape from Alcatraz, where he was serving a life sentence, and Lloyd Barker, following parole from Leavenworth, was later killed by his wife.

Alcatraz, with its Kansas connections, was yet another indicator of the times. It was changed in 1934 to a federal prison from a U.S. Army disciplinary barracks. The U.S. Justice Department intended to use "The Rock," a twelve-acre island in the middle of San Francisco Bay, to hold the worst federal inmates, so rampant was crime across the nation at the time. Among the earliest of the nation's "worst of the worst" to be shipped to Alcatraz were fifty-two inmates, including Al Capone, sentenced to eleven years in 1931 for income tax evasion. The largest delegation of the "worst" federal prisoners, 102 strong, came from the federal prison in Leavenworth, and included the famous George "Machine Gun" Kelly, whose real name was George Barnes. Many Alcatraz residents had committed crimes in Kansas.

In addition to the notorious gangster Al Capone, destined to die of syphilis, and the college-educated bootlegger, bank robber, and kidnapper "Machine Gun" Kelly, who would die of a heart attack in 1954 at Leavenworth, and the Kansas scourge Arthur "Doc" Barker, killed in an escape attempt from Alcatraz, among the most famous early residents of Alcatraz was Kansan Alvin "Creepy" Karpis. Karpis was actually born Albin Karpowicz in Montreal. His name was changed to Alvin Karpis by a Topeka elementary school teacher. Detested by guards and inmates alike wherever he served prison time, Karpis would spend twenty-six years, a record, at Alcatraz.

Given the above roster of frequent travelers across Kansas, it is not surprising that, from 1929 until 1939, thirty-two Kansas law enforcement officers were killed in the line of duty.[10] Fifteen died as a result of adversarial action between 1920 and 1929.

Into such times and because of such times, the KBI was born.

For many, World War II officially started on September 1, 1939, with Hitler's invasion of Poland and the declarations of war against Germany two days later by Great Britain and France. Others might suggest that it actually started long before 1939, with Japan's invasion of Manchuria in 1931, and/or the Japanese invasion of China in 1937, or with Italy's invasion of Ethiopia in 1935, or with the Spanish Civil War, 1936–1939.

In any event, Americans cared little about such external events of 1931–1939. We remained occupied with the Great Depression and its consequences. Indeed, as late as May 1941, after the British, standing alone, had been engaged in a desperate fight with the Germans for twenty months, a Gallup poll reported that 80 percent of Americans still opposed any entry into the war. It was, they said, none of our business. It was strictly foreign business.

World War II was thrust on Americans on Sunday, December 7, 1941, by the Japanese sneak attack on Pearl Harbor and the subsequent declarations of war against us by the Germans and Italians. Still slowly emerging from the ravages of the Depression, America was ill prepared to fight a war. By the evening of December 7, half our Pacific fleet lay at the bottom of Pearl Harbor, and we were reeling from the loss of 2,400 killed and more than 1,000 wounded in Oahu, Hawaii, on that tragic Sunday morning.

Our woeful military strength was suddenly even less than before and the worst was yet to come. The Japanese would run unimpeded across the Pacific for a year, quickly conquering British, French, Dutch, and American territories throughout Asia and the South Pacific. Their success mirrored Hitler's sweep across Europe and North Africa the previous two years. French Indochina had already been occupied by the Japanese. The Dutch East Indies and British Hong Kong and Singapore fell quickly to invading Japanese. In the surrender of the British "fortress" of Singapore to the Japanese in February 1942, there proved to be more captives than captors, prompting Winston Churchill's famous lament, "Defeat is one thing; disgrace is another."

Americans, as well, experienced early defeats, but not disgrace, at the hands of invading Japanese. Our small Pacific outpost on Guam, defended by 500 marines and native troops armed with World War I helmets, rifles, and ammunition, was overrun by 5,400 Japanese on December 10, 1941. The courageous 500 or so marines and sailors on tiny Wake Island held out sixteen days before being overwhelmed by the vastly superior force of Japanese invaders. There were far more casualties among the captors than the captives. In the Philippines, gallant American and Filipino troops fought without reinforcements, and with little food, ammunition, and medicine, until May 1942, stalling the Japanese onslaught and buying precious time for a staggered America. Thousands of sick and starving Americans and Filipinos died at the hands of the Japanese in the infamous Bataan Death March that followed the surrender of Bataan earlier in April 1942. General Jonathan "Skinny" Wainwright would be forced to surrender his remaining troops the next month, when Corregidor fell to the Japanese. General Wainwright would barely survive the next three years of Japanese captivity. Many of his courageous troops would not.

Defeat was one thing and patriotism another. Never before and not since has there been such an extended patriotic era in American history—or such instant and prolonged unity across the nation. As Senator Robert Dole of Kansas reminisced years later about young Kansans like himself and other Americans who joined the military following the Depression and/or at the outset of World War II: "It was a good deal; you got a good deal; you got a good pair of boots, three meals a day, new clothing, a new rifle. It was the most many young Americans had ever had."[11] Americans were also frightened and bewildered. Germans dominated Europe and North Africa. Their submarines routinely patrolled the waters off our east coast. The Japanese controlled Asia and the Pacific.

Rationing of gasoline, butter, meat, sugar, tires, shoes, coffee, and cheese, which began on the American home front in 1942 and 1943, would not end until 1945. Americans carried ration cards, held scrap metal drives, and purchased war stamps and bonds to help the national war effort. Men headed to military service. Women, most of whom had never worked outside their homes before, also headed to factories to manufacture equipment and materials for war.

With many Kansas law enforcement officers joining other Kansans in the long lines at military recruiting stations across the state throughout December 1941 and the months that followed, the KBI became even more important to the Kansas law enforcement community and to the Kansas criminal justice system. Congress had passed the Selective Service Act on September 14, 1940, providing for the drafting of all able-bodied men between the ages of twenty-one and thirty-five. In November 1942, during the war's first year, the minimum draft age would be lowered to eighteen by a desperate Congress and president.

When the Japanese attacked Pearl Harbor, without warning or a declaration of war, and plunged America into war, all nine KBI agents and their director were well above the maximum draft age of thirty-five. Ace fugitive hunter Joe Anderson was fifty-seven. Clarence Bulla was forty-three, Herb Henderson fifty, Roy Dyer forty-five, Ron Fowkes fifty-one, and Director Lou Richter was forty-eight. Most of the original KBI agents, like their director, already had military service in World War I to their credit.

Although few in number and too old for the military draft, the KBI agents, all experienced lawmen, became critically important to undermanned Kansas law enforcement agencies in general and to the FBI in Kansas in particular during the war. The KBI's help was especially needed because Kansas quickly became a vital arsenal for the war effort, with a massive military presence in our state demanding law enforcement attention.

Kansas, already important to the nation's aviation industry because of icons such as Walter and Olive Ann Beech, Clyde Cessna, Lloyd Stearman, Amelia Earhart, and Wichita's Boeing Corporation, quickly became a key military aircraft manufacturer and trainer. The state sent pilots, planes, Dwight David Eisenhower, and more than 215,000 young Kansas men and women to the war. (More than 3,500 would be killed in action.)[12] Fort Riley and Fort Leavenworth trained and shipped thousands of troops overseas. Navy pilots and crewmen trained at naval air stations at Hutchinson and Olathe. Their Army Air Corps bomber counterparts (B-17, B-24, and B-29) trained at various air bases built across the state in Herington, Wichita, Salina, Great Bend, Pratt, Dodge City, Garden City, Coffeyville, Liberal, Topeka, Hays (Walker), Winfield, and Independence. Thousands of construction workers poured into the state to build those air bases. The 35th Infantry Division, consisting of National Guard troops from Kansas, Nebraska, and Missouri, fought across France, Belgium, and into Germany in 1944 and 1945, with General George Patton. The division suffered 2,947 killed and 12,935 wounded.[13]

"Rosie the Riveter" wasn't just a character in a 1942 song or the figure in a popular wartime Norman Rockwell poster. She truly existed in Kansas during World War II. Thousands of "Rosies" worked at the Sunflower Army Ammunition Plant near DeSoto, Kansas. A settlement known as Sunflower Village was built across the road from the plant to house many of the 20,000 people who worked there during the war. Many of those workers came from Missouri, Oklahoma, Arkansas, Iowa, and Nebraska.

Boeing's Wichita factories were producing more than 40 percent of all the invaluable B-29 "Superfortresses" sent to World War II—more than 1,600 of the huge bombers—while providing employment to thousands of Kansas citizens, including many "Rosies," and also to immigrants from Oklahoma, Arkansas, Missouri, and Texas. By 1944, there were 55,000 aircraft workers in Wichita alone. Boeing's Stearman Division built more than 8,500 of the Stearman Kaydet trainers, the most common aircraft trainer of World War II. Wichita's 14,000 Beechcraft workers produced 7,400 AT-7 and AT-11 aircraft during the war. They were used to train thousands of navigators and bombardiers. Boeing employment alone peaked at more than 35,000 during B-29 production in 1945, with almost 50 percent of the Boeing workforce being women.[14]

More than 6,600 B-25 twin-engine medium bombers were manufactured by "Rosies" and their male counterparts (mostly boys and older men) in the Kansas City, Kansas, North American Aviation plant during the war.[15] That

U.S. Army Air Corps workhorse medium bomber was made famous by the Jimmy Doolittle raid on Japan in 1942. By autumn 1943, 23,500 employees labored in the Fairfax Industrial District plants of Kansas City, Kansas, on the B-25 bombers. Almost 40 percent were "Rosies."

A German prisoner-of-war camp was built in Concordia, Kansas. One of the largest such camps in America during World War II, it opened in 1943 and closed at war's end in 1945. It was guarded by 800 troops and housed as many as 5,000 German prisoners, mostly captives from the German Army's "Afrika Corps," survivors of the fighting in North Africa, and German Navy U-boat survivors. The second largest camp in Kansas was Camp Phillips, near Salina, which held approximately 4,000 German and Italian prisoners. A branch of Camp Concordia, holding 150 to 200 prisoners, was established in Peabody, Kansas, to provide prisoner-laborers to area farms and businesses badly in need of workers.[16] Similar small camps were also established, some quite temporary, in Lawrence, Cawker City, Council Grove, El Dorado, Elkhart, Eskridge, Hays, Hutchinson, Neodesha, and Ottawa. Prisoners in the Lawrence camp not only happily worked on farms in 1945, but some German prisoners who had been stone masons in previous civilian life worked on the construction of Danforth Chapel, a landmark on the University of Kansas campus. Stockades at Fort Leavenworth and Fort Riley held prisoners of war considered the most dangerous and/or the greatest escape risks.

The state's universities and colleges trained officers and various military specialists during the war. With such substantial military presence in Kansas and the state so involved in the war effort, KBI agents were frequently called on to assist the undermanned FBI in locating and apprehending selective service violators, military deserters, servicemen absent without leave, and draft dodgers. The KBI, on behalf of its federal counterparts, also became involved in investigations involving theft of government property, black market fences, fraud against the government, and the occasional escapee from the prisoner-of-war camps in the state.

More often, with serious meat rationing in place, the agents were needed to identify, apprehend, and prosecute cattle thieves, who were plentiful and who roamed across Kansas, Colorado, Nebraska, Oklahoma, and Texas in the early years of the war.

Theft of precious drilling equipment and petroleum in the vital Kansas oil fields also became an investigative priority for the KBI, as did the theft of grain from Kansas farms, silos, and storage elevators, given the food shortages of the day at home and the demand for food for our troops.

Today, a review of official KBI investigations entered in the *Kansas Bureau of Investigation Case Record* during the war years of 1942 through 1945 provides insight into KBI investigative activities during that period. The most common entries in the large directory of investigations during World War II refer to arrests of military deserters, theft of oil field equipment, larceny of livestock, fencing and receiving stolen property (often automobile tires and tubes), liquor violations, theft of ration books, and, of course, the more traditional crimes of robbery, forgery, burglary, and murder.

Though few in number, KBI agents were everywhere across the state and, when necessary, across the nation. As Director Richter reported to the Kansas livestock commissioner, Will J. Miller, in a letter dated January 13, 1943, "The Bureau has apprehended cattle thieves operating in five of the surrounding states. The Bureau makes it a practice to follow up evidence not only within the confines of the state, but over other states of the union. It has apprehended fugitive criminals, such as bank robbers, murderers, etc., as far east as the state of Massachusetts and as far west as California."[17]

Commissioner Miller was probably even more impressed by Director Richter's 1943 report to the Kansas legislature a month later, summarizing the KBI's activities in its first forty-one months of existence. Headlining the bureau's accomplishments since its creation were the convictions of sixty-three cattle rustlers. Richter had consistently complained that 90 percent of all cattle thefts in Kansas involved unbranded cattle, even though a state-registered brand cost only two dollars. He waged a one-man campaign with Kansas ranchers and cattlemen to encourage branding and registration. The campaign was working.

In the same period the KBI solved all twenty-eight homicides assigned to the agency and successfully closed 656 of the 716 major criminal matters referred to it. It arrested thirty-two fugitives, worked sixty-three forgery cases, forty-five robberies, one hundred and fifteen cases involving grand larceny and/or receiving stolen property, sixty-two narcotic investigations, twenty-one auto thefts, fifty-four burglaries, twelve embezzlements, three kidnappings, thirty-eight prostitution cases, and five jail breaks around the state.

Among the busiest of the busy nine KBI agents working for Richter was Special Agent Joe Anderson. A bachelor, Anderson clearly had no home life. He had been undercover with Hight and Wetherick for several weeks in Colorado, of course, before standing beside Richter in front of the Macksville bank. Thereafter, he had specialized in homicide cases, fugitive investigations, and theft of oil field equipment.

Fittingly, Joe Anderson was the first KBI special agent to be mentioned in a Kansas Supreme Court decision, *State of Kansas v. Fred L. Brady*, in 1943: "Joe Anderson, an experienced operative connected with the Kansas Bureau of Investigation."[18] Anderson had participated in the arrest and interrogation of Brady, who had murdered a man in Winfield, Kansas, on January 9, 1943.

Thereafter, the reports of the Kansas Supreme Court, and other court decisions, would routinely describe the significant contributions of KBI personnel to the Kansas criminal justice system. But Special Agent Anderson was the first. The *Brady* decision, in 1943, was the earliest state supreme court reference to the young KBI.

Anderson was earning his top agent's pay, but he was not the only one with a superb work ethic or special expertise. Most of the impressive statistics related to the apprehension and prosecution of cattle thieves were results of the investigative efforts of Ron Fowkes and Charles Maupin. Director Richter had assigned those cases almost exclusively to Fowkes and Maupin. Fowkes had worked as an investigator for the Kansas Livestock Commission and then as deputy sheriff for the Wabaunsee County Sheriff's Department, specializing in cattle theft, prior to becoming a special agent with the KBI. Maupin, prior to joining the KBI, had worked many cattle rustling cases as sheriff of Graham County. Clarence Bulla, former sheriff of Bourbon County, and Jack Huse, former Riley County deputy sheriff and former assistant chief of police of Manhattan, spent months investigating an organized theft ring operating in central Kansas that targeted copper, brass, and other metals essential to the war effort. Bulla and Huse's work paid off when they helped to send the two men most responsible for the metal thefts, primarily from public utility companies in Dickinson, Saline, McPherson, Pawnee, and Phillips Counties, to Lansing. Herb Henderson, who had been an investigator for the prestigious Pinkerton Detective Agency prior to his KBI hiring, had contacts across Illinois, Indiana, and Ohio. For three months he worked a multi-state case involving the theft of $10,000 worth of tires at Wichita. That was a considerable quantity in that day. Tires were heavily rationed, due to their demand for the war effort. Henderson's efforts resulted in the arrest and prosecution of three Chicago men and their incarceration in Lansing.

KBI business, unfortunately, was good. There was plenty of crime to go around. All nine agents and their boss were well occupied, individually and collectively, during World War II. The sight of a KBI agent walking into a Kansas sheriff's office or police station in those days was an especially welcome one, given the depleted resources of local law enforcement during the war.

The KBI, still in its infancy in those years, was handling its wartime responsibilities quite well. The *Kansas City Star* noted, "One of the by-products of the KBI is a sudden diminution of cattle rustling in Kansas."[19] Richter's vision for placing emphasis on cattle branding among Kansas ranchers was bearing fruit. In 1941, the Kansas brand commissioner, at the urging of the Kansas livestock commissioner and Richter, published the first book of 6,021 registered brands over 214 pages, issuing a copy to all 105 Kansas county clerks and printing 500 for sale to Kansas cattlemen at two dollars each. Meanwhile, state and county livestock associations posted rewards ranging from $250 to $1,000 for the arrest and conviction of cattle thieves. Rewards for bank robbers, in contrast, ranged from $50 to $500.

The theft and transportation of live cattle became so risky for the rustlers that Director Richter noted, "Because of the rationing of meat, and public demand which fosters the black market, cattle thieves are now butchering what they steal and selling the meat as quickly as possible, rather than sending live animals to community sales or stock yards. In many instances, especially in isolated sections of the state, stolen animals are butchered on the spot."[20]

Meanwhile, as the KBI worked to help make the Kansas home front safer and more secure, America and its allies were winning the war in Europe and the Pacific.

Victory came first in the European theater, where President Roosevelt had appointed native Kansan Dwight David Eisenhower, of Abilene and West Point, as Supreme Commander of Allied Forces. But before victory in Europe was achieved on May 8, 1945, places like Anzio, Utah Beach, Bloody Omaha, Malmedy, Sainte-Mère-Église, the Bulge, Remagen, Buchenwald, and Dachau would be added to Americans' geographic vocabularies. In the Pacific, Pearl Harbor, Wake Island, Bataan, and Corregidor would be avenged with Japan's surrender on August 14, 1945. American blood that had been shed at Midway, Guadalcanal, Tarawa, Saipan, Iwo Jima, and Okinawa, among other battle sites, made the victory over Japan possible. Atomic bombs dropped from B-29s on Hiroshima and Nagasaki made it certain.

Meanwhile, the KBI braced for the inevitable postwar boom—with one director, nine agents, and one support person.

Following the end of the war, much of Richter's efforts went into strengthening his now firmly established KBI. He accepted every public-speaking invitation his schedule would permit across the state. He became a fixture at Kansas Livestock Association dinners, Kansas Bankers' Association events, conferences and meetings of the Kansas State Peace Officers' Association, and local civic group affairs in every corner of the state. His message was consistent. The KBI was doing a great job and it deserved more resources and manpower and better pay for its agents. His eloquence, popularity, and reputation were partially rewarded. By 1950 he had persuaded the legislature to give him a total of sixteen agents and two more support personnel.

Richter established certain qualifications for the additional special agents he was bringing on board. Each man would have a high school diploma and a minimum of five years of law enforcement experience and be at least twenty-eight years old. The director also emphasized that successful applicants must want a career, not a job. When asked by a reporter what sort of man he was seeking for his new additional special agents, Richter replied, "More of the same" and then explained:

> He needs a keen understanding of human nature, imagination, curiosity, persistence, intelligence and a broad general education. He should be able to get along with those who use four-letter words as well as with those who use four-syllable words. He should keep an open mind and get in the habit of hard work. He should be sympathetic and tactful. Tact is the ability to accomplish things pleasantly without friction. He should be optimistic and co-operative, have courage without foolhardiness, and be ambitious both for himself and the department, and amenable to discipline. He should be honest and more than that, honorable. He should never make a promise to a criminal or an informer unless he is willing to carry it out.[21]

The veteran director pointed out that he had no place in the KBI for any man who would insult or physically abuse a prisoner. He described law enforcement's physical abuse of a suspect as "an evidence of weakness."

Kansas media became the KBI's most vocal and consistent lobbyist. In a story on January 10, 1954, the *Topeka Daily Capital* called the growing agency a "powerful little band against crime." The writer complimented the agency's head by noting:

> Richter runs his department quietly and with little publicity, which is the way his agents work. They are not headline hunters. And probably nowhere does the state get more value for money spent than in the KBI. . . . Richter believes strongly that the country should be run from the grass roots, and the KBI never moves in unless invited, and never usurps the authority the people have placed in the hands of their elected officials. But a sheriff or county attorney has only to make a quick call to the KBI in Topeka to receive the help of a special agent, highly trained and experienced.[22]

The *Hutchinson News-Herald* had expressed similar sentiments on December 15, 1953:

> Nothing speaks higher of KBI Chief Lou Richter than he has run his little department quietly through several administrations and never once

has been dragged in, or poked his nose in any of the successive political dogfights that liven up the capitol. . . . Nowhere do Kansans get more for a dollar invested in state government. . . . We're happy to join . . . in a tribute to the KBI whose latest feat was the difficult solving of a string of western Kansas wheat thefts.[23]

The end of the war brought a dramatic decrease in cattle rustling and other black market–related crimes. And there had been few bank robberies in the state since the attempt at Macksville. The end of the war had also brought predictions from Richter that other crime, in particular juvenile delinquency, would be increasing in the next few years. He announced at the end of the war that juvenile delinquency among girls had already increased an incredible 60 percent between 1941 and 1945 in the state. Most crime in Kansas during the war, however, he attributed to paroled convicts and military deserters.

In August 1947 Richter warned a Smith Center civic group that crimes committed by persons under the age of twenty-one had already increased by 9 percent in 1946 and would increase even more. "If I had my way I'd blast delinquent parents a little more. . . . Winning the war abroad will have been of no particular value if we lose the fight against crime within our own borders."[24] That situation was still bothering the director in August 1951 when he told the *Topeka Daily Capital*, regarding spiraling juvenile crime and crime by young adults, "You can trace the history of a great many of these youths back to the World War II period. Fathers and mothers got high-paying jobs in war industries. This left youngsters who were 10 to 14 without proper home supervision, and most of those who turned to crime later quit school before entering high school. Then they drifted into crimes such as the burglaries which trouble us today."[25]

Indeed, burglary was a problem in the early 1950s. The KBI helped arrest an Oklahoma City group of four men and a woman in 1950 and charged them with burglaries of liquor stores in Lyons, Chase, Selden, Timken, Victoria, Albert, Collyer, and Englewood. Local Kansas officers arrested two of the men and the woman. KBI agents arrested the other two men in Oklahoma City. All were eventually convicted.

Another, more sophisticated group of burglars in 1951 caused the KBI and other Kansas law enforcement agencies considerable concern for several months with burglaries of Veterans of Foreign Wars and American Legion clubs in seventeen Kansas cities and towns prior to their capture by the KBI and local officers. The same group had hit similar veterans' clubs in Missouri, Colorado, and Nebraska.

The KBI, in conjunction with the attorney general's office, also conducted a series of raids on illegal gambling establishments and bookie joints in Topeka, Wichita, Leavenworth, and Kansas City in 1951, in a brief respite from their burglary investigations. They arrested sixteen individuals and seized considerable gaming paraphernalia.

Meanwhile, the agency was building an impressive collection of fingerprint records, significant criminal history files, and photographs of criminals. Moreover, Richter was using some of his additional agents to assist him in training Kansas law enforcement officers. State-mandated police training would not come to Kansas until 1969, with the creation of the Kansas Law Enforcement Training Center at the old Hutchinson Naval Air Station, and the legislative requirement that Kansas officers receive prescribed basic training and annual in-service training. The KBI teamed with the Kansas State Peace Officers' Association and the University of Kansas to set up annual law enforcement training seminars each summer at the University of Kansas starting in 1947. Director Richter and other KBI agents served as instructors in those seminars. The 1951 seminar program listed Director Richter and KBI Special Agents Vernon Dillon, Harry Felker, D. K. Fitch, and Ron Fowkes among the scheduled instructors. Another instructor was the undersheriff of Finney County, Al Dewey, a future KBI agent. KBI involvement in the training of Kansas law enforcement officers continues today.

Richter also assisted the U.S. Secret Service with escort protection for President Eisenhower on his occasional trips home to Kansas. Richter and other agents that he hand-picked were often seen walking or running next to the presidential automobile in parades whenever the president returned to his home state.

During this postwar period, Director Richter hired several new agents to replace some of his original nine who were retiring, and also to fill the additional positions permitted by legislation. Some of the shoes to be filled were especially large. Harry Neal had left the agency in 1943, Jack Huse and R. L. Griffith in 1945, and Charley Maupin in 1947. Joe Anderson and Herb Henderson, who joined together on the KBI's first day of operation, also stepped down together, on June 30, 1955.

Added to the KBI agent rolls were D. K. Fitch and Eldon Fisher in 1945, Wayne Owens in 1946, Vernon Dillon and Roy Church in 1947, Wendell Cowan and a Kansas sheriff named Logan Sanford in 1948, and Harry Felker, Tom Stowers, and Vance Houdyshell in 1949. Added in 1955 were Al Dewey, Howard Docker, Clarence Duntz, and Harold Nye.

On Thursday, September 13, 1956, almost fifteen years after he had faced Hight and Wetherick in Macksville, Louis Phillip Richter, the only director the KBI had known, died in a Topeka hospital at the age of sixty-three. He had been hospitalized a week earlier after a fall in his home in which he had broken an arm, having already lost his right leg to the cancer that had confined him to his home since July.

In his tenure as director, Richter had faithfully served six governors, five attorneys general, and a generation of Kansans. The attorneys general he had served went on to positions of distinction, including governor and state supreme court justice. Their associations with Richter and the KBI had only enhanced their political careers and personal reputations.

Richter had kept his word to Governor Payne Ratner, Attorney General Jay Parker, and the 1939 Kansas legislature. He had sought and achieved professionalism in the ranks of the KBI and had taken those ranks only where requested and needed. He had remained true to his vow to not enter a case unless other law enforcement officials requested KBI assistance. He had avoided all appearance of impropriety and had steered his agency around anything resembling politics. Yet he was at ease with congressmen, governors, army generals, attorneys general, state legislators, and a president. He had created an elite investigative ally for Kansas prosecutors and law enforcement. No scandal or blemish had tarnished his beloved KBI. Indeed, he had developed a state law enforcement investigative agency, one of the first in the nation, so respected and so highly regarded that it was often compared to the FBI. It was a compliment that delighted Richter, a strong admirer of his national counterpart, J. Edgar Hoover.

The son of a German immigrant mother and Kansas farmer, Richter was survived by his wife of thirty-seven years, Ella, also a native of Marion County. Funeral services were held in Marion and burial was in Hillsboro, where Richter had attended high school. There was standing room only in the Marion Presbyterian Church. The overflow filled the funeral home across the street from the church as well. The funeral services were piped into the funeral home by a special sound system extending from the church. Pallbearers included KBI Special Agents Logan Sanford, Roy Church, Vance Houdyshell, Wayne Owens, and Roy Dyer, one of the original nine. Also present were the current attorney general, John Anderson Jr., Jay Parker, the former attorney general who was now a justice of the Kansas Supreme Court, and in addition another justice, Harold Fatzer. Perhaps most notably, among the honorary pallbearers were five more of Richter's original nine special agents, Harry Neal, Joe Anderson, Clarence Bulla, Ron Fowkes, and Herb Henderson.

Kansas newspapers, mourning Richter's passing, echoed sentiments of the Kansas criminal justice system in referring to him in such terms as "legend" and "hero." All recalled that September morning in 1941 when the director had himself stood with other law enforcement officers in the Macksville street in the KBI's first gun battle.

He had served seventeen years as director of the KBI. No other director has served longer.

As Richter was battling his illness, Attorney General Anderson named Will Johns, an investigator for the office of the attorney general, as acting director of the KBI. Following Richter's death, the attorney general announced that Johns would continue as interim KBI director pending a final decision on a formal replacement.

The final decision was announced in April 1957, and the announcement surprised many. Anderson announced that, effective April 23, the second director of the Kansas Bureau of Investigation would be KBI Special Agent Logan Sanford, the former sheriff of Stafford County, Kansas, then assigned as an agent in St. John, Kansas. Anderson had reached past the KBI's executive staff and other political recommendations to select as director the former sheriff who had stood with Richter and his agents in front of the Macksville bank in 1941.

Logan Sanford had returned home following World War II after receiving his military discharge in November 1945. He again ran for sheriff the following year, polling the highest vote count of any candidate for any position in the November 1946 election in his home county. Sanford's dream of becoming a KBI agent, born in September 1941, was fulfilled on January 1, 1948, when Richter appointed him as special agent and assigned him to the region of the state covering his home county, permitting his continued residence in St. John with his wife, Doris, and three daughters, Margaret, Bonnie, and Corine.

Sanford had proven as effective and popular in his new position as he had been as sheriff, and his investigative accomplishments soon validated Richter's faith in him. That faith led Richter to nominate Sanford for the FBI National Academy in Quantico, Virginia. J. Edgar Hoover had created the FBI National Academy to provide leadership and management training for carefully selected local law enforcement officers, those who were expected to be the future leaders and/or administrators of their respective agencies or other such agencies. Sanford had been one of the first from Kansas selected and Lou Richter, with his FBI connections, was instrumental in that selection. Sanford's appointment to the special FBI school, more than three months in duration, was one of Richter's last official acts, in 1956, prior to his illness.

Those who recalled that impressive honor for Sanford and who understood the friendship between him and Richter were not surprised by Attorney General Anderson's announcement in April 1957. Those observers were confident that Richter would have been pleased with the selection of his successor.

The similarities between the two men, physically, as well as professionally, were striking. Both were large, dark-haired, handsome men. Each was a
product of rural, small-town Kansas. Each came from an agricultural background. Neither was a politician, yet both understood politics and people
very well. Between them they were elected Kansas county sheriff seven
times, and had there not been an ill-conceived law forbidding Kansas sheriffs from serving more than two consecutive terms, each would probably have
been sheriff several more times. It was then typical, if not traditional, for a
popular sheriff to be succeeded by his wife or his carefully selected undersheriff every third term before legally running for office again. Both Richter
and Sanford were popular in their home counties, and each could easily have
been elected sheriff more often.

They shared many of the same values and philosophies. Each ran the KBI
quietly, with as little publicity as possible, and with great modesty. It was the
practice of each to permit the local sheriff, police chief, or county attorney
to issue any press release regarding a joint investigative effort. Neither was a
headline hunter. Headlines, however, came easily to both.

Each was a no-nonsense administrator, firmly believing in policies, rules,
regulations, and discipline. Yet both were very much admired and respected
by those whom they directed. Both enjoyed excellent reputations across the
state within the Kansas law enforcement community. Each was elected president of the Kansas State Peace Officers' Association, the largest law enforcement association in the state. Richter had been elected the association's president in 1936 while serving as sheriff of Marion County; Sanford served in the
position in 1964 while he was still KBI director.

The similarities between the two didn't end with career accomplishments.
In response to a question at a Kansas City Rotary Club dinner in 1945, Richter blamed juvenile delinquency on parents and absence from church. He
urged parents to "exercise more supervision of young people. . . . Juvenile
delinquency can be laid directly at the door of the parents. . . . In my home
and I know it's not a general practice in homes producing delinquents, we
had a prayer in the morning and again at night and grace was said at meals."[26]
In 1966, when a reporter asked Sanford what he considered important de-
terrents to crime, he replied, "Personal pride, pride in the family and the
sure disgrace that follows conviction as a criminal, rank right behind the
good influence of the church, the family and the schools in shaping a clean,
productive citizen's life. I believe the influence of churches to be the greatest
deterrent to crime, especially when combined with good environment."[27]

Each one's administration was forever inextricably linked to a single major
crime. With Lou Richter it was a southwestern Kansas bank robbery. With
Logan Sanford it would be a western Kansas quadruple homicide.

CHAPTER FOUR

Clutter: "Cold Blood" in Western Kansas, Justice on Lansing's Gallows

The Clutter case, which more than any other symbolizes the KBI, started in a cell in Lansing in June 1959—not on a farm near Holcomb, Kansas, in November 1959. It would also end in Lansing, but not until April 14, 1965. It would end on the gallows at Lansing.

In many respects, it has not ended. It remains probably the most infamous crime in Kansas history (with the possible exceptions of Missourian William Quantrill's bloody pro-slavery raid on Lawrence on August 21, 1863, when some 200 mostly unarmed and defenseless men and boys were murdered, the city business district destroyed, and almost 200 homes torched;[1] and the modern-day "BTK" saga of Wichitan Dennis Rader, Kansas's most famous serial killer, 1974–2005).

Thanks in large part to the flamboyant Truman Capote's best-selling book *In Cold Blood*, described by Capote himself as a nonfiction novel based on the crime, its investigation, and the prosecution, the KBI continues to receive more media and researcher inquiries on the Clutter case than on all other KBI investigations combined. There have been so many, in fact, that during my tenure as director, 1994–2007, the responsibilities of one KBI supervisor at headquarters included the response to all such inquiries.

Capote's book, published in late 1965 by Random House, had been serialized in four issues of the *New Yorker* (in September and October of 1965). In turn, the book was adapted into a 1967 Oscar-nominated movie of the same name, with John Forsythe as KBI Special Agent Al Dewey and Robert Blake and Scott Wilson as Perry Smith and Richard Hickock, respectively.

The most popular display case at KBI headquarters during public tours remains the one that contains Hickock's shotgun and knife, Smith's boot, photographs of Hickock and Smith, photographs of the Clutter family, and the actual bloody sole imprint from the scene.

There have been several documentaries and one television miniseries on the Clutter case. Those imitations pale in comparison with Capote's book and the original movie, in my opinion, but they nevertheless reflect the continuing interest in the events of November 15, 1959, at Holcomb, Kansas. *In Cold Blood* remains required reading in the journalism, literature, and criminal justice classes of many schools and colleges across the nation.

The National Institute of Justice Conference on Science and Law in San Diego in October 2000 featured presentations and discussions of the Clutter case with KBI forensic and investigative involvement. Participants at the conference came from across the nation and represented the U.S. Department of Justice, the American Academy of Forensic Sciences, the National Center for State Courts, the National District Attorneys Association, and the National Academy of Sciences. Special guests of honor and featured presenters were KBI Special Agent in Charge Larry Thomas (later Assistant Director Larry Thomas), the resident expert on the famous case at KBI headquarters, and Senior Special Agent Ray Lundin, then of the KBI Cold Case Squad.

Herbert Clutter had been a nationally respected and successful farmer in Finney County, Kansas. In 1950, U.S. Secretary of Agriculture Charles Brannon appointed this popular Kansas farm leader to the National Grain Advisory Committee. President Dwight Eisenhower, also a Kansan, appointed Clutter in 1953 to the newly created Federal Farm Credit Board. He had also been a board member of the Consumers Cooperative Association in Kansas City, Missouri, and served on the board of the Garden City Cooperative Association for twelve years, ten of them as president. He was the first president of the Kansas Association of Wheat Growers and also the first president of that association's national counterpart.

Moreover, forty-three years after his murder and the murders of his wife, daughter, and son, Clutter received another honor for his well-known previous leadership in Kansas and U.S. agriculture. On March 31, 2003, he was posthumously inducted into the Kansas Cooperative Hall of Fame, which recognizes Kansas farm leaders who have been instrumental in the agricultural cooperative philosophy in Kansas and the nation. Clutter's two surviving daughters accepted the award in Hutchinson, Kansas, and the award was placed in a display case in the Pride of Kansas Building on the Kansas State Fairgrounds.

William Floyd Wells, KSP 14323, on the other hand, had no national recognition or admirable achievements to his credit. He had succeeded at nothing, not even burglary.

In June 1959, Wells was serving a sentence of three to five years in Lansing for the burglary of an appliance store in Labette County. His cellmate in June and July 1959, prior to the latter's parole on August 13, was twenty-eight-year-old Dick Hickock of Johnson County, Kansas.

Hickock's success story was no brighter than Wells's. He had also succeeded at nothing, including worthless checks, which had landed him in Lansing. What Richard Eugene Hickock was good at was storytelling. He especially liked to tell stories of his claimed exploits in athletics, his passing of bad checks, and his countless sexual conquests of women, even though many, including KBI agents, would later consider him a latent pedophile. He also enjoyed predicting future "big scores" after his upcoming parole. Those plans always included his buddy and former Lansing cellmate Perry Smith, who had received his Lansing parole on July 6, 1959, having served three years of a five-to-ten year burglary sentence.

To counter Hickock's constant claims of criminal intelligence and "big score" information, Wells told Hickock about the wealthy western Kansas farmer for whom he had worked as a farmhand ten years earlier. One of the richest and most successful farmers in the Midwest, Wells told Hickock that Herbert Clutter at any given time would have ten to twenty men working for him on his farm near Holcomb and $10,000 in cash in the safe behind his desk in the office in his home. Hickock was immediately interested in everything Wells knew about Clutter and his money, believing that this could be the "big score" he had been unsuccessfully pursuing for so long.

Finally feeling important and knowledgeable about something, Wells did nothing to discourage Hickock. Indeed, he drew a map for Hickock showing how to reach the Clutter farm from Garden City and Holcomb. He also drew a diagram of the two-story farm home, highlighting Clutter's office, where the alleged safe was located. Wells explained that ten years earlier Herb Clutter and his wife, Bonnie, had two older girls, who were probably gone now, and another daughter, Nancy, and a son, Kenyon, both of whom were now probably in high school and still living at home.

When Hickock shared his plans with Wells, he predicted that he and Perry Smith might have to leave no witnesses behind at the Clutter farm. Wells dismissed such robbery and murder predictions, he later told KBI agents, because Hickock was the biggest blowhard and braggart he had ever known. Hickock was paroled to his parents in Olathe, Kansas, in August. Wells told nobody in Lansing about his departed cellmate's "big score" plans.

Richard Eugene Hickock, KSP 13651, twenty-eight in 1959, three years younger than Perry Edward Smith, was a native Kansan. Smith, KSP 12649, called Nevada home, but he had lived in many places, including Alaska. He was in prison for a burglary in Phillips County, Kansas, committed as he traveled through Kansas from Nevada en route to New York. Otherwise he had never been in Kansas.

Both came from poor families—Smith's considerably more dysfunctional than Hickock's. Two of Smith's three siblings had committed suicide. His mother had died an alcoholic and his father had abandoned the family repeatedly. Smith never completed grade school and claimed physical abuse at both an orphanage and at a shelter for neglected children. Two motorcycle accidents had left his already physically strange body even stranger with legs of different length. He was five feet four in height but emphatically claimed to be five feet five inches tall. He fancied himself an artist, songwriter, and poet. He had never married.

Hickock had been a good high school athlete. Following graduation he worked at a variety of menial jobs, usually something connected with automobiles, his true love, most often repairing or painting them. He had also been injured in an accident—automobile rather than motorcycle. He had married twice, divorced twice, and was the father of three sons. Hickock considered women and passing worthless checks his foremost talents.

Smith, following his July parole from Lansing, had maintained contact with Hickock, awaiting the latter's release. Hickock, after his parole in August, did three things quickly. He bought a new 12-gauge pump shotgun at a Western Auto store in Olathe on credit, bought a black 1949 Chevrolet, and wrote to Smith, then a truck driver in Idaho, telling him to catch a bus to Kansas City, explaining he had identified the perfect "big score" for them.

In response to Hickock's letter, Smith telephoned him, advising he was en route to Kansas City on a Greyhound bus. Smith arrived on November 12. Hickock met Smith at the bus station and found him a motel room. He thoroughly briefed Smith on Wells's "big score" information. For a couple of days they worked on the 1949 Chevrolet, patronized Kansas City prostitutes, and planned trips to western Kansas and Mexico.

On the afternoon of November 14, 1959, they placed Hickock's new shotgun and his hunting knife in his 1949 black Chevrolet and, using money Hickock had obtained passing a dozen or so worthless checks in the Kansas City area, they started the 367-mile trip from Olathe to Holcomb, Kansas. At Burlingame they gassed up the car and bought gloves. At Emporia they purchased rope and tape. Shortly after midnight, on November 15, 1959, they purchased gasoline outside Garden City, Kansas, and then followed Floyd Wells's directions to the Clutter farm, near Holcomb.

Sometime around 1:00 A.M., with Smith carrying the shotgun and Hickock a hunting knife and flashlight, they entered an unlocked door into Clutter's office and searched that room, unsuccessfully, for a safe. They went into the first floor bedroom and found Herbert Clutter asleep, alone. They awakened him and took him to his office, ordering him to show them his safe. As Smith cut telephone lines on the first floor, Clutter insisted to Hickock that there was no safe anywhere in his home. He gave Hickock thirty dollars from his wallet, all that he had, and offered to write them a check. Disbelieving Clutter's claims of no safe and no other money, they became angry and forced him upstairs, where his wife, teenaged daughter, and teenaged son were asleep in different bedrooms. Each was awakened.

Each family member denied the existence of a safe, and the search of that floor, like that of the first floor, revealed no safe. More cash, eleven dollars, was found, bringing the total cash loot to forty-one dollars. When asked about the whereabouts of the rest of the family, Mr. Clutter quietly and calmly explained that there were two older daughters, one married and in Illinois and the other a student in the University of Kansas School of Nursing in Kansas City.

It was becoming apparent to both Hickock and Smith that Floyd Wells had lied. There was no $10,000. Herb Clutter didn't appear to be rich. There was no safe. And the two of them were looking at parole violation, new criminal charges, and an inevitable return to Lansing.

Subsequent statements and admissions to both the KBI and Truman Capote never clarified who made the initial decision at the scene. Most agree that had either Hickock or Smith attempted the robbery alone, the final crime would have been just that, attempted robbery. Together, however, without speaking to each other about the decision, the two men together decided to leave no witnesses, as Hickock had predicted to Wells in their cell in June. Years later Al Dewey would say that Perry Smith was the follower until the pair crossed the Clutter threshold. After entry into the home, he became the dominant force.

However the decision was reached, five months after Floyd Wells told Dick Hickock about his previous employer and his rumored wealth, and had drawn diagrams and maps to assist Hickock and Smith, the popular, highly regarded agricultural visionary Herbert Clutter and his wife, daughter, and son lay slaughtered in their western Kansas home, in what KBI Director Logan Sanford would soon describe as the most brutal crime in Kansas history.

Using the rope and tape purchased in Emporia, Herbert, Bonnie, Nancy, and Kenyon Clutter were each bound and gagged. Bonnie and Nancy were left in their respective upstairs bedrooms. Herbert and Kenyon were bound and gagged in the basement of the home. Smith cut Mr. Clutter's throat with the hunting knife and shot him in the head with the shotgun. He then shot Kenyon in the head, before going upstairs to execute both Nancy and Bonnie in the same manner, a shotgun blast to the head at very close range. Hickock had followed Smith every step of the way, holding the flashlight on every victim as Smith shot them in the darkened house. He also helped Smith pick up each of the four shotgun shell casings as Smith ejected them after each killing.

They took the forty-one dollars in cash, Kenyon's Zenith portable radio, and Herbert's binoculars, then departed their "big score." North of Garden

City, toward Scott City, they paused long enough to bury some of the homicide paraphernalia in a ditch before returning to Kansas City.

Alvin A. Dewey is arguably the best-known special agent in KBI history. The Clutter case and Truman Capote made that so. Only Directors Richter and Sanford, or maybe Joe Anderson, could challenge the dark-haired, handsome Dewey for such a claim to fame. The irony is that all four were quiet, modest gentlemen. None sought fame.

On November 15, 1959, Dewey was the resident KBI special agent in Garden City. He had previously been a special agent with the FBI. While an FBI agent in New Orleans in 1941, he met the lovely Marie Louise Bellocq, a New Orleans native and a stenographer in the FBI office. They were married on June 28, 1942, in New Orleans. Al and Marie Dewey left the FBI and moved to Al's hometown, Garden City, Kansas, in 1945. He served as undersheriff and sheriff of Finney County, Kansas, prior to being appointed KBI special agent on January 15, 1955, by Director Lou Richter. Dewey was assigned to his native western Kansas, where he knew every sheriff and police chief.

Following discovery of the awful homicide scene at the Clutter farm by two of Nancy Clutter's girlfriends, who had intended to accompany her to church that morning, Finney County sheriff Earl Robinson's first call was to his friend and predecessor Al Dewey of the KBI. The former G-man and personal friend of the Clutter family, as the resident KBI agent, assumed leadership of the investigation. His office was in the Finney County sheriff's office in the Garden City courthouse. For the next six years, until the case was finally settled on the gallows in Lansing, the Clutter murders would consume his time and mind throughout his waking hours and cost Dewey considerable sleep and, some said, much of his health.

Every KBI agent in the agency at that time would eventually work on the quadruple murder investigation, but Director Sanford assigned primary investigative responsibility at the outset to KBI Special Agents Al Dewey, Clarence Duntz, Roy Church, and Harold Nye under Dewey's direction. And, as always with the KBI, those agents worked closely with local Kansas law enforcement agencies. The KBI command post for direction of the case was at the Finney County sheriff's office throughout the investigation.

One of the first things that intrigued Al Dewey and the other officers at the terrible scene near tiny Holcomb, Kansas, was the contradictory nature of the treatment of the four victims by the killer or killers. A degree of compassion had been extended to the victims, it appeared, in that, in the basement, forty-eight-year-old Herb Clutter's body was lying on a large cardboard box that had previously contained a recently purchased mattress, and fifteen-year-old Kenyon, Herb's son, was on a basement couch. They were not lying on the cold concrete basement floor. Upstairs, Herb's forty-five-year-old wife, Bonnie, and Nancy, their sixteen-year-old daughter, were in their respective bedrooms in their beds. Neither had apparently been sexually molested. On the other hand, in the most brutal fashion any of the veteran investigators present had ever observed, each victim, bound and gagged, had been shot in the head at extremely close range with a large, probably 12-gauge, shotgun. In addition, Herb's throat had been cut. The house was, as one investigator noted at the scene, "a bloody mess."

If robbery were the motive, then the crime was not much of a success, the investigators agreed. Everyone knew Herb Clutter kept no cash. He paid for everything with checks. Probably less than fifty dollars in cash had been in the house. Kenyon's portable radio and Herb's binoculars, often used by Kenyon for coyote hunting, could not be found in the house or in Kenyon's truck.

Clearly a shotgun and knife had been used. Neither was found at the scene. Nor were any shotgun shell casings. Two separate weapons usually meant two killers, but only one boot print, a "Cat's Paw" sole, had been found in Herb's blood on the mattress box.

Such brutality and savagery at a murder scene often indicated revenge or passionate hatred. Yet the Clutters were respected people. Herb's reputation as a fair man and a Christian was without qualification. At any given time, as many as fifteen or twenty men worked on the Clutter farm, most during wheat harvest. No worker had ever complained of poor treatment by the Clutters. Individually and collectively, the family's reputation was above reproach.

Dewey and Robinson held a news conference at the Garden City courthouse the day following the discovery of the murders. Autopsies were not yet completed, and several KBI agents and local investigators were still laboring at the Clutter home. The two veteran lawmen told the public assembly what little they knew that they could share and issued an appeal to anyone who might have pertinent information to come forward.

The Clutter murders quickly captured the interest of national media, including the Kansas City radio station whose news program Floyd Wells was listening to in his Lansing cell on Monday, November 16, 1959. "Damn," he would later say of his first thoughts. "Damn, I don't believe it. Just like Dick said he would do." Then he thought of the Christmas several years earlier when Mr. Clutter had given him an extra fifty dollars for the holiday. But he did nothing except to continue monitoring news reports until days later, when the newspaper in Hutchinson offered a reward of one thousand dollars for any information leading to the capture and conviction of the person or persons guilty of the Clutter murders.

More than a thousand people attended the Clutters' funeral services, including several KBI agents, who were most interested in the attendees. The problem was they weren't sure what a quadruple murderer looked like. Al and Marie Dewey were present, of course, as friends of the Clutters and members of the same Garden City Methodist Church. No clues were forthcoming from the funeral.

The autopsy reports did not tell the investigators anything new either, except that Mr. Clutter's throat had been cut before he was shot. A 12-gauge shotgun had been used on all the victims, and the medical examiner confirmed that neither Mrs. Clutter nor Nancy had been sexually assaulted.

Brilliant, meticulous crime scene work by Garden City's Assistant Chief of Police Rich Rohleder provided the first good news on the evidence front when his crime scene photographs were developed. In an unusual underexposed photograph, a second boot print, not visible to the naked eye at the scene, was revealed. Someone wearing boots with unique diamond-patterned soles had walked in the dust around Herb's body on the mattress box. "Cat's Paw" and diamonds. Two different boot soles. There had been at least two killers.

Possible suspects were being eliminated almost as quickly as they were suggested. Nancy's boyfriend, Herb's business associates, area natives with criminal records, anyone who was suggested, were all checked out and eliminated in the next weeks. Photos of the crime scene and descriptions of the modus operandi were sent to law enforcement agencies in other states. KBI agents contacted every informant they had and visited with local law enforcement in their respective assigned areas across the state.

Meanwhile, Robinson, Dewey, Duntz, Church, and Nye had decided to concentrate on all the farmhands who had worked for the Clutters in the past ten years. Herb Clutter's farm records and employee files had been meticulously maintained. It could be done. It would simply take time to locate and interview everyone who had worked for Herb. There were almost one hundred names on the list. Should they go chronologically or alphabetically? Either way it would have taken awhile to get to Floyd Wells. But the Clutter investigators were headed toward Wells, methodically, slowly, inevitably.

On December 4, 1959, Warden Tracy Hand in Lansing telephoned Director Sanford at KBI headquarters: "Logan, I have an inmate in my office right now. His name is Floyd Wells and I think you guys should hear the story he's been telling me." The warden briefly summarized Wells's story and agreed to hold him in isolation for his own protection until KBI agents could arrive to formally interview him. Director Sanford assured the warden that that would be soon. After directing Special Agent Wayne Owens to Lansing, Sanford telephoned Al Dewey in Garden City to brief him on the Lansing story. Files were being pulled on Richard Eugene Hickock and Perry Edward Smith, and copies, along with photographs of Hickock and Smith, would be driven west to Dewey that day by a KBI agent.

Both Sanford and Dewey had noted the name Floyd Wells on the alphabetical and chronological rosters of former Clutter farmhands, and both felt good about this new lead. Sanford sent Special Agent Harold Nye to Johnson County to interview Hickock's parents in Edgerton, and his last employer, an Olathe auto body shop operator. In his interviews Nye used the pretext that he was looking for Hickock for a parole violation in connection with seven worthless checks he had passed in the Kansas City area on November 20, accompanied by Perry Smith.

The Johnson County interviews didn't produce information about the current whereabouts of Hickock and Smith, but they did establish that Hickock and Smith had left the area on Saturday, November 14, ostensibly to go to Fort Scott, Kansas, to visit Smith's sister. They had returned the afternoon of Sunday, November 15, reporting that Smith's sister had apparently moved. They had not been able to find her, they said. The pair left the area again together on November 21, destination unknown to the interviewees, and had not been heard from since.

Nye had pretended to admire the new 12-gauge Savage shotgun, a model 300, in the corner of Hickock's parents' living room. Dick had purchased it for pheasant hunting, Mr. Hickock told the agent. His son had only paid fifteen dollars down and the store had been calling about the balance. Nye examined the gun and was strangely, instantly, convinced that it had killed the Clutters. He was reluctant to put the gun back in the corner of the room but knew he had no choice. He memorized the serial number and disguised his excitement and interest in the gun.

The search for the Clutters' killers officially started on December 5, 1959. But the wanted notices and all-points bulletins issued nationwide by the KBI for Hickock and Smith reflected nothing about suspicion of murder. The charges listed were parole violation and passing worthless checks. The KBI didn't want to tip their hand to the pair of fugitives and also didn't want the media frenzy that would surely follow any murder charge announcement.

Unknown then to the KBI, Hickock and Smith had fled first to Acapulco, Mexico, and then Mexico City, where they quickly ran out of the money from the worthless checks and sold Kenyon's radio, Mr. Clutter's binoculars, and Hickock's 1949 Chevrolet. Then, in early December, about the time of Wells's Lansing disclosure, they took a bus across the border to California and proceeded to hitchhike across the country. Sightings of them were soon reported in Florida, Nevada, Wyoming, Nebraska, and Iowa. In Iowa they stole a 1956 Chevrolet and drove it to Kansas City, where Hickock replaced the Iowa license plate with a stolen Kansas license plate and passed more bad checks. The KBI was now a day or two behind them, but once again the pair made it out of Kansas undetected, despite new, revised wanted notices about them, the car, and the Kansas license plate.

The KBI promptly shared whatever information it obtained about Hickock and Smith with Nevada authorities, given that Smith had shown a propensity for heading to Las Vegas, Reno, and Elko. Information regarding the Iowa stolen car and the Kansas plate was teletyped to all three Nevada municipal police departments and the Nevada State Police.

The KBI did not know that, prior to their departure from Mexico, Hickock and Smith had placed most of their belongings in a large box and mailed it to Perry Smith, via general delivery, in Las Vegas. Those belongings included Smith's "Cat's Paw"-soled boots and Hickock's boots with the diamond-patterned soles.

On December 30, 1959, forty-five days after the murders and twenty-six days after Floyd Wells gave his story to Wayne Owens, Hickock and Smith, riding in the car they had stolen from Iowa bearing the stolen Kansas license plate, were arrested by two Las Vegas police officers on behalf of the state of Kansas. The fugitives were arrested only a short time after they arrived in Las Vegas that same day.

The Las Vegas Police Department officer who telephoned Sanford minutes after the arrest of the pair at 6:25 P.M. Kansas time noted that Hickock and Smith had readily admitted the car theft, the parole violations, and the worthless checks. They had been separated in different cells after being allowed to select their own property from a large box they had picked up at the local post office minutes before the wanted car was spotted by the two patrolmen. And they had waived extradition to Kansas.

Pursuant to Sanford's instructions, Al Dewey, Clarence Duntz, Roy Church, and Sheriff Robinson immediately left Garden City in two automobiles en route to Las Vegas. Harold Nye flew from Kansas City to Las Vegas the following day.

On January 2, 1960, at the Las Vegas Police Department, in separate interrogation rooms, at 2:00 P.M. Las Vegas time, Al Dewey and Clarence Duntz interviewed Smith and Harold Nye and Roy Church interviewed Hickock. Although the U.S. Supreme Court didn't require warnings or advice of rights until its decision in *Miranda v. Arizona* some six years later, the KBI, like the FBI, already had such a policy in place for custodial interrogations. Accordingly, Hickock and Smith, in their separate interrogations, were advised that they had the right to remain silent, that anything they said could be used against them in court, and that they had the right to an attorney. Each understood and waived his rights. Smith added that Lansing had taught him his rights.

After listening to Hickock talk about their travels to Mexico and around the country, about auto theft and worthless checks, celling with Smith in Lansing, and trying to find Smith's sister in Fort Scott on November 14, Church and Nye stopped Hickock at 5:30 P.M. and admitted they didn't really care about auto theft, checks, and parole violation. They were there, they advised Hickock, to "clear up the Clutter murder case." Instantly, a shaken Hickock denied any knowledge of that crime and angrily terminated the interview. He was returned to his jail cell for the night, separate from Perry Smith.

At 1:30 P.M. the next day, the agents interviewed him again after advising him again of his interview rights, which he again waived. For an hour he attempted to persuade the agents of the November 14–15 alibi involving Fort Scott and Smith's sister, and his ignorance of the Clutter case. When told there was a living witness to the Clutter murders who would testify against him, Hickock paused and said, "I'll tell you this, I won't testify to it in court nor will I sign a statement, but Smith killed the Clutter family."

In the written and taped confession that followed, Hickock admitted he had originally obtained information about Herbert Clutter from a Lansing cellmate, Floyd Wells, and had contacted Smith about the "big score." The robbery was his idea, he acknowledged, but he insisted Smith had cut Herb Clutter's throat with Hickock's hunting knife and had shot all four family members with Hickock's shotgun. Both the knife and gun were at Hickock's parents' home. He also admitted he had worn boots with diamond-patterned soles during the crime. And Smith had worn boots with "Cat's Paw" soles.

Meanwhile, Smith was denying everything about the Clutters in Las Vegas interviews on January 2 and January 3. However, as he rode in the car with Dewey and Duntz on January 4 en route to Garden City, Smith was told of Hickock's statement, after which he admitted their involvement in the murders and promised he would furnish a formal statement to that effect when they arrived in Garden City.

In a lengthy statement at the Finney County sheriff's office in Garden City on January 6, recorded by a court reporter, Smith waived his rights and admitted that he had cut Herb Clutter's throat and shot him and Kenyon. He claimed that Hickock had also stabbed Mr. Clutter and shot both women. He also claimed that he had prevented Hickock from raping Nancy prior to her murder.

The preamble of Smith's recorded statement in Garden City reflects the fact that the KBI warned Smith of his rights:

> Q Perry, you know that I am A. A. Dewey of the Kansas Bureau of Investigation and that the man sitting there is Mr. C. C. Duntz of the Kansas Bureau of Investigation and that the lady to my left here is Mrs. Lillian Valenzuela, the court reporter here at Garden City, Kansas?
>
> A Yes.
>
> Q Perry, you also know that you do not have to make any statement?
>
> A Yes, sir.
>
> Q And that anything you say can be used in court against you?
>
> A I do, sir.
>
> Q And no threats, promises of rewards or immunity have been made by Mr. Duntz or myself to obtain this statement?
>
> A That's correct, sir.
>
> Q You also realize you have the right to be represented by an attorney?
>
> A Yes sir, I do.
>
> Q And, in view of what I have stated above, you are willing to make a statement?
>
> A Yes, sir, I am willing to.

By any legal standard of the day, more than six years before the U.S. Supreme Court handed down the landmark decision regarding custodial interrogation in *Miranda v. Arizona,* Dewey's advice of rights to Smith was exceptional and a fine example of the KBI's professionalism.

The following evening Dewey received a telephone call from a jailer telling them that Smith wanted to see Dewey and Duntz again. The two agents went to the jail about 8:00 P.M. Smith told them that he wished to change his statement to admit that he had killed all four Clutters himself. Hickock had not killed anyone, he insisted, and he didn't want Hickock's elderly mother to think he had.

Hickock and Smith appeared in Finney County District Court on January 7 and each was charged with four counts of first-degree murder. They waived preliminary hearings and were bound over for trial.

The KBI retrieved the shotgun and knife from the home of Hickock's parents. On January 13, 1960, Hickock and Smith directed agents to the locations of the four 12-gauge shotgun shell casings, three pieces of nylon cord, and a partial roll of adhesive tape in a ditch between Scott City and Garden City, where the duo had buried the items following the murders. All that recovered evidence was later forensically connected to the shotgun and crime scene.

District Court Judge Roland Tate, who would preside over the trial, appointed local attorneys for Hickock and Smith's defense on January 8, 1960. Despite their previous admissions, they each entered pleas of not guilty on February 9, 1960, in state district court in Garden City. The defense attorneys had little choice other than to argue temporary insanity for both defendants and beg for mercy.

The lead prosecutor was Finney County Attorney Duane West, who, at six feet four, towered over both Hickock and Smith. He also towered over his assistant counsel, special assistant prosecuting attorney Logan Green. West and Green elected to pursue the death penalty.

Initially, Hickock moved to be tried separately from Smith. However, on March 9, each defendant agreed to be tried together. The trial started March 22, 1960, and lasted three days, although the defense required less than two hours. The jury deliberated forty minutes, after which Hickock and Smith were each found guilty of four counts of first-degree murder. They were sentenced to hang in Lansing, where the tragic scheme had been born.

Hickock and Smith appealed their convictions to the Kansas Supreme Court on a variety of grounds, including temporary insanity, lack of change of venue, moving the trial out of Garden City (although the defense never requested a venue change), and failure of the district court judge to continue the trial date, due to the illness of Hickock's father, a subpoenaed character witness.

On July 8, 1961, the Kansas Supreme Court rejected the appeals and affirmed the convictions and sentences. The U.S. Supreme Court also later rejected their appeals on three separate occasions and, finally, the Kansas Supreme Court, with all appeals exhausted, scheduled the defendants' executions for April 14, 1965. On that cold, rainy night, in a warehouse in Lansing, the two killers were executed by hanging, first Hickock and then Smith.

On November 28, 1966, Truman Capote hosted 540 guests at the New York Plaza Hotel. The formal occasion, "The Black and White Ball," was to honor his longtime friend Katharine Graham, publisher of the *Washington Post*, but also to celebrate *In Cold Blood* being listed on all the best-seller lists at the time. The center of interest for many there were KBI Special Agent and Mrs. Al Dewey of Garden City, Kansas. Al and Marie had become close friends of Capote and Capote's childhood friend Nelle Harper Lee while the two stayed in Garden City researching Capote's eventual runaway best seller. Capote and Lee, author of *To Kill a Mockingbird*, had been frequent guests in the Dewey home during the research. Both Capote and Dewey had been witnesses at the executions in Lansing on April 14, 1965, as were Church, Duntz, and Nye.

Truman Capote died on August 25, 1984, of liver disease complicated by alcohol and drugs. The four KBI agents, Al Dewey, Roy Church, Clarence Duntz, and Harold Nye, all retired: Church in 1963, and Dewey, Duntz, and Nye in 1975. Harold Nye served as KBI director from September 1969 to January 1971. Roy Church died on January 20, 1971; Al Dewey died on November 6, 1987; Clarence Duntz died on August 25, 1991; and Harold Nye died on August 27, 2003, the last survivor of the famous quartet of Clutter investigators.

Interest in the tragic events of November 15, 1959, and their investigative and prosecutorial aftermath continues unabated today. It seems likely that the Clutter case will remain the most famous investigation in KBI annals and that Truman Capote, Perry Smith, and Richard Hickock will forever be prominent figures in the history of the agency. Recent evidence of this unending interest can be found in two more movies about the true-crime classic *In Cold Blood* and its talented, openly gay, diminutive (five foot three) author.

The first film, *Capote*, released in October 2005, starred Philip Seymour Hoffman in the title role, Catherine Keener as Nelle Harper Lee, and Kansas City's own Chris Cooper as Special Agent Al Dewey. It was filmed in Canada. The movie received four Academy Award nominations. Hoffman won Best Actor for his startling portrayal of Truman Capote. Keener received an Oscar nomination for Best Supporting Actress for her portrayal of Lee, Capote's Alabama childhood friend and neighbor and Kansas companion and research assistant. The film also received Best Picture and Best Director nominations.

The second film, *Infamous*, filmed in Texas and released in 2006, featured Sandra Bullock as Lee, Jeff Daniels as Dewey, and Toby Jones as Capote, as well as Gwyneth Paltrow and Sigourney Weaver.

In Cold Blood, the original movie, was filmed in Kansas—in Holcomb, Garden City, Lansing, and Johnson County, where it all happened and where *In Cold Blood*, the book, was researched by Truman Capote and Nelle Harper Lee.

As recently as May 28, 2006, the literary classic ranked first on the New York Times best sellers list (for nonfiction paperbacks), and number 15 on that list as late as October 8, 2006. Interest in the KBI's most famous case shows little evidence of waning.

CHAPTER FIVE

Sanford: KBI Growth, 1957–1969

At the age of twenty-one, during the summer of 1928, Logan Sanford worked for the police department in Kinsley, Kansas, as a motorcycle patrolman. That fall he entered the University of Kansas as a freshman. He attended classes in the morning and worked as a patrolman for the Lawrence Police Department during the afternoons, evenings, and weekends. But money was tight and he wasn't able to complete his college education. He returned home to Stafford County and farmed, as he had been raised. He married Doris Nelson, the beautiful daughter of a Stafford County farmer, in 1933, and they continued to farm, throughout the Depression, until 1940, when law enforcement again beckoned him. That year he was persuaded by friends to run for sheriff of his home county, and he won easily. He never left law enforcement again, except for military service in World War II. After winning the sheriff's election, he moved his wife and three daughters to St. John, the county seat and location of the sheriff's office.

When he ran for reelection in 1942, after his first two-year term as sheriff, his major campaign effort consisted of the following poem that he wrote and which the *St. John News* gladly printed:

The Sheriff's Job

Now, this sheriff's job is a curious one
Like the housewife's work, it's never done.
Calls come by night and come by day.
They may be near or miles away.
Today we hunt evidence and dig up the facts.
Tomorrow we struggle with delinquent tax.
Next day we're hunting a mottled face cow.
That night we referee a nice family row.
Next day we have court and the lawyers all rave.
The defendant sits there in need of a shave.
"Where were you," they beller, "on the first of September?"
The defendant replies, "I don't remember."
They argue around 'till half-past three.

Then the jury goes out and fails to agree.
The judge sends them back 'till their duty is done.
But eight hours later they're still eleven to one.
We set out to catch him and we do our best.
We get our percentage and lose all the rest.
We don't get 'em all, for some leave no clue.
They don't leave their cards, like the candidates do.
So it's quite a game, if you stay right in.
You'll get a pat on the back or a sock in the chin.
But I still like it all and I'm shedding no tears.
And I'd like to be sheriff for another few years.[1]
   —*Sheriff Logan Sanford*

Sheriff Sanford again won reelection easily but resigned his position in 1943 to enlist in the army, although his age, family, and his law enforcement employment would have kept him out of the draft. He was honorably discharged in 1946, returned home, and was appointed undersheriff. That fall he again ran for Stafford County sheriff and was easily elected to the office. He served as sheriff until January 1, 1948, when his friend Lou Richter appointed him special agent with the KBI and assigned him to St. John to help cover parts of central and western Kansas.

Although oversight of the Clutter investigation may be the contribution to the KBI legacy for which Logan Sanford is best remembered, it was not his only contribution. When Attorney General John Anderson Jr. appointed Sanford as director on April 23, 1957, the KBI had nineteen special agents and three office personnel. When he retired, twelve years later, on December 1, 1969, the agency, thanks to his efforts, had a roster of thirty special agents and fourteen office personnel. Moreover, during his tenure as chief of the KBI, he established the KBI forensic laboratory; hired the first laboratory director; initiated the *KBI Bulletin*, a monthly publication for Kansas law enforcement; created a KBI polygraph program; set up the agency's first photography section; assigned special agents across the state, placing them, when possible, in their hometowns because Sanford felt "they know the area and the people"; and was actively involved in the creation of the state's first statewide law enforcement teletype system.

He had brought many of his innovative, progressive ideas from the FBI National Academy in Quantico, Virginia, having graduated from that law enforcement executive program's 57th Session in 1956. He was already an experienced administrator, having not only been elected sheriff of Stafford County three times but also having served as chief of a counterintelligence unit in the U.S. Army during the war.

Furthermore, as Director Sanford continued his predecessor's policy of using the KBI in the training of local Kansas law enforcement officers. He also was a leader in the successful effort to persuade the state legislature to mandate Kansas police training and create the Kansas Law Enforcement Training Center in 1969. He served on the predecessor of the Kansas Law Enforcement Training Commission, today's Kansas Commission on Peace Officers' Standards and Training. Sanford also spent considerable time and effort, at the request of Colorado law enforcement officials, in a campaign to persuade the Colorado legislature that Kansas's western neighbor needed their own version of the KBI.

In a special feature on August 23, 1966, the *Denver Post,* lamenting the lack of progress in the recent unsolved murder of a University of Colorado coed, urged the creation of a Colorado Bureau of Investigation, similar to what its Kansas neighbor had created almost thirty years earlier. The feature story, a response to a dialogue that week between representatives of the city of Boulder and Colorado Governor John Love, was eight pages in length and full of glowing references to the KBI. The city of Boulder had asked for state assistance in the college student's murder and the governor had replied, "We are powerless. We have no help to offer."[2]

The answer to a wave of unsolved Colorado homicides, according to both Governor Love and the *Denver Post,* was the creation of a Colorado Bureau of Investigation. Governor Love explained that he had conferred in his Denver office the previous month with Director Logan Sanford of the KBI, and he believed such an agency was needed in Colorado. If reelected, he noted, he would propose the creation of such an investigative body to the 1967 session of the Colorado General Assembly.

The governor and the newspaper both admitted that not everyone agreed with them. Three years earlier, an advisory committee of Colorado lawmen had concluded, "There is no need for any Colorado bureau of investigation, and it is not feasible."[3] They did not want, they said, "outsiders" coming in to take over their investigative responsibilities and share the credit when crimes are solved.

The *Denver Post,* however, countered with a survey the newspaper had completed only days before the feature story, wherein fifty-four of sixty-two Colorado sheriffs reported they were in favor of the formation of a Colorado Bureau of Investigation to assist them. Most made it clear they wanted a small, expert group of investigators, which would come only when called. Many of the Colorado sheriffs, especially those in eastern Colorado near the Kansas line, who had previously worked with KBI special agents, held up the KBI as an example of how a CBI could and should work.[4]

Sheriff William Howard of Cheyenne County, Colorado, said he would be for a Colorado bureau "if it would be a parallel to the KBI. I think the KBI is a very good organization. I've worked with them over a number of years."[5]

Sheriff Eugene Kelley of Kiowa County, Colorado, agreed when asked for his opinion of a future CBI: "I'm for it. I've worked closely with the KBI for nearly twenty-two years. They're a well trained group and they don't come into the county until you call them."[6]

And Sheriff Ernest Price of Yuma County, Colorado, volunteered, "We work with the KBI quite a bit and the KBI doesn't take any rights away. . . . I think it would be all right if it worked something like that."[7]

Sheriff Alfred Clark of Lincoln County, Colorado, was even more emphatic: "I'm 100 percent for it. I've worked quite a bit with KBI boys and I think they're a fine setup. About as good a setup as you could get."[8]

Sheriff Vince Bianco of Logan County, Colorado, continued the theme: "I'm very much in favor of that. . . . We've had some wonderful cooperation from the KBI."[9]

Denver Bland, the chief of police of Thornton, Colorado, and formerly the sheriff of Sedgwick County, Kansas, where he had been accustomed to KBI services and assistance, told the *Denver Post*, "There's something lacking in Colorado law enforcement." The KBI, or its equivalent, was what was lacking, he said.[10]

With Governor Love and the Colorado legislature seeking the advice, counsel, and testimony of KBI Director Logan Sanford almost every step of the way, the Colorado Bureau of Investigation became a reality. Director Sanford's direct participation in the birth of the CBI developed a kinship between the two state bureaus that continues today.

Two years later the KBI received similar high praise from another non-Kansas newspaper. On January 27, 1968, in part two of a series of stories urging the creation of a state bureau of investigation to combat New Mexico crime, the *Albuquerque Journal* noted, "Probably the best example of a statewide investigative body in the immediate vicinity of New Mexico is the Kansas Bureau of Investigation (KBI)." The editor explained, "While the KBI doesn't operate with the showmanship of the Texas Rangers, our neighboring state's clue seekers, it has a prestige of its own. The agency even gained its first taste of national fame in Truman Capote's book, *In Cold Blood*. Capote was visibly impressed by the law enforcement work of KBI officers in solving the four murders he immortalized." The story continued, "The KBI was created by an atmosphere much like that hanging over New Mexico today. It was brought about by demands from the legal profession, cattlemen, law officers, and the public, all reacting in alarm to criminal violence plaguing Kansas during the 1930s. Born in 1939, the KBI has functioned since and has been the pattern for other . . . states as they have set up similar agencies."[11] Unlike Colorado, New Mexico was not successful in its pursuit of a state bureau of investigation. But it was clear that the KBI had achieved an admirable national reputation and was well respected by neighboring states.

While Logan Sanford, like his legendary predecessor, was able to accomplish exceptional feats with limited resources, he and his successors were never able to achieve adequate salaries for their dedicated employees. This tradition, unfortunately, continues in today's KBI.

One of Director Sanford's strongest supporters, Bill Hazlett of the *Wichita Beacon,* tried to help the KBI with its salary woes in an editorial on January 30, 1960: "Stingy Pay for Excellent Work."

Hazlett mailed the director a personal copy of the editorial and wrote in the margin, "Logan: Thought we might be able to help you guys a little bit with an editorial boost. This editorial appeared, at my request, in *The Wichita Beacon* Saturday, January 30, 1960. See you at the Clutter Murder Trial." The editorial asserted:

> The work of Kansas Bureau of Investigation agents to solve the murder of the Herb Clutter family of near Garden City was an outstanding example of professionalism in the police field. It comes as a shock to learn that these talented, experienced agents receive salaries that can only be described as stingy.
>
> Prospective KBI agents must have the following qualifications:
>
> 1. They must be between 24 and 45 years of age.
> 2. They must be residents of Kansas for five years before application.
> 3. They must have a minimum of five years in law enforcement work.
> 4. They must be of good moral character and have no record of felony convictions and no indictments against them.
> 5. They must pass stiff physical and mental examinations.
>
> The applicant who can meet these requirements starts at salary grade A-$358 a month. The highest salary he can achieve is grade H-$505 a month. It is almost unattainable.

A recruit policeman, with no previous experience, receives $340 a month in Wichita. In 4½ years, he can reach $416. Many departments pay much more than Wichita.

Logan Sanford, KBI director, had to go to the Legislature to ask for $4,000 in emergency money to cover expenses of the investigation of the Clutter murders. The bureau, it seems, just doesn't have funds for anything unusual.

Well, as John Ruskin, the English philosopher, observed, "Work worth doing is either underpaid or not paid for at all." The 18 agents of the KBI obviously stick to their job because they believe that the work is worth doing. It is likely that they will always be underpaid—but do they have to be as underpaid as they are now?[12]

Brutal and senseless homicides of national significance characterized the KBI administration of Logan Sanford. There had been the challenging Clutter case with Perry Smith and Richard Hickock in 1959, of course. There was also a pair of teenaged army deserters, George Ronald York of Florida and James Douglas Latham of Texas, who, in May and June 1961, went on a six-state crime spree following their escape from the army stockade at Fort Hood, Texas. The two escapees, full of adrenaline and hate, committed robberies, stole vehicles, and murdered seven men and women in Florida, Tennessee, Illinois, Kansas, and Colorado over fifteen days before being captured at a police roadblock in Utah, where they were stopped and arrested in a vehicle stolen from one of their victims. At the start of their rampage they had beaten a man nearly to death in Louisiana. They strangled two women to death in Florida and shot and killed a man in Tennessee, two men in Illinois, and another man in Kansas. Their last victim was an eighteen-year-old motel maid, sexually assaulted, shot, and killed in Colorado. Most of their victims were cruelly and severely beaten before being put to death. The duo gave new meaning to the old law enforcement phrase "just mean."

The Kansas victim was Otto Ziegler of Oakley, Kansas. Mr. Ziegler was a popular, friendly, outgoing sixty-two-year-old grandfather employed by the Union Pacific Railroad. Known for a readiness to assist others, it was his misfortune to stop to assist two young teenaged boys who appeared to be having car trouble. He didn't know the car was fine, or that the car had been stolen in Illinois, or that the Kansas license plate had been stolen the previous night in Dorrance, in Russell County, Kansas, or that the two harmless-appearing young men had recently killed five people. They each shot the would-be Good Samaritan, stole his fifty-one dollars, and left his body next to railroad tracks near Sharon Springs in rural Wallace County, Kansas.

Wallace County Sheriff "Buck" Sullivan immediately called for KBI assistance. Director Sanford ordered Clarence Duntz and Joe Baker from Topeka to join Jack Ford from Ulysses at Sharon Springs. Ford, a U.S. Marine Corps veteran of the Pacific campaign in World War II, would be the case agent and lead investigator. He had been sheriff of Grant County in Ulysses prior to being appointed a KBI agent in 1960. He would later end his distinguished career in 1987 as KBI assistant director. Baker had started with the bureau in 1959. Duntz, of course, was a veteran of the Clutter investigation.

Few cases in KBI annals provide a better example of the results of old-fashioned police work—crime scene examination, development of witnesses, asking questions, beating the bushes, wearing out shoe leather—than the Ziegler investigation. Thanks to the work of Sheriff Sullivan, Jack Ford, Joe Baker, and Clarence Duntz, as well as railroad detectives and other local officers, witnesses were quickly located who provided physical descriptions of two young white males who had been seen in the area in a red 1960 Dodge with Russell County license plates. Shell casings, later connected to the guns of both York and Latham, were recovered at the scene. Latent fingerprints were removed from pop bottles at a café in nearby Wallace, Kansas, where York and Latham spent some of Ziegler's money, and from his truck. Those fingerprints from the two pop bottles and Ziegler's truck would be connected to the two army deserters. Many witnesses would later testify that the two strangers had been seen in Wallace and near Sharon Springs, in sparsely populated Wallace County, at the time of the Ziegler homicide. The resulting interstate broadcast of the vehicle description led to the eventual capture of the killers at the Utah roadblock, but not before they had claimed their last victim, the Colorado motel maid.

Florida, Illinois, Tennessee, Colorado, and Kansas had the death penalty at the time and each of those states wanted to prosecute York and Latham. The U.S. Army, the FBI, and Louisiana also wanted the pair, but for crimes far less serious than those in the five capital punishment states. Prosecutors in the different jurisdictions agreed that Kansas, because of the quick and thorough investigative efforts in Wallace County, had the best evidence of guilt and the best prosecutorial case. Accordingly, Utah turned over the two fugitives to KBI Special Agents Jack Ford and Clarence Duntz, who transported them back to Kansas for trial, after the pair waived extradition.

On November 7, 1961, in state district court in Russell, Kansas, both defendants were convicted of first-degree murder. On December 2, 1961, that court sentenced York and Latham to hang in Lansing for the murder of Otto Ziegler. On June 22, 1965, slightly over two months after Perry Smith and Richard Hickock were hanged in Lansing, York and Latham were hanged there for the Kansas portion of their interstate crime spree, thereby saving several other jurisdictions the time, effort, and expense of trials.

Kansas has not executed anyone since 1965. No other KBI director, since Logan Sanford, has been involved in an execution.

By the end of 1963 Director Sanford had been able to increase his special agent complement to twenty-two. Like his predecessor, he continued to show a preference for Kansas sheriffs or deputies whenever he had the opportunity to hire an agent, which wasn't often. Although Sanford required a minimum of five years of law enforcement experience as a prerequisite for a special agent, the agents he hired averaged eight years of experience. As he told a reporter in December 1963, his agents received no special training when appointed because "they've got the know-how or they wouldn't have been hired in the first place."[13]

The director persuaded the 1968 Kansas legislature to increase the number of special agents to thirty. Again he pointed out to a reporter that the new ones would come mostly from medium-sized Kansas police departments and sheriffs' departments. "We watch a man develop over the years, watch how he operates and then pick him up. We want the all-around man with lots of experience, the man who has dealt with every conceivable crime. The good medium-sized department is better because in large departments they tend to specialize."[14]

In August 1969, Logan Sanford announced his retirement, effective December 1, 1969, in a letter to Kansas Attorney General Kent Frizzell, who reluctantly accepted the request from the sixty-one-year-old KBI director and responded with this letter:

Mr. Logan Sanford, Director
Kansas Bureau of Investigation
Statehouse
Topeka, Kansas

Dear Logan:
    Your thirty years of service in the field of law enforcement have made their mark on Kansas history. Few men can claim such influence.
    The Kansas Bureau of Investigation was unique at the time of its inception. It has grown from an embryo containing a staff of ten agents to an organization containing thirty highly respected, professional agents and an efficient well-run office staff of fourteen. Many other states now

have bureaus patterned after the Kansas Bureau of Investigation and look to Kansas for still further guidance.

The twelve years that you have served as Director to this outstanding agency have been the most progressive in the history of the Bureau. They have seen the establishment of the laboratory and the installation of sophisticated equipment which have greatly enhanced crime detection techniques. They have seen the installation of a statewide communication network joining all law enforcement agencies and a mandatory and uniform crime reporting system. They have seen improvement of the filing system in the Bureau and the faster location of records. They have seen the elevation of the agents to civil service status taking them out of the realm of political influence.

These are but a few of the achievements of the Bureau under your direction. To list them all would be impossible. But more important than what you have done, is how you have done it. Your modest demeanor and quiet guidance have provided leadership in a field which sorely needs the image which you have created.

I would like, for myself and the other citizens of Kansas, to acknowledge the large debt we owe you and to congratulate you on a record of outstanding service.

Sincerely,
Kent Frizzell
Attorney General

August 29, 1969

On July 18, 1994, at KBI headquarters in Topeka, Attorney General Robert Stephan administered the oath of office to a new KBI director before 200 guests. Most of the onlookers were law enforcement officials from across the state, mainly police chiefs and sheriffs, and/or KBI personnel and KBI retirees. Attorney General Stephan and the new director were longtime friends, having known each other more than twenty years, since the former was a state district court judge in Wichita and the latter a special agent with the FBI in Wichita. Attorney General Stephan had offered the KBI directorship to his friend more than two years earlier. That offer had been reluctantly declined, after a period of a month of deliberation and soul-searching.

On the occasion of July 18, 1994, two of the ceremony's attendees shared a rather unusual and historical relationship. They had both been present in Macksville, Kansas, on September 16, 1941, when two Lansing escapees had attempted to rob a bank. Their respective roles in the events of that day were dramatically different, and the older participant might not have even noticed the other in the aftermath of that attempted bank robbery, the only occasion that day when they were in close proximity to each other.

One was a special guest of honor at the ceremony. He was there at the personal invitation of the incoming director. That special guest, Logan Sanford, the second director of the KBI, surrounded by several of his own family members, was seated in the front row, directly in front of the podium. He was present to watch a protégé being sworn in as the tenth director of his beloved KBI. The tenth director would be the second director from St. John and Stafford County, Kansas.

The second spectator, who, like Logan Sanford, was at Macksville, Kansas, on September 16, 1941, also enjoyed a special relationship with the new director. She was his wife of almost thirty-nine years. At the age of five, Shirley Barnes had been shooed home by her father, Oscar Barnes, when he saw her in the growing crowd of onlookers near the bodies of two would-be bank robbers following the KBI gunfight. She, like her father and the other onlookers, had also been watching the bigger-than-life Stafford County sheriff, Logan Sanford, his undersheriff, Wes Wise, KBI Director Lou Richter, and the other KBI agents present. Shirley would always remember the dead criminals more clearly than the live lawmen.

I was that newly appointed director of the KBI, and Logan Sanford was one of my special guests. A native of St. John, I had gone to school with Logan's daughters, Corine, Bonnie, and Margaret. Bonnie and I were classmates. Later, as a KU undergraduate, and then as a law student at KU, I had traveled to Topeka a few times to visit Director Sanford at KBI headquarters. The best chance to become an FBI agent would be with a law degree, he and others had continually counseled. On my graduation from KU Law School in 1961, Director Sanford served as one of my references when I obtained an appointment to the FBI Academy in Quantico, Virginia, from FBI Director J. Edgar Hoover.

Sanford had tried, unsuccessfully, to obtain a waiver for me from the statutory requirement at that time that required a minimum of five years of law enforcement experience to become a KBI special agent. With two degrees from the University of Kansas I was qualified to become an FBI agent, but not a KBI agent. Sanford beamed on the day I became director when I told that true story to those assembled. To a reporter he added afterward with a smile that, finally, after thirty-three years in law enforcement, and a bachelor's degree and a law degree from KU, I was qualified for KBI service.

Following the ceremony on July 18, 1994, Logan Sanford would return to KBI headquarters one more time. I had observed at the swearing-in ceremony and afterward, to my disappointment, that Sanford was not well known to current KBI employees. Few KBI retirees seemed well acquainted with him either. Of course, he had retired twenty-five years earlier. But, if the KBI had a Mount Rushmore, surely the second face thereon would be that of the man who had carried Lou Richter's baton so well for twelve years. Logan Sanford had presided over the Clutter case and stood beside Richter at Macksville. I vowed to correct that deficiency in recognition. Accordingly, with the assistance of Logan's three devoted daughters, Margaret, Bonnie, and Corine, the KBI and his family hosted an open house at KBI headquarters on August 8, 1995, to honor the second director of the KBI. In attendance were former Attorney General and Mrs. Robert Stephan, Attorney General Carla Stovall, and many KBI retirees, including almost all living former directors. The occasion was used to unveil a new display case in the Hallway of Honor at KBI headquarters, featuring memorabilia of Sanford's tenure. That display case was intentionally placed between the display case honoring Director Richter and the display case depicting the attempted robbery of the Macksville bank. Logan and his family, including grandchildren and great-grandchildren, received a special tour of KBI headquarters. The former director was pleased, proud, grateful, and, as always, modest and gracious. He especially liked the covered-dish luncheon provided by his KBI family to the 200 guests.

Only four months later, on December 12, 1995, Logan Sanford died in Stafford. Nine miles from St. John. Twenty-two miles from Macksville. In Stafford County.

The message went out across the Kansas law enforcement community on the teletype system he had helped create: "Regret to advise Logan Sanford, age 88, Director, KBI, 1956–1969, died in his sleep, early A.M., December 12, Stafford, Ks. Arrangements pending. Welch, KBI, 12/12/95."

A media release followed later that day from KBI headquarters:

PRESS RELEASE
December 12, 1995
  Larry Welch, Director, Kansas Bureau of Investigation, Topeka, Kansas, advised today that Logan Sanford, age 88, Director of the KBI from 1956 until his retirement in 1969, passed away in his sleep at his home in Stafford, Kansas, during the early morning hours of December 12, 1995.

  Welch advised that Mr. Sanford was the second director of the KBI and presided over the agency during many of its formative years and during many of the historical events which eventually helped shape the agency, i.e., the Clutter murders; creation of a statewide teletype system; development of the KBI Laboratory; development of the central repository for criminal records; the executions of Smith, Hickock, York and Latham, the last criminals executed in Kansas.

Only Lou Richter, of the ten KBI directors, the first director of the KBI, served longer than Logan Sanford as director.

Former Director Sanford had recently been honored, on August 8, 1995, with an open house at KBI Headquarters in Topeka. That event was attended by many family members, retired KBI agents, former Attorney General and Mrs. Bob Stephan and Attorney General Carla Stovall.

Director Sanford was a former sheriff of Stafford County and a graduate of the FBI National Academy at Quantico, Virginia.

He was preceded in death by his wife Doris in 1992 and is survived by three daughters and a host of grandchildren and great grandchildren.

The funeral will be Friday, December 15, 1995, at 2 P.M., Minnis Chapel, Stafford, Kansas, with the burial at Stafford.

An error in the KBI archives at the time mistakenly listed Director Logan Sanford's tenure as director as 1956–1969, instead of the correct 1957–1969, thus causing the tenure error in the teletype, the media release, and, later, in my eulogy at Logan's funeral services. I was honored when Logan's daughters asked me to deliver the legendary Kansas lawman's eulogy and to serve as an honorary casket bearer with former KBI directors Tom Kelly and Jim Malson and other KBI retirees Ron Blum, Charles Buchanan, Jack Ford, Floyd Gaunt, Ray Macey, Ron Klingenberg, Jess Gragg, Jack Williams, and Jim McCubbin.

CHAPTER SIX

Directors: KBI Directors, 1969–1994

From the creation of the KBI in 1939 through my own tenure that ended in 2007, ten directors, including Lou Richter and Logan Sanford, have served at the pleasure of fourteen Kansas attorneys general.

Richter and Sanford served a combined twenty-nine years as directors of the KBI at the pleasure of eight of the fourteen attorneys general (all eight were Republicans). Richter served Kansas Attorneys General Jay Parker, A. B. Mitchell, Ed Arn, Harold Fatzer, and John Anderson in his seventeen years. Logan Sanford served Kansas Attorneys General John Anderson, William Ferguson, Robert Londerholm, and Kent Frizzell in his twelve years.

The next seven directors would serve at the pleasure of four Kansas attorneys general in their combined twenty-five years of KBI directorship. Robert Stephan served as the state's attorney general for sixteen years, from January 1979 to January 1995. No other Kansas attorney general has served in that position as long. In part because of Stephan's unusually long tenure, none of the next seven KBI directors following Richter and Sanford served more than one attorney general as director.

It was my privilege as the tenth director to have served at the pleasure of four Kansas attorneys general, Robert Stephan, Carla Stovall, Phill Kline, and, briefly, Paul Morrison. I thus became the second-longest-serving KBI director, with nearly thirteen years on the job, exceeded only by Richter's seventeen years, which, I predict, will never be surpassed.

On September 1, 1969, Harold "Nappy" Nye, a KBI assistant director, was appointed by Attorney General Kent Frizzell to replace the retiring Logan Sanford. Sanford had named Nye assistant director in 1961 and placed him in charge of the bureau's investigative division. Nye's role in the Clutter case was likely a reason for that appointment. Months before Sanford's retirement, the director reassigned Nye to the head of the bureau's record, identifications, and communications division for additional administrative experience.

Attorney General Frizzell, on making the announcement on Sanford's successor, noted that he had received eleven applications from eleven "top-notch law enforcement officers." "Nappy" Nye, well known in Kansas law enforcement circles, was chosen from a pool of five finalists. The other four were Harry Felker and Jack Williams of the KBI, former Kansas Highway Patrol Superintendent J. H. "Rip" Reeves, and Atchison Chief of Police Gus Wood.

A native of Oakley, Kansas, Harold Nye started his law enforcement career as a night marshal in Oakley. He had grown up on a farm near that small western Kansas town. After a year he resigned to accept a position with the Garden City Police Department. From 1948 to 1951 he served as a patrolman with that department. He joined the Hutchinson Police Department, serving from 1951 to 1955, as captain of detectives and then as assistant chief of police.

Nye was appointed a special agent with the KBI on July 1, 1955, by Director Lou Richter and served as agent until being promoted to assistant director on June 15, 1961. He was then sent to the Southern Police Institute in Louisville, Kentucky, for management and leadership training, and graduated on December 1, 1961. While director, in 1970, he was elected president of the Kansas Peace Officers' Association, formerly the Kansas State Peace Officers' Association. Nye moved KBI headquarters out of its crowded space in the state capitol in 1970.

Vern Miller, the first Democrat to preside over the KBI as attorney general, named Fred Howard to replace Nye as director in January 1971. Nye retired from the KBI on July 22, 1975, and moved to Oklahoma City. On August 27, 2003, Harold "Nappy" Nye, the last surviving member of the legendary quartet of KBI agents that had worked on the famous Clutter *In Cold Blood* case in Holcomb, Kansas, died following surgery in Oklahoma City at the age of seventy-seven. He was buried in Oakley, Kansas.

A native of Strong City, Kansas, Fred Harris Howard was appointed the fourth director of the KBI on January 11, 1971, by Attorney General Vern Miller. Miller, the former sheriff of Sedgwick County, had become good friends with Howard, who had been a Kansas Highway Patrol sergeant in Wichita at the same time.

Howard had briefly attended both the University of Kansas and Kansas State University and had served eighteen years with the Kansas Highway Patrol in various assignments across the state, most recently in Wichita. While with the state patrol he attended Northwestern University's Law Enforcement Supervision and Command School in Evanston, Illinois.

As KBI director, Fred Howard created the bureau's narcotics division in 1971 and laid the groundwork for creation of the agency's second forensic laboratory in Great Bend in 1975. He resigned in January 1975 to accept the post of chief of police in Topeka. He was elected president of the Kansas Peace Officers' Association in 1979 and retired from the Topeka Police Department in 1981. Enjoying retirement on his farm near Harveyville, Kansas, in rural Wabaunsee County, Howard served three terms as county commissioner. He died on January 14, 2011, at the age of eighty-two and was buried at Cottonwood Falls in his native Chase County. Shirley and I attended his funeral services in Emporia.

A native of the Wichita-Augusta area and a U.S. Navy veteran of the Pacific theater in World War II, William L. "Bill" Albott is the only KBI director to have also served as superintendent of the Kansas Highway Patrol. He served the state patrol from December 1, 1951, until his retirement from that agency on January 18, 1975. He was superintendent from 1969 until his retirement and, like Logan Sanford, was a graduate of the FBI National Academy in Quantico, Virginia.

Albott was appointed the fifth director of the KBI by Attorney General Curt Schneider, a Democrat, on April 1, 1975, and served in that capacity until his retirement on January 8, 1979.

Like Nye and Howard before him, Bill Albott was well known and highly regarded within the Kansas law enforcement community and the criminal justice system, and he was a strong supporter of the fledgling Kansas Law Enforcement Training Center in Hutchinson, where he was a frequent instructor in the state-mandated training of Kansas law enforcement officers. All three also served on the predecessor of the Kansas Law Enforcement Training Commission (then known as the Governor's Advisory Commission on Law Enforcement Training), today's Commission on Peace Officers' Standards and Training.

Bill Albott retired in Topeka and died at the age of seventy-nine on April 13, 2000. Many retired and active KBI and Kansas Highway Patrol personnel were in attendance at his funeral service in Topeka on April 18, 2000. Retired KBI agents Ray Macey, Jack Ford, and Jack West served as pallbearers, and speakers included Kansas Highway Patrol superintendent Don Brownlee and me.

Attorney General Robert Stephan, a Republican, appointed five of the first ten KBI directors. The first of those five was Thomas E. Kelly, appointed on January 8, 1979. A native of Topeka, Tom Kelly received a bachelor's degree and a law degree from Washburn University in Topeka. He served in the Army Air Corps in World War II and was appointed special agent with the

Federal Bureau of Investigation on March 15, 1948. Over the next twenty-eight years his FBI service took him to the FBI's Philadelphia, Newark, and Kansas City Divisions. Most of his FBI service, 1959 until his retirement in 1976, was in the FBI resident agencies of Hutchinson and Topeka in Kansas. During that FBI tenure, like some of his KBI director predecessors, he was a frequent and popular guest lecturer in the Kansas Law Enforcement Training Center near Hutchinson. Following his retirement from the FBI and prior to his appointment as director of the KBI, Kelly served as executive director for the Governor's Committee on Criminal Administration.

In 1984 Kelly moved KBI headquarters to its current location at 1620 S.W. Tyler in Topeka. The first college graduate and the first of three FBI retirees to preside over the KBI, Tom Kelly retired from the KBI on June 30, 1987. He died on March 24, 2011, in Topeka at the age of ninety. His funeral was attended by many KBI and FBI representatives. Shirley and I were also in attendance.

The seventh director of the KBI, following Kelly, was David E. Johnson, appointed by Attorney General Stephan on July 1, 1987. Johnson, a native of Ottawa, Kansas, attended the University of Kansas and Ottawa University. His law enforcement career started with the Ottawa Police Department in 1952. He was appointed special agent with the KBI on February 1, 1964, by Director Sanford, following nine years as investigator with the office of attorney general. A graduate of the Southern Police Institute in Louisville, Kentucky, he retired from the KBI as an agent on April 9, 1984, to accept a position with the Kansas State Insurance Department.

Johnson, however, was lured back to the KBI by Attorney General Stephan to assume the reins of director, and he served in that capacity from July 1, 1987, to December 9, 1989.

During his law enforcement career, Dave Johnson also served more than twenty years with the Kansas National Guard, eventually retiring with the rank of captain in an artillery unit. Following his final KBI retirement in 1989, Johnson spent ten years with the Kansas Racing and Gaming Commission as its director of security before retiring in Topeka.

James G. Malson, a native of Chanute, Kansas, would serve as the KBI's eighth director, replacing Dave Johnson. Following Sanford, Nye, and Johnson, Malson was the fourth person to be named director after serving as an agent of the KBI. Malson had attended Neosho County Community College and Kansas State University before service with the U.S. Army in Germany from 1956 to 1960. Following military service, he began his law enforcement career with the Kansas Highway Patrol, serving in Chanute and Kansas City from 1960 to 1962. He resigned from the state patrol in 1962 to become a deputy sheriff with the Johnson County Sheriff's Department in Olathe.

On March 1, 1969, Malson, then a detective with the Johnson County Sheriff's Department, resigned his post to accept an appointment from Director Sanford as a special agent with the KBI. Assignments as special agent followed in Pratt, 1969–1970; Olathe, 1970–1972; and Ottawa, 1972–1989. He was then promoted to assistant director by Director Johnson, shortly before the latter's retirement. Malson was appointed director by Attorney General Stephan on December 9, 1989, and retired from the KBI on April 30, 1992. Today he resides on his farm in Franklin County, near Ottawa, Kansas.

On a Saturday morning early in March 1992, Bob Stephan, a friend from our days in Wichita when he was a state district judge and I was with the FBI, called me at our home in Goddard, Kansas. Bob confided in me that Jim Malson had informed him that he would like to retire by May. Stephan said he wanted me to come to Topeka and take over the KBI on Jim's retirement. I was surprised, flattered, and interested. He urged me to give my strongest consideration to his offer and volunteered to give me as much as a month, if needed, to consider it. I promised to discuss the opportunity with my family and to respond as quickly as possible.

I had retired after twenty-five years in the FBI in 1986 to accept the associate director's position at the Kansas Law Enforcement Training Center (KLETC), a unit of the Division of Continuing Education of the University of Kansas, located south of Hutchinson, near Yoder, Kansas. KLETC was, and is, a wonderful facility and very important to the Kansas law enforcement community. Robert Senecal, then dean of KU's Division of Continuing Education, a great boss and strong supporter of Kansas law enforcement, and well respected at KU and across the state, promoted me to KLETC director in 1989. It was like having my cake and eating it too. I worked for my alma mater, the University of Kansas, which had oversight over mandated Kansas law enforcement training and KLETC, and also worked with my best friends, Kansas police chiefs, Kansas sheriffs, and Kansas law enforcement in general. Dean Senecal and KU had supported us in our promises to Kansas law enforcement that physical and staff improvements would be forthcoming at KLETC. We were already involved in the early phases of an ambitious program of new construction at the state's central law enforcement academy.

Moreover, our family had recently built a new home in Goddard, west of Wichita, where Shirley and I had raised our three children. I had assured

Shirley, my high school sweetheart, that there were no more moves in our future. KLETC was but a few miles from Goddard and my position at KLETC was probably the most secure and most stable in the Kansas criminal justice system. I would be a fool to leave such security, and my promises to Kansas law enforcement were far from fulfilled. I felt like a traitor even considering a departure from KLETC at that time, given my promises to Kansas police chiefs and sheriffs and the kindness shown to me by Bob Senecal and KU.

I wrestled with the agonizing decision for the full month given to me, changing my mind an embarrassing number of times during my deliberations. We owed Kansas law enforcement so much more at KLETC, and then there were the promises to my wife, who had been subjected to eight transfers in our first nine years with the FBI. Then, too, there was my obligation and responsibility to the great staff KU had permitted me to assemble at KLETC. I had persuaded close friends Ed Pavey and Dick Burch to leave comfortable law enforcement positions to join me as assistant directors. In the end, despite my reluctance to decline Bob Stephan's once-in-a-lifetime invitation to head up an agency I admired and respected, I called him to decline the opportunity he had extended to me. The timing was just not right, no matter how much I wanted to be the ninth director of the KBI. Bob expressed disappointment and understanding. Because he had asked me to have a name ready for his consideration if I did eventually decline the position, I was prepared when he asked for another nomination. I highly recommended to him a former FBI colleague of mine, also retired, then residing in Taos, New Mexico, Robert (Bob) Davenport, a native of Bowling Green, Kentucky, and a 1962 graduate of the University of Tennessee.

In his distinguished career of twenty-five years in the FBI, in addition to special agent assignments in Nebraska and Pennsylvania, Bob Davenport had served as assistant special agent in charge of the FBI's Salt Lake City division and as special agent in charge of the Springfield, Illinois, and Kansas City divisions. Furthermore, he had retired from the FBI as deputy assistant director at FBI headquarters in Washington, D.C., in charge of Congressional and Public Affairs. One of Bob Stephan's prerequisites had been that he wanted someone who could interact easily and effectively with Kansas legislators and state government officials. I told Bob Stephan that if Bob Davenport could deal with Congress and the White House, he could certainly interact effectively with our legislative folks in Topeka.

Moreover, when Davenport had served as special agent in charge of the FBI's Kansas City office, covering western Missouri and all of Kansas from August 1982 to May 1988, he had been popular with law enforcement in both states and had been considered a true gentleman and good leader by all. He had been my boss during his Kansas City tenure until my retirement in 1986. Given Davenport's qualifications, Bob Stephan requested that I contact him to see if he might be interested in heading up the KBI. I agreed to do so.

Although he had been my boss for a few years in my FBI career, Bob Davenport was also a friend of mine and of Shirley's, too. He had been in our home and had joined us as a guest for KU ball games. We had visited him and dined with him on trips to Washington, D.C., when he was at FBI headquarters. We had maintained contact after his retirement to New Mexico in 1990. I called Bob immediately, and the rest is history. My friend in New Mexico was, as I had deduced, bored in retirement. It was an easy sell. He had enjoyed his Kansas service with the FBI and respected Kansas law enforcement in general and the KBI in particular, and agreed to meet Stephan in Topeka. Divorced for several years, he had no family constraints. Only the one meeting between Davenport and Stephan was required. The two were both true gentlemen and natural leaders, and each was impressed with the other immediately. It was a good fit.

I attended Bob Davenport's swearing-in ceremony at KBI headquarters on April 30, 1992, as he became the ninth director of the KBI.

Irony came full circle almost two years to the day after Bob Davenport became KBI director when he called me at home on a Friday evening in May 1994. He explained that an opportunity for a lofty corporate position in the private sector, which he had not expected for two more years, had become available suddenly. It was his if he acted quickly. He said he planned to advise Stephan the next morning that, reluctantly, he must step down sooner than he had anticipated. Bob said it would be easier telling the attorney general of his resignation in the morning if he could tell him at the same time that he had spoken with me and that I now was willing to accept the KBI directorship.

A little more than two months earlier I had undergone double bypass heart surgery. In addition, Bob Davenport and I were both aware that Stephan was not running again for reelection as attorney general, instead retiring after sixteen years in the Kansas top law enforcement office to enter private law practice. I was not acquainted with any of the candidates for the attorney general position that he would vacate in early January 1995. Thus, I could only be assured that I would remain KBI director until then, when a new attorney general would be likely to appoint someone known to him. In other words, I would be director for mere months. It was foolish. I thanked Bob Davenport but declined, dreading Shirley's disappointment if I accepted, given her concern about my recent heart surgery and any move from Goddard.

The next morning, a Saturday, I received phone calls from both Davenport and Stephan—Davenport advising me that Stephan would be calling, and Stephan, for the second time, offering me the head position of the KBI. He told me up front what I already knew, that he could guarantee me the position only through December 1994. After that, I was on my own, at the pleasure of the new Kansas attorney general, whoever that might be. He urged my acceptance this time, but, recalling my month-long deliberations the first time, he requested my decision by Monday morning, so he could announce my impending appointment at the same time as Bob Davenport's resignation, effective in June. I promised to call him at his home on Sunday evening with my decision. Shirley was convinced as well as hopeful that my decision would be to decline for a second time the wonderful privilege of directing the KBI, and, for most of the weekend, that was how I was leaning. But following our return from church in Goddard that Sunday morning, I walked in the country near our home on the western edge of Goddard for more than an hour. Foolish as it seemed for so many reasons, I decided to leave my beloved KLETC and end my law enforcement career as director of the KBI, however brief that privilege might turn out to be. Shirley was surprised and a bit disappointed, but only out of concern for me. Being the greatest wife ever, she noted she had followed me to Tennessee, Washington, D.C., Florida, Puerto Rico, Texas, and Kansas City, and she would follow me to Topeka, knowing my immense respect for the KBI.

Silently, she probably was questioning my sanity or intelligence. Not only was my tenure as KBI director guaranteed for a mere five months, and not only would I be surrendering the most secure law enforcement post in Kansas, but she would have to stay behind at first and sell the home we had recently built in Goddard. Furthermore, the KBI director's salary was less than the salary I was receiving at KLETC as director, and Stephan had informed me there were no provisions to pay our moving costs and no possibility of per diem payments as I lived in Topeka in temporary quarters. Shirley may have questioned my sanity or intelligence, but she never expressed such doubts. She knew how much I really wanted to lead this agency I had admired so much for so long.

Bob Davenport publicly announced his resignation the next day, effective June 30, 1994. I replaced him on July 18, facing the very real possibility that my tenure would end in December. Fortunately for me, and, I hope, for the state and the KBI, the tenure proved to be a bit longer—almost thirteen years.

It was my privilege to have known eight of the previous nine KBI directors. I never had the pleasure of meeting Lou Richter. My relationship with

Logan Sanford, my hometown mentor, is already documented herein. As an FBI agent, I worked with "Nappy" Nye on several joint KBI-FBI endeavors, prior to our respective retirements, and "Nappy" visited KBI headquarters more than once during my directorship. I first met Fred Howard in our mutual involvement in the Kansas Peace Officers' Association many years ago, where we were both life members. I knew Bill Albott in both his Kansas Highway Patrol and KBI days and was privileged to speak at his funeral. Tom Kelly was an FBI colleague and, indeed, as an FBI resident agent in Hutchinson, Tom conducted my FBI background investigation in St. John and KU in 1960 and 1961. Tom was a frequent visitor to KBI headquarters. I have also known and respected Dave Johnson for many years, and he too was an occasional KBI visitor. I have known Jim Malson for several years as well, and Jim, like Sanford, Kelly, and Johnson, honored me with his presence when Attorney General Stephan administered my oath of office at KBI headquarters on July 18, 1994.

All nine previous directors were good and honest men, veteran lawmen, and very capable, qualified administrators. All were intelligent. All were fiercely devoted to the Kansas law enforcement community and to the KBI. Their respective administrations were scandal free, and each remained steadfast in adhering to the Richter-Sanford principle of coming when called; of sending KBI special agents where and when summoned by the attorney general, governor, prosecutor, police chief, sheriff, or just cause. None postured for the media and none attempted to set public policy. None was a master of self-congratulation. None ever moved quickly into a publicity vacuum. Each attempted to avoid the entanglements of politics, yet each, necessarily, worked closely with the Kansas legislature, on both sides of the aisle. None of my nine predecessors lacked integrity and each embraced the tradition of noblesse oblige.

The KBI continues to be a unit of the office of the Kansas attorney general, as it was in 1939, and the director continues to serve at the pleasure of the attorney general, as he did in 1939. Attorney General John Anderson's only instruction to Logan Sanford when he asked the agent to step up to director and move to Topeka in 1957 was, "You take over. You run it. If I have any objections, I'll let you know."[1] That simple admonition has characterized the relationship between the Kansas attorney general and the KBI director from 1939 to the present day. There has never been a signed contract between the two offices and there has never been any guarantee of longevity for the director. There has only been a simple oath, a handshake, and confirmation by the Kansas senate.

CHAPTER SEVEN

Samaritan: The KBI Helps Overturn Two Criminal Convictions

With rare exception, requests for KBI investigative and forensic assistance come from Kansas sheriffs, police departments, prosecutors, or the attorney general. On at least one occasion the request came from a Kansas district court judge who feared justice had not prevailed in a recent trial in his courtroom, had the courage to say so, and, like William Blackstone (1723–1780), believed that "it is better that ten guilty persons escape than one innocent suffer."

The letter from Harry G. Miller Jr., Kansas district court judge of the 29th Judicial District, Division 3, Kansas City, Kansas, dated January 30, 1969, was received at KBI headquarters in Topeka the next day. Judge Miller, departing from normal protocol, directed the letter to KBI Special Agent Wendell Cowan rather than Director Logan Sanford. The judge's departure from protocol was, no doubt, occasioned by the fact that he was acquainted with Special Agent Cowan and well aware of the agent's reputation as a KBI polygraph operator. It seemed to the judge that the KBI polygraph would clarify the situation he described in his letter:

Dear Mr. Cowan:

During the past several weeks . . . two women were sent to the State Industrial Farm for Women at Lansing on a charge of robbery in the first degree. They were convicted by a jury although both defendants had considerable alibi evidence that they were elsewhere. Both have steadfastly denied any participation in the robbery. Both have requested lie-detector tests and were refused.

Since the trial, their counsel have obtained some information of a similar robbery or two in Kansas City, Missouri, by two women similar in description who are now being prosecuted in Missouri.

The conviction was obtained in my court on the sole testimony of the victim who identified the two women. . . .

For all these reasons and some others, I have a definite un-easy feeling about the conviction. I would like to request that you give a lie-detector test to both of these women and advise me. If you will do this, I will have our probation officer send you his report and all the background material you may need.

Yours very truly
Harry G. Miller[1]

The agent dutifully ran the letter by Director Sanford, who quickly approved Judge Miller's request for KBI assistance. Sanford and Cowan had entered on duty with the KBI together in 1948.

Cowan met with Judge Miller, who elaborated on his suspicions and made available to the agent all relevant court records and the trial transcript. Following his review of those materials, the KBI agent studied the case file at the Kansas City Police Department and interviewed the arresting officer, Chief of Detectives Boston Daniels, later police chief of Kansas City, Kansas.

The armed robbery in question had been of Reed Liquor Store on Chelsea Trafficway in Kansas City, Kansas, at 9:30 P.M. on September 18, 1968. The proprietor of the liquor store had claimed that two young African American females, one heavy, one slender, robbed the store while he was there alone. The heavier one pointed a pearl-handled pistol at him while he handed the slender one the cash in a bag. The heavier woman was wearing a black dress and the slender one a pink print dress. The heavier one ordered the slender one to check the cash register to ensure that the store owner had placed all the money in the bag. When satisfied they had all the loot, they left.

Detective Daniels had passed on the young women's physical descriptions to some of his informants, who, like Daniels and the liquor store owner, were also African American. The next day one informant telephoned the detective and advised that the two suspects were then sitting side by side on stools in a downtown Kansas City (Kansas) bar. Detective Daniels, with other officers, proceeded to the bar, arrested the women, and took them to the police station. He telephoned the liquor store owner and asked that he come to the station to identify the robbers. The armed robbery victim identified both women in a lineup and, despite their protests of innocence and alibi claims, they were charged with the liquor store robbery. The liquor store owner again identified both defendants in the jury trial four months later. Generally speaking, the victim's identification of the robbers and his testimony represented the prosecution's entire case.

The defense consisted of fairly extensive alibi testimony. Both defendants testified and both denied any involvement in or knowledge of the crime. Both women claimed they spent the entire evening in question in a bar across town. Although friends, they were actually not together that night. The owner of that bar, a woman, testified on behalf of the defendants, claiming that both had been in her establishment most of that evening. She had even posted the bail bond for one of the young women, who had previously been one of her employees. Three other witnesses also testified for the defense, claiming to have seen the defendants throughout the evening in the bar. One witness noted that she and one of the defendants had arrived together at that bar via taxicab at about 8:00 P.M., and, at the end of the evening, she had loaned that defendant four dollars in cab fare to go home because the latter had no money.

Clearly, the jury had not believed the two defendants, the owner of the bar, or the other three defense witnesses. The only person the jury apparently had believed was the liquor store owner.

Even Detective Daniels had expressed his own doubts to Special Agent Cowan about the guilt of the pair, having relied completely on his own informant's reliability and on the liquor store owner's positive identification of both women. The detective's case file consisted of three pages, and the officer admitted that he had conducted no investigation regarding the defendants' whereabouts that night, their relationship, their alibi claims, the cab drivers, or anything else. He had marked the investigation closed when the victim identified the pair and the prosecutor had expressed satisfaction.

Special Agent Cowan, unfortunately, couldn't interview the bar owner, a key defense witness. Three weeks following the trial, she had been shot and killed during an armed robbery of her bar. He was, however, able to interview the other defense witnesses who had testified in the trial. The veteran agent found their stories credible. He also interviewed both defense attorneys and found that both were convinced of the innocence of their respective clients and that justice had been thwarted in the trial. Each attorney was grateful for the intervention of Judge Miller and the KBI. What really impressed Special Agent Cowan was not the defense attorneys' belief in their respective clients' innocence, but rather the information that one of the attorneys, Karen Johnson, had developed about a similar armed robbery of a liquor store, an hour or so later on the night of September 18, 1968, across the river in Kansas City, Missouri. It was Johnson's understanding that two young African American women had been arrested by the Kansas City, Missouri, Police Department for that liquor store robbery. She believed they were of similar physical description to the two Kansas robbers, one heavy, one thin. One had been wearing a black dress. One had been wearing a print dress. Only one had been carrying a gun. Johnson, impressed with the apparent coincidences, had attempted to obtain information from the Missouri police but had been unsuccessful in her efforts. She did, however, have the name of one attorney who had represented one of the Missouri defendants.

Beginning to share Judge Miller's "uneasy feeling" about the two Kansas women's convictions, Cowan went to Kansas City, Missouri. The police department provided the entire case file to him. Both of those defendants, unlike the defendants in the Kansas case, had entered pleas of guilty to the robbery of the Missouri liquor store. Although the ages of the four defendants, thirty-one and twenty-four for the Kansas women and twenty and sixteen for the Missouri women, didn't really fit, their physical descriptions did. And the manner of the Missouri robbery matched exactly the modus operandi of the Kansas liquor store robbery.

Special Agent Cowan contacted the Missouri attorney whose name had been furnished to him by Karen Johnson. Cowan explained the situation and requested the opportunity to interview the attorney's client. The lawyer was agreeable but predicted the agent was wasting his time. He explained that Johnson had shared her concerns with him and, accordingly, he had interviewed his client about the Kansas robbery. He noted she denied any involvement in that crime. Since she had admitted the Missouri robbery, he had no reason to believe she was lying about the armed robbery to the west. But he would ask her if she would be willing to talk to the KBI agent. The attorney called Cowan later that day to inform him that the interview was scheduled in three days. His client had, indeed, been willing to speak to the Kansas officer, much to the surprise of her lawyer and Cowan.

The sixteen-year-old Missouri defendant had already been lodged in the Missouri State Training School for Girls, at Chillicothe, Missouri, following her plea of guilty in court. The agent telephoned that facility and arranged an interview of the juvenile in a week, four days after his scheduled interview of her codefendant.

Then the agent discussed the situation with the prosecutor in the Wyandotte County attorney's office who had handled the Kansas prosecution. Cowan wanted to know the following: if he could persuade the two young Missouri women to admit their responsibility for the Kansas liquor store robbery, could the Kansas prosecutor assure him that the Kansas women would go free and the Missouri women, given their Missouri convictions, would not be prosecuted for the Kansas robbery? Cowan added that all was conditional on the Kansas women each passing a polygraph examination. The prosecutor, like the judge and the KBI agent, being interested in justice and not merely prosecution, quickly agreed. He appreciated the KBI agent's interest in the case and promised to support Cowan's eventual conclusion.

The interview of the older Missouri female had been scheduled in her attorney's office in downtown Kansas City, Missouri. She had earlier pleaded guilty, but she would not be sentenced until the state had completed her presentence investigation and her record of arrests and outstanding charges, if any, had been thoroughly reviewed for the sentencing judge. Another charge of armed robbery, from Kansas or anywhere else, was not what she needed at that particular time. Cowan knew the interview would be difficult, if not impossible.

Cowan interviewed the young woman in front of her attorney. He described the two young Kansas women and showed their photographs to her. He described the Kansas robbery, the paucity of evidence and investigation in the case, and the trial itself. He showed her the judge's letter, told her of the prosecutor's agreement, and advised her of his interviews of the defense witnesses. He told her bluntly that he and others believed she and her teen-aged accomplice had robbed the Kansas liquor store about an hour before they robbed the Missouri liquor store across the river separating the two cities of Kansas City. While she continued to deny that she and her associate had robbed the Kansas liquor store, Cowan was encouraged by her body language, by her invitation to him to interview her again after her sentencing, and also by her somewhat strange suggestion that he first interview the sixteen-year-old, already confined in the Chillicothe juvenile facility. He told her that interview was already scheduled. That information seemed to please her. The agent concluded in his report of the interview,

> I asked her if after her case was settled, whether she had to go to the penitentiary or was paroled, would she talk to me again about this robbery in Kansas, and she agreed. She denied being in Kansas that night or involved in the robbery of the Reed Liquor Store, but not very convincingly, and as far as I am concerned, her answers to my questions and her demeanor is a tacit admission of her involvement in the robbery of Reed's Liquor Store.[2]

The next day, February 18, 1969, the agent drove to the women's farm at the Kansas State Penitentiary in Lansing. He first met with the superintendent, Mrs. Marian Phillips, with whom he had earlier made telephone arrangements to interview and polygraph the two recent arrivals who had been convicted of the Kansas City liquor store robbery. She also appreciated his interest in the two young women, confiding that she and her staff "had a feeling that they were telling the truth and that these girls were not guilty,"[3] as Cowan reflected later in his report.

He administered polygraph examinations to each of the two women, separately, in a private interview room. His concluding statements in each of the two interview reports were identical: "It is the opinion of this examiner that this subject told substantially the truth during her polygraph examination."[4] Both had emphatically denied robbing the Kansas liquor store.

On February 26, 1969, now completely convinced of the innocence of the two young Kansas women, Cowan drove to Chillicothe, Missouri, and to the Missouri Training School for Girls. He went first to the office of Robert Scott, a supervisor at the school, with whom he had earlier made arrangements for the interview of the juvenile liquor store robber. Mr. Scott explained the rules. Scott would have to remain present during the interview, and he would have to advise the teenager of her rights to not be interviewed by Cowan. Additionally, Cowan could not take a written statement from her or ask her to sign anything. The KBI agent agreed to all the conditions.

The youthful but exceptionally mature young inmate was then brought into Scott's office where she was introduced to Cowan. Scott identified him as a KBI special agent and carefully explained to the inmate Cowan's interest in the Kansas liquor store armed robbery and Cowan's belief that she and her accomplice were responsible for that crime, for which two Kansas women had been convicted. Scott then advised her of her *Miranda* rights to silence and counsel. As Cowan's report later reflected, Mr. Scott closed his remarks to the teenager by telling her "that she didn't have to answer any of my questions, but that he hoped she would cooperate and tell me the truth as he felt that this case justified some truth telling."[5]

Scott then gave permission for Cowan to speak to the youthful offender, who to that moment in the interview had not spoken a word herself. Cowan's subsequent report reflected:

> I informed her of my mission, that I was here not to hurt her in any way, but to plead the cause of two colored girls who were in the penitentiary in Kansas for a robbery that I knew they did not commit. . . . I told her that I had talked to [her fall partner] but that she couldn't tell me anything, as she was still under a pre-sentence investigation for a parole, but that she had asked that I come to see her. I explained . . . that two colored girls, very closely fitting the physical description of her and [her fall partner] robbed the Reed Liquor Store in Kansas City, Kansas on the 18th of September last year about forty-five minutes before she and [her fall partner] robbed the Monarch Liquor Store in Kansas City, Missouri. I told her that it would be a 1,000 to 1 chance that two different people did these two robberies. I informed her that these two girls had been tried in court and were convicted of the armed robbery of the Reed Liquor Store on the sole testimony of the victim who was the only witness to the robbery.[6]

At that point, the Missouri teenager interrupted Cowan to correct him. "That's a lie, because there was another witness to that robbery," she said. The surprised Cowan asked her if she meant the Kansas robbery. "Yes," she replied. He then asked her if she was involved in the robbery of the Reed

Liquor Store in Kansas City, Kansas, the night of September 18, 1968. Again the reply was "yes." And she added that so was her codefendant, readily admitting, as Cowan had suggested, that they robbed the Kansas store about an hour before they robbed the Missouri store, for which they were arrested and prosecuted.

The young woman then described in detail the Kansas robbery, including her partner's black dress and pearl-handled pistol, and her own brown print (not pink) dress. She described how she accepted the sack of money from the male proprietor and how her partner instructed her to check the cash register to make sure the man had placed all the cash in the sack. The only detail Cowan had wrong, she advised, was that a woman was also present during the robbery. They had presumed it was the owner's wife. "A colored girl," she was wearing a yellow mini-dress and had a black purse and a pack of cigarettes in her lap. She smoked a cigarette all through the robbery as though nothing unusual was happening. The two robbers talked about that strange behavior afterward, she recalled.

The next afternoon Cowan went to the Kansas liquor store to talk to the proprietor who had identified the two Kansas women for the police and in the trial. He was not present. Only his wife was present. Cowan identified himself to her and explained what he had been doing in recent days in connection with the robbery of their store. He asked how it was that her husband had been able to identify the two young local women as being responsible. Cowan's subsequent report reflected her response: "She told me that was easy, as you don't find two colored girls of that description going around robbing places very often. I asked her if there were any witnesses to the robbery besides her husband and she told me no. I then left."[7]

The fourteen-page report of KBI Special Agent Wendell Cowan to Judge Harry Miller was dated March 4, 1969. In the report, Agent Cowan pointed out there was one final lead he intended to pursue. As soon as the pre-sentence investigation was completed on the twenty-year-old Missouri woman, Cowan intended to try again to obtain her admission to the Kansas liquor store robbery. He would advise the judge when that interview had been conducted.

On July 29, 1969, the twenty-year-old Missouri defendant furnished a signed statement to Cowan in her attorney's office, admitting her involvement in the armed robbery of the Kansas liquor store at 9:30 P.M. on September 18, 1968. She confirmed the version of events furnished earlier to Cowan by her teenaged associate. Cowan personally delivered that signed statement to Judge Miller's chambers the next day, thereby closing the KBI's involvement in the case. There was, however, no need for that statement. Judge Miller had already set aside the jury verdict and the convictions of the two Kansas women after receipt of Cowan's March 4 investigative report.

Defense attorney Karen Johnson beautifully summarized the situation in her letter to Cowan on March 11, 1969:

Dear Mr. Cowan:

On behalf of my client . . . and myself, I want to thank you for your thorough investigation of the Reed Liquor Store and Monarch Liquor Store robberies. Because of your interest and efforts her innocence has been established, her record cleared and she is no longer incarcerated.

It is gratifying to know that the Kansas Bureau of Investigation will work as hard to reverse the conviction of an innocent person as it will to prosecute and obtain a conviction of one who is guilty.

I am glad I had the opportunity to meet you. I hope I will see you again, and if I can ever be of help to you in any way, please do not hesitate to call on me. It would be a pleasure to work with someone as capable as you.

Again, my thanks for your interest, your investigation and your beautiful report to Judge Miller.

Yours very truly,

(Mrs.) Karen I. Johnson

Wendell Cowan retired on November 30, 1970, after twenty-two years of service as a special agent with the KBI. He died on March 20, 1987.

CHAPTER EIGHT

Pyle: Homicide without a Body

At 5:15 A.M., Thursday, April 8, 1971, an interstate truck driver stopped a deputy sheriff on Highway 54 in Greensburg, Kansas. The trucker told the officer that a few minutes earlier, as he was coming through Haviland, twelve miles east of Greensburg, he had seen a fire far in the distance, south of Haviland. He stated that, based on the size of the glow in the darkness, the fire might be a barn or a house.

The Kiowa County deputy radioed the Pratt County sheriff's office and a deputy was dispatched west of Pratt on Highway 54. He soon reported that he was unable to locate any fire in that area.

The Haviland city marshal was called out, and he drove south. Twelve miles south of Haviland and two miles northwest of the small community of Belvidere, he discovered a pasture on fire. The dispatcher's radio log would later reflect that the city marshal had notified the dispatcher at 5:55 A.M. that he had arrived at the scene of the fire. He was joined within minutes by firemen and other officers whom he had summoned as he had proceeded south and first observed the glow on the horizon.

Before he stepped from his pickup truck, he realized it was not just a pasture fire. The ranch house that had previously occupied the center portion of that pasture was gone. Burning rubble was now in its place. The well-known ranch house of Golda (Goldie) Millar had burned to the ground, and neither Goldie nor her ever-present German shepherd, Brandie, were to be seen.

If Kiowa County, Kansas, in 1971, had a matriarch, it was the seventy-eight-year-old, popular, well-to-do, physically large widow and rancher Goldie Millar. She previously had raised cattle and wheat on the ranch's 3,100 acres. In recent years she had primarily leased out most of the ground to area cattlemen for pasture. The ranch, in early 1971, had been conservatively appraised at more than $340,000.

Bill Hogan, sheriff of Kiowa County, watched the firemen poke through the ashes of the house. It was light now and the rubble had cooled enough to permit closer examination of what was left of Goldie Millar's home. The sheriff recalled that he had spoken with Goldie earlier that week, on Monday, and he knew she was recovering from a bout of the flu. It had, as she told Hogan, "knocked her for a loop." Perhaps, thought the sheriff, Goldie's daughter had come from Colorado and taken Goldie back home with her to care for her mother, who lived alone.

As Hogan was deep in that thought, a deputy called out to him from the basement of the house. "Bill, here's the dog." The sheriff returned to reality. "What's that?" The deputy repeated, "I said, here's Goldie's German shepherd."[1] The sheriff walked over to the edge of the basement and looked down to where the deputy was pointing the toe of his cowboy boot. Sheriff Hogan now saw the charred, massive head of Brandie. The deputy kicked aside more rubble to reveal the remainder of the big dog's badly charred body. The sheriff removed his western hat and leaned over the edge. "Well then, boys, look close. Goldie's here somewhere. She and that dog are never far away from each other." The dog's fierce devotion to her mistress was legend. No stranger approached Goldie unless she told the dog to stay back. Brandie slept at the foot of her bed and rode with her in the cab of her pickup truck. Brandie had bitten more than one person who had come too close to Goldie.

The house, what was left of it, and also the surrounding area were searched for hours. No trace of Goldie or anything resembling human remains could be found. Goldie's .22-caliber revolver had been found in the basement and closer examination of the German shepherd had revealed an unusual thing. A .22-caliber shell casing was imbedded in the dog's head. The cartridge bore no firing-pin mark and had apparently exploded from the heat of the fire. The dog had not actually been shot, in the strictest sense. But what had killed the dog and where was Goldie? Hogan decided to call KBI Special Agent Duane Bell, who lived in nearby Pratt.

The matriarch of Kiowa County was a lifelong native. She had many friends and she had two daughters. Both daughters had declined to embrace the ranch life of their parents. One lived on the East Coast and one lived in Colorado Springs. Goldie also had grandchildren. One of those grandchildren was Michael Duane Pyle, Goldie's twenty-six-year-old grandson.

Mike Pyle had a troubled childhood. When he was a small boy, his father had committed suicide. He became a discipline problem and had assaulted several younger boys, including his own brother. At the age of twelve, he was placed in the famed Menninger's Clinic, in Topeka, Kansas, for psychiatric evaluation. Five years in a military school followed that and, after attempts at higher education proved unsuccessful, Mike was sent in 1964, at age nineteen, to live on the Kansas ranch with his grandmother.

The situation proved to be harmonious for a few years. The grandmother was a positive influence and Mike turned into a pretty good ranch hand. Things went so well that, in 1967, Goldie had her will drawn up and left the ranch and the land to Mike, generally excluding the two daughters and other grandchildren.

In 1968, Mike married and brought his bride to live with Goldie and him on the ranch. Harmony ended and lives changed. Relations between Goldie and Mike's wife soon became strained, and, within a year, relations between grandmother and grandson deteriorated to the point that, on at least two occasions, Mike severely beat Goldie. She declined to press charges. Later, however, during another violent argument, Goldie called Sheriff Hogan to the ranch. During that confrontation, the sheriff suggested that Mr. and Mrs. Mike Pyle should leave the ranch. Mike reluctantly complied, but unwisely predicted to the sheriff, "This is my ranch and I am going to have it, one way or another."

Soon thereafter, without telling Mike, Goldie revoked a power of attorney she had given him and, in her attorney's office, also revoked her last will and testament. On Thursday, April 8, 1971, Michael Duane Pyle mistakenly thought he was still the primary beneficiary in the last will and testament of Mrs. Golda "Goldie" Millar.

Mike and his wife moved to Pratt, thirty miles away. He continued to frequent the ranch and still had his mail delivered to the post office at Belvidere, two miles from the ranch, as did Goldie. The relationship worsened and twice Goldie threatened to prosecute Mike for theft of property from the ranch—once, some tools; on another occasion, a water pump.

During the week before April 8, 1971, Mike seemed to go out of his way to try to persuade neighbors, friends, and associates of Goldie that his grandmother had started drinking heavily and was becoming mentally incompetent. While no one believed Mike's new assertions, they also didn't dispute them. No one liked Mike Pyle anyway and all wondered why Goldie just didn't run him off once and for all.

KBI Special Agent Duane Bell was the first KBI agent to join Sheriff Bill Hogan at the scene of the fire. He arrived late morning before noon. Special Agent Al Dewey drove in from Garden City and arrived mid-afternoon. KBI Director Fred Howard, who had been appointed director only three months before, had called Dewey, at Bell's request, and asked him to proceed to Kiowa County to assist. It was clear to Hogan, Dewey, and Bell that they had, at the very least, an arson and a missing person case on their hands. All three suspected worse.

The sheriff briefed the two agents on events at the ranch the past few years and explained, as best he could, the relationship between Mike and Goldie. Hogan also told them that his last personal contact with Goldie was on Monday, April 5. He had telephoned Goldie about 6:00 P.M. that day and told her that he had just received a Pratt County arrest warrant for Mike on bad-check charges. He wondered if Mike was at the ranch. Goldie informed the sheriff that Mike lived in Pratt, but she expected Mike at the ranch that evening and she would tell him to see Hogan about the arrest warrant the next day.

As Sheriff Hogan and KBI agents Bell and Dewey visited, a young man and a woman pulled into the ranch yard in a pickup truck about 5:30 P.M. Hogan turned to Bell and Dewey and said, "Here's Mike and his mother now." As the couple approached the three law enforcement officers, the sheriff quietly told the agents that he would take the mother, Goldie's daughter, aside and visit with her. That would give Bell and Dewey an opportunity to visit with Mike Pyle to see if they could get a reading on him, as the sheriff put it.

Pyle and the two agents leaned against his pickup truck and visited while they watched searchers continuing to poke through the rubble of Goldie's home. When, during that conversation, one agent asked Pyle when he had last seen his grandmother, both agents were surprised with the answer that he had last seen her shortly after midnight early that very morning. He explained that he had been en route to Colorado Springs from Pratt the previous night and had detoured by the ranch to check on his grandmother's welfare. He had arrived at the ranch shortly before midnight and had departed for Colorado Springs shortly after midnight. Pyle claimed he had stayed only minutes because he had found Goldie very drunk. In fact, he noted, she had been on a three-week drinking binge. Everybody knew about it, he claimed. He said the house was full of Old Charter whiskey bottles. He had no idea how many she had emptied. He volunteered that he had not learned of the fire until he had arrived at the home of his mother and stepfather in Colorado Springs about 8:15 A.M., Colorado time, or 9:15 A.M., Kansas time. His stepfather had received a phone call from a neighbor of Goldie only minutes before he had arrived.

Pyle suggested that the fire was possibly caused by a defective furnace that had been causing trouble a long time. But, he admitted, it might have also been caused by rats chewing through electrical wiring. At any rate, he repeated—Bell and Dewey thought for emphasis—that he left his grandmother shortly after midnight, disgusted with her intoxicated condition. He drove straight through to Colorado Springs to visit with his mother and stepfather "about business and about Goldie." He was, he recalled, speechless when they told him the ranch had burned to the ground. An hour later, joined by his mother, he headed back to Kansas and the ranch.

Shortly afterward, Mike and his distraught mother took their leave of Hogan, Bell, and Dewey and drove to Pratt to get Goldie's daughter a motel room.

In the days that followed, the ashes were sifted and resifted. The ranch was searched by men on foot, in trucks, and on horseback. Divers searched area ponds and aircraft crisscrossed the whole region. Missing-person bulletins were widely circulated and state news media let all know that Goldie Millar was missing. Since she was one of the most successful ranchers in the area, some recalled the Clutter family at Holcomb and wondered if Goldie had been the victim of a robbery, or worse.

On Thursday, April 8, 1971, Goldie Millar, age seventy-eight, of rural Kiowa County, Kansas, disappeared. She was never seen again.

Duane Bell and Al Dewey believed Goldie was dead. They were pretty certain they knew "why" and "who," but they did not know "when." The "where" was troubling too. If she had been killed at the ranch, where was her body? Why wasn't her body lying alongside Brandie? The agents decided to retrace Goldie's movements for the week preceding the fire to see if they could establish the "when." Maybe the "where" would then become clear, too. They started with two of Goldie's closest friends—two ladies she had known most of her life and saw almost daily. One was the postmistress in Belvidere and the other operated the general store and gas station in the town. Both ladies said they last saw Goldie on Thursday, April 1, a week before the fire. She had picked up her mail and visited briefly with both. She had seemed fine and in good spirits. She appeared to be recovering nicely from the flu. Neither had seen her since, although the postmistress had spoken with her on the phone, Monday, April 5.

It was also determined that on Friday, April 2, three different cattlemen spoke to Goldie in her ranch yard. One of them stopped by again the next day, on Saturday, April 3, when he saw her in the yard. A fourth cattleman had spoken with her on the phone during the evening of Saturday, April 3. None of the men had seen Goldie or talked to her since those two days. The agents were unable to identify anyone who saw or spoke to Goldie on Sunday, April 4.

Sheriff Hogan had told the KBI agents about his phone conversation with Goldie on Monday evening, April 5, when the sheriff was trying to locate Mike Pyle to serve him with the Pratt County bad-checks warrant. That was about 6:00 P.M. Bell and Dewey located an individual who spoke with Goldie that same Monday evening on the telephone, after the sheriff had spoken with her. The call, between 7:00 and 7:30 P.M., was about a fencing job at the ranch the next day. Goldie had informed the caller that the necessary fencing materials would be in the yard at the ranch ready to go the next day. Shortly afterward, Goldie had received a third phone call, this one from the Belvidere postmistress, who reported that she was working late that evening at the post office. Mike had just called her from Haviland to see if she was still there so he could come by and pick up his mail. After she had hung up from Mike, it had occurred to her that Goldie might like Mike to pick up her mail too since she hadn't made it by the post office that day. Mike could then drop it off for her. Goldie advised her friend that she would very much appreciate the favor. All who had spoken with her or had seen her in those days in early April described Goldie as cheerful, normal, and sober.

Two things had become clear to Bell and Dewey. First, since the three phone calls she had received at the ranch Monday evening, April 5, no one had seen or spoken to Goldie Millar, except Mike Pyle. And secondly, Goldie, as they had suspected, while considered a heavy drinker by some, was not considered a drunk. Only Mike had claimed to see her intoxicated those last days.

At 8:30 P.M. on Monday evening, April 5, Mike did pick up his and Goldie's mail at the Belvidere post office.

On Tuesday, April 6, the man who was to put up a new fence at the ranch appeared at Goldie's house. The materials were not in the yard, as Goldie had said they would be, and no one seemed to be around. The man left. On the same day, between 9:00 A.M. and 10:00 A.M., Mike and his wife appeared at her sister's residence in Sawyer, Kansas, twenty miles east of the ranch. The wife asked her sister if she could stay with her while Mike went out to the ranch to check on the report of a fire. Later, that afternoon, Mike called his wife at her sister's home and informed her there was no fire after all.

On Wednesday, April 7, Mike and his wife were seen at an area farm sale, and later that morning he picked up his mail at Belvidere. The postmistress asked him about Goldie's flu. Mike laughed and replied, "She gets her flu in pint bottles." Goldie's friend did not appreciate or believe Mike's flippant response to her question.

Mike's stepfather had confirmed that, during the early afternoon of Wednesday, April 7, he had received a phone call from Mike advising that he wanted to come to Colorado Springs the following day to discuss some business.

At 5:00 P.M. on Wednesday, April 7, Mike and his wife were in the Belvidere general store. When the proprietor asked about Goldie, Mike informed her that his grandmother had been on "a helluva binge." In fact, he said, Goldie was probably passed out at the ranch as they spoke. He said he had been very worried about Goldie and he was going to Colorado the next day to see his mother and see what could be done for Goldie. He then dialed Goldie's number on the store phone in front of the owner. He let it ring several times and received no answer. He concluded aloud, for all in the store to hear, that Goldie was probably passed out and couldn't answer the phone. After Mike and his wife left the store, Goldie's friend wondered why Mike was saying such things. Goldie liked bourbon, but her friend didn't appreciate talk about Goldie being a fall-down drunk, especially from a ne'er-do-well grandson.

The next morning, at 5:15 A.M., the truck driver reported the fire that turned out to be Goldie Millar's home.

The early investigative efforts of Dewey, Bell, and Hogan had convinced the trio that Mike Pyle had probably killed his grandmother late Monday night, April 5, or in the very early morning hours of Tuesday, April 6. Nobody had seen her or talked to her since Mike had apparently took her mail to her that Monday night. The fencing materials were not out as Goldie had promised they would be the next day, Tuesday. That was the same day Mike had strangely claimed that he had to check out a report of a fire at the ranch. Bell and Dewey theorized that Mike probably started a fire that Monday night in the house, presuming and hoping that after he left the house would burn down that night or early the next morning. For whatever reason, the fire had gone out, as the disappointed Mike learned the next day, Tuesday, when he left his wife at her sister's place. Therefore, Goldie was probably murdered that Monday night after Mike had brought her the mail. She was certainly killed before the night of the real fire, although that could have been the night Mike disposed of the body. But where and how?

The first real break came when Bell and Dewey interviewed the manager of the apartment building in Pratt where Mike and his wife lived. She advised the agents that on Thursday morning, April 8, at 7:00 A.M., Mike had telephoned her, said he had an emergency, and needed to speak to his wife. After being summoned to the phone, Mike's wife, in front of the apartment building manager, suddenly became hysterical. She hung up the phone and told the manager, "That was Mike and he said his grandmother burned up in a fire."

Mike had claimed he learned of the fire at 8:15 A.M., Colorado time, or 9:15 A.M., Kansas time, when his stepfather gave him the news in Colorado Springs that had rendered him speechless. Yet at 7:00 A.M., Kansas time, he notified his wife at Pratt about the fire.

While they had not yet conducted a formal interview with Mike, Bell and Dewey had visited with him on several occasions following their first meeting at the ranch after the fire. He was always quite talkative, very composed, and without emotion—until one meeting in the street in Belvidere when Dewey had casually asked Mike if he had been aware that Goldie had revoked her will. As the two KBI agents watched him, the color seemed to drain from Mike's face, his jaw seemed to tighten, and he appeared to be in a trance. He did not answer the question, but the KBI agents looked at each other and realized the revocation of Goldie's last will and testament had truly been news to Mike. Bad news. Surprising news, it appeared.

Actually, they had already known the answer to that question. When they had interviewed his mother about her recollections of Mike's behavior as she rode with him from Colorado Springs to the ranch, she had recalled that, during that trip, Mike had once turned to her suddenly and said, "Don't forget, I don't want to cause hard feelings, but the will is made out to me. Your sister and you get one thousand dollars apiece, and I think Carla and Bill [Mike's sister and brother] get something, but it's all mine."

She also recalled wondering aloud what could have caused the fire. Mike had suggested it might have been Goldie's practice of hanging her clothes on the hot water heater or maybe all that gasoline she kept around the house.

About the first of May, Mike Pyle hired Harold Herd, an attorney in the town of Coldwater in an adjacent county. Herd, later a justice of the Kansas Supreme Court, was highly respected and was considered one of the finest attorneys in southwestern Kansas.

The KBI agents continued to press the investigation. They interviewed more than a hundred people, many of them several times. Bell and Dewey's first formal interview of Pyle began at 1:00 P.M., May 11, 1971, in Herd's office at Coldwater. After Bell had advised Pyle of his rights to remain silent, according to the 1966 U.S. Supreme Court decision *Miranda v. Arizona,* and Pyle, in the presence of his attorney, had acknowledged and waived those rights, Dewey promptly confronted him with their knowledge of his premature telephone call to his wife in Pratt the morning of the fire, two hours before he claimed to have learned of the fire from his stepfather in Colorado Springs. Immediately, a shaken Pyle requested that he be permitted to confer with his attorney privately. It was almost an hour before Herd and Pyle returned to the room. The interview resumed but again ended quickly when Pyle asked to be excused for a moment. He returned ten minutes later and asked Herd to step outside the room with him. Herd complied but returned quickly with the news that he had just been informed by his client that Pyle had taken an overdose of pills in a suicide attempt. The agents transported Pyle to the Coldwater hospital emergency room, where a physician induced vomiting. Particles of a single capsule of Librium, a tranquilizer, were recovered. Pyle had lied about the overdose.

Pyle asked the doctor and the two nurses to step outside and leave him alone with the agents. He told the agents, "I don't know how much Mr. Herd would want me to tell you men, but I am going to tell you exactly what happened." He then gave his version of the relationship between his grandmother and himself. The recent bitterness stemmed, he said, from Goldie's hatred of his wife. Goldie, he claimed, had threatened his wife's life. When he dropped by the ranch en route to Colorado that Monday evening, Goldie, intoxicated, urged him to divorce his wife. She even offered to pay for it. When he declined, Goldie threatened to "get rid of her in one way or another," or so Pyle claimed.

Following a heated argument about his wife, Pyle alleged that Goldie passed out on the living room floor. He went to the garage and returned with three one-gallon jugs of transmission fluid. He poured it on the floor, threw a match on it, and left as the room exploded in flames. He said he had arrived about 11:00 P.M. and left a little after midnight. He admitted he had prematurely called his wife from a small town in Colorado.

The two agents did not interrupt him as he told his story. Pyle concluded by turning to Bell and saying, "I hope you and Mr. Dewey will understand why I had to kill my grandmother." Bell paused and then responded, "But Mike, if that story is true, where is Goldie?" Pyle declined to answer and the agents formally placed him under arrest for the murder of Mrs. Golda Millar. They lodged him in the Commanche County jail. They called Herd, then KBI headquarters in Topeka, and finally Sheriff Hogan. Pyle was permitted to call his wife.

Michael Duane Pyle gave, in all, six confessions, or admissions, or statements against interest, in the three days of May 11, May 12, and May 13, 1971. He consistently admitted he was responsible for Goldie's disappearance and for the arson of her home. He was just as consistent in his refusal to identify the method of murder or the disposition of the body.

Three of the admissions came on the same day, May 12, following the first confession in the hospital emergency room. Bell and Dewey went back to the Coldwater jail the following morning. They wished to reduce to writing the oral confession given to them by Pyle. After again being advised of his rights to remain silent, he repeated his previous statement, which was then put in the form of a signed statement, although Pyle declined to sign it without his attorney present. A friend was permitted to visit Pyle in jail that day. In their conversation about Goldie, Mike told his friend that he had "burned her up." The third admission of the day occurred when Sheriff Hogan drove to Coldwater to visit Pyle in jail. The sheriff advised him of his rights again and then discussed things with him for an hour and a half. The first hint as to the method of the murder came in that conversation between Hogan and Pyle. In discussing his relationship with his grandmother, Mike calmly noted, "I should have cut her throat one other time." This comment was the only time Pyle suggested a cause of death for Goldie other than the fire.

On May 13, Mike was moved to the Kiowa County jail in Greensburg. He had requested cigarettes from Bell, so the agent visited him with the cigarettes that morning. Pyle thanked him for his generosity and said, "Mr. Bell, I haven't been completely honest with you. I've decided to tell you where Mrs. Millar's body is. It's so gruesome and horrible I only want to tell it once. Will you go get Bill Hogan and bring the sheriff in so I can tell you both at the same time?"

The KBI agent went to tell the sheriff the news they had desperately wanted to hear. His joy, however, was short-lived. Mrs. Pyle was then with the sheriff and, when Bell told Hogan that Mike wanted to visit with them again, she insisted that she be allowed to speak to him first. Due to excessive compassion or an underestimation of her influence, they permitted her to see Pyle first. Forty-five minutes later, when the sheriff and the agent finally did see their prisoner, his only statement to them was this: "I've changed my mind. She died in the fire."

The sixth and final admission came later that day in the Kiowa County Court House immediately before Pyle's arraignment. Also present were Herd, Dewey, and Bell. He repeated the original story he had given in the emergency room, but with one variation. This time he claimed he had a change of heart. He said that he had returned to the burning house to pull Goldie to safety but was driven back by the heat and flames and then, regretfully, drove to Colorado.

Pyle remained in the Kiowa County jail, charged with first-degree murder and aggravated arson. It was clear that for whatever reason he was not going to reveal the location of Goldie's body or the cause of death. The family was very distressed and wanted to provide an appropriate burial for their mother and grandmother. Pyle declined every plea from the family.

On one occasion, Bell wondered aloud if Pyle thought they would not be able to prove murder without the body and that was the reason for his silence on that issue. Dewey looked at Bell and Hogan and commented that, inasmuch as the Kansas criminal justice system had never charged anyone with murder, let alone convicted anyone of murder, without the "corpus delicti," the victim's body, Pyle might be right. Many prosecutors had declined to take such a case into court.

The Kiowa County Attorney's office and the appointed special prosecutor, Jack Focht of Wichita, later one of the most successful defense attorneys in Kansas, however, agreed that the circumstantial case put together by Bell, Dewey, and Hogan was impressive and deserved to be heard.

It was July 1972 when the case went to trial in the tiny Kiowa County court-room in Greensburg. The courtroom was packed daily and the only specta-tors not acquainted with Goldie Millar were Focht, Dewey, Bell, and Herd.

There was still a complete absence of any evidence relating to the body of the alleged murder victim. There were no crime scene photographs. There was no autopsy and no report from a pathologist. No cause or place or time of death. No coroner's findings. No homicide case, without the victim's body, had ever gone to court in Kansas, and few had been tried anywhere else.

The jury had two issues to decide. Was Mrs. Golda "Goldie" Millar mur-dered? If so, did Michael Duane Pyle commit that murder? Despite able de-fense by Harold Herd and the absence of the "corpus delicti," the jury was persuaded by the impressive testimony of Bell, Dewey, and Hogan, and the overwhelming circumstantial evidence. Yes, said the jury, Goldie Millar had been murdered, and yes, Mike Pyle had murdered her, beyond any reason-able doubt.

On July 5, 1972, Judge Ernest Vieux sentenced the defendant to life im-prisonment for first-degree murder and five to ten years for aggravated ar-son. He was moved to Lansing on July 14, 1972.

Herd appealed the verdict to the Kansas Supreme Court. He disputed the confessions and the venue or location of the murder but primarily appealed to the "corpus delicti" issue. How, he argued, could you prove a murder without a body?

On March 1, 1975, the Kansas Supreme Court affirmed Mike Pyle's con-viction, victim's body or no victim's body. The court concluded:

> While we have no reported murder case in this state in which no por-tion of the victim's body was found . . . it is well-established . . . the corpus delicti itself may be proved by direct testimony or by indirect or circumstantial evidence, or a combination of both. . . . In this case there was ample evidence, independent of Mike's admissions, from which first the court and later the jury might infer that Goldie was dead, and that she had been the victim of foul play. Such evidence included: the fact that she was never heard from after April 5 by her friends and customary associates; the strained relations between Mike and Goldie; the carefully constructed alibi consisting of his fabricated charges of drunkenness and the all-night trip to Colorado; the false-alarm fire of two days before; Mike's avowed intention to get the ranch "one way or the other"; and

ultimately his premature display of knowledge of the fire and her death. Some of this evidence served a dual purpose; it not only showed that Goldie was dead by criminal means, but pointed the finger of guilt at Mike.[2]

The Pyle case, a fine example of methodical investigative efforts and of the potential of circumstantial or indirect evidence, was nonetheless not a celebrated case. It did not receive considerable publicity, and the importance of the case has been greatly underestimated through the years, except on the judicial precedent front. The successful prosecution of Michael Duane Pyle, without the "corpus delicti" of the crime, represented the first time that the Kansas criminal justice system had supported a murder conviction without any evidence of the victim's body. Since then there have been several successful murder convictions in Kansas without evidence of the victim's body. All the other cases have cited *State of Kansas v. Michael Duane Pyle.*

Dewey, Bell, and Hogan believed that Pyle deposited the body, probably dismembered, somewhere between the Kansas ranch and Colorado. Family members, the KBI agents, and Sheriff Hogan attempted repeatedly to persuade Pyle to divulge the body's location, both following his arrest and following his conviction. He resisted all such efforts, even later in prison.

Special Agent Dewey retired on November 17, 1975, six months after the Kansas Supreme Court ruled on the Pyle case. He died in 1987. Al was a friend and I attended his funeral services at Garden City. Special Agent Bell retired on August 20, 1979. He died in 1989. Duane was also a friend and I have long regretted having been unable to attend his funeral services.

Harold Herd continued a very successful law practice in southwestern Kansas until his appointment to the Kansas Supreme Court in 1979. Justice Herd retired in 1993 and died in his beloved Comanche County, Kansas, on April 23, 2007. Jack Focht, the lead prosecutor, continues to practice law in Wichita. Following his retirement, Sheriff Bill Hogan died of cancer.

Michael Duane Pyle continues to serve a life sentence in the Kansas penal system. In an attempt to avoid public scrutiny and enhance his chances for parole, he legally changed his name in prison to Daniel Lee Kirwan. At last check he was lodged in the Larned State Mental Health Facility.

Goldie Millar has never been given a proper burial, and *State v. Michael Duane Pyle* (1975) remains the state's leading judicial authority on homicide prosecution without the victim's body.

CHAPTER NINE

Nemechek: Serial Murder in Rural Kansas

The nationwide teletype issued by KBI headquarters in Topeka read as follows:

> On January 13, 1975, bodies of two female adults and one small boy were found in Graham County, Kansas. Location is 12 miles north of the Interstate 70 and Ogallah interchange. Victim number one was a white female 19 years of age shot with shotgun in left side. Victim was undressed and had had sexual intercourse. Possibly forced. Victim number two was a white female 21 years of age, also undressed, and death was caused by two gunshot wounds in the right side. This victim may have had an act of sodomy committed upon her. Victim number three was a small boy 3 years of age. Died from exposure. No apparent injuries. The purses and contents and clothing of victims one and two were left with the bodies. It is requested that any department having a case with similar M.O. contact the Kansas Bureau of Investigation, Topeka, Kansas, attention Pruter or Macey.[1]

The teletype need not have been issued nationwide. The man responsible for the brutal murders lived less than twenty miles from the crime scene. He had lived within twenty miles of that crime scene all twenty-four years of his life. Before his identification and arrest a year and a half later he would murder two more young white females in western Kansas near Interstate 70. Those murders would occur in two other Kansas counties, and each of those two crime scenes would also be within twenty miles of the killer's hometown of Wakeeney, Kansas. The five homicides would provide the KBI with its most daunting investigative challenge yet.

Cheryl Lynn Young, her three-year-old son, Guy William Young, and her friend Diane Lynn Lovette had been visiting various relatives in Colorado in early December 1974. On December 12, the trio departed the home of Cheryl's grandparents in her new red Toyota en route to the young women's respective homes in Iowa. Cheryl's car still had a California license plate on it, the last remnant from her residence and marriage in California. She had moved back to her original home in Iowa months earlier after filing for divorce in California, but she had not yet registered her car in Iowa.

Cheryl and Guy Young resided in West Point, Iowa. Diane Lynn Lovette's home was in Fort Madison, Iowa. Both the young women were attractive. Cheryl, twenty-one, was a blonde and only five feet one and 95 pounds. Brown-haired Diane, nineteen, was even smaller at four feet nine and 100 pounds. Guy was a handsome little boy, towheaded and fair-complected.

They departed Denver between 4:00 P.M. and 5:00 P.M. on December 12, 1974, intending to drive straight through to Fort Madison while alternating drivers frequently. The journey would instead end tragically in remote, rural western Kansas, a few hours later.

Early on January 3, 1975, Cheryl Young's father in Tahoe City, California, telephoned Cheryl's grandfather in Denver. The family had become concerned because Cheryl, Guy, and Diane had apparently never arrived in Iowa. The girls had contacted no one since their departure from Colorado, and telephone calls and letters to them had gone unanswered. Now Cheryl's father was advising her grandfather that he had been notified that Cheryl's car was being stored at the Triangle Truck Stop in Wakeeney, Kansas, having been found abandoned nearby on Interstate 70 on December 13, 1974. Storage costs were mounting.

Cheryl's grandparents rented a tow-bar in Denver and drove to Wakeeney on January 4, 1975. They stayed in a local motel that evening and the next morning went to the Triangle Truck Stop to claim Cheryl's Toyota. The car was full of gasoline but the battery was dead. The right rear tire was shredded, apparently having blown out, and the ignition key was missing. The fears of her grandparents increased when they observed Cheryl's brown leather driving gloves on the dashboard in front of the steering wheel and found Guy's favorite toys, his coat, shoes, and socks, and the coats of Cheryl and Diane still inside the car. Confused and concerned, they towed the car back to their residence in Denver. There, new keys were made by a Denver Toyota dealer, permitting the car's trunk to be opened, revealing all three suitcases of the travelers, still packed. Where were Cheryl, Guy, and Diane? And what had caused them to abandon the new automobile?

At approximately 11:00 A.M. on January 13, 1975, Sheriff Don Scott of the Graham County Sheriff's Department in Hill City, Kansas, received a telephone call indicating that two trappers had just made a grim discovery south of Hill City and just north of Interstate 70 on a remote, abandoned farmstead known locally as the Joe Faulkner place. They said they had stumbled on the body of a small blonde girl near the old Faulkner farmhouse and had then discovered the bodies of two women on the second floor of the farmhouse. Sheriff Scott's first telephone call was to the Kansas Bureau of Investigation.

As Kansans give directions, the crime scene was eight miles south, four miles east, five miles south, one mile east, and one mile back north from Hill City in sparsely populated Graham County.

Sheriff Scott and other local officers were joined at the crime scene at approximately 3:45 P.M., January 13, 1975, by KBI agents Ray Macey and Earl Maudlin. The first body, the small child described by the trappers, was lying on the ground just a few feet from the old, abandoned two-story plaster and concrete farmhouse. Thirty-five years earlier it had been the Faulkner family home. The small structure was now without doors, and no glass remained in any window. There were no apparent injuries on the body of the barefoot, coatless, towheaded child. Even in death the small child's long, bright yellow hair contrasted sharply with the dark ground on which the body lay. Early indications were that the child had died of exposure, apparently having been left to die in the brutal Kansas winter. But the trappers were wrong. The child was a little boy, not a girl, a mere toddler. Veteran officers at the scene looked away from the little boy's body with moist eyes during the three-hour crime scene investigation that followed that afternoon.

The sheriff and an area state game warden led the two KBI agents upstairs in the old farmhouse where the bodies of the two women had been found. The two women were lying next to each other. One, brown-haired, lying on her back, face up, was nude except for shoes and socks. The other, a blonde, lying on her side, face down, was completely nude. It was apparent to the veteran officers that both women, each young and attractive, had been shot with a shotgun, and probably sexually assaulted. Women's clothing, a baby's blanket, and purses were next to their bodies. A search of the first purse yielded an Iowa driver's license issued to Diane Lynn Lovette. A California driver's license in the second purse identified its owner as Cheryl Lynn Young.

Other KBI special agents, including Jack Ford and Duane Bell, quickly responded to the crime scene to join Sheriff Scott, Macey, Maudlin, and others in the initial investigation. Among the latter were Graham County Attorney Randall Weller; Scott's undersheriff, Earl Wood; the Kansas game warden, Bud Crumrine; Chief of Police Ken Roy of nearby Wakeeney; Trooper Kenny McGlasson of the Kansas Highway Patrol; and Undersheriff Larry Wade, Trego County Sheriff's Department, Wakeeney.

The first-day examination of the scene and area was stopped a little after 6:00 P.M. due to darkness, shortly after the bodies were removed. A deputy remained to ensure the security of the remote crime scene, and the examination continued the next morning at first light.

Autopsies performed on the three bodies in Hutchinson, Kansas, the next morning, January 14, were attended by KBI Special Agents Don Burns and Tom Lyons. The medical examinations confirmed much of what the crime scene investigators had suspected. Little Guy Young, born on March 16, 1971, had no injuries or wounds. He had been left to die of exposure in the cold, barefoot and coatless, motherless and alone. As also indicated by pools of blood under each victim and by blood spatter on one wall at the farmhouse, the autopsies reflected both women had been shot standing up, at that scene. Cheryl Young had been shot twice on her right side with a shotgun. Diane Lovette had died instantly of a shotgun blast to her heart. Lovette had definitely been forcibly raped, prior to death, and Young had probably been sodomized, postmortem. Cloth removed from Young's wounds during the autopsy indicated that someone had disrobed her after she was shot. None of his mother's blood was found on little Guy. The medical examiner attributed the remarkable cleanliness of the little boy's bare feet to moisture falling on the body. Sheriff Scott determined through the weather bureau that three inches of snow had fallen in that area on December 14; two inches on December 26; and less than an inch each day on January 2, January 5, January 9, and January 10. Temperatures had fallen as low as 9 and 10 degrees several days throughout December and early January. The cold weather had helped to preserve the three bodies.

An area newspaper, the *Salina Journal,* would later write of the triple homicide, "Now known as the Lovette-Young murder case by lawmen, it rivals in brutality the Clutter case . . . of the late 1950s at Holcomb which resulted in the conviction and hangings of 2 men, Richard Hickock and Perry Smith."[2] Pressed for a comment, Bob Clester, the KBI's western region supervisor in Great Bend and now in charge of the investigation, would only say that the triple-slaying was in the KBI's "real active" file.

KBI Director Fred Howard, in his last days in office, was sparing no effort. He gave the case top priority and granted all of Supervisor Clester's requests for resources and personnel, as would his successor, Bill Albott. Special Agents Macey, Maudlin, Ford, Burns, Bell, and Lyons were quickly joined by Special Agents Leonard Pruter and Jock Murray. All were veteran, experienced investigators. The investigation became a coordinated, multi-agency effort, with area sheriffs and police chiefs contributing what modest resources and manpower they could spare to Sheriff Scott's department and the KBI. The FBI and the Kansas Highway Patrol assisted as well.

Thanks to the intensity and scope of the investigation in its first hours, some of the mystery surrounding the abandonment of Cheryl Young's red 1974 Toyota began unraveling. KBI contacts with the families and friends of Lovette and Young in Iowa, California, and Colorado revealed what had happened to the abandoned car on Interstate 70 near Wakeeney the month before. At 8:30 A.M. on December 13, 1974, Kansas Highway Patrol Troopers Keith Denchfield and Kenny McGlasson had observed the car parked in the median on the north side of the eastbound lane of the interstate at the Ogallah exit, with the right rear end extending into the roadway. The driver's window was down and no key was in the ignition. There was a heavy coat of frost on the car, indicating it had been parked in that location for several hours. A check for any stolen report on the basis of the vehicle identification number and the California license plate was negative. Papers in the car reflected the owner to be Cheryl Lynn Young of either Fort Madison or West Point, Iowa. Teletypes sent to both cities requesting contact of the owner were unsuccessful. A registration check was also initiated on the basis of the California license plate, not necessarily a rapid police inquiry in 1974. Considering the car a traffic hazard, and awaiting results of the license plate registration request in California, the troopers ordered it towed into Wakeeney, sixteen hours after the vehicle had departed Denver with its three occupants, unbeknownst to the Kansas lawmen on December 13, 1974. Repeated checks with the National Crime Information Center (NCIC) in the ensuing days continued to be negative regarding any stolen report for the vehicle anywhere in the nation. Local law enforcement officers remained puzzled. It was a brand new automobile. Surely it had been stolen. Why had it not been reported?

The triple-slaying received considerable media exposure, statewide and nationally. The next few weeks and months found KBI special agents following leads and tips across the state and nation resulting from the media coverage. The leads went nowhere. Most area residents figured the killer was now on the East Coast or West Coast, but certainly not in their God-fearing, law-abiding midst.

But how, wondered Sheriff Scott and the KBI, would a killer from California or New York, simply passing through the area, have found the old Faulkner homestead? It was, after all, eight miles south, four miles east, five miles south, one mile east, and one mile back north, from Hill City, in the remotest part of Graham County, and not visible from Interstate 70, although close in proximity.

Therefore, early in the investigation, a local resident considered as a possible suspect was Francis Donald Nemechek of Wakeeney. The investigation determined at the outset that Cheryl Young had obtained the full tank of gasoline in her Toyota late on the night of December 12 at the Triangle Truck Stop in Wakeeney. Employees there had recalled Cheryl, Diane, and Guy in the truck stop before midnight buying gasoline, drinks, and snacks. When pressed by law enforcement officers to recall other customers also present then, one of the names suggested more than once was Francis Donald Nemechek. Witnesses could not be certain, but Nemechek, known as a heavy drinker, was usually in the Triangle at that time of night buying beer. He certainly could have been there that particular night and therefore might have seen the Iowa trio. In fact, late one night earlier in December, Nemechek had been ordered out of the truck stop restaurant because he was drunk and yelling profanities.

Nemechek was a farmhand for Joe Faulkner. He knew Faulkner's land and properties well. Moreover, he was the first person after the two trappers who actually stumbled on the homicide scene to come forward the morning of January 13, 1975. He had volunteered his services to Sheriff Scott and had commented that, in the course of his duties for Faulkner, he had been by the homestead previously in December and the bodies were not there. This was curious, noted Sheriff Scott to himself later. Clearly the old farmhouse was the scene of the murders and the medical examiner had estimated the deaths to have occurred approximately one month prior to the discovery of the bodies. How could Nemechek have missed that homicide scene?

Investigators learned that Nemechek had a drunk-driving arrest on his record earlier in 1974 in Galveston, Texas. He had also been arrested at a Salina truck stop in February 1974 in the act of having intercourse with a juvenile female in the cab of his truck. The juvenile and her family declined to complain and Nemechek was merely charged with disorderly conduct. Then there had also been a couple of complaints of indecent exposure against him in Wakeeney, wherein he had exposed himself to young women in separate incidents. The incidents were reported to authorities, but Nemechek had not been charged.

Accordingly, on January 17, 1975, only four days after the discovery of the bodies, Nemechek was interviewed in a Wakeeney motel by KBI Special Agents Leonard Pruter and Floyd Gaunt and given a polygraph examination. He denied being at the Triangle Truck Stop the night in question and denied any knowledge of the murders. The results of both the interview and the lie detector examination were inconclusive. Nemechek was strange, to be sure, but of more than that investigators could not be certain. Francis Donald Nemechek remained a suspect and at liberty.

At approximately 1:30 A.M. on January 1, 1976, shortly after many across the country had celebrated New Year's Eve, a Colorado family left the Triangle Truck Stop in Wakeeney, Kansas, and headed east on Interstate 70. They had filled their car with gasoline and availed themselves of the rest rooms at the truck stop. Immediately after pulling on to I-70 they were followed extremely closely by a pickup truck. They slowed significantly, hoping the vehicle would pass them, which it eventually did. But then it slowed in front of them, forcing them to pass it. Such maneuvering continued for two or three miles before the strange vehicle sped up, passed them again, and disappeared into the darkness, but as the vehicle went around them, they heard a "backfire."

Relieved, the Colorado travelers dismissed the pickup driver as someone who had celebrated New Year's Eve too much and was probably intoxicated. Seconds later their fears returned as they saw the pickup truck parked with its lights off on the exit ramp at the Ogallah interchange. The white male driver, the lone occupant, was standing by the pickup, driver's door open, as they passed. And as they passed the menacing vehicle, they heard three more backfires or loud pops, which they then realized were actually gunshots. They hurried east to the next interstate exit in Hays, Kansas, without being followed by the pickup, and reported the incident to the Hays Police Department.

The descriptions of the pickup truck furnished by the four adults in the Colorado car in separate interviews were similar and very precise. The pickup was a late model, perhaps new, GMC, maroon or dark red over white in color. It was equipped with a light-colored or white camper shell, had a Kansas license plate, "west coast" mirrors, three CB radio antennae, and an expensive heavy-duty rear bumper with "Hays, Kansas" imprinted on it.

The Hays Police Department confirmed four bullet holes in the vehicle of Walter Wright of Lakewood, Colorado, probably .22-caliber, and interviewed Mr. Wright, his wife, and their passengers, Robert and Virginia Wright, also from Colorado. They found the travelers' stories credible, corroborated by the four obvious bullet holes in the Colorado vehicle. Since the incident had occurred in Trego County, the Hays authorities promptly furnished the Wrights' statements and their descriptions of the suspect's pickup truck to the Trego County Sheriff's Department in Wakeeney. The truck's description had not been familiar to Hays authorities.

When Trego County Undersheriff Larry Wade, one of the first officers involved in the Lovett-Young case, read the Wrights' statements and saw their description of the suspect's vehicle, his thoughts immediately turned to a local resident who had recently bought a new 1975 GMC pickup truck. Wade knew that pickup to be reddish-brown over white in color and fitted with a white fiberglass camper shell. It also had three CB radio antennae, a heavy-duty rear bumper, and a Kansas license plate. Most important, Wade and a local Wakeeney police officer had been in the Triangle Truck Stop at 1:30 A.M. on January 1, drinking coffee. The local owner of that pickup, so similar in description to the suspect's vehicle, was also present at that time in the truck stop. Maybe, thought Wade, they finally had something on Francis Donald Nemechek. He telephoned KBI Special Agent Leonard Pruter.

In school, Nemechek had been the opposite of his popular, smart, athletic, older brother, his only sibling. A loner, "Donnie" had not been popular. He was often a disciplinary problem, a poor student, and, finally, a dropout. He had held a variety of jobs since then—ranch hand, custom wheat cutter, truck driver, welder. He was a farm worker for Joe Faulkner in December 1974. He had married a local girl and fathered a little boy. The child was approximately the same age as Guy Young. Nemechek had been abusive and cruel to his wife during their brief marriage. He had beaten her often, once breaking an eardrum. He also once held his .22-caliber handgun to her head and threatened to kill her. On another occasion, when she was pregnant with their child, he pushed her down a flight of stairs in their home after an argument about a divorce. During a fight in the winter of 1972, following the birth of their son, Nemechek forcibly undressed his wife and shoved her outside in the bitter cold. She remained there for an hour, nude. A year later, when she complained about how fast he was driving as they returned late at night from a wedding dance, he opened the passenger door of their car and shoved her out. The fall broke her tailbone. And throughout their marriage, as his wife would later admit, he sexually assaulted her frequently. The wife-initiated divorce was final on October 22, 1974, less than two months prior to Nemechek's assault on the Iowa women. The ex-wife was interviewed by Special Agent Pruter on January 6, 1976, the week of the sniping incident. A profile of Nemechek was becoming clear.

At 9:30 A.M. on January 8, 1976, Undersheriff Larry Wade and KBI Special Agents Leonard Pruter and Tom Lyons interviewed Nemechek at the Kansas Highway Commission Building in Wakeeney. He had left Joe Faulkner's employ and now worked for a local welding shop. He agreed to meet them at the neutral site rather than at the sheriff's office, police department, or

his new place of employment. Nemechek denied any knowledge of the sniping incident, as it had come to be known in the area. He stated that he had
finished at the welding shop about 6:30 or 7:00 P.M. on New Year's Eve and
had gone to a local club, where he celebrated with friends and relatives until almost 2:00 A.M. Then he went to the Triangle Truck Stop, bought gas,
and drove to his uncle's residence, next door to his own in Wakeeney. He
remained there visiting with family members until 3:00 A.M., when he went
home to bed. He agreed to another polygraph examination, and again results
were inconclusive. (By this time the lawmen were convinced of his guilt and
were frustrated by Nemechek's apparent ability to fool the polygraph.) He
signed consent search waivers permitting searches of his residence and his
pickup truck for a .22-caliber weapon. None was found. A 12-gauge Rem-
ington Model 11 automatic shotgun, however, was found during the search
of his residence. The officers recalled that Diane Lovette and Cheryl Young
had been killed with a 12-gauge shotgun. Half of Trego County, of course,
owned 12-gauge shotguns.

The officers had not believed Nemechek's alibi for the early morning of
January 1, 1976. Indeed, they believed he had attacked the Wrights, and they
also believed he was responsible for the Lovette-Young homicides a year
earlier. They decided they had a good circumstantial case on the sniping
incident. If they could get Nemechek to jail, he might break. They could
continue to work on his alibi witnesses and continue to pursue the .22-caliber
weapon they believed he possessed. Special Agent Pruter could go to Colorado to show the Wrights photos of Nemechek and his truck. Trego County
Attorney David Harding agreed. On January 12, 1976, an arrest warrant was
issued charging Nemechek with aggravated battery in connection with the
sniping case. At 9:40 a.m.,that day, Undersheriff Wade and Special Agent
Pruter arrested Nemechek at the welding shop. They transported him to the
Trego County jail. He continued to deny any involvement in the Wright case.
He was booked into jail, fingerprinted, and photographed. He was then arraigned before District Court Judge David Rhoades, who ordered him held
in lieu of $20,000 bond, a sizeable bond at that time. His preliminary hearing
was scheduled for January 21. At least the mean-spirited bully would be off
the streets and roads of the area and no longer a threat to travelers, or anyone
else, thought Wade and Pruter.

At 12:30 P.M., three hours after the arrest, Undersheriff Wade telephoned
Special Agent Pruter to advise him that Nemechek's father had pledged his
home for the $20,000 bond. Nemechek had walked out of jail.

Pruter drove to Colorado. The Wrights were unable to positively identify
Nemechek's photograph; however, they said the photographs of his pickup
truck bore a striking, frightening resemblance to that of their assailant.

Nemechek's trial on the sniping matter was originally set for June 7 and later rescheduled for September 8. He was still the main suspect in the Lovette-Young case and that investigation continued as well.

On June 30, 1976, shortly before midnight, the worried parents of Carla Baker, an attractive twenty-year-old junior at the University of Kansas, home in Hays for the summer, reported to the Hays Police Department that their daughter was missing. They explained that Carla had gone for an evening bicycle ride earlier, as was her custom, but had not returned. A search across Hays, concentrating on her usual biking course, by family, friends, and neighbors for more than two hours, had been unproductive. She had not taken her purse, wallet, money, or any other personal items with her. She had departed the family residence on her bicycle at approximately 8:00 P.M. A missing-person's report was broadcast by Hays Police Department.

At 2:45 A.M. on July 1, 1976, Carla's expensive ten-speed Raleigh bicycle was found in a ditch in north Hays, not far from Interstate 70, less than forty miles east of Wakeeney. The location was considered a crime scene and carefully examined, diagrammed, and photographed. The bicycle was removed to the Hays Law Enforcement Center and processed for latent fingerprint impressions. In the following days, the area was searched on foot, in various vehicles, on horseback, and in aircraft. Missing-person posters bearing Carla Baker's photograph were placed at truck stops along Interstate 70 from Limon, Colorado, to Lawrence, Kansas, home of the University of Kansas, and at the Triangle Truck Stop in Wakeeney. No sighting of Carla Baker was ever reported.

On Saturday, August 21, 1976, less than two months after the disappearance of Carla Baker in Hays, sixteen-year-old Paula Fabrizius, a state park rangerette at Cedar Bluff Reservoir in Trego County, was reported missing to Larry Wade, now sheriff of Trego County. She was last seen at her state park gate position at 6:40 P.M. Only fifteen minutes later she was missing from her assigned gate position. Her eyeglasses and her unused spray can of Mace were found lying near her automobile. An extensive search of the state park by scores of searchers found no further evidence of the popular Ellis High School student and cheerleader. One of the volunteer searchers was Francis Donald Nemechek.

At 1:10 A.M. on August 22, Sheriff Wade awakened KBI Special Agent Leonard Pruter with a telephone call to advise him about the missing girl, "just in case," he said. Pruter didn't return to bed. He made coffee and awaited

Sheriff Wade's second call, which both anticipated. At approximately 9:30 A.M., August 22, two teenagers on a motorcycle near Castle Rock, a popular large rock formation in Gove County, Kansas, about twenty-five miles from Cedar Bluff State Park, saw the body of a young nude female lying at the base of a large bluff. The body appeared to have been pushed over the bluff, and the teenagers reported seeing articles of clothing and personal effects strewn around the body down below.

Following Sheriff Wade's second telephone call to Pruter, the sheriff was joined at Castle Rock by Pruter, Duane Bell, Jock Murray, Lanny Grosland, and Steve Couch of the KBI, and Wakeeney Police Chief Ken Roy among others. The crime scene examination and the subsequent autopsy determined that Paula Fabrizius had been strangled and sexually assaulted. Cause of death was a single stab wound to the heart, but there were several other knife wounds as well. Some of them were postmortem and some were sexual in nature.

Among the items of clothing and personal effects strewn around Paula's body had been a warranty card for a recently purchased CB radio found by Ken Roy. Investigation soon determined that Paula Fabrizius had not purchased a CB radio. The warranty card and other crime scene evidence were transported immediately to the KBI Forensic Laboratory in Great Bend.

Meanwhile, witnesses reported having seen Francis Donald Nemechek in his conspicuous pickup truck at two separate Cedar Bluff locations on August 21 prior to Paula's disappearance, and a less certain report indicated he might also have been seen headed toward Castle Rock later that day.

On August 24, two weeks before his sniping trial was scheduled to begin, Nemechek was again visited by special agents from the KBI. Special Agents Leonard Pruter and Tom Lyons went to the welding shop in Wakeeney where Nemechek was employed. They interrupted him in the act of washing his pickup truck, inside and out. A broom and bucket of water were positioned near the truck's rear bumper. Portions of the cab, in particular the seats, the passenger's door, seatbelts, and floor mats, were still wet.

For the third time in his life, Nemechek was advised by a KBI agent of his rights to consult an attorney and to remain silent, and, for the third time, he agreed to talk. The interview started in the welding shop office at 3:00 P.M. Nemechek admitted the purchase of a new CB radio in Hays on August 21, the day of Paula's disappearance. He had installed it in his truck at the Wakeeney welding shop the same day. He wasn't sure where the warranty card was but guessed he might have already mailed it to the manufacturer. He admitted being at Cedar Bluff and being near Castle Rock the same day. He even recalled seeing Paula at her gate that day and visiting briefly with her at that location. About an hour into the interview, Steve Couch, a KBI forensic scientist, arrived and informed his KBI colleagues that he had developed a latent fingerprint impression on the CB radio warranty card. The latent print had been identified as that of Francis Donald Nemechek. The forensic process had also revealed a boot print on the card. The agents noted that the boot sole impression was very similar to the footwear Nemechek was then wearing. Nemechek was placed under arrest for the murder of Paula Fabrizius, and, also, although the words were not spoken, for the murders of Cheryl Young, Guy Young, and Diane Lovette.

The sniping trial was postponed again.

When it was learned that Nemechek had been arrested for the rape and murder of Paula Fabrizius and suspected of the Lovette-Young rapes and killings, feelings were running high in the four rural Kansas counties affected by his brutal rampage. Citizens of Ellis, Graham, Trego, and Gove Counties were ready for justice. The day that Nemechek was transported from the Trego County jail in Wakeeney to the larger, more secure facility in Hays, hanging nooses were seen on the interstate overpasses between the two cities. Nemechek's father told the *Hays Daily News* that the family would not be posting the $250,000 bond for his son. The family believed jail would be the safest place for him. In the same newspaper story, a former classmate of Nemechek was quoted: "If I had to describe Donny Nemechek in one word, that word would be 'evil.'"[3]

The evil one's world was finally collapsing. A fellow inmate in the Ellis County jail later informed the Ellis County attorney that Nemechek was claiming credit not only for the Fabrizius, Lovette, and Young murders, but also for the killing of Carla Baker, whose body could be found at a particular location in Cedar Bluff, near where Paula Fabrizius had been abducted, according to Nemechek's story to his cellmate.

A piece of cloth found by the KBI in Nemechek's otherwise pristine truck was identified as coming from the blouse Carla Baker had made herself and was wearing the day of her disappearance. Blood they found on the truck's carpeting, despite the cleaning by Nemechek, was determined to be human and type A. Fabrizius's blood type was O positive. Unfortunately, Baker's blood had never been typed. Investigators strongly suspected it was type A. Nobody had yet heard of DNA testing.

On September 21, 1976, in a remote, secluded area of the Cedar Bluff State Park, KBI agents, county prosecutors, and local officers, following the cellmate's directions, found human skeletal remains and long hair. They also found pieces of clothing and a wristwatch that the Baker family identified as belonging to Carla. A Hays dentist, through dental examination, confirmed the remains were those of Carla Baker. No cause of death could be determined.

On October 8, in a special consolidation hearing in court in Wakeeney, Nemechek was also formally charged with the three Lovette-Young murders by Graham County authorities and with the murder of Carla Baker by Ellis County authorities. Eventually, on a motion for change of venue by the defense, which claimed no fair trial could be held in the four counties in question, the trial was moved to Salina in Saline County, with District Court Judge Steven Flood presiding.

The trial was held February 14 through February 18, 1977. Defense psychiatrists argued that Nemechek was insane when he murdered the four young women and left little Guy Young to freeze to death. One testified that Nemechek had dressed in women's clothing as a teenager, was confused about his own gender, and became uncontrollably violent whenever rejected by women. Nemechek's insanity defense didn't impress the jury and he was found guilty on all five counts of first-degree murder after only four hours of deliberation.

On March 7, 1977, with the death penalty not available at that time in Kansas, Nemechek was sentenced to five consecutive life sentences. The sniping charge was dismissed. Curiously, on the same day, even though he vowed to appeal the sentencing, Nemechek agreed to a final interview by Sheriff Scott, Sheriff Wade, and Special Agent Pruter. In that interview in the Ellis County jail in Hays, Nemechek admitted four of the murders. He denied much recollection of little Guy William Young, and he denied any recollection of the New Year's Day sniping incident. The assaults on Cheryl Young, Diane Lovette, Carla Baker, and Paula Fabrizius, however, he recalled vividly.

Nemechek recalled he had been drinking beer on December 12, 1974—a lot of beer. He was angry with his former wife and still bitter about the divorce earlier that summer. He positioned himself, late that night, on an overpass on Interstate 70 at the Ogallah interchange, halfway between Wakeeney and Hays. With his .22-caliber rifle he fired a round into the tire of an approaching car. Then he hurried down to the interstate to assist the puzzled occupants of the suddenly disabled automobile. The occupants were two young attractive women from Colorado. He offered to help them with their flat tire. They seemed frightened of him, however, and repeatedly declined his offers of help. He became angry, returned to his vehicle, and retrieved his shotgun. He forced the frightened women into his pickup truck and noticed for the first time that one was carrying something wrapped in a small blanket. He had decided to take the women to the old Faulkner place, an old homestead of his then-employer, and rape both of them.

En route, the woman without the blanket attempted twice to open the passenger door and jump from the moving truck. Angrily, after the second attempt, he stopped and forced her to remove her blouse. He pointed out to her that it was bitterly cold that evening and she had no coat and now no blouse. He recalled that he was pleased she had not been wearing a bra. Upon arrival at the old, abandoned farmhouse, he forced the two women upstairs into the house as he carried a flashlight. He stated that he had learned on arrival there that the blanket concealed a baby. The blanket and baby, he claimed, were left on the seat of his truck with his shotgun.

On the second floor of the house he ordered both women to disrobe. He raped the one whom he had forced to remove her blouse during the trip, because he was angrier at her. After he raped the first woman, however, he was kicked by the second. He then went to his truck, noticed the baby was sleeping, picked up his shotgun, and returned to the house, where he shot both. His exact words were: "I turned my head and shot once at each of the women. I thought I had missed. I went downstairs and got another shell and came back up and shot again." He recalled shooting one twice, because she wasn't dead after the first shot. He didn't recall sexually assaulting the victim he had not raped. He did recall becoming ill and vomiting in the house as he departed. He claimed the little boy was not in the truck when he returned to his vehicle and he could not explain why the blanket in question had been found upstairs near the bodies. He declined further discussion of the child. But he added, "It was just like a dream. I never gave it any more attention."

On the day he abducted Carla Baker in Hays, Nemechek again claimed to have been drinking beer heavily, alone. He drove from Wakeeney to Hays for no reason. In Hays, on a side street, he stopped to urinate, and as he was relieving himself he saw an attractive young woman approaching on a bicycle. He exposed himself to her. She became angry and yelled at him. He became angry, grabbed her by the hair, and pulled her off the bicycle. He dragged her, fighting and screaming, to his truck and forced her into it. He drove her to the vicinity of the Cedar Bluff Reservoir, tore off much of her clothing, and attempted to rape her. She, however, kicked him in the groin and, in a fury, he stabbed her with his large hunting knife. He denied raping or molesting her, but the interviewers were convinced he had sexually assaulted her after death. As he put it, "I did expose myself to her as she rode by. She turned and said, 'You stupid bastard, you think you are funny.' I then reached up and grabbed her and pulled her down. . . . We did not have intercourse although I tried. She tried to kick me again. At that time, I pushed the knife in. I wiped the knife off on her clothes and left."

On August 21, 1976, Nemechek recalled he had been drinking beer most of the day. He had installed a new CB radio in his truck and then went driving in the Cedar Bluff area. He saw the young state park employee at the gate entrance. He visited with her briefly and, suddenly, became strongly attracted to her physically. He acted on his urges and grabbed the frightened girl, forcing her into his truck. He drove first to a storage building on some land owned by his father. The building was locked, however, and since he had no key he drove the girl to the Castle Rock area where he forced her to disrobe. He noted that Paula Fabrizius, like Carla Baker, physically fought him in resisting his sexual advances. He eventually raped her and, because she continued fighting him, he stabbed her to death with the same hunting knife he had used on Carla Baker. He admitted repeatedly stabbing her and cutting her, even after death, because of his anger over her strong physical resistance. As he explained it, "I don't know what it was. I just snapped. I opened the door and grabbed her and then took off." After raping the pretty, young ranger he recalled, "When I went to put on my shirt, she picked up a rock and threw it. I went over and slapped her and choked her. She started cussing, so I got my knife and pushed it into her. I pulled her to the edge and threw her over the side, along with her clothes, and left." He denied emphatically that he had sexually assaulted her postmortem. And he found nothing strange in his volunteering as a searcher for Paula after raping and murdering her.

On April 1, 1978, the Kansas Supreme Court rejected Nemechek's appeal and affirmed his conviction and the five consecutive life sentences. In a period of twenty months he had murdered four attractive young women, ages sixteen, nineteen, twenty, and twenty-one, and had left a barefoot, coatless three-year-old boy to freeze to death.

He was denied parole in 1991, 1994, and 1997. On the third occasion the Kansas Parole Board received a petition signed by 15,016 people, mostly residents of Graham, Trego, Ellis, and Gove Counties in western Kansas, opposing any possible parole.

Every KBI agent and every other law enforcement officer who participated in the Nemechek investigation has since retired. Don Scott was the last. Serving his native Graham County as sheriff since 1973, he retired in 2007. He was the most senior in tenure among all 104 Kansas sheriffs when he stepped down. A good sheriff and highly respected, Don easily won election to the Graham County Commission and, at the time of this writing, he continued to serve his home county as a public servant.

In July 2007, Francis Donald Nemechek, serving five consecutive life sentences for first-degree murder, was again denied parole by the Kansas Parole Board. In June the board had received a petition signed by almost 15,000 western Kansas residents opposing parole for Nemechek. He must wait until 2017 to again apply for parole. By then the Kansas serial killer will have served forty years in prison. He remains confined in the Lansing Correctional Facility, with many of the worst in Kansas.

CHAPTER TEN

Stephanie: "Stephanie's Law"
Born in Tragedy

On June 30, 1993, Stephanie Rene Schmidt was nineteen years old. She was four days short of her twentieth birthday on July 4. She was blonde, five foot two in height, weighed 115 pounds, and had hazel eyes. She was bright and beautiful. She was a student at Pittsburg State University in Pittsburg, Kansas, between her sophomore and junior years. Although it is the largest community in southeast Kansas, Pittsburg was rural compared to her native Johnson County, and Stephanie loved that. She was a good student, had a great work ethic, and was a member of a college sorority. She was the daughter of Gene and Peggy Schmidt of Leawood, Kansas, both alumni of Pittsburg State. She was the older sister of Jennifer, her only sibling, better known as Jeni, by two years. Stephanie was much loved by her parents, her sister, her Leawood neighbors, her college sorority sisters, her friends, coworkers, and classmates from both high school and college—indeed by all who knew her. She was truly the mythical "girl next door."

On June 30, 1993, Donald Ray Gideon was thirty-one years of age. He was five feet seven in height, weighed 150 pounds, had brown hair, brown eyes, and a temper he often could not control. He had an eighth-grade education, was a loner with no close friends, and had spent more than one-third of his life in penal and/or mental health facilities. His arrest record dated to age thirteen and, on November 5, 1992, he had been released on parole from the Kansas prison system, having served almost ten years of a ten- to twenty-year sentence for the 1982 rape and aggravated sodomy of a college coed at Labette County Community College in Parsons, Kansas, his hometown, near Pittsburg, in southeastern Kansas.

Stephanie Rene Schmidt and Donald Ray Gideon had nothing in common except that she worked part-time and he worked full-time at the same Pittsburg restaurant. He was a dishwasher, on state parole. She was a popular waitress, working her way through college. Unfortunately, Stephanie knew little about Gideon's extensive criminal record. She, like most of her fellow waitresses at the restaurant, knew he had been in jail—for fighting, someone had said.

Certainly no one could be expected to know that he had raped again, on April 16, 1993, only five months after his release from prison. That recent victim, a local Pittsburg woman, had elected to not report Gideon's sexual assault on her until later, after June 30, 1993, too late to serve as a warning to Stephanie and other young women in southeast Kansas. She had not promptly reported her rape because she believed Gideon's threats to kill her if she reported his angry assault on her. He was not, he emphasized to her, going back to prison.

Stephanie had originally decided to remain in Pittsburg during the summer of 1993, take a few summer classes, and work in the restaurant. She had promised, however, to return to Leawood on July 2 for a long weekend at home to celebrate her birthday with her family. A nagging sore throat had delayed her summer school participation, however, causing her to miss the first few days of classes. Consequently, she had changed her plans and would spend the rest of the summer at home, when she returned to her suburban Kansas City home on July 2. Accordingly, some of her coworkers and college friends insisted, since she was leaving for the summer, that they would celebrate her birthday early with a final evening together for dinner and drinks. Stephanie agreed, even though she still didn't feel well. The celebration would be on the evening of June 30 at a restaurant in nearby Frontenac, with drinks following at a popular Pittsburg bar.

When by the afternoon of July 2 Stephanie had not arrived at her Leawood home and had not telephoned, and her parents were unable to reach her by phone, they became concerned. Their daughter was not one to keep them in the dark or to not follow through on plans, especially family plans. When he continued to reach only her telephone recorder at her apartment, Gene Schmidt started telephoning friends of Stephanie and of the family in Pittsburg, attempting to learn Stephanie's whereabouts and confirm her welfare. When those attempts failed to locate her, he called the Pittsburg Police Department at 5:30 P.M., on July 2, 1993, to report his daughter missing.

Two Pittsburg police officers, together with Stephanie's boyfriend, Matt, and Dr. Ron Seglie, a family friend, both of whom had already been searching for her, went to Stephanie's apartment. They found two newspapers on her front porch, from that morning and from the day before. They found her car there and, inside the apartment, her purse, with checkbook and credit cards, on the kitchen table. All her personal effects and clothing seemed to be there and nothing appeared out of place.

As the four contacted coworkers and friends, it gradually became apparent that none of them had seen Stephanie since the early morning hours of July 1, when she was seen by several people leaving the Pittsburg bar where her post-dinner birthday celebration had been held.

Two of her girlfriends informed the police that they had picked up Stephanie at her apartment, following return from the Frontenac dinner, and took her to the bar for a nightcap. They recalled that Stephanie had taken from her apartment only her Kansas driver's license, her keys (car and apartment), and an ATM card. At her request, en route to the bar, they stopped at a bank ATM where she withdrew twenty dollars. She was wearing a plaid green and blue top, blue jeans shorts, and tan sandals. Her girlfriends noted too that Stephanie had not been feeling well, but had gamely gone with them for phase two of her scheduled pre-birthday evening, the post-dinner nightcap at the bar. Shortly after midnight, however, she told her companions that she felt so bad she wanted to return to her apartment and go to bed. She declined their offer to drive her home, saying that their coworker Donald Gideon, who was at the bar, had already offered to give her a ride home. Gideon said he was leaving anyway and therefore Stephanie wouldn't have to have her friends leave early. She thanked them for the evening and left. They had assumed she left with Gideon.

The next morning at the restaurant Gideon told other employees that he had not taken Stephanie home the night before. He had made the offer and had walked out of the bar thinking she had accepted, but, he said, when he walked toward his pickup truck, she, without comment, walked in the opposite direction in the parking lot. He had assumed one of her female companions was taking her home after all.

Efforts by the police to contact Gideon for an interview were unsuccessful on July 3 and 4. They left notes on his apartment door requesting a telephone call, and were unable to locate anyone, including his family, who had seen him since he had been observed filling up his pickup truck at 5:00 P.M. on July 2 in Pittsburg. He had claimed to be going fishing, but there was no fishing equipment in his truck at that time, according to witnesses. Gideon's mother and uncle joined in the unsuccessful search for him. They told police they were unaware of any fishing plans, and they were further mystified when Gideon did not attend a long-planned family picnic at an area lake on July 3. Gideon's parole officer had not seen him since June 28, and then Gideon did not report for work on July 3. He was scheduled to contact his parole officer on July 6.

On July 4, five police officers executed a search warrant at Gideon's apartment. Nothing was found indicating Stephanie Schmidt had ever been there, and there were no clues pointing to Gideon's whereabouts. On July 6, it was determined that he had closed his savings account at a Pittsburg bank on July 2, withdrawing $1,002. He had still not reported to work at the restaurant, a condition of his parole. On July 6, his parole was revoked and an arrest warrant was issued for him, charging him with parole violation. On the same day, he and his 1974 Ford pickup truck, faded blue-gray in color, Kansas license plate FQV633, were entered into the FBI's National Crime Information Center (NCIC). Also, on the same day, law enforcement officers in Crawford County initiated a large-scale search for Stephanie Schmidt, Donald Gideon, and Gideon's vehicle around the communities of Frontenac and Pittsburg. An aerial search was added to that effort on July 7, concentrating on parks, rivers, lakes, and the area's many strip pits.

Pittsburg and Crawford County authorities also requested KBI assistance, which KBI Director Robert Davenport quickly authorized. Special Agent in Charge Bill Delaney of the bureau's Overland Park office, the bureau's eastern region supervisor, assumed command of the KBI effort. Carl Carlson, Steve Koch, and Kelly Robbins of the KBI's forensic laboratory would assist, and Delaney eventually assigned Special Agents Bruce Adams, Scott Teeselink, Tom Williams, Delbert Hawel, George Johnson, Scott Ferris, Allen Jones, and Randy Ewy to the investigation. Several, including Delaney himself, were involved from the outset.

On July 5, Donald Gideon had attempted to enter Canada at Blaine, Washington. He was turned back by suspicious Canadian authorities. If he had attempted the entry one day later, NCIC would have reflected his fugitive status and, presumably, he would have been apprehended and his cross-country flight terminated. Instead, he drove to Coos Bay, Oregon, abandoned his vehicle, and boarded a bus.

On July 7, Gideon's mother informed investigators that her son had telephoned the previous evening. She had tearfully told him that he was wanted for questioning regarding "that Stephanie Schmidt girl," that he was on television and in the newspapers, and that law enforcement officers had been contacting her daily regarding his whereabouts. He responded that he had not killed anybody and hung up. She would recall later that she had not said anybody was dead. The phone call had come from a pay phone in Crescent City, California.

Soon, Oregon law enforcement officers were processing Gideon's pickup truck as a crime scene for Kansas authorities. Law enforcement agencies in California, Oregon, Washington, Alaska, and Canada were pressing the search for Gideon at the request of Kansas authorities, emphasizing Crescent City, California, and Coos Bay, Oregon. Gideon's bus took him southeast, however, not deeper into the Pacific Northwest. He arrived in Daytona Beach, Florida, on July 10.

When Kansas U.S. Attorney Jack Williams authorized the filing of an Unlawful Flight to Avoid Confinement arrest warrant by the FBI for Gideon on July 13, the search went national. Until then, local officers had carried the heavy load in the investigation, especially Detectives Ken Orender and Mark Leonard of the Pittsburg Police Department, and Officers Doug Sellars and Mike Swift of the Frontenac Police Department. Now the KBI and FBI were assisting.

More valuable assistance was received when John Walsh agreed to feature Donald Gideon and Stephanie Schmidt on his *America's Most Wanted* television program on Friday evening, July 16. Gene and Peggy Schmidt, still confident Stephanie was alive somewhere, were interviewed on the program and pleaded for their daughter's safe return. But the only person who knew the answer to the question about the well-being of Stephanie Schmidt was watching the television program in Florida.

The next morning, Saturday, July 17, at approximately 6:00 A.M., Donald Ray Gideon telephoned the Volusia County, Florida, sheriff's office and told them he would be waiting at a telephone booth in Ormond Beach, Florida. He explained that he was the man featured the previous evening on *America's Most Wanted* and he wanted to surrender. At 6:19 A.M., Sgt. Jean Absher and Investigator Cliff Williams of the Volusia County sheriff's office appeared at the telephone booth and took Gideon into custody on the Kansas parole violation warrant and the federal unlawful flight warrant. The chase was over. The investigation was not.

The first law enforcement officer to ask questions of Gideon about his knowledge of Stephanie Schmidt was FBI Special Agent Todd Rowley. Shortly after his surrender to Florida officers, the FBI assumed temporary jurisdiction over Gideon on the basis of the federal unlawful flight warrant, pending formal extradition, or waiver thereof, to Kansas. Gideon was interviewed by Agent Rowley in the district office of the Volusia County Sheriff's office in Ormond Beach, Florida. The FBI agent advised Gideon of his *Miranda* rights to remain silent and to be represented by an attorney. Although he declined to sign the waiver form furnished to him by the agent, he acknowledged that he understood his rights and was willing to be interviewed—not an uncommon response.

Gideon readily admitted knowing Stephanie, inasmuch as they worked together at the same restaurant in Pittsburg, Kansas. He denied emphatically having kidnapped her or injured her in any manner. He also denied knowing her whereabouts or physical condition, and he claimed to resent being featured on *America's Most Wanted* the evening before. He complained that, because of the television program, the entire nation was now convinced of his guilt. He insisted he was innocent of any wrongdoing involving Stephanie Schmidt, of whom he said, "I liked Stephanie. She was a sweet girl. I would not hurt her."[1] Special Agent Rowley would later note that, during the interview, Gideon always referred to Stephanie in the past tense.

Gideon did admit violating terms of his parole. He claimed that the only reason he left Kansas without permission and traveled around the country the last several days was the death of a friend in Pittsburg in an automobile accident. When pressed by the agent, Gideon admitted that the accident victim was more an acquaintance than a friend. But still he had felt the need to get away to sort out things about life in general. He said he had driven to Mount Rushmore in South Dakota and then to Idaho, Oregon, Washington, and the Canadian border. He had no explanation for abandoning his truck in Oregon and boarding a bus to Florida. He admitted seeing Stephanie and her friends in the Pittsburg bar early on the morning of July 1. He also admitted offering her a ride home but said that, in the parking lot, she had walked to another vehicle. He presumed she was driven home by one of her girlfriends. He also admitted drinking heavily that night. He was, he said, "really drunk, really lit." Gideon told Rowley that he anticipated waiving extradition to Kansas. He wanted to return to Kansas to get the matter hanging over him settled.

Kansas Attorney General Robert Stephan, a friend of the Schmidts, advised them of the apprehension of Gideon. Their hopes soared. A KBI agent and a Pittsburg detective drove to Florida to bring back the Kansas parole violator, who was still the only suspect in the disappearance of Stephanie Schmidt.

At approximately 9:30 A.M. on July 22, 1993, Special Agent Scott Teeselink of the KBI and Detective Ken Orender of the Pittsburg Police Department appeared at the Volusia County sheriff's office in Daytona Beach, Florida. They provided copies of the Kansas arrest warrants for Gideon to Sgt. Absher of the Volusia County Sheriff's Office, who reiterated to the Kansas officers the circumstances of Gideon's surrender. She turned over to Teeselink and Orender all of Gideon's luggage and personal effects he had in his possession at the time of his surrender and also additional property she had later retrieved from his motel room. Nothing therein, the Florida officer told the Kansas officers, seemed to connect the fugitive to the Kansas girl, insofar as she could determine. Within minutes, jail personnel escorted Gideon to an interview room Sgt. Absher had arranged for the KBI agent and Pittsburg detective.

Gideon again waived his *Miranda* rights and agreed to be interviewed, although again declined to sign the formal waiver of rights. In this interview of slightly less than an hour, Gideon repeated almost verbatim his story to FBI Agent Rowley five days earlier. He admitted violation of his parole by leaving Kansas without permission. But, he reiterated, the only reason he left was to drive and mentally sort out things relating to the death of an acquaintance in an automobile accident. He denied any knowledge of Stephanie Schmidt's whereabouts since he left the Pittsburg bar with her sometime after midnight on July 1. He had offered to drive her home, but apparently she went with somebody else. He had been very intoxicated, but not so intoxicated that he did not know he had not abducted or harmed Stephanie in any manner. Gideon eventually became angry when pressed by the Kansas officers regarding certain parts of his story and the interview was concluded. At 10:30 A.M., the trio began the return trip to Kansas.

During their travel together, the Kansas officers emphasized to Gideon how important it was to the Schmidts to learn the status of their daughter, even if the news was tragic. It was important to them, as parents, to know Stephanie's fate. Similarly, Teeselink pointed out to Gideon, it was important for the latter to communicate with his own mother. Gideon agreed, and that evening, while they stopped for gasoline, Teeselink permitted Gideon to telephone his mother. She was not home and Gideon asked if they could try again the next morning. Absolutely, replied the KBI agent, carefully building rapport with his prisoner.

Shortly before midnight on the first day of travel, they stopped in Paducah, Kentucky. The officers placed Gideon in the McCracken County jail for the night and they stayed in a local motel. Prior to departure the next morning, Gideon was permitted a long telephone conversation with his mother back in Kansas.

They arrived in Topeka, Kansas, late in the day on July 23. Gideon was placed in the Shawnee County jail. The next morning Teeselink visited Gideon, reminded him of his *Miranda* rights, and emphasized again to him that the law enforcement search for Stephanie was going nowhere and they needed help. Gideon looked at the KBI agent and then, after a brief pause, asked, "Well, will you come back tomorrow and see me? I've got to think about it."[2] That was their best news yet.

The hopes, however, were short-lived. On the morning of July 25, after once again waiving his *Miranda* rights, Gideon told Teeselink, "I thought about it. I just can't do it. I thought you were talking about a plea."[3] Disappointed but still determined, Teeselink withdrew and telephoned FBI

Special Agent Mike Napier in the FBI's Kansas City office. Napier, a long-time friend and former FBI colleague of mine, was a highly regarded FBI criminal profiler, investigator, and interrogator. He agreed to join Teeselink the next day at the Shawnee County jail to participate with the KBI agent in yet another interview of Gideon. Gideon had not yet requested an attorney or invoked his right to remain silent. Teeselink wanted to keep trying until Gideon finally did close the "Constitutional" door of opportunity.

On July 26, 1993, a different Donald Ray Gideon was seated in the interview room of the Shawnee County jail with Teeselink and Napier. As always, he waived his *Miranda* rights. But this time he also signed the rights waiver presented to him and he initiated the conversation. As he did so, he appeared to be setting certain conditions prior to making any admission. For starters, he wanted media in the Pittsburg area to publicize a letter he planned to write to explain his conduct in this matter. No problem, agreed Teeselink, the official KBI media liaison and spokesman. He informed Gideon that that could be easily arranged.

Second, Gideon wanted to be placed in the Hutchinson Correctional Facility, not Lansing. He had been confined at "Hutch" before and wanted to return there, where he still had associates and friends, and he definitely wanted to avoid Lansing. Teeselink explained that his eventual penal location would ultimately be up to the department of corrections. The KBI agent, however, promised to make known Gideon's wishes about being placed at Hutchinson.

Third, he wanted Stephanie's parents to have considerable input in his sentencing. No problem there, both agents agreed.

Thereafter, in order, he wanted visits and books from his mother in the Crawford County jail, where he anticipated he would soon be temporarily lodged; the return to him of a necklace and also postcards and photos from his recent travel; the opportunity to tell his mother what he had done before she learned of it from the media; back pay owed to him by his Pittsburg employer; a promise from the agents that they would tell Stephanie's parents that he was very sorry for what he was about to tell the agents, and that Stephanie's last words, when she knew she was going to die, were that she loved them.

Following the officers' agreement with his prerequisites, Gideon provided a written and signed confession, as well as a taped confession, admitting the abduction, rape, sodomy, and murder of the beautiful young college student. He also admitted the recent rape of the other Pittsburg woman, belatedly reported to law enforcement. Gideon explained that his problem was his temper. He described it as rage, especially when combined with hard liquor and/or drugs. With some pride, he pointed out that, while serving his prior rape conviction at Hutchinson, he had written an anger-control booklet for that facility's Sex Offender Treatment Program, of which he was a graduate.

Gideon admitted that he had driven Stephanie Schmidt from the Pittsburg bar at her request. He did not, however, drive her home as she had requested. He intended to drive her to his uncle's cabin in a remote, rural area of nearby Cherokee County, but he quickly realized he didn't have enough gas in his truck for such a trip. He also admitted he fully intended to rape her. He insisted, however, that he had not intended to kill her. When Stephanie realized Gideon was not headed toward her apartment, she protested and asked that he let her out. When she placed her hand on the door handle, he physically grabbed her and speeded up. He drove to rural Cherokee County and pulled well off the road. He assaulted Stephanie, tearing her blouse and forcibly removing her shorts, before raping and sodomizing her in the cab of his pickup.

He again attributed his behavior to uncontrollable rage caused by his sexual urges, temper, and liquor. He then walked the nude, frightened young girl to a nearby field in the dark of that tragic night, where, after telling her several times in answer to her questions that he was not going to kill her, he strangled her. To make sure she was dead, he then tied her bra tightly around her throat. He noted that Stephanie, despite his repeated denials, knew he was going to kill her, as she stood nude in that field with him, because she asked him to tell her parents she loved them.

On July 27, 1993, the day following his confession, Gideon led KBI and FBI agents and local law enforcement officers to the body of Stephanie Schmidt in rural Cherokee County, Kansas. Attorney General Stephan made the sad telephone call to the Schmidts.

On October 6, 1993, Donald Ray Gideon appeared in Cherokee County District Court before Judge David Brewster and entered pleas of guilty to charges of first-degree murder, aggravated kidnapping, aggravated criminal sodomy, and rape, avoiding trial.

On November 18, Judge Brewster, before sentencing, commented:

> The Court finds that the defendant committed this murder in an especially heinous, atrocious or cruel manner. The defendant drove his victim into the country in the dark of night, raped her and sodomized her, forced her from the vehicle, made her stand naked in the dark and . . . humiliated her, terrorized her and finally took her life. It's reasonable to conclude that all this time she knew that she would die. And whether it took five minutes or five hours is irrelevant. In my view it was a heinous and atrocious and cruel offense and nothing else can be said about it.[4]

Judge Brewster then sentenced Gideon to 40 years, 408 months, 154 months, and 154 months, respectively, for each of the four offenses, and ordered the sentences to run consecutively, not concurrently, thereby ensuring that Gideon would remain in prison the rest of his life.

On April 28, 1995, the Kansas Supreme Court affirmed Gideon's sentence. Gideon was ordered confined at Lansing, not Hutchinson.

In 1993, the death penalty was not available to Gideon's primary prosecutor, Assistant Attorney General John Bork. Kansas had not yet restored the ultimate punishment after the U.S. Supreme Court ruled the death sentence constitutional in 1976, reversing its 1972 "unconstitutional" decision. Kansas had executed no one since 1965, when Perry Smith, Richard Hickock, James Latham, and George York were hanged at Lansing.

In 1994, the death penalty (lethal injection) was reinstated by the Kansas legislature, in part because of Gideon. Governor Joan Finney testified against the death penalty, but when the legislation passed she did not veto it and permitted it to become law without her signature.

From the day of their daughter's disappearance, Gene and Peggy Schmidt turned their backs on their successful advertising business and devoted themselves to helping find Stephanie. After Gideon's arrest, the recovery of their daughter's remains, and Stephanie's funeral, they devoted themselves exclusively to another endeavor: speaking out for Stephanie. They sought the answer, for Stephanie, to this question: Why did not someone tell her and her female coworkers and fellow students that in their midst was a convicted sexual predator only recently released from prison after serving less than half of his rape-sodomy sentence?

With the assistance of their other beautiful daughter, Jeni, Peggy and Gene's determination, dedication, eloquence, and passion have contributed much to the Kansas criminal justice system. The Schmidt crusade, whose foundation is officially entitled Speak Out for Stephanie (SOS), has become the worst nightmare of rapists and rapist-murderers, not just in Kansas, but across our nation as well.

With the help of Kansas Attorney General Robert Stephan and, later, Kansas Attorney General Carla Stovall, and key Kansas legislators, the Schmidts lobbied for the passage of Kansas's Stephanie Schmidt Sexual Predator Act, better known as Stephanie's Law, and related legislation. Stephanie's Law was successfully and masterfully defended before the U.S. Supreme Court by Attorney General Stovall in *State of Kansas v. Hendricks* in 1996. The law provides that persons convicted of sex crimes may be held longer than their court-imposed sentences, if psychiatrists find they remain too dangerous for release. Other states quickly copied the Kansas law after the U.S. Supreme Court, in 1997, agreed with Attorney General Stovall's argument that it was constitutional. Other states also adopted the philosophy of the Kansas Sex-Offender Registration Act, which permits the KBI's public release of photographs and addresses, and other background information of convicted sex-offenders, also thanks in part to the efforts of the Schmidts.

Because of their tireless efforts, Peggy and Gene Schmidt count among their close friends people like John Walsh of *America's Most Wanted* and famed FBI profiler John Douglas (the model for the FBI profiler in Thomas Harris's novel *The Silence of the Lambs* and the film based upon it) and his frequent coauthor, Mark Olshaker. John Douglas, a friend of mine and a former FBI colleague, devoted two chapters to Stephanie in the best-seller *Obsession* in 1998. My favorite line in that work on rapists and killers comes near the end of the book: "We shouldn't be more interested in the privacy and reputation of convicted sexual offenders than we are in the safety of our children."[5] That simple statement captures the essence of Speak Out for Stephanie.

On May 24, 1999, a large crowd filled the auditorium at KBI headquarters as we honored Stephanie's memory; celebrated Stephanie's Law; recognized the officers of the twenty law enforcement agencies involved in the investigation, capture, and prosecution of Stephanie's killer; and unveiled the latest display case in a historic line of notable criminal cases involving the KBI and other law enforcement agencies.

The display case had been designed, at my request, by Peggy Schmidt. It remains today the brightest, most colorful, and most artistically appealing of all the KBI display cases. Peggy arranged the official agency patches of all twenty law enforcement agencies in a pyramid that points upward toward Stephanie's photograph. Donald Gideon's wanted poster and photographs of Attorney General Stovall, Gene, Peggy, and Jeni are also included, with a copy of the legislation creating Stephanie's Law.

Present were most of the KBI agents and KBI forensic scientists who had worked on the 1993 investigation. Special guests from Florida were Lt. Jean Absher and Officer Cliff Williams of the Volusia County sheriff's office, to whom Gideon had surrendered the morning after seeing himself on *America's Most Wanted*. Miss Kansas of 1998, Jennifer Vannatta, a close friend of the Schmidt family, was also present, as were administrators and/or officers from all of the twenty law enforcement agencies, such as Pittsburg Police Chief Mike Hall and Sheriff Sandy Horton of Crawford County. U.S. Attorney Jack Williams, who had authorized the unlawful flight arrest warrant for Gideon in 1993, was present, too.

John Walsh sent a letter of apology, lamenting that his schedule did not permit his attendance at the ceremony. I read his letter to the audience:

Dear Gene, Peggy and Jeni:

Although I can't be there with you to dedicate the memorial to Stephanie, with law enforcement and the Kansas Attorney General, I didn't want to miss the opportunity to send my warmest wishes to you and everyone in attendance.

I am so proud of the three of you. You have fought so hard in Stephanie's memory to make sure she did not die in vain. Each of you, along with those who have fought by your sides have proven yet again that one person can make a difference. I know Stephanie is proud of you too.

God bless you.

Sincerely,

John Walsh

Host

America's Most Wanted[6]

My remarks to the audience followed:

Thank you for your very special presence on this very special occasion.

Today we unveil the latest in a historic line of display cases representing criminal investigations involving the KBI and Kansas law enforcement and, in today's case, even law enforcement outside our state.

Today we unveil the beautiful display case featuring the investigative, prosecutive, legislative and judicial achievements which arose from the tragic murder of Stephanie Schmidt in July, 1993.

Perhaps no other case in the annals of the Kansas Bureau of Investigation has had the far-reaching implications of this case.

On July 27, 1993, Jennifer Schmidt, Stephanie's sister, wisely predicted to her father, "You know, dad, something good is going to come from all of this."

Jeni's prophecy was wise beyond Jeni's years. Indeed, the fulfillment of her prophecy is a primary reason for our assembly today.

It is truly remarkable, as Jeni predicted, that so very much good has come from so very much bad.

So, today we recognize not only the efforts of the more than twenty agencies involved in the initial search for Stephanie and then the search, the capture, and the prosecution of her previously convicted killer. We recognize more. We recognize the historic efforts of the Schmidt family and others, such as then-Attorney General Bob Stephan, which resulted in the Kansas Sexual Predator Law, better known to us today as "Stephanie's Law." And we recognize more. We recognize the masterful defense of that legislation by Attorney General Carla Stovall before the U.S. Supreme Court in 1997. That victory by Attorney General Stovall prompted similar legislation in other states across our nation, thereby providing protection for far more than would-be future Kansas victims. An awesome tribute to Stephanie Schmidt.[7]

Then, together, before the assembled media and approximately 200 guests, Attorney General Stovall and the Schmidts unveiled the tribute to Stephanie and to her family's efforts in her behalf.

There was more than just legislative achievement for Gene, Peggy, and Jeni. Former U.S. attorney general Janet Reno presented the 1998 National Crime Victims Service Award to them. Former Kansas attorney general Carla Stovall gave them the 2000 Kansas Crime Victim Advocacy Award, and FBI Director Robert Mueller honored them with the 2002 FBI Community Leadership Award.

In one of the most logical political appointments ever, Attorney General Phill Kline named Gene Schmidt the Kansas State Victims' Rights Coordinator, effective July 1, 2003. Ten years to the day after his own daughter was the victim of a cruel, tragic, senseless crime, and ten years after he and Peggy and Jeni began their efforts on behalf of crime victims, Gene was named to the state post that officially placed him in charge of what he and Peggy had been unofficially doing a long time, speaking out for Kansas victims and their families.

When the media asked for my thoughts on Gene's appointment, I was more than pleased to share them: "People who know Gene Schmidt and have followed Gene Schmidt for a few years know that he literally is typecast for this position. I can't imagine a more appropriate appointment than Gene Schmidt to work on behalf of victims and victims' families. . . . It won't be a job with him, it will be a commitment and dedication."[8] In November 2004, however, impatient with state efforts in support of victims' rights, Gene Schmidt resigned from his state position to return to his own national advocacy and speaking efforts.

Scott Teeselink, a fine interrogator, retired on April 1, 2001, after thirty years with the KBI.

Jeni Schmidt married in November 2003. She and her husband, Jim, reside in Johnson County, Kansas. They have two beautiful little girls, Lyda Rene and Willa.

The U.S. Supreme Court has upheld Stephanie's Law three times. Thanks to Gene, Peggy, and Jeni Schmidt, Stephanie's Law, requiring registration of first offenders and making the registration accessible to the public, preceded the more nationally prominent Megan's Law.

Stephanie Rene Schmidt never reached her twentieth birthday. Gene and Peggy Schmidt continue speaking out for her and for the rest of us.

On April 28, 1995, following the decision of the Kansas Supreme Court in *State of Kansas v. Donald Ray Gideon,* Justice Bob Abbott commented: "If the sentences imposed are affirmed and the defendant earns the maximum good time available to him, he will first be eligible for parole sometime after his 119th birthday." Donald Ray Gideon has not yet reached his 119th birthday and, therefore, is not yet eligible for parole. He remains in the Kansas penal system.

CHAPTER ELEVEN

Carrie: Second Coed's Slaying Leads to Death Row

Less than one year after the Kansas Supreme Court affirmed that Donald Ray Gideon should remain in prison until his 119th birthday for raping, sodomizing, and strangling Stephanie Rene Schmidt, another recent parolee brutally murdered another Pittsburg State University coed.

This time, a paroled killer forcibly entered the apartment of the young college student a block from campus. He beat her, attempted to rape her, tied her to a chair, and stabbed her to death—to avoid returning to prison, he would later say. He had been drinking heavily and was on drugs, he was full of rage, and, he later claimed, he could not control overwhelming sexual urges. He stabbed her seven times, after stomping on her chest as she lay on the floor, attempting to strangle her, and breaking her jaw. He then fled to another state. Never had déjà vu been so cruel. At least not in Pittsburg, Kansas, the close-knit community of 17,500, or on the city's college campus of 6,500 students.

Carrie Arlene Williams was born in Parsons, Kansas, on April 27, 1975. She was raised in the Wesley United Methodist Church and attended Parsons schools. She graduated from Parsons High in 1993 and Labette County Community College in 1995, where she was an honors student, a standout softball player, and a record-setting tennis player. After community college she left Parsons and transferred to nearby Pittsburg State University to complete her degree in home economics and fashion merchandising.

Carrie was five feet four inches tall, weighed barely 100 pounds, and had blonde hair. As a junior at Pittsburg State, she worked part-time at the local J. C. Penney's department store. On March 30, 1996, she was less than a month away from her twenty-first birthday on April 27th. Carrie was engaged to Mike, her high school sweetheart, and, just days before her murder, she had called her minister, Reverend J. C. Kelly, to reserve the Wesley United Methodist Church in Parsons for her wedding on March 22, 1997, during what would have been her senior year in college.

Like Stephanie Rene Schmidt, Carrie Arlene Williams was young, beautiful, loved, respected, and already a success in life. Her longtime tennis coach said of her, "She wasn't very fast. She wasn't very big. She just didn't give up."[1] Indeed, she never did give up in her short life. Not even as she was being murdered.

Gary Wayne Kleypas, like Donald Ray Gideon, was not a success. He too had a violent past and a prison record. Kleypas was born on October 8, 1955, in Missouri. He was six feet one inches tall, weighed over 200 pounds, and had brown hair. When Carrie Williams was less than two years old, on January 23, 1977, Kleypas beat to death a seventy-eight-year-old woman in Galena, Missouri. He lived near her and had worked at odd jobs for her. Technically, he beat her to death. Actually, she suffocated on her own blood after he beat her severely in her home, following an unsuccessful sexual assault. He avoided Missouri's death penalty when a judge found mitigating circumstances. Kleypas had pleaded insanity and had claimed alcohol and drugs were responsible. He was convicted of second-degree murder and sentenced to thirty years in a Missouri prison.

Kleypas was denied parole in August 1984 and was turned down on three subsequent occasions. In October 1992, after serving fifteen years of his thirty-year sentence, he was paroled to Pittsburg, Kansas. He planned to work and enter Pittsburg State University's Nursing School. He wanted to be a nurse and help others, he said. He immediately resumed his frequent use of alcohol and drugs, however, ensuring that his rehabilitation and commitment to others were both short-lived.

In January 1994, less than two years after he was paroled from the Missouri prison, he held his girlfriend hostage and sexually assaulted her in the apartment they shared in Pittsburg, following an argument. The girlfriend informed police that she and Kleypas had been drinking at a Pittsburg bar. She claimed that, on their return to the apartment, Kleypas had lost his temper, put his hands around her throat, threatened her with a knife, and sexually assaulted her. The county attorney was uncertain the girlfriend would make a good witness and declined to prosecute Kleypas on that occasion. He continued to be free on parole and to abuse alcohol and drugs.

On several occasions prior to March 30, 1996, Carrie and/or her roommate, Robyn, had returned home to find their apartment door open. On one such occasion, money and Robyn's camera were discovered missing. The camera contained film with photographs Robyn had taken on a trip with friends to Padre Island, Texas, and it had had sand in its viewfinder since that trip. The girls had also been continually harassed by obscene telephone calls from an unidentified male. The male caller used their names and was very explicit in his sexual threats, especially to Carrie. The girls requested that their apartment door's lock be changed, and the obscene calls stopped after Carrie's mother had a caller identification unit installed on the apartment's telephone.

During the evening of March 29, Carrie and her best friend, Tiffany, watched a video in Carrie's apartment (Robyn was away for the day) before Carrie drove her friend home at about 1:00 A.M. Shortly after 2:00 A.M., Mike, her fiancé, returned an earlier call and they spoke briefly. Because Carrie had promised to go shopping with Tiffany at 8:00 A.M., she told Mike she had to go to bed.

Tiffany arrived at Carrie's apartment punctually at 8:00 A.M. that morning, but no one answered the door. She presumed that Carrie had elected to sleep in and skip the shopping trip. Tiffany went shopping alone and then attempted to call Carrie. She left messages and continued to call because she knew Carrie was scheduled to work at J. C. Penney's at 1:00 P.M., and Carrie never missed work. Tiffany called both Mike and then J. C. Penney's without locating her best friend. Concerned, she went back to Carrie's apartment and knocked on the doors and windows, but again received no response. Now quite frightened for Carrie's welfare, she went to the apartment manager's residence next door to Carrie's apartment. The manager and her son accompanied Tiffany back to the apartment and the manager unlocked the front door. Tiffany led the trio into the apartment, calling out loudly for her friend with every step. She saw Carrie's bedroom door was closed and realized she had never before seen that door closed. She was now very afraid and told the manager so. The latter offered to open the door. Tiffany declined, insisting she should do it. She called out her friend's name a final time and opened the door.

The physical beating her petite friend had endured, and a blanket wrapped around the victim's head, discouraged immediate positive identification. Nonetheless, Tiffany knew at once. Carrie Arlene Williams would not reach her twenty-first birthday. Tiffany's best friend was a lifeless figure on the floor.

Three hours earlier, Gary Wayne Kleypas had gone to two Pittsburg stores and cashed small checks. He then withdrew one hundred dollars from his bank account and, with that small amount of cash and Carrie's engagement ring, removed from her lifeless hand, he headed to Springfield, Missouri, where he had family.

The first Pittsburg officer responding to the apartment manager's telephone call to police was Officer Henry Krantz. He entered from a side door and found Carrie's body on the floor of her bedroom. Her head and upper body were wrapped in a blanket. Blood was on her body and also spattered on at least one wall. She had been stabbed repeatedly and her face and body reflected considerable trauma. Articles of her clothing were tied around one of her legs and also around a chair in the room. The officer confirmed that the body was cool to the touch and that rigor mortis had set in. He secured the premises and retreated carefully from the apartment to report his findings to arriving detectives.

A search warrant was obtained for Carrie's apartment at 113 W. Lindberg, Pittsburg, Kansas. During the ensuing search, closer examination of the body revealed at least six stab wounds to the chest. The autopsy would later confirm seven. Carrie's face and head reflected considerable bruising. She had been severely beaten as well as stabbed. Even so, it was obvious she had not submitted meekly. The apartment showed signs of a fierce struggle and Carrie's hands were badly bruised.

Officers noticed with special interest that one of the names on Carrie's caller ID unit was Gary Kleypas, accompanied by his telephone number. Officer Steve Rosebrough knew that name and he knew that Kleypas lived at 117 W. Lindberg, two buildings from Carrie's apartment. He knew also that Kleypas was a nursing student at Pittsburg State University. More important, he knew Kleypas had, in recent years, been paroled to Pittsburg from a murder conviction in Missouri. The caller ID indicated that Kleypas had telephoned the victim's apartment at 1:48 A.M. that morning. Criminals are presumed innocent, not intelligent. Pittsburg Chief of Police Mike Hall telephoned the KBI as Officer Rosebrough obtained a search warrant for the apartment of the missing Kleypas.

Meanwhile, the Crawford County prosecutor, learning Kleypas was a prime suspect in the murder of Carrie Williams, reconsidered the 1994 rape allegations of Kleypas's then-girlfriend. Though still not impressed with that case's merits, the prosecutor considered it to be a good vehicle in the pursuit and apprehension of Kleypas until all the evidence in the Carrie Williams case could be sorted out. Accordingly, on March 30, 1996, the day Carrie's body was discovered, an arrest warrant was issued for Kleypas charging him with the alleged 1994 rape. Kleypas was entered into the FBI's National Crime Information Center (NCIC), and notices were broadcast across Kansas and Missouri. The crime and Kleypas's wanted status were front-page news in papers across Kansas, Missouri, and Oklahoma.

On March 31, 1996, the Pittsburg Police Department secured 117 W. Lindberg all night, until a search team entered Kleypas's apartment to initiate what would prove to be a four-day search, with secured interruptions each night (the officers were left at the scene each night as the search was halted to safeguard its integrity). The search team consisted of a Pittsburg officer, Tim Anderson; two KBI forensic scientists, Steve Koch and Lisa Villalobos; and KBI Special Agent Bruce Adams. Before the case was over, Special Agent in Charge Bill Delaney and Special Agents Terry Morgan, Dave Schroeder, and Tom Williams were working on it. In addition, Deputy Director Terry Knowles would assign KBI Forensic Scientists Carl Carlson, John Horn, Gretchen Kurtz, Dennis McPhail, and Dwain Worley to the investigation before its completion.

The investigation caught the attention of Kansas Attorney General Carla Stovall. Stovall had received her bachelor's degree from Pittsburg State, prior to her law degree from the University of Kansas, and had been the first female county attorney in Crawford County. She wanted Kleypas in custody quickly. I assured her that this would indeed happen.

The search of Carrie's apartment determined that a window had been broken and the screen removed and thrown in the trash can behind the apartment. Some of the screen, strangely, had also been found in Carrie's bedroom clothes hamper. Blood had been recovered from the inside doorknob of the front door, and a bloody handprint was found on the bedroom wall. Considerable blood was also found on a pillow that was believed to have been used to cover Carrie's face.

Moreover, early on the morning of the murder, a neighbor had found a roll of film on the ground by Kleypas's car. When developed, that film yielded photographs of Carrie's roommate, Robyn, and several of her friends, as well as three photographs taken inside Kleypas's apartment. The photographs had obviously been taken with Robyn's camera.

The search inside Kleypas's apartment found blood on the building's outer door and blood elsewhere inside his apartment. The searchers removed from his apartment a shower curtain, a pair of shoes matching a shoe print outside Carrie's window, considerable drug paraphernalia, and a wooden box with a false bottom containing numerous syringes.

Kleypas did not report for work at the Pittsburg restaurant where he was employed on Saturday, March 30, or on Sunday, March 31. Those absences were violations of his parole conditions. Shortly after his deadly assault on his young neighbor, he had driven a Ford pickup truck, borrowed from a friend, to Springfield, Missouri. He went no further because he had less than two hundred dollars in cash and only Carrie's engagement ring to pawn. Leaving the state of Kansas was another parole violation.

His brother was surprised to see him in Springfield when Kleypas contacted him the evening of March 30. They spent a few hours playing pool in a Springfield tavern. Kleypas told his brother that the scratches, bruises, and abrasions on his face and neck were the results of a bar fight in Pittsburg the night before. The brother was concerned for Kleypas's future when Kleypas added that he had stabbed his assailant during the fight. The brother helped him locate a motel room and told him he would return the following morning to help Kleypas sort out his future.

The next morning, at 6:00 A.M., Kleypas telephoned his brother. He sounded as though he was under the influence of alcohol or drugs, and he told his brother that he was "checking out." An hour later he telephoned his mother and informed her that he had once again "done something stupid," and he didn't want to put his family "through all this again." Meanwhile, his brother was mentally interpreting what Kleypas had meant by "checking out,"[2] and the brother became more concerned for his welfare. He drove immediately to the motel and found a bleeding Kleypas on the motel room floor, suffering from what appeared to be self-inflicted cuts on his wrists, ankles, and neck. The brother telephoned 911 and reported an apparent suicide attempt, as Kleypas admitted to his brother he had not been honest about the Pittsburg bar fight story.

Springfield police quickly arrived to find Kleypas struggling with his brother, who was trying to prevent Kleypas's continued attempts to commit suicide with razor blades. Kleypas then fought with the officers, threatening them with the razor blades and then begging them to do what he didn't have the heart to do: kill himself. He was soon subdued and transported to a hospital for treatment of his superficial self-inflicted wounds. Toxicology would show that he had consumed considerable amounts of cocaine.

On April 1, 1996, the Springfield, Missouri, Police Department telephoned KBI Special Agent Tom Williams and advised him that they had the Kansas fugitive Gary Wayne Kleypas in custody. Williams and Detective Stuart Hite of the Crawford County Sheriff's Office in Pittsburg then headed to Springfield. Williams had already been planning a drive there because, shortly before the police called, he had learned from Kleypas's mother in Iola, Kansas, that her fugitive son had telephoned her from Springfield an hour earlier that morning. He sounded drunk and/or impaired in some manner and had apologized for again embarrassing the family. He had repeatedly vowed that he was not going back to prison. She was worried about his state of mind and whatever he had done or was doing.

Williams and Hite visited Kleypas in the Springfield hospital. His only statement as he held up bandaged arms for them to see was that he wished "this had worked."[3] He declined to waive his rights or to be interviewed but did not request an attorney. His wounds were determined not to be life-threatening and he was moved to the county jail, pending extradition to Kansas.

In the motel room, officers found a bloody note, "Check brain. Full autopsy please."[4] Also recovered were cocaine, syringes, and a camera with sand in the viewfinder.

Williams and Hite, persistent in their efforts, followed Kleypas to the Springfield jail from the hospital. This time, as he waived extradition to Kansas, he acknowledged his rights and said he would discuss matters with them in the car on their way back to Kansas. During the trip back to Kansas, he admitted the sexual assault and murder of Carrie Arlene Williams the night of March 29–30. He also admitted to numerous obscene phone calls to Carrie and her roommate over several months in the recent past and one call the night of the murder in which he did not speak. He promised to provide more specific details in a formal interview in Kansas.

On April 2, 1996, at the Crawford County Sheriff's Office, Kleypas waived his *Miranda* rights again and confessed more fully to Williams and Hite. Kleypas admitted to a 1:48 A.M. telephone call to Carrie on March 30. He went to her apartment shortly thereafter. He rang her doorbell, stepped back out of sight, and heard her call out "Mike" in a questioning tone as she opened the door. Seeing no one, she closed the door. Kleypas again rang the doorbell and again Carrie called out "Mike" as she opened the door. Now confronted by Kleypas, she attempted to close the door, but Kleypas slammed the door into her face, knocking her back as he entered and temporarily stunning her. He added that, minutes before, he had unsuccessfully attempted to enter the apartment through a window. He had removed portions of the screen and tossed them into a trash can in back of the residence. As he started breaking the window he decided the front-door entry would be easier and quieter.

Once inside he pushed his victim into the bedroom with his knife and forced her to undress. He sexually assaulted her before beating her, tying her to a chair with items of her clothing, attempting to strangle her, and then stabbing her "more than once." He removed her engagement ring and sixty or seventy dollars from Carrie's purse. He admitted that his facial scratches, bite marks, bruises, and abrasions were from Carrie, who even while bound to the chair continued to fight with him while he strangled and stabbed her. He also acknowledged that his victim had admitted to him, before he killed her, that she recognized him as "the man who lived in the green house down the street." He estimated that Carrie's ordeal had lasted ninety minutes, and he admitted previous break-ins of Carrie's apartment and thefts of money and a camera. He claimed not to recall what he did with Carrie's engagement ring. After noting that he then went home and showered, he was asked if there was anything in conclusion he wanted to add. He replied, "I'm guilty," and he asked for forgiveness. Neither officer responded.[5]

Later, during the evening of April 2, KBI Special Agent Bruce Adams obtained a search warrant for the person of Gary Wayne Kleypas, authorizing the search and seizure of Kleypas's body to obtain blood, hair, urine, saliva, fingerprints, and fingernail scrapings; casts, molds, photos, and dental X-rays; complete body measurements; examination casts and molds of bite marks on his body; photographs of his body; and a complete medical examination. Pittsburg Police Officer Tim Anderson, pathologist Dr. Erik Mitchell, and forensic odontologist Dr. Daniel Winter assisted Special Agent Adams in the execution of that search warrant in the county jail at about 11:30 P.M. Prior to the warrant's execution, Kleypas asked Adams if he could first consult with an attorney. When Adams denied the request and explained that the warrant was, in effect, a command of the court and not a request, Kleypas reluctantly agreed to cooperate. The body search revealed, among other things, that Kleypas had shaved his pubic area and scrotum to prevent the collection of such DNA evidence prior to his attack on Carrie. That act was, of course, an indication of premeditation.

The next morning, April 3, as Adams prepared to fingerprint Kleypas, the confessed killer remarked, "I don't know why you guys are going through all this trouble. I'm going to plead guilty and spend the rest of my life in prison."[6] He would change his mind later regarding the self-proposed plea of guilty, when he learned he would be facing Kansas's reinstated death penalty.

Carrie's funeral was held at Wesley United Methodist Church in Parsons, where she and her family had worshipped all her young life and where her wedding had already been scheduled. She was buried in Springhill Cemetery, just south of her hometown.

The next day, April 5, 1996, when Kleypas was arraigned in Crawford County District Court on charges of first-degree murder, rape, criminal sodomy, aggravated robbery, aggravated burglary, burglary, and theft, deputy sheriffs had to protect the defendant from the victim's distraught father and fiancé. Both attempted to grab him as he was escorted by officers into the courtroom. Despite his earlier confession, Kleypas entered pleas of not guilty to all charges. On July 3, 1996, the charges against Kleypas were amended to include capital murder. He would be the first person to face the death penalty in Kansas since 1972.

On October 11, 1996, Crawford County District Judge Don Noland, at Pittsburg, ruled that Kleypas's earlier confession, though strongly contested by the defense, was admissible. On January 3, 1997, Judge Noland ruled that the prosecution could not mention Kleypas's previous murder conviction in trial. Six days later, he granted a change of venue for the trial as requested by the defense, due to concerns with adverse pretrial publicity against Kleypas in Pittsburg. The trial would be held in Wyandotte County District Court in Kansas City, Kansas. Carrie's parents were disappointed with the ruling, which placed the trial for their daughter's killer 150 miles from their home.

The trial began July 8, 1997, in Kansas City. The defense argued that Kleypas had experienced blackouts the evening before and the morning of the murder (apparently not while he was shaving his pubic area) and that he suffered from a progressive, uncontrollable sexual disorder that had started with window peeping when he was sixteen, triggered by drugs, stress and/or alcohol and that resulted in uncontrollable rages. Moreover, his brain, according to defense medical experts, had been damaged by chronic cocaine and methamphetamine use. Other problems, rendering him not responsible, according to the defense, were severe alcoholism, paranoia, voices in his head, and an abusive father. One defense psychiatrist testified, however, that Kleypas did feel "severe remorse" and was obsessed with the question, "Why do I do these brutal things?" In addition, it was noted that the defendant routinely wept during his psychiatric interviews.

The defense attorneys also argued that the KBI agent and deputy sheriff had duped Kleypas into confessing through clever "confabulation," wherein Kleypas, because of his blackouts, had to rely on the officers' version of the events inasmuch as he allegedly had no personal recollection himself of what had transpired. In short, they offered every possible defense except for "he didn't do it."

Assistant Attorney General John Bork, the lead prosecutor in the Gideon prosecution, once again served as lead prosecutor, teamed with Crawford County Attorney Barry Disney. They countered defense arguments by emphasizing the cruelty and brutality of the crimes against Carrie Williams, and they had their own array of expert witnesses, primarily from the KBI.

KBI Forensic Scientist Lisa Villalobos testified that she was able to identify blood on the front doorknob of the victim's home, on Carrie's mattress, on the blanket wrapped around Carrie's head, on the pillow used on Carrie's face, and on the sock that had bound the victim to a chair as Kleypas's blood. All this was possible due to Carrie's aggressive physical resistance, and the infliction of blood-letting wounds on her assailant. She also identified saliva on Carrie's body as belonging to Kleypas. DNA was a key determinant.

Special Agent Adams testified about Kleypas's statement to him following the arrest, when the defendant predicted he would just plead guilty and spend the rest of his life in prison.

The prosecution also introduced into evidence a large, color crime-scene photograph of the battered and bloodied face of the victim. The prosecutor told the jury, "Look, it's battered almost beyond recognition. Look at those pictures. Do you see any mercy at all?" Wyandotte County jurors wept openly.

Equally effective was the videotaped confession of Kleypas taken during his interrogation by Williams and Hite. The jury saw and heard Kleypas calmly and without emotion comment about his dilemma following his sexual assault on Carrie: "I was not sure what to do. I was scared. She knew who I was. She made a comment about knowing me and that I lived two houses down." So, he said, after attempting to strangle her, and after he beat her and stomped her and stuck a sock in her mouth, "I cut and stabbed her repeatedly. I cut myself."

In the courtroom in Kansas City in order to give moral support to Carrie Williams's parents and family were Gene and Peggy Schmidt, parents of Stephanie, murdered by Donald Gideon. "We kind of felt like we should be here," Peggy replied to a reporter's question. And, when asked if she thought the capital punishment facing Kleypas was cruel and unusual, she responded, "No, cruel and unusual punishment is what Stephanie Schmidt and Carrie Williams got." When asked by another reporter what he thought the toughest part of such a trial was for a parent, Gene Schmidt stated, "The hardest part is seeing your loved one treated as evidence."[7]

On July 25, 1997, following two days of deliberation, the jury returned with a verdict of guilty of capital murder. In addition, they found Kleypas guilty of attempted rape and aggravated burglary. Strangely, the jury of six men and six women acquitted Kleypas of aggravated criminal sodomy, aggravated robbery, burglary, and theft.

Prosecutors Bork and Disney were jointly named Kansas Prosecutors of the Year for 1997. Bork died of cancer on September 25, 2006. No prosecutor was ever more popular with KBI agents and forensic scientists.

The death sentence imposed by the jury was upheld by Judge Noland on March 11, 1998. The judge described the crime in graphic detail and agreed with the jury that the evidence supported the death sentence.

Kleypas then launched appeal after appeal, creating an appellate nightmare. The issue was whether Kleypas, confined at the El Dorado Correctional Facility as inmate number 0066129A, would spend the rest of his life in his one-man cell there or be moved to Lansing to receive the lethal injection he had earned.

On December 28, 2001, the Kansas Supreme Court, after considering legal briefs totaling more than 3,000 pages, arguing ninety-five issues and sub-issues, and reviewing 232 defense motions and the corresponding prosecutorial responses, issued a 338-page decision. The court ruled in favor of the prosecution on all but two issues. Kleypas's conviction for capital murder was affirmed; however, the death sentence was vacated and he was remanded for resentencing. The court upheld the Kansas capital murder statute as constitutional, but ruled it had been applied unconstitutionally in the Kleypas case. The basic issue was that a majority of the court construed the Kansas death penalty statute to require that aggravating circumstances must outweigh mitigating circumstances before the death sentence could be imposed. In the Kleypas case it was found that there was an equal balance of aggravating and mitigating circumstances, which meant only a life sentence could be imposed. Chief Justice Kay McFarland and Justices Robert Davis and Bob Abbott dissented. The matter was sent back to the trial court to decide the sentencing issue of death or life sentence.

When he murdered Carrie Williams, Kleypas was only two months away from finishing his nursing degree. Because of him, a new law went into effect on July 1, 1997, providing that no one convicted of "crimes against people" could be licensed as a nurse in Kansas. Some refer to it as Carrie's Law.[8]

Steve Rosebrough, the young police officer who obtained the crime scene search warrant on March 30, 1996, is now a KBI special agent assigned to Pittsburg. Tom Williams retired from the KBI in 2003 and was elected sheriff of Allen County, Kansas. Carla Stovall, after serving two terms as Kansas attorney general, retired from public life and politics and married. Pittsburg Police Chief Mike Hall retired and resides in Maryland with his lovely wife, Cate. Bruce Adams, another fine KBI agent, retired in 2007.

To further tighten the legal entanglements of *State v. Kleypas*, the Kansas Supreme Court on December 17, 2004, in *State v. Marsh* found the Kansas death penalty statute unconstitutional on its face. The court ruled that aggravating circumstances must outweigh mitigating circumstances in order for a Kansas jury to impose the death sentence, consistent with its death penalty ruling in the Kleypas case. Chief Justice McFarland and Justice Davis again dissented, joined by recent bench arrival Justice Lawton Nuss.

Attorney General Phill Kline appealed the *Marsh* ruling to the U.S. Supreme Court. The Kansas legislature was poised to rewrite the death penalty law if the state lost in the U.S. Supreme Court or if the U.S. Supreme Court declined to hear the appeal, which most thought likely. If it fell upon the

Kansas legislature to rewrite the statute, it could not be applied retroactively to Kleypas. He would simply spend the rest of his life in the Kansas penal system, like Donald Ray Gideon, preferably in Lansing.

Attorney General Kline immediately filed a motion to stay the Kansas Supreme Court's *Marsh* ruling. On December 20, 2004, the Kansas Supreme Court granted that stay.

On May 31, 2005, the U.S. Supreme Court surprised many by granting Attorney General Kline's request for certiorari, or writ of review. On July 21, the Court scheduled arguments in *State v. Marsh* for December 7, 2005. Fifteen states with similar death penalty statutes and equal concern filed friend-of-the-court briefs in support of Kansas. The appeal was argued by Attorney General Kline. Following the recent retirement of Justice Sandra Day O'Connor, that argument ended in a 4–4 deadlock. The legal status of Gary Wayne Kleypas and Michael Marsh, convicted of brutally murdering a twenty-one-year-old mother and burning alive her nineteen-month-old daughter, as well as that of six other men on Kansas's death row, remained in doubt.

Following the appointment of Justice Samuel Alito to fill the O'Connor vacancy, a second hearing of *Marsh* and the constitutionality of the Kansas death penalty statute was scheduled for April 25, 2006. Again, Attorney General Kline appeared extremely effective in his arguments before the Supreme Court in defense of the Kansas statute. His efforts were rewarded on June 26, 2006, when, in a 5–4 decision, the U.S. Supreme Court reversed the *State v. Marsh* decision by the Kansas Supreme Court and upheld the Kansas death penalty statute as constitutional on its face.

With all the legal entanglements regarding the Kansas death penalty statute resolved, Kleypas's resentencing trial was scheduled for September 2008, again in Wyandotte County District Court. Crawford County District Judge Donald Noland presided again, with a Wyandotte County jury. On September 15, 2008, following a week of testimony, the jury again returned the death sentence for Kleypas, rejecting the defense plea for a life sentence and the defense excuse of mental illness. On December 3, 2008, pursuant to the jury's recommendation, Judge Noland reimposed the death sentence for Kleypas, which had been set aside in 2001.

Carrie's killer now resides with other residents of Kansas's death row at the state's correctional facility near El Dorado.

CHAPTER TWELVE

Shannon: The KBI Goes to Costa Rica

The telephone at the residence of Brad and Jeanette Stauffer in Topeka, Kansas, rang at 6:30 A.M. on Mother's Day, May 13, 2001. Jeanette answered. The caller asked, "Are you Jeanette Stauffer?" "Yes," she replied. The caller continued, "Are you the mother of Shannon Lucile Martin?" Now with heart sinking, Jeanette Stauffer responded fearfully, "Yes." The male caller then spoke the words that would change forever the lives of the Stauffer family. "I have very bad news. Your daughter has been murdered."[1]

Shannon Lucile Martin was an honors student at the University of Kansas in Lawrence. A member of the Phi Beta Kappa National Honor Society, she was scheduled to graduate with high academic honors at KU in seven days with her younger sister Sheri. Her bachelor's degree would be in biodiversity, ecology, and evolutionary biology. Botany was her special interest and, following graduation, she was to begin a plant ecology research internship at the University of Minnesota, en route to a graduate degree in physiological plant ecology. Her honors thesis was entitled "Investigation of the Potential for Crassulacean Acid Metabolism in a Family of Epiphytic Ferns, the Vittariaceae." She was a serious student with a bright future.

Shannon, winner of numerous science awards and various scholarships at KU, was as attractive as she was intelligent. A member of the KU Student Senate, the former gymnast was at age twenty-three still a petite five foot four and 102 pounds. Shannon loved her family, the University of Kansas, biology and botany, her friends and classmates, and Brutus, her family's twelve-year-old German shepherd. In addition to ferns, she liked to study flowers, tropical forests, squirrel monkeys, coral reefs, and mangrove swamps. She was fluent in Spanish. Another of her loves was Costa Rica, the nation considered by many to be among the most progressive in Latin America.

Seemingly destined for a brilliant career as a biologist, botanist, or research scientist, the young KU coed had her life and promising career brutally, prematurely, and suddenly ended when she was attacked by three assailants and stabbed fifteen times. Evidence would reveal that Shannon fought bitterly, but, in the end, was overwhelmed by the number of her attackers and at least one knife. It would be months, however, before those facts were known.

The bearer of the sad news who called Jeanette Stauffer on Mother's Day, 2001, about her daughter's murder was Mark Culliane of the U.S. Embassy in San José, Costa Rica. Shannon Martin had been murdered in Golfito, Costa Rica, not in Kansas. She had been a KU Study Abroad Student in spring and summer 2000 in Costa Rica. She was back in Golfito in 2001, where she had studied in 2000, to obtain additional ferns for her honors' program research thesis. She would be there only one week, according to plans, and would then return to Lawrence for her May 20 graduation, joined by many of her family and friends. Now, however, the long-awaited, well-deserved university graduation would be replaced with an unexpected funeral.

Costa Rica is slightly smaller than West Virginia. Golfito is a small Costa Rican port city of 14,000 on the Pacific side of the country, adjacent to Panama. The community is 105 miles south of San José, the nation's capital. Thanks to America's United Fruit Company and the banana, the area had enjoyed relative prosperity from 1935 until 1985. Its economy had suffered, however, in recent years. Some journalists, covering the story of Shannon's murder and its investigation, often referred to the town as impoverished or economically depressed. Unemployment was high. Crime was increasing. Drugs were a growing problem, as were robbery, theft, and assault.

Because of the shock and accompanying confusion, it would require several more telephone conversations between Culliane and the Stauffers to clarify the circumstances of the crime. Shannon's brutalized body was found during the early morning hours of May 13, 2001, along an abandoned airstrip access road. The scene was less than a city block, thirty yards at most, from her host family's home where she was spending the week, and with whom she had lived the previous year. They had become close family friends of the Stauffers. Jeanette and Sheri had visited the Costa Rican family and Shannon during the summer of 2000.

The murder scene was approximately 200 yards from a club where Shannon had gone dancing with friends and other U.S. college students the night of her attack, intending to resume her collection of ferns in the morning. The club's unisex restroom was out of order and, when the need arose, Shannon told companions she was going to her nearby host family's home to use the restroom rather than use Mother Nature's facilities as did other club patrons. She vowed to return promptly. She did not.

To compound the Stauffers' anguish, they faced tremendous bureaucratic hurdles at every turn. The day following the murder they were instructed to wire $5,200 in cash through Western Union to Costa Rica to ensure that Shannon's body could be prepared for burial and transportation to the United States in time for the scheduled funeral in Topeka, Kansas. That telephone procedure alone required four heart-rending hours.

In simply seeking information regarding the homicide investigation there were expenses, confusion, and more painful frustration, thanks to the great distance and the differences in language and culture. There were daily telephone calls to the U.S. Embassy in San José; to the Costa Rican Embassy in Washington, D.C., to U.S. congressmen; to the U.S. State Department; and to every other American and Costa Rican agency the persistent, frustrated Jeanette Stauffer could think of or that had been suggested to her. She sought help from KU officials, the FBI, and the Organization of Judicial Investigation (OIJ), Costa Rica's FBI.

There were countless calls to Shannon's Costa Rican host family, O'dette and Marciel Porras, who had reciprocated the love Shannon felt for them. It fell to Mr. and Mrs. Porras, whom Shannon affectionately called "mama and papa," to identify her battered body and to select, for the family, the casket in which Shannon would return to Kansas.

In the beginning of the ordeal Jeanette had been frustrated by the paucity of information she was able to obtain about the circumstances of Shannon's death and the steps being taken to solve the crime and ensure some degree of justice. Within three weeks her frustration had turned to anger and despair. She was receiving no comfort whatsoever from the information she was able to collect about the initial phase of the homicide investigation in Golfito. A quick trip to Costa Rica had done nothing to restore her confidence in the quality of the investigative efforts being taken to identify Shannon's killer, or killers. The solution of Shannon's homicide had been in doubt from the outset. Nobody was in custody and there were no suspects.

Jeanette Stauffer first shared her concerns with me in my office in late May 2001. Special Agent in Charge Larry Thomas, head of our KBI Cold Case Squad and an exceptional homicide investigator in his own right, had requested the meeting. The Thomas and Stauffer families were acquainted, having shared the same Topeka school district for their children. Jeanette had called Larry Thomas with general questions about homicide investigation, and I quickly agreed to the meeting he suggested. Her exceptional determination, intelligence, and persistence were evident. She holds a law degree and has the communications skills and common sense to succeed in anything she chooses. When I first met her, she was determined to solve her daughter's murder. It was clear that afternoon in May 2001 that even with no suspects in the case or any real reason for optimism, she would never rest until the crime was solved.

I suggested that, if her opinion of the investigation's progress didn't improve soon, I would be willing to send Larry Thomas to Golfito on a brief fact-finding mission to establish liaison with the investigators themselves, or, at least, with the appropriate law enforcement officials in Costa Rica, to acquire a more accurate picture of what was or was not being done. We would never have taken such a step to interfere with the law enforcement or government of any country. It simply seemed appropriate to me to consider such a measure to assist Kansas citizens. If a Costa Rican citizen were murdered anywhere in Kansas, I would have immediately assured the victim's family and the Costa Rican government that any Costa Rican law enforcement officer would be welcomed by the KBI and afforded every professional courtesy in our homicide investigation. I would have assigned a KBI agent to host the law enforcement visitor during his or her stay. Law enforcement is law enforcement. Justice is our common objective. There's no other way to approach the problem than through such cooperation, no matter the differences in culture, language, and geography.

Larry Thomas was anxious to go. I considered it a logical KBI assignment and was willing to pay his salary and permit him the time to carry it out. I knew Kansas Attorney General Carla Stovall and Kansas Governor Bill Graves would support such an action, and I hoped, given our tough KBI budget situation, that between the governor and the attorney general they could perhaps even find the money for the flight and per diem expenses, if I couldn't myself. As I believed she would, Stovall, always a fierce and persuasive advocate for Kansas crime victims, liked my idea almost as much as Jeanette did when I shared it with her in late May 2001. The attorney general shared my confidence in Larry Thomas.

But soon, the reports from Costa Rica seemed to improve. Jeanette was receiving assurances from all levels of authority in both Washington and Costa Rica that the case was finally receiving the attention it deserved and required. The need for direct KBI involvement seemed to be disappearing. So be it. With sixteen of my eighty-one special agent positions then vacant for budgetary reasons, I was happy to not have to send one of my best to Central America indefinitely. We could track Costa Rican developments by merely following the stories in the Kansas media. Jeanette had learned early that the media could be a powerful ally in such a situation. She used the Kansas media and the media was pleased to assist by reporting developments or the lack thereof. They recognized a story when they saw it and the brutal unsolved murder of a bright, beautiful KU coed thousands of miles from Kansas was a powerful story, which the entire state followed with tremendous interest.

One of Jeanette Stauffer's most reliable sources for news from Costa Rica about the homicide investigation became Tim Rogers of the *Tico Times,* a respected English language newspaper in San José, Costa Rica. Rogers eventually became a friend, not merely a source.

In June 2001, Jeanette, thanks to her own tireless efforts, was receiving assurances that the investigation was proceeding well. She had learned that there had been a torn shirt found near Shannon's body and hair recovered from Shannon's hand. There were conflicting reports, too, of a knife found at the scene.

On Thursday, June 14, Jeanette spent two hours on the telephone with Director Lineth Saborio of the OIJ and U.S. Embassy officials in San José. On a first-name basis with the director of Costa Rica's FBI by then, she told the *Kansas City Star,* "Lineth was very responsive, was very respectful and I believe they're interested in trying to find an end to this."[2] She reported also that she had relayed FBI and KBI offers of help to the Costa Rican officials. There had been no immediate acceptance of the offers of investigative and/or forensic assistance, but things seemed to be progressing. Jeanette was cautiously optimistic.

Jeanette told the *Topeka Capital-Journal* on June 14, "I believe the OIJ is doing everything they can to solve Shannon's murder."[3] There did seem to be some concern by the Costa Rican officials, however, about the possible expense of DNA testing of the evidence. That, I confess, concerned me as well. As the *Topeka Capital-Journal* reported on June 15, 2001:

KBI director Larry Welch said Thursday he was stunned to hear that finances might impede a homicide investigation. "I couldn't believe there should be a problem like that," Welch said. "It seems to me if that's all it took, I ought to send a KBI agent down there. We've got one of the finest forensic labs in the country, for gosh sakes." Welch said the KBI had contacted the FBI in Washington, D.C., and he will remain in touch with Stauffer until the investigation reaches a satisfactory end. Kansas Attorney General Carla Stovall has offered her support to jump-start the investigation, and Welch said he thought Governor Bill Graves also would back the effort. "We're not in the business of interfering with another country," Welch said, "but I guarantee you the KBI will step in if nobody else is prepared to."[4]

Jeanette's joy was short-lived. The day following her lengthy telephone conversation she was notified that Costa Rica would not pursue DNA testing of evidence in Shannon's case because of the expense. Angry does not adequately describe the distraught mother's response to the puzzling, frustrating news. As the *Lawrence Journal-World* reported on June 16, 2001, "I'm livid," Jeanette Stauffer said. "Here we've got someone who was brutally murdered and nothing is being done, all over a small amount of money."[5]

In addition to the bad news about the prospects for DNA testing, Jeanette also learned that five suspects had been arrested and released in the weeks since the slaying for lack of evidence. Yet the shirt, knife, and clutched strands of hair in Shannon's hand remained untested.

Then, within a week, Jeanette was notified that Costa Rican officials had relented. The evidence would be sent to the FBI forensic laboratory in Washington, D.C., for examination. To preserve the chain of custody, a Costa Rican diplomat would carry the evidence in a diplomatic pouch to the United States. There had been disagreement, apparently, between OIJ and the Supreme Judicial Council of Costa Rica over the handling of the evidence and who would pay to have it transmitted. At any rate, it appeared the evidence would finally be Washington-bound, according to the U.S. Embassy.

A week later Jeanette telephoned to see what, if anything, Costa Rican officials had heard from the FBI about the examination of evidence. She was told the evidence was still in Golfito. It had not been sent anywhere.

Now stripped of the last of her patience, Jeanette lashed out at everybody. As the *Topeka Capital-Journal* reported on June 27:

Stauffer said she no longer felt she could trust promises of Costa Rican investigators or FBI officials. She said she would like the Kansas Bureau of Investigation to send its scientists to Costa Rica to test the samples. KBI Director Larry Welch has said he would be glad to assist with the investigation if U.S. and Costa Rican officials ask. Stauffer also said she wanted KU to consider suspending its study abroad program in Costa Rica until an investigation into Martin's death had been sufficiently completed. Stauffer said she believes it is time for schools who are sending students abroad to send a message to Costa Rica by suspending programs until her daughter's homicide has been solved. "She loved Costa Rica," Stauffer said. "She loved the people and the climate and the environment, and they don't even care enough to solve her brutal murder."[6]

On June 28, 2001, Jeanette sadly reminisced with some reporters about recent events. Shannon had flown to Costa Rica on May 10. Jeanette had last spoken with her by telephone on May 11. The happy daughter, calling from Costa Rica, had been ebullient: "My mama and papa are spoiling me again! I love seeing all my Costa Rican friends. They are so nice to me." Two days later, May 13, Shannon was murdered. On May 16, Jeanette had been told the evidence was being appropriately examined. On June 28, the evidence was still in Golfito, with, apparently, nothing having been done forensically.

Then, once again, the news improved. On June 30, 2001, the evidence was finally delivered to the FBI. No one was in custody yet and there were still no solid leads or suspects, but Shannon's family was cautiously optimistic again. Jeanette was seeing progress—glacial in speed and sporadic at best—but progress nonetheless. The evidence was finally being examined. Meanwhile, University of Kansas officials had promised her a review of the study abroad program in Costa Rica to ensure the safety and security of future KU student-researchers.

On July 6, however, Jeanette's hopes suffered yet another reversal. Most of the hair evidence had been determined to be from Shannon herself and the remaining few strands, when compared to five suspects earlier arrested and released, did not match any of them.

Then, the emotional roller coaster ride that characterized the homicide investigation for Jeanette Stauffer hit another high when she was invited to appear in Washington on Friday, July 13, 2001, to meet not only with Ambassador Jaime Daremblum but also with the president of Costa Rica, Miguel Ángel Rodríguez Echeverría. President Rodríguez had been scheduled to come to the United States to confer with President George W. Bush and, therefore, the U.S. Embassy took advantage of that opportunity to arrange a brief fifteen-minute conference for Jeanette at the Costa Rican Embassy.

Always organized and prepared, Jeannette spent the week before flying to Washington preparing questions and thoughts for her meeting with President Rodríguez with the help of KBI Special Agent in Charge Larry Thomas. She wanted to make maximum use of the fifteen minutes allotted to her. She and Thomas decided it would be most expedient for her to have a letter prepared to hand to the president. Thomas had previously assisted her in preparing pertinent questions about the Costa Rican investigation for her telephone conversation with the OIJ director.

The final draft of the letter Jeanette prepared for President Rodríguez read as follows:

July 13, 2001

President Miguel Ángel Rodríguez
San José, Costa Rica

Dear President Rodríguez:

My family, my community, and I deeply appreciate and respect you for your efforts to resolve the questions regarding the murder of my daughter. I also want you to know that your taking this time to meet with me is very much appreciated.

I have given a lot of time to the questions that I am privileged to ask you. I wanted to spend time getting to know you as a person, and it would be impossible in the short amount of time that we have to express the concerns of a mother for a daughter who has been murdered. Therefore, I thought it would be most appropriate to prepare these questions in writing so that with greater calm and time you could review them.

Answers to these few questions will provide me with some degree of comfort. Your efforts in obtaining answers, as you can imagine, are of great personal importance to all of us who loved her.

What steps to your knowledge are being taken to conduct a thorough investigation?

Do you believe these steps to be sufficient and appropriate or would you suggest that anything else be done?

Who in your administration may I please contact so that I don't have to bother you concerning questions that may arise?

Mr. President, I am also pleased to advise you that I have received word from the Kansas Bureau of Investigation that they are willing to assist in whatever manner the Costa Rican authorities desire. If not you, to whom should this offer be addressed?

As you can imagine, the worst thing for your country and mine is the perception that serious crime is not investigated. With that in mind and on behalf of my family, my community, and me, let me express to you our deepest appreciation for your attention to these questions and for your support.

Very truly yours,
Jeanette C. Stauffer
Mother of Shannon Martin

The meeting, which was unlikely to have been held in the first place, and which was scheduled for only fifteen minutes, stretched easily to forty minutes. Even the president of Costa Rica could not resist the determination and persuasion of the little lady from Topeka, Kansas. Jeanette hailed it as a successful meeting and praised President Rodríguez as very personable, understanding, courteous, and sympathetic. He told her that he also knew something about the tragic loss of a child. He had had a fifteen-year-old son who had been killed in an accident.

A week after Jeanette Stauffer's meeting with Costa Rica's president and ambassador, her optimism appeared to have finally been rewarded, at least briefly, with the news that an FBI agent would soon be headed to Costa Rica to confer with local investigators, and that he would be accompanied by a Miami homicide detective assigned to a Miami FBI task force. A U.S. Embassy spokeswoman in Costa Rica initially confirmed that the officers would review and assess the homicide case.

In August, Jeanette received a formal letter in response to her hand-delivered letter of July 13. President Rodríguez didn't specifically respond to her questions but did suggest that she contact Costa Rican Prosecutor Eric Martínez Trejos at Golfito for answers to those questions in her letter. She made arrangements to fly to Costa Rica on August 27 to speak personally with Trejos and to determine the feasibility of establishing a reward fund to assist the investigation as well. She returned from that trip disillusioned anew. No one seemed to be investigating her daughter's homicide, and her questions as to why the investigation was not more aggressive continued to go unanswered.

She would eventually travel to Costa Rica seventeen times. Brad, her retired military husband, made many of the flights with her. The stepfather would have accompanied his wife on all the flights, but family resources wouldn't permit it. The determined mother brought volumes of newspaper accounts and copies of police reports and investigative files back from each trip, most of which the Stauffers then had translated into English at considerable expense. She shared everything she brought home with Larry Thomas, who examined it all. She also shared her notes from countless conversations with Golfito neighbors, bar patrons, witnesses, and town residents.

Several facts were becoming clear. First, there had been no knife recovered at the scene. There had been considerable talk about a knife. No one, however, seemed to know whose or where it was. It was also clear that many people had trampled through the homicide scene. People had been observed walking around the body even after the police arrived. The site had not been effectively protected. Witnesses claimed the police had not worn gloves at the scene. Others said potential evidence had been left at the scene when police departed. The prosecutor, in unexplained haste, had declined to wait for daylight to raise and move Shannon's battered body, contrary to most accepted homicide-scene procedures. Almost none of the KU and other American college students present in the bar had been interviewed, and neither had most residents in the neighborhood. But, most important, it became apparent that while many names of suspects had come and gone, three names had surfaced early, and many citizens of Golfito continued to tell Jeanette and occasionally the police that those three people were probably responsible for Shannon's murder.

These three suspects appeared to be Rafael Zumbado Quesada, aka "Coco," age 52; Luis Alberto Castro Carrillo, aka "Caballo" ("Horse"), age 33; and Kattia Cruz Murillo, aka "La Panteonera" ("The Grave Robber"), age 29. "Caballo," greatly feared in Golfito, was a notorious drug dealer and thief, with a long arrest record. Kattia Cruz, the only female, was a crack cocaine addict, known to always carry a knife. She was a fixture on Golfito streets begging for money. "Coco," a drug addict and drug dealer, was also a suspect in another homicide, the killing of a drug dealer who had dared venture into "Coco" territory. The rival drug dealer had been hacked to death with a machete.

Some of the police reports obtained by Jeanette indicated Shannon had been stabbed thirteen times. Others indicated fourteen times. The autopsy revealed fifteen stab wounds. It also determined she had not been sexually assaulted. It was believed that earrings she had been wearing were missing. She had carried little money. The motive for the attack remained elusive. Robbery seemed possible, but if that were the case the crime could scarcely be called successful. Little of material value had been taken. Indeed, little of material value had been available, or apparent, to any would-be robber.

The events of September 11, 2001, followed, which distracted from Shannon's cause. On November 11, 2001, however, Costa Rican police quietly made an arrest. Kattia Cruz was officially taken into custody and formally charged with the murder of Shannon Lucile Martin. She had been the primary suspect in the minds of both Jeanette Stauffer and Larry Thomas. There were two other suspects as well, still free; nonetheless, 2001 turned into 2002 with growing hope for justice for Shannon—at least in Kansas.

Larry Thomas continued to assist Jeanette in developing questions she could pose to the prosecutor and investigators in Costa Rica. He pored over the reports and materials she regularly brought from Golfito, including, occasionally, Costa Rican answers to questions he had previously drafted. He was examining the English language translations of all those materials as soon as Jeanette's translators completed their work in Topeka. The long-distance approach to homicide investigation frustrated him greatly, and he longed to personally put questions to the investigators, the prosecutor, witnesses, and especially to Kattia Cruz. Larry Thomas is no ordinary criminal investigator. He is blessed with boundless energy and professionalism. He holds a bachelor's degree from Central Missouri State University in Warrensburg and joined the KBI as a special agent on March 1, 1984. I promoted him to special agent in charge on December 18, 1994, and sent him to the prestigious Royal Canadian Mounted Police College in Ottawa, Canada, in 1997. He graduated from the FBI's Central States Law Enforcement Executive Development School in 1998 and from the FBI National Academy in Quantico, Virginia, in 1999. He commanded the KBI's Cold Case Squad and later directed the KBI's participation in the BTK Task Force in Wichita. In 2001 Thomas was an assistant director waiting to happen.

The "boom and bust" experience continued for the Stauffers as the other two suspects, Zumbado and Castro, were also taken into custody in July 2002. Now, finally, "Coco," Kattia, and "Caballo" were all where Jeanette had long thought they should be, in the Golfito jail. All three were actually incarcerated pursuant to a rather unique arrest provision of Costa Rican law, called "preventive custody." It can best be compared to an arrest without formal charges, not unlike the old U.S. law enforcement "Vagrancy Investigation" arrests of the 1930s and 1940s.

Jeanette continued to travel to and from Costa Rica and continued to meet with Larry Thomas and her translators after each return, often at KBI headquarters.

Then, on Sunday, November 30, 2002, Tim Rogers of the *Tico Times* telephoned to tell her that "Coco" and "Caballo" had suddenly been released by the police. Only Kattia Cruz, the original arrestee, remained in custody, and the reporter suggested that Kattia's continued confinement appeared uncertain. Justice for Shannon continued to elude her family as 2002 turned into 2003.

The beginning of 2003 was better than the end of 2002. In early February Jeanette was excited to learn that "Coco" was again in custody, arrested for murder. Her enthusiasm was dampened a bit when she was advised that the murder for which he was charged and jailed was not that of Shannon but of the rival drug dealer he had allegedly hacked to death. Still, he was in custody. So was Kattia Cruz.

The turning point in Jeanette's crusade for justice for Shannon came in April 2003, when a law student, a young American named Jeff Thomas, interning in the courthouse at Golfito, innocently suggested to Jeanette that she should become a "querellante," another interesting and uniquely Costa Rican provision in their law. He explained that she could file a motion for her own legal representative, her own attorney, to work in conjunction with the prosecutor. She and her attorney could legally confer with the prosecutor, participate in any investigative and/or pretrial conferences, and sit at the prosecutor's table in any legal proceeding, hearing, or trial. Jeanette was stunned. Those rights and privileges were exactly what she had been seeking in all her visits to Golfito. Why, she asked the young legal intern, was she just then being advised of such a wonderful possibility? The young man sheepishly confided in her that the prosecutor had described her to his staff as a busybody American to whom he had no legal obligation to tell anything and, therefore, he wouldn't waste his time doing so.

On May 3, 2003, Kattia Cruz, Rafael Zumbado Quesada, and Luis Alberto Casto Carrillo, also now in custody, were all afforded preliminary hearings, formally charged with Shannon's murder, and bound over for trial. More important, also on that day, Jeanette Stauffer stood in the same court, flanked by a Costa Rican attorney she had hired and to whom she had granted power of attorney to represent her in Shannon's case and by a Spanish-speaking attorney who had accompanied her from Kansas. She petitioned the Costa Rican court to become a "querellante," an actual participant in the homicide prosecution. Much to the dismay of the prosecutor, the court granted Jeanette's motion. The investigation was still woefully incomplete, but justice was finally headed in the right direction. Jeanette was buoyed as never before by the recent positive legal developments.

Now legally entitled to see the 960-page prosecutor's file, she paid to have it copied and brought it home to Kansas with her. She turned it over to Jesse Ybarra, her primary Topeka translator, and Larry Thomas. For a week at KBI headquarters Thomas reviewed the file as quickly as Ybarra translated it. Together they discovered that some evidence had still not been forensically examined and persons identified as potential witnesses had never been interviewed. The whereabouts of the murder weapon, the knife, were still unknown, and many reports in the file contradicted others or were incomplete.

It was clear that Thomas and Ybarra needed to be in Golfito. I made it an official KBI assignment and authorized Thomas to accompany Ybarra and Jeanette Stauffer. Thomas would be on official duty and we would continue his salary. With serious budgetary problems at the time, however, the KBI had no money for Thomas's travel and per diem expenses, much to my dismay. Neither did the state. Jeanette found the money in her own savings and loans.

Thomas spent nine days in Costa Rica in June 2003, ten days in September 2003, ten days in October 2003, seven days in November 2003, and five days in June and July 2004. In all, he would eventually make twelve trips to Costa Rica. The Stauffer family paid for every flight and for his per diem expenses, a terrible financial burden. Jeanette said many times that it was the best money they ever spent. I still regret that she and her husband had to pay the travel expenses of a KBI agent.

Thomas's first flight to Costa Rica was on June 22, 2003, with Jeanette and Ybarra. He quickly visited the scene of the crime, interviewed many potential witnesses, and reviewed the available evidence. He met with officials at the U.S. Embassy in San José and with Costa Rican police and forensic scientists.

When the trio departed for Costa Rica on Sunday, June 22, Thomas responded to reporters' questions by saying, "I won't be intervening with the local investigation. But I'll observe, and if I have any comments or recommendations or offers of assistance, I hope they'll be considered as the case moves forward."[7] He exceeded those modest goals.

Despite the necessity of almost all communications between Thomas and witnesses, officials, and police passing through an interpreter, Thomas established quick and easy rapport with the Costa Ricans. Together, Jeanette Stauffer's persistence, Jesse Ybarra's linguistic aptitude, and Larry Thomas's homicide experience and expertise paid great dividends. The trio was much appreciated by Jeanette's Costa Rican attorney, Juan Carlos Arce, who often traveled with the three Topekans on their investigative journeys around Costa Rica. All information and evidence developed by the Kansas investigators were promptly and faithfully shared with Arce, who in turn provided it quickly to the chief prosecutor. That pattern of sharing continued through all the investigative trips to Costa Rica.

Rumors had persisted that the murder suspects had escaped the scene of the homicide by taxicab. Local officials had neglected to pursue even that simple lead and, during her earliest solo trips, Jeanette had pleaded through Costa Rican media for the cab driver, who had suddenly left that employment without a forwarding address, to come forward. It had been to no avail.

Witnesses now confirmed the taxicab story for Thomas. A man and a woman definitely hurried from the homicide scene in Golfito cab #57. That information led to the identification, location, and interview of the cab company employee who had cleaned cab #57 in the cab company's garage the night Shannon was murdered. The employee recalled a reddish-brown substance in the cab's back seat and on a rear interior door handle. He also recalled the male and female passengers who were with the cab driver when the latter checked the cab in for the night. In particular, he recalled how nervous and excited the two passengers were and how they ran from the cab when it arrived at the garage. Furthermore, he remembered realizing the reddish-brown substance must have been blood when he heard about the murder of the American female college student the next day, and the rumors that the suspects escaped in a taxicab. Lastly, he recalled the name of the driver of cab #57, who seemed acquainted with his final passengers that night, and who quit his job and moved from Golfito shortly after Shannon's murder. When Thomas asked the helpful employee why he had not previously reported all the information regarding cab #57, he shrugged and replied that the KBI agent was the first to ask him questions about the incident.

Thomas was excited about the possibility of still finding residual blood in cab #57, almost two years after the murder, if in fact the cab cleaner was correct in his presumption that the reddish-brown substance he observed was actually drying blood—Shannon's blood.

The first problem was that the cab company no longer owned cab #57. The second problem, Thomas and his colleagues discovered as they traced the automobile through various owners, was that one subsequent owner had wrecked the vehicle and sold it for salvage. Eventually, and incredibly, the rear seat and both rear doors of what was once cab #57 were found in a dilapidated shed in the country many miles from Golfito. Thomas called OIJ's crime lab in San José and requested that a forensic team join them at that site to process the automobile parts now covered with rust, dirt, and debris. The Kansans waited hours for the forensic team to arrive and then patiently watched as they processed the parts, unsuccessfully, for human blood. There was no trace evidence. Apparently the cab cleaner's efforts, along with the elements and the passage of time, were too much to overcome.

Undeterred, the investigative team from Kansas simply changed its focus from the cab to the driver of the cab. The driver's trail took them from Golfito through two smaller rural communities and, eventually, to San José, the nation's capital, 105 miles from the homicide scene.

Juan Carlos Arce, Jeanette's Costa Rican attorney, traveled with them to San José, and his knowledge of that city proved helpful. He had attended college and law school there while on scholarship for playing *fútbol* (soccer).

Finding the driver was difficult enough, thanks to geography and language impediments. The difficulty was compounded by the driver's secondary employment as a small-time drug dealer. The driver was nervous and reluctant to speak with the Americans on the street corner where they first found him. They coaxed him to a nearby hotel room for a more in-depth interview.

During preliminary inquiries in Golfito, some witnesses at the homicide scene and the cab cleaner had suggested the two taxicab passengers were Luis Alberto Castro Carrillo and Kattia Cruz Murrillo. The cab driver, in the hotel room, reluctantly confirmed that rumor. Then he added a fact that no one else had volunteered. There had actually been three people that night running toward his cab, apparently following the murder of Shannon Martin. Only two, Castro and Cruz, hailed his cab and became passengers. The third, who ran by the taxicab and disappeared into the night, was Rafael Zumbado Quesada, aka "Coco," known to the frightened driver as a crack cocaine addict and major drug dealer. Clearly, the driver feared the notorious Zumbado, but eventually and reluctantly he agreed to testify in Shannon Martin's homicide trial about his actions and recollections the night she was murdered. His fear of Zumbado, however, proved greater than his commitment to civic duty. He later fled to Panama and could not be located again.

In subsequent trips, Thomas retrieved one earring of Shannon pawned by Kattia Cruz; interviewed Kattia's brother; interviewed every witness identified in the prosecutor's original file, a file that was now growing rapidly in size; found and interviewed new witnesses; located the phantom knife believed to be the murder weapon; and reviewed the autopsy photographs. Thomas also continued Arce's crash course in "KBI Homicide Investigation 101," as Larry would later describe it, and Arce was receiving passing grades from the veteran KBI investigator.

Jeanette Stauffer was happier, but not satisfied. As she described the situation later to the Kansas legislature:

> The Kansas investigation team discovered a taxicab, knife, and pants with human blood that should have been examined by the OIJ crime lab but never were tested. Hair samples were not taken from all of the suspects to be compared to the five unmatched hair samples found in Shannon's hand. Thomas and Ybarra talked with over thirty people who should have been interviewed in the beginning. Agent Thomas asked my Costa Rican attorney to motion the court to have the taxicab, knife, and pants tested. . . . During the first two trips, they (Ybarra and Thomas) interviewed more people and collected more evidence than had been gathered by the prosecutor on the case and Costa Rican investigators during the previous two and a half years.[8]

Jeanette was very pleased with the work of the Kansas investigation team, but her elation truly had no bounds when, on November 20, 2003, Juan Carlos Arce petitioned the trial court to allow Larry Thomas to be designated a trial consultant and permitted to sit at the prosecution's table during the trial of Cruz, Castro, and Zumbado. The court quickly approved Arce's motion and more history was made. The KBI would officially assist in the prosecution of killers of a Kansas citizen in a criminal trial in another nation, a first for the KBI and, I think, for all Kansas law enforcement.

The case against Kattia Cruz had always been considered the strongest of the cases against the three defendants. The case against Zumbado relied heavily on the frightened cab driver. That case was dealt a serious blow when that witness fled in fear to Panama prior to the trial. The strong case against Castro would later be attributed by Arce and Jeanette to the investigative efforts of Ybarra and Thomas.

It had been estimated that the trial would last five or six days. Instead, it lasted two weeks. Kattia Cruz and Luis Alberto Castro Carillo were each convicted of "simple homicide" and sentenced to fifteen years in prison. Rafael Zumbado Quesada was acquitted, due to lack of evidence, by the three-judge panel handling the trial. The head judge explained the verdicts: "This is not because we believe in Zumbado's innocence, but because we are judges of the Republic and of the law and not of conscience. . . . We know that Kattia and Luis Alberto killed Shannon. This is clear."[9] Ironically, Zumbado was already serving thirty-five years for his unrelated murder conviction.

"Simple homicide," a charge similar to second-degree murder in most states, automatically draws a fifteen-year sentence in Costa Rica. "Qualified homicide," a charge similar to first-degree murder in most states, can draw a thirty- or thirty-five-year sentence in Costa Rica. The prosecution appealed the sentences on the ground that the convictions should have been for "qualified homicide," not "simple homicide," thirty or thirty-five years, not fifteen years.

The appeal for review of the sentences was granted in April 2004, and Jeanette Stauffer and Larry Thomas returned to Golfito on June 29, 2004, for the sentence-modification hearing. Thomas consulted with Arce and the prosecutor, and he helped them prepare a persuasive argument for "qualified homicide." They succeeded. Each defendant's sentence was changed to thirty years, creating a larger measure of justice for Shannon, although far from the full measure Jeanette sought.

The trial, like the investigation, did not reveal the motive for Shannon's senseless murder, although it was probably robbery. Given the savage nature of the assault and the profiles of the defendants, the attack was probably drug-induced. No evidence was ever developed indicating that Shannon might have known her attackers. The investigation, the trial, and the appeal cost the Stauffer family more than $255,000 and three years. Not surprisingly, Jeanette Stauffer's dauntless efforts on behalf of her murdered daughter did not end with the convictions of the two killers.

Thanks to Jeanette's tireless efforts, the Shannon Lucile Martin English Language Center was opened in Shannon's beloved Golfito. The center was built inside the Costa Rican Coast Guard Academy to teach English free of charge to Golfito residents and Coast Guard Academy cadets. Naturally, Jeanette had gone straight to the top. She persuaded the national commandant of the Costa Rica Coast Guard to donate the space. Then she solicited support from thirty Golfito businesses. The response was overwhelming. Since American tourism is the main industry in Golfito, the city was anxious for its residents to learn English. At one time there was a waiting list of 300 to enter the language center named after the KU student from Topeka, Kansas.

In a letter to several Kansas newspapers on November 14, 2004, Jeanette Stauffer wrote in praise of recent Kansas legislation that had amended the Kansas Crime Victims Compensation Act to include Kansans who are victims of violent crime in another country. She had testified in support of the legislation. The final paragraph of her letter read, "The state of Kansas has been very supportive. If it were not for the Kansas Bureau of Investigation, the murder of Shannon would not have been solved. And, if it were not for Kansas legislators and the office of the attorney general there would be no legislation in place to help victims and families victimized by violent crime in another country."[10]

On April 4, 2005, Kansas Attorney General Phill Kline, flanked by former attorney general Bob Stephan and Jeanette Stauffer, announced at a news conference that Jeanette Stauffer would be the new Statewide Victims' Rights Coordinator for Kansas. Who better? She served well in that capacity for eighteen months before leaving to pursue other interests.

In August 2005, I promoted Larry Thomas to KBI assistant director. In September 2005, KSN-TV in Wichita aired an hour-long program in primetime on Shannon's murder and the investigation, featuring Jeanette Stauffer, Jesse Ybarra, and Larry Thomas.

In late March 2006, a concerned Jeanette Stauffer telephoned Larry Thomas to advise that her Costa Rican attorney had just notified her that Kattia

Cruz and Luis Castro had been granted appeals to challenge their murder convictions of 2003 and the thirty-year sentences of 2004. There was a new prosecutor on board who was completely unfamiliar with Shannon's murder investigation and prosecution. Jeanette's attorney was not confident of the appeal's outcome without Jeanette and her "Kansas investigation team" being present in San Isidro, Costa Rica, on April 7, 2006, to assist with the final appeal argument.

Back to Costa Rica went Jeanette Stauffer, Jesse Ybarra, and Larry Thomas. On April 6, the trio met with Jeanette's attorney and the new prosecutor to plot strategy. The strategy was simple. Both attorneys would speak, as would Jeanette herself. Both defendants' attorneys and both defendants would also speak if they wished.

On April 7, 2006, at 9:30 A.M., the appeal hearing commenced before a three-judge panel in the San Isidro court. The new prosecutor spoke first, followed by Jeanette's attorney and the defendants' attorneys. Jeanette closed for the prosecution, eloquent and passionate as always.

Then Kattia Cruz spoke to the court and surprised all present. She was extremely remorseful and she apologized to the court and personally to Jeanette for her part in the murder of Shannon Martin. She blamed her action that tragic night in May 2001 on her addiction to drugs. She professed to be a different person now and she tearfully begged Jeanette's forgiveness, which was not forthcoming.

The last to speak was Luis Castro. Defiant as ever, he insisted he was innocent and was being used as a scapegoat because an American had been killed and someone had to pay. He demanded a full apology from Jeanette Stauffer. The apology, like the request for forgiveness from Kattia Cruz, did not materialize.

The tribunal of judges ended the hearing and promised to reconvene at 3:30 P.M. that afternoon to deliver its ruling. When they resumed, they announced that the conviction and thirty-year sentence of Kattia Cruz would stand. They also affirmed the conviction of Luis Castro. Then they announced that his penalty was being changed from the thirty-year sentence. Jeanette and her team immediately feared the worst. They need not have, because the tribunal quickly added that the defiant, unremorseful Castro would serve a thirty-five-year sentence, the maximum possible sentence under Costa Rican law, rather than the thirty-year sentence imposed by the lower court. At the conclusion of the appeal hearing, each of the judges thanked and congratulated Jeanette Stauffer's Kansas investigation team for its assistance in achieving justice in Golfito for Shannon Martin.

During the evening of May 19, 2006, in the large banquet room of the Airport Hilton in Wichita, approximately 450 members and guests of the Kansas Peace Officers' Association, the Kansas Sheriffs' Association, and the Kansas Association of Chiefs of Police (KACP) attended the annual KACP Awards Banquet honoring Kansas law enforcement officers for exceptional performance in 2005. Kansas Attorney General Phill Kline and several Kansas legislators were in attendance, and it was my privilege to preside over the banquet and awards ceremony as master of ceremonies for the evening. That evening one of the Kansas officers honored by his peers for exceptional performance was KBI Assistant Director Larry Thomas. The award was given "for what is believed to be the first time a Kansas law enforcement officer helped investigate and helped prosecute killers in a foreign country who had murdered a Kansas citizen in that country." A special guest that evening, in that large crowd, seated at a reserved table up front with Larry Thomas and others, was a beaming, proud, and happy Jeanette Stauffer. When I introduced her to the audience as Larry Thomas received his award, the modest, determined mother of Shannon Martin received a standing ovation.

The KU–Costa Rica Exchange Program, created in 1958, is the longest continuously operating student-faculty exchange between universities in the United States and Latin America, In fact, one of the author's grandsons, a Spanish language major at the University of Kansas, studied at the University of Costa Rica in San José in the KU–Costa Rica Exchange Program in 2011.

On May 6, 2008, the Supreme Court of Costa Rica once again affirmed the convictions and sentences of Kattia Cruz and Luis Castro, thereby exhausting all appeals for the pair.

CHAPTER THIRTEEN

Liz: The KBI Assists in a Very Cold Case

She was the only daughter and the oldest of the four children of Al and Kay Wilson of Prairie Village, Kansas, a nice suburb of Kansas City. On Sunday, July 7, 1974, she was thirteen years old, having reached that young milestone less than two weeks earlier. She was known to giggle frequently, as little girls do, and all who knew her considered her a delight. She was barely five feet tall, weighed about ninety pounds, and had blue eyes, reddish-brown hair, and lots of freckles. On that last day of her short life, Lizabeth Ann Wilson was wearing a red, white, and blue swimsuit with white sandals. She was carrying a large multicolored beach towel and a green tennis ball. While a cute, cheerful, and popular girl, she was certainly not yet a sexy young woman. She was still a little girl, with no obvious feminine charms. Unless, of course, the viewer is a pedophile.

It was a typical Kansas summer day, and the temperature in Prairie Village on July 7, 1974, reached 94 degrees. Liz and her brother John, age eleven, had been doing what Kansas kids have always done during the hot summers. They had been swimming at the municipal swimming pool. In a departure from their usual regimen, they did not swim that Sunday afternoon. Instead, they went to the city pool at 6:00 P.M., following an early dinner, with parental instructions to be home no later than 8:00 P.M. At approximately 7:15 P.M., Liz and John were headed home because the brother and sister had a disagreement in the pool. Liz was upset with her brother and threatened to tell her parents that he had jumped on her in cannonball style in the pool and hurt her. She had cried as a result of her brother's action. In fact, she wouldn't stop crying and John intended to beat her home in order to give his version of the event first and then hope for the best.

Shawnee Mission East High School was 200 yards from the swimming pool and four blocks from the Wilson home. The school was midway between the pool and their home. Liz and John always walked to the pool and returned to their home through the school grounds, together. Their instructions from their strict parents were to always walk together, both to and from the pool. But on this occasion, due to the trouble in the pool, when Liz angrily and tearfully announced she was going home, John had decided to hurry home ahead of his sister to argue his cause first.

During the summers, even during the evenings, the front doors of Shawnee Mission East High School were left open as the school janitors performed their chores. Janitors routinely permitted passing children to step inside the front doors of the large high school to drink from the water fountains located fifty feet inside.

John had run nearly one-third of the way across the school's large parking lot before he stopped to look behind him to determine Liz's progress. He saw her just entering the edge of the parking lot and he could see she was still crying. He ran past the school's main front entrance doors, not pausing for the usual drink. But he needed to catch his breath before the last leg of the race home, so he hid next to a wall in front of the school. He would wait for Liz and then beat her home with a final burst of speed. He waited a minute, then two or three minutes. No sister. He stood and looked behind him. And then in all directions. Somehow Liz had changed her route, no doubt in a clever move designed to reach home first, he thought. Now frantic, John ran all the way home. He was home by 7:30 P.M. No Liz. His luck was really holding, however, because their parents were also not yet home. Mr. and Mrs. Wilson had told Liz and John that they should all be home by 8:00 P.M. The parents arrived home within minutes of John's arrival. Still no Liz. 8:00 P.M. came and went. Liz had still not returned.

John had planned to reason with Liz before she could speak to their parents. He would make all the promises necessary if his sister would not snitch on him. He was beginning to think Liz had gone to the nearby home of her girlfriend who had been at the pool with them. All the better; it would be more time for Liz to cool off and/or forget, or forgive John for what he had done to make her cry. He suggested to his parents that Liz had stopped at Dorothy's home when shortly after 8:00 P.M. they asked him about her whereabouts.

The Wilsons regarded Liz as an exceptionally responsible child and, while disappointed she had not called, they were not yet alarmed about her absence. However, by 9:00 P.M., Liz's parents were upset with her and telephoned her friend's home. When advised that Liz had not come home with Dorothy, the Wilsons were instantly alarmed. Al Wilson telephoned the Prairie Village Police Department and reported their daughter missing.

An intense search was immediately launched by the Prairie Village Police Department and by friends and neighbors of the Wilsons. The search concentrated on the swimming pool, the area between the pool and the school, the school itself, and the Wilsons' neighborhood, several blocks in all directions. The search continued through the night and throughout the next day, joined by FBI agents, the Metro Squad—a major-crimes squad of officers from Missouri and Kansas law enforcement agencies in the Kansas City metropolitan area—and officers from the Johnson County Sheriff's Office.

A complete search of the interior of the large high school was conducted with dogs and countless officers. The dogs were also used at the pool, across the school grounds, and throughout the residential neighborhood. Efforts were made to identify and interview everyone who had been at the pool. Officers knocked on every door in the large residential area the first two days. Kansas Highway Patrol aircraft flew overhead looking for a small body that might be attired in red, white, and blue. No physical evidence of Liz Wilson was found in Prairie Village except for several reddish-brown hairs recovered in the television room of the high school by FBI agents, later found to be "microscopically . . . similar" to hairs from Liz's hairbrush in her home, given the limits of such forensic science in 1974. No other physical evidence was found in those early searches; however, several youngsters reported suspicious conduct by a high school janitor the evening of the disappearance. Strange or weird were probably more accurate descriptions of John Henry Horton's behavior than suspicious.

John Wilson had not seen Horton watering trees in front of the high school that evening, but other children had. The custodian had demonstrated an unusual interest in young girls and had a reputation for his attempts to engage young girls in conversation as they passed or entered the school. In fact, during the evening in question, it was learned that Horton had approached cheerleaders practicing at the school and exhibited unusual and unwanted interest in them. Additionally, officers identified two more young attractive girls, both teenagers, who had been playing tennis at the courts near the school and pool. After tennis and shortly before Liz Wilson's disappearance, they walked by the school and were confronted by a man in a school custodian uniform, later identified as John Henry Horton. Horton acted strangely and had told the girls he was looking for another custodian, because he needed someone to stand on his shoulders to turn off an elevated water spigot at the school. Both girls agreed he seemed to be asking one of them to stand on his shoulders to perform the described task. A bit frightened, the girls hurried away, they told officers. An inquiry confirmed that there were no elevated water spigots at the school and that no other custodian was on duty that evening. Only Horton.

Horton was the closest thing to a suspect on the first evening. The next morning, officers went to Independence, Missouri, to interview him at his home. Horton, age twenty-seven, was six feet in height, 170 pounds, with brown eyes, brown hair, and numerous tattoos on his arms. Originally from New York, he had eight arrests across Kansas and in the state of New York, primarily for burglary but also for larceny, vagrancy, and interfering with a police officer. He had served two sentences for burglary at the Elmira Correctional Facility in Elmira, New York, in 1966 and 1968. He was released in 1970 and in 1971 joined the army, but later he was restricted to his North Carolina army base and ordered to forfeit three months' pay for an AWOL violation. He was discharged in 1973, as unsuccessful in the military as he had been as a burglar.

When interviewed in his home the morning following Liz's disappearance, Horton denied any knowledge of Liz or her disappearance. His answers, however, were often evasive and contradictory. The officers agreed with the school children. Horton was weird. He had cuts and scratches on his arms, forehead, and neck. His explanation was that he always got such cuts and scratches at work. He consented to a search of his car. In a white canvas bag in the trunk of his car, the officers found three bottles of chloroform, one can of ether, one bottle of sulfuric acid, and a butcher knife. Strange stuff for a school janitor. Inside the car the officers found more strands of hair that would later be determined to be "microscopically . . . similar" to those of Liz Wilson. Another consensual search inside his home located a pair of his undershorts on which there appeared to be blood. Later, forensic examinations verified it as human blood, but typing and classification were no help because Liz Wilson's blood had never been typed.

Horton continued to give evasive and conflicting answers to questions about his precise whereabouts the entire evening of July 7, 1974, about the strange items in his car, and about the blood on his undershorts. The officers, unable to obtain any admissions from him, pushed him to take a polygraph examination. He agreed and twice underwent polygraph interviews. Both examinations determined him to be deceptive in his answers. He admitted theft of the items from the school's chemistry laboratory found in his car and theft of television tubes from the school's television room where the suspicious hairs had been found, but emphatically denied any knowledge of Liz's whereabouts. He described himself as a "scrounger" rather than a thief.

The FBI laboratory, in those pre-DNA days, was unable to make anything more incriminating out of the hairs found in Horton's car, or those from the television room at the school, to which he had access.

Horton remained the primary suspect, but the case went nowhere until 3:25 P.M. on January 7, 1975, seven months to the day after Liz's disappearance. Agents of the Federal Bureau of Alcohol, Tobacco and Firearms, on a routine inspection of a dynamite storage shed for a construction company, discovered a small human skull with five teeth in a large twenty-five-acre alfalfa field in Lenexa, Kansas, approximately ten miles from Shawnee Mission East High School. Thirteen other human bones were found scattered 300 yards from the skull. No other physical evidence was located in the resulting extensive search. Through dental records the remains were identified as those of Lizabeth A. Wilson, age thirteen, of Prairie Village. No cause or manner of death could be determined from the skeletal remains. The recovery of Liz's remains was important to the Wilsons, who were devout Catholics. Liz was laid to rest in Humboldt, Iowa, Kay Wilson's original home. Al Wilson was promoted by his company, B. F. Goodrich, and the family moved to Chicago.

Liz had been abducted in Kansas and, apparently, murdered in Kansas. There was, it seemed, no interstate transportation or federal kidnapping involved, and therefore no FBI jurisdiction. Lacking jurisdiction, the FBI withdrew from the case. The Prairie Village Police Department continued as the agency of jurisdiction, with John Henry Horton still the only strong suspect. The case went cold.

Twenty-five years later, informal talks between Captain John Walters of Prairie Village and Special Agent in Charge Larry Thomas of the KBI eventually led to a thorough review of the case by Corporal Kyle Shipps of the Prairie Village Police Department and Senior Special Agents Ray Lundin and Brad Cordts of the KBI's Cold Case Squad. Countless hours were spent locating and reading investigative reports of the Prairie Village Police Department, as well as the Liz Wilson files of the Kansas City FBI, the Johnson County Sheriff's Department, and the Kansas City Metro Squad. The reviewers' collective opinion was that the investigators of 1974 and 1975 had been on the right track. John Henry Horton was the logical suspect. The case warranted reopening and deserved fresh investigative attention. The official request for the assistance of the KBI Cold Case Squad came in a letter from Police Chief Charles (Chuck) Grover in January 2002. Though facing significant budget constraints and a severe shortage within our special agent ranks at the time, due to the budgetary restrictions, I gave my approval to Larry Thomas's plea that we join Prairie Village in the reopened case. Officer Kyle Shipps and Senior Special Agent Brad Cordts of the KBI would serve as the lead investigators. Sergeant Craig Caster of the Prairie Village Police Department and Larry Thomas would supervise under the oversight of Chief Grover.

Several KBI personnel would eventually cover leads and conduct interviews in the case. Foremost among them were Thomas and another special agent in charge, Bill Delaney, as well as KBI agents Angie Wilson, Bill Halvorsen, and Ray Lundin, the latter, with Cordts, a member of Thomas's three-man KBI Cold Case Squad. The agents were assisted by the analytical support of KBI Crime Analysts Jeff Muckenthaler and Katie Schuetz. The bulk of the effort, however, came from Shipps of Prairie Village and Cordts of the KBI. Little supervision and oversight were ever needed.

The two veteran officers agreed between them that the first order of business was to locate and visit the parents of Liz Wilson to officially advise them that the case would be reopened, solicit their support and assistance, and thoroughly reinterview them and their son John about the events of July 7, 1974. They knew that the Wilsons had left Prairie Village shortly after Liz's kidnapping and murder and moved to the Chicago area, in connection with Al Wilson's promotion by the Goodrich Company. It was also determined that the Wilsons had moved to the Chicago suburb of Itasca, where Kay had opened Carol Kay Interiors and they raised their three sons while continuing to struggle with the unanswered questions concerning their only daughter's death. Later, with Kay's health in decline, they moved to Arizona.

On June 27, 2002, Brad Cordts and Kyle Shipps met with Al and Kay Wilson in their Scottsdale home. The Wilsons were grateful for the new attention offered to Liz's case and appreciated the officers' emphasis that they did not wish to raise any false hopes on the part of the parents, but they vowed to give the case their best investigative and, they hoped, prosecutorial efforts. Cordts, using KBI DNA kits he had brought with him, took saliva and blood samples from the Wilsons, in case their DNA was needed in the future, and the officers interviewed the parents about their memories of July 7, 1974. They were unable to add anything of significance to what they had told officers at the time of the crime. The Wilsons agreed to call the officers if they recalled anything further and they advised that their son John lived in Bradenton, Florida, employed by a trucking company.

Eight days later Cordts and Shipps interviewed John Wilson in Prairie Village. He had volunteered to come to them. John relived the troubling events of July 7, 1974, for the investigators and accompanied them to the pool, the school, and the old neighborhood in an effort to improve his recollection of the events of that day so long ago. He remained positive, as he had been twenty-eight years earlier, that he saw no one, other than Liz, anywhere in the school parking lot that terrible day during his hurried trip home. He tried hard to be of assistance in her homicide investigation. When Brad Cordts dictated his notes from the interview with John Wilson, the report turned out to be four pages long. Clearly, Liz's brother had forgotten nothing.

Cordts and Shipps were determined to concentrate on John Henry Horton until proven wrong. There was only one problem. They didn't know where he was. They started their search for his current whereabouts in Independence, Missouri, where the 1974–1975 investigative reports had left him. They knew he had been fired at Shawnee Mission East High School, shortly after Liz Wilson's disappearance, due to his theft admissions. They quickly determined that he no longer lived in Independence.

In the next few weeks they backtracked Horton from Independence to Lee's Summit; then Moberly; Bevier; Callao; Brookfield; Hannibal; and, finally, Canton, all in Missouri. In the course of that investigative effort they learned that Horton had three vehicle accidents while briefly residing in Independence. They also learned from the police chief in Bevier, Missouri, that Horton was the only suspect in a series of incidents in 1992 and 1993 involving a window peeper and numerous teenaged girls in that community. All were convinced that Horton was the peeper, but they were never able to catch him in the act. The complaints stopped when he moved from Bevier. They were informed by authorities in Callao that Horton had, in fact, been arrested in that community in 1993, charged with and convicted of trespass and resisting arrest, having been caught window peeping on young girls there. There had been numerous complaints involving a series of such incidents, prior to Horton's arrest, wherein young girls reported a man dressed completely in black watching them at night and then running from the scenes. So convinced were the local officers that it was Horton that they placed a surveillance on him for several evenings and finally caught him following a brief chase on foot from the residence of one young girl where he was observed by officers looking through a bedroom window, dressed entirely in black. Horton entered pleas of guilty to charges of trespassing and resisting arrest and was fined five hundred dollars. He and Sharen Horton, his wife, moved from Callao. Officers later noted that a series of arsons, which had suddenly started after Horton moved to Callao and became a volunteer firefighter, ended abruptly when Horton moved away.

Horton's reputation for strange behavior had followed him since 1974 and was apparently deserved. When Cordts later interviewed the officer who arrested Horton in Callao, the officer advised that, during the surveillance, he watched Horton come out of his own residence dressed in black and go to the residence in question, climb over a tall fence, and position himself next to a bedroom window. When arrested, Horton admitted to the officer that he had a fascination for young girls and had been window peeping a long time. The officer further informed Cordts that young girls and young women in Callao had been quite afraid of Horton, who spent considerable time in a local park near his residence watching them. Horton would later deny that he had made such admissions to the Callao officer.

When Shipps and Cordts first resumed the Liz Wilson homicide investigation focusing on John Henry Horton, one of their primary missions was to not let Horton know that he was being investigated again—at least for as long as possible. They intended to confront him eventually, but when that occasion arrived, they wanted their appearance to be a complete surprise. Their initial investigative efforts determined that John and Sharen Horton then resided near Canton, in northeast Missouri, where Horton worked for a small manufacturing company. They would not contact that employer until they were ready to confront Horton. Throughout the spring and summer of 2002, however, they contacted many former employers and former coworkers of Horton across Missouri. Indeed, they contacted every known former place of employment for Horton since his termination at Shawnee Mission East High School.

A common theme developed with contacts at many of the past employments. Coworkers and even one former employer were reluctant to discuss the homicide suspect. Not because of friendship or respect, but because they were persuaded, due to his own false claims, that he was a former motorcycle gang member and they feared retaliation. Former custodians at Shawnee Mission East High School had no such reluctance to describe their recollections of him, however. The remembered him as lazy and excessively interested in young girls. Furthermore, they had considered him a chronic liar and a braggart. They spoke of his claims of heroic combat service in Vietnam and his boasting of many personal enemy kills there. None had believed him. They also remembered that he liked to take his frequent breaks during summer months in the bleachers at the nearby swimming pool to watch the young girls. During the school term he was especially attracted to the cheerleaders in short skirts. His fellow custodians also recalled his claim of strong associations with members of the Hell's Angels motorcycle gang. He often told stories to any custodians who would listen about numerous fist fights that he consistently won, beating up others, especially law enforcement officers. Actually, most considered him a coward, and none was surprised he was considered a suspect in Liz Wilson's disappearance. Some were only surprised he had not been arrested and charged at the time.

Cordts was able to locate and interview the FBI agents, now all retired, who had worked on the 1974–1975 investigation. He spoke to the agents who had located the "microscopically . . . similar" hairs in the school's television room and in Horton's car. He located and interviewed the FBI forensic examiner (retired in North Carolina) who had forensically compared those hairs with hairs recovered from Liz Wilson's hairbrush and pronounced them similar. The bad news was that all those hairs had, inexplicably, been destroyed on September 15, 1975, according to records in the FBI's Kansas City office, after the FBI had closed its case, lacking further jurisdiction. The retired FBI agents and forensic laboratory examiner shared Cordts's surprise and disappointment after learning of the inadvertent destruction of those items of evidence. Each FBI agent who had worked on the case had strongly believed

John Henry Horton was responsible for Liz Wilson's death. And, depending on future judicial rulings, if the case reached prosecution, the forensic examiner's case notes, reports, and worksheets regarding the missing hairs were available in FBI laboratory files, if the retired forensic examiner would be permitted to testify without the actual hairs over strong defense objections, no doubt, if at all.

The problem of the missing hairs wasn't the only forensic challenge to eventual successful prosecution that Shipps and Cordts identified. In January 1975, the skull and thirteen bones found in Lenexa, Kansas, had been identified as the remains of Liz Wilson, based on the opinion of Liz's dentist in Prairie Village, who had compared the teeth in the skull to his dental records and X-rays for Liz that confirmed her identity. Cordts learned, however, that the dentist had died ten years ago. Attempts to locate Liz's dental records from the dentist who had taken over that dental practice, the deceased dentist's widow, and the Kansas State Dental Board were unsuccessful. The records were presumed to have been destroyed. Successful prosecution of Liz's killer could depend on the introduction of evidence in trial proving that those remains buried in Humboldt, Iowa, in 1975, were indeed those of Liz Wilson. Without the dentist and the dental records, there might be a problem.

DNA evidence, unknown in 1974 and 1975, could save the day now, the officers decided. Cordts had obtained DNA swabs from Liz's parents when they were interviewed in Arizona, just in case their DNA would be needed. He contacted the Wilsons and requested their permission to exhume Liz's remains in Iowa and to submit the skeletal remains to DNA analysis for comparison to the DNA of the Wilsons. They quickly gave Cordts their blessing for such action. Cordts traveled to Humboldt, Iowa, and coordinated the exhumation process. He then transported the remains to the offices of Dr. Erik Mitchell, a forensic pathologist in Topeka. Dr. Mitchell examined the skeletal remains with Attorney General Phill Kline, Larry Thomas, and Brad Cordts in attendance, and he selected appropriate samples for DNA comparison. Within weeks it was forensically determined that the remains were those of a female offspring of Al and Kay Wilson, namely Liz Wilson. Another prosecutorial hurdle was successfully cleared.

Meanwhile, in 2002 and 2003, other potential trial witnesses were identified and interviewed, or in some cases reinterviewed. During the summer of 2002, Shipps and Cordts twice reinterviewed the woman who had been the fifteen-year-old tennis player confronted by Horton outside the school with a bizarre story about needing someone to stand on his shoulders to turn off a water spigot at the school. This important witness, now forty-four years of age, walked the route she had taken from the tennis courts near the pool on

July 7, 1974, accompanied by Shipps and Cordts. She showed them the actual spot by the school where the custodian had spoken to her and her girlfriend. The officers reasoned that the confrontation occurred only a few minutes before Liz Wilson was abducted near that same location. The woman had seen John Wilson running by the school only a minute or two after she hurried away from her strange encounter with Horton. She recalled that Horton had no visible scratches or cuts on his face during her conversation with him. She identified a photograph of Horton in a 1974 photo display as the custodian who had engaged her in the strange conversation the evening Liz Wilson disappeared. Her friend, with whom she had been playing tennis and who had also been present during the incident with Horton, corroborated her friend's story and the photograph identification. Neither woman knew the photograph they individually selected was of John Henry Horton. They only knew the photograph depicted the custodian who confronted them outside Shawnee Mission East High School the evening of July 7, 1974.

It cannot be said that Sharen Rebecca Horton was expecting such a knock on her door, because the visit clearly surprised, shocked, and then angered her. On August 7, 2002, Senior Special Agent Ray Lundin of the KBI and Detective Darrell Thompson of the Prairie Village Police Department stood on the front porch of the Hortons' rural residence northwest of Canton, Missouri. The color drained from her face when Lundin identified himself and his partner and informed her that they were there to discuss the 1974 homicide of Liz Wilson in Kansas. Surprise and shock quickly gave way to anger after Sharen Horton stammered, "I wasn't even there." Then she demanded, repeatedly and unsuccessfully, an explanation as to how Kansas law enforcement had found them after so many years, indicating that the Hortons had made an effort to keep their whereabouts to themselves. Her anger never subsided during the brief discussion, which could not be described as an interview. She continued to express intense dislike of all law enforcement, but especially Kansas law enforcement. She complained that Kansas law enforcement and the Liz Wilson case had caused her husband to lose his job at the Kansas school and caused her family to go hungry. She had no love for either Kansas police or Kansas itself. She insisted that her husband of thirty years was innocent. She trusted him completely, she claimed. When she paused to take a breath, Lundin used the opportunity to ask her about her husband's arrest in Callao. That question also surprised her and, clearly flustered, she attributed that arrest to "politics" and the fact that her husband had "ruffled political feathers" in Callao. Her husband was no window peeper, or killer, or child molester, she maintained. He was simply the victim of incompetent Kansas police. Lundin didn't get the chance to point out that Callao was in Missouri, not Kansas, because Sharen Horton terminated any further discussion at that point.

In his usual, understated style, Lundin, the KBI's quiet, exceptional investigator, interrogator, and hostage negotiator, best summarized the "interview" of Sharen Horton in the last sentence of his report of their meeting: "The interview of Sharen Horton was very limited due to the uncooperative spirit she displayed toward the investigative effort being made in this case."[1]

At the same time that Lundin and Thompson were confronting the uncooperative Sharen Horton at the Hortons' rural residence, Thomas and Cordts, according to plan, were in Canton, Missouri, in their parked car next to John Henry Horton's car in his employer's parking lot, waiting for the suspect to emerge from work. At 4:10 P.M. on August 7, 2002, Horton walked from the building to his car. When the two KBI agents got out of their car to confront him, he was as surprised, if not as angry, as his wife had been minutes before and a few miles away. Cordts told the nervous, surprised Horton that he and Thomas were from the KBI's Cold Case Squad. He further explained that the KBI and the Prairie Village Police Department had reopened the Liz Wilson murder investigation. Since Horton had been a major player in the original investigation, Cordts explained, they wanted to reinterview him about Liz and the events of July 7, 1974.

Horton's first response was, "Liz Wilson? Liz Wilson? Oh, that's been a long time ago. I can't remember anything about that." However, he expressed a willingness to talk to them and tell them whatever he could remember. The KBI agents told Horton they had a room at the Holiday Inn across the river in Quincy, Illinois, where the interview could be conducted more privately than in his workplace parking lot. Horton agreed that he was anxious to leave the parking lot. He reiterated that he would speak to them, but he claimed he had something he needed to do at the American Legion in Canton before he could visit with them in Illinois. Accordingly, Thomas and Cordts followed him to the American Legion Club. No one else was present when they joined him inside the club. He told them he had telephoned his wife and informed her of the agents' request to interview him in a motel in Illinois. She was en route, he explained.

Within minutes, as the agents and Horton engaged in light conversation, Sharen Horton walked into the club carrying a small child, presumably a grandchild. She was still angry from her own earlier brief encounter with the Kansas investigators, and she expressed her displeasure about the presence of Cordts and Thomas in Canton as well. She confronted the agents and criticized them for "stirring up this case again." Horton sat quietly as his wife vented anew her lack of respect for law enforcement. She complained that the

Liz Wilson case had nearly ruined their lives. Her innocent husband had lost a good job at the school in Kansas, and they had been forced to move from the area because of the bad publicity. Eventually, Horton's wife calmed down and she ended her second tirade of the day. Then, in front of the agents, the pair openly discussed whether they needed an attorney. They decided they did not. Thomas invited Sharen Horton to accompany them to the motel in Quincy and wait there for her husband while the agents interviewed him. She declined the invitation and decided instead to return home with the child. Horton would leave his car at the American Legion and ride with the agents to Quincy, and they would later drive him back to Canton following the interview.

Thus it was that a shaken John Henry Horton found himself in a room at the Holiday Inn in Quincy with Cordts and later, both Cordts and Larry Thomas. Horton agreed that the interview could be videotaped. Although it wasn't a custodial interrogation requiring a waiver of *Miranda* rights, the agents thought that there was a strong possibility that Horton might confess to his violation of Liz Wilson. Therefore, to be safe, Cordts advised Horton of his rights to remain silent and to be represented by an attorney, pursuant to the *Miranda v. Arizona* Supreme Court decision of 1966. Horton waived his rights and signed the *Miranda* card at 5:50 P.M. Before the interview commenced, however, the nervous Horton asked to use the motel room's restroom.

Horton then stated that his only involvement in the Liz Wilson case was that he was a janitor at the Shawnee Mission East High School, near where she had disappeared. He advised that he became a suspect because he was the only custodian on duty that particular evening, working his usual 3:00 P.M. to 11:00 P.M. shift, and the investigators who interviewed him at his home the next day found "stuff" in his car that they thought had been stolen at the school. He identified the "stuff" as primarily school athletic trophies he had recovered from a school trash bin, obviously thrown out by school officials. He emphasized that he was a "scrounger" all his life. He often went through people's trash, looking for "stuff." He was a "scrounger," not a thief, he insisted, just as he had said to other officers in 1974. When Cordts pressed him and pointed out that the "stuff" taken from his car the day after Liz's disappearance didn't include any athletic trophies, at least as reflected in the original investigation file, but rather a butcher knife taken from the school's home economics room and bottles of ether, chloroform, and sulfuric acid stolen from the school's chemistry laboratory, Horton did what he would do throughout the interview: he fell silent for a minute or two and then said he didn't recall, and/or he couldn't explain.

When Cordts asked what he actually recalled about the circumstances of Liz's abduction, Horton replied that all he knew was that she had been killed and her body had been found in Kansas. He recalled that agents of the FBI and detectives from the Prairie Village Police Department had interviewed him the day following the little girl's disappearance and then again, months later, after her remains had been recovered. He had cooperated with them but was unable to help them because he knew nothing. He had consented, in 1974 and 1975, to a search of his car, polygraph examinations, interviews, and even investigative hypnosis by an FBI psychiatrist, because he had nothing to hide, he emphasized. He had also agreed to be photographed. In return, he noted, he lost his job at the school because of the school property found in his car, and he eventually had to move from the Kansas City area because everyone thought he was a child molester or worse.

After reciting his past employments and past places of residence (leaving out Callao, Missouri, where he was arrested for window peeping), Horton asked to go the restroom again at 6:20 P.M.. When he returned to resume the interview, Cordts asked Horton if he was okay, noting that he seemed very nervous and somewhat uncomfortable. Horton explained he had glaucoma and might need to eat soon. Cordts assured him that food could be brought to him. Horton declined the offer of food and said he could continue.

In response to background questions, Horton stated that he had been born in New York City and went to high school there, although he later received a GED in the military and did not graduate from high school. He said he was in the U.S. Army from 1970 to 1973, had one AWOL violation and had never served in combat or anywhere outside the United States, contrary to boastful claims he had made at various times to different people through the years. He said that, following his 1973 military discharge, he and Sharen lived briefly in North Carolina. He worked at Kmart and then at Burlington Mills before moving to Independence, Missouri, and finding work as a custodian at Shawnee Mission East High School across the state line in Kansas. He acknowledged that a sixteen-year-old niece, Cindy Owens, lived with them briefly in their small, crowded home in Independence. He made her leave, however, when it was discovered she had cookies, chips, and pop stashed in her room and was not sharing with his wife and son. She moved out and, soon thereafter, gave birth to a baby boy, he recalled. He denied any sexual improprieties with Cindy Owens.

Regarding the events of July 7, 1974, he insisted that, to his knowledge, he never saw Liz Wilson or her brother. He claimed to not even recall there was a municipal swimming pool close to the high school, even though the investigation had determined he was known to spend time at the pool while on duty as a school custodian, apparently to watch the girls in their swim attire. Cordts pressed him with the information that other custodians had noted that Horton regularly took his work breaks and lunch breaks at the pool during the summer months and sat in the bleachers, openly admitting that he liked to watch the girls in their scanty swimsuits. Horton denied those claims, insisting he recalled no nearby swimming pool and claiming he always ate his meals in the school's janitors' room.

He also claimed that July 7, 1974, was one of those rare days when he didn't eat the lunch he had brought from home. He recalled that he had brought chicken but had decided he was not in the mood for it. Thus, because he had a little money on him, another rare occasion, he recalled, he drove somewhere for a sandwich in his unreliable 1969 Ford Fairlane. The car broke down on the way back to the school and, consequently, he was more than two hours late returning to work, having to repair his car in a grocery store parking lot. All that transpired, he insisted, during the time the agents claimed Liz Wilson disappeared.

At 7:17 P.M., Brad Cordts told Horton he had another idea to refresh Horton's memory, and the interview was moved to an adjoining room that Cordts had already cleverly set up. But first, Horton had to use the restroom again. In the other room was not only another video camera but also items of evidence from the case. The actual bottles of chloroform and ether stolen from the school in 1974 had been strategically placed. There was a photograph of the butcher knife taken from the school's home economics room and found with the ether and the chloroform in Horton's car. There were crime scene diagrams prominently placed in the room depicting the high school, the school grounds, and swimming pool, and the various routes across the school grounds of different witnesses who had been interviewed. There were also more aerial photographs of the entire area.

Horton appeared to be overwhelmed when he first entered the second motel room and saw the display of evidentiary material. He sat down and looked around the room for at least a minute in silence. When he finally spoke, he observed that the school's trophies he allegedly took from a school trash dumpster were missing. Cordts reiterated that he knew nothing about any such sports trophies being involved in the case. Horton then recalled that he had definitely found the bottles of chloroform and ether in a school dumpster, like the phantom trophies. He insisted he did not steal the chemicals from the school's chemistry laboratory, despite prior admissions.

Cordts continued to press Horton for his best recollection of his activities on July 7, 1974. Horton recalled that he arrived at school that day to start his shift at 1:00 P.M. Cordts corrected him. He had clocked in that day at 2:51 P.M., according to school records. "OK," responded Horton. He then said that he went to work inside the school. Again, Cordts corrected him. No, Horton had talked to a young female jogger outside the school not too long after arriving. He had asked her if she had seen another custodian, even though he knew no other custodians were on duty at that time. And, Cordts told Horton, they knew that at 5:00 P.M. that day he had visited with some female cheerleaders outside the school. Horton could not recall such events, he said. But, after further questions from Cordts, Horton stopped denying he had stolen the butcher knife and the bottles of chemicals from the school. He then maintained he did not know why he took the knife. Such theft was "weird," he admitted. He then acknowledged the chemicals came from a locked cabinet. He simply didn't recall breaking into the cabinet. He recalled, however, placing the bottles of chemicals, the knife, and the mysterious school trophies in two canvas bags and, eventually, in his car. Yet he insisted he had no recollection of conversations with kids outside the school that afternoon or evening. Those kids had identified him in the photograph as the custodian with whom they had had a conversation, bearing in mind that no other custodian was working at that particular time. But, he said, if the kids said they did talk to him, then it must have happened.

Cordts asked him if he recalled the attractive seventeen-year-old female tennis player to whom he had called out as she walked near the school, asking if she had seen another custodian. Then, Cordts continued, Horton had explained to her that he needed help turning off a very high water spigot. Horton had asked her, Cordts insisted, that since he couldn't find the nonexistent second custodian, to get on his shoulders so she could turn off the water for him. Horton thought for a time. He didn't recall such an incident, he claimed, but he thought if the girl said it happened, it probably happened. He admitted there were no elevated water spigots at Shawnee Mission East High School. Cordts then added that a tennis-playing female companion of that girl had arrived during that particular conversation. She had confirmed that the conversation Horton now described as "weird" had taken place. Horton said, again, "OK." Then Cordts pointed out that both those young attractive girls insisted that incident occurred immediately outside the school at 7:20 P.M. on Sunday, July 7, 1974. "OK," Horton acknowledged. Cordts displayed to Horton photographs of Horton taken on July 8, 1974, depicting scratches on his arms, back, forehead, thigh, and behind an ear. Horton said he did not recall the scratches or how they came to be on his body. The KBI agent also pointed out that the incident with the two tennis players, at 7:20 P.M., occurred at approximately the same time Liz Wilson would have walked home, past the school, from the pool. "OK," agreed Horton. But he never saw her, he insisted.

Cordts pressed Horton again. Not only had Horton seen Liz Wilson, he had killed her and stuffed her body in a canvas bag in his car. He had scratches on him that night and the next day because Liz Wilson had fought as he strangled and raped, or attempted to rape, the little girl. He assaulted her in the school and killed her because she was a witness, or Horton had used too much chloroform in his assault and that chemical overdose had killed Liz. At first Horton didn't respond. Then he denied Cordts's allegations. Why did Horton go to an employment agency the day after Liz Wilson's disappearance expressing a desire for a new job? Why was hair similar to that of Liz Wilson found in his car on July 8, 1974? Why did he strangle her instead of using the butcher knife? After those rapid-fire questions went unanswered, Cordts told Horton there was no mystery regarding who killed Liz. The only unresolved questions related to how and why. After a long period of silence, Horton replied, "I didn't do it."

Cordts pointed out that Horton's lifelong reputation included a well-known fondness for young girls and improper advances toward them. Even recently in Callao, Missouri, Horton had confessed to the arresting officer that he was physically attracted to young girls. Showing the most emotion of the evening, Horton denied making that statement to any officer, and he emphatically denied stalking girls in Callao or window peeping on any of them.

Cordts made a final plea to Horton, pointing out that the Wilson family needed some degree of closure. They needed to know why and how Horton killed their thirteen-year-old daughter on July 7, 1974, on her way home. Horton paused and muttered, "I don't know what to tell you."

Thomas then speculated that Horton had simply panicked after sexually assaulting her. Horton did not respond. Thomas asked Horton if he remembered being caught by Sharen with his hand down his niece Christine's panties when Christine, Cindy's sister, was fifteen years old. Horton laughed nervously and then shook his head negatively, without speaking. That bit of new information had been relayed to them earlier in the day by the other agents.

At 9:05 P.M., Horton suddenly said he was going to have his wife get him an attorney. The interview was promptly terminated. Thomas offered to call an attorney for him at that time. Horton declined, saying he preferred to have his wife select one. Horton was then transported back to his car at the American Legion Club in Canton, Missouri, arriving at 9:35 P.M. The dejected KBI agents later agreed there had been occasions that evening when they believed John Henry Horton was very close to confessing to the murder of Liz Wilson.

On the same day, August 7, 2002, that Lundin and Thompson contacted Sharen Horton and Cordts and Thomas interviewed John Henry Horton, KBI Agents Bill Halvorsen and Angie Wilson located Cynthia (Cindy) Owens, the niece who had been living with the Hortons at the time of Liz Wilson's disappearance. Owens, sixteen years of age when she resided briefly with the Hortons in Independence, Missouri, was now living near Keytes-ville, Missouri, with a female roommate. The agents explained their pres-ence and Horton's niece agreed to be interviewed about her recollection of the events surrounding the story of Liz Wilson. She advised that she had not seen the Hortons in more than two years and acknowledged that her mother was John Horton's sister. She recalled the Horton household as one that would not have won any Good Housekeeping awards. The small home was seldom clean, with dirty clothes and dirty dishes everywhere, even though Sharen Horton did not work outside the home. Owens's room was a makeshift space in the attic. She noted that she "hung out" with John more than with Sharen or Horton's young son. She stated that she often rode on Horton's motorcycle with him and was aware that Horton occasionally stole chloroform from the school with which to "get high" and sometimes sold drugs on a small scale. She suspected him at the time of burglarizing a veterinarian's clinic in their Independence neighborhood to get drugs to sell. She also suspected him of window peeping in their neighborhood in the evenings, although he claimed he was simply running for exercise during his frequent late evening absences from home.

Owens denied that Horton was ever sexually inappropriate with her, but thanks to the rapport that Halvorsen and Wilson established with her, she made their day with the unanticipated admissions that her own sister had confided in her recently that Horton had been inappropriate with her when they were young girls. Owens explained to the agents that her sister, Chris-tine, had told her only that Horton had touched her inappropriately, provid-ing no details of the incident. Owens furnished her sister's married name and current address to the interviewers.

Then Owens gave the name of a young girl, Joy, who had lived across the street from the Hortons during Owens's brief stay with them. She de-scribed Joy as fourteen years of age at the time and Owens's only friend in the neighborhood. Prior to Liz Wilson's disappearance, Horton had one eve-ning invited Joy and Owens to accompany him to a nearby golf course to "get high." The trio walked to the golf course and sat under a tree. Horton produced chloroform in a bottle and gave some to Joy on a rag or paper towel. At Horton's insistence, Joy sniffed it and then passed out. Owens denied she herself breathed any chloroform and denied any further recollection of what subsequently happened to her unconscious friend.

Owens did recall the night of Liz Wilson's disappearance. She said that Horton returned home from work that night looking shaken and as though "he had seen a ghost." He went straight to bed without eating anything and without visiting with Sharen or with her. The next morning several police officers appeared at the Horton home. They took hair samples from Horton, his wife, their son, and Owens, and searched Horton's car, finding bottles of chloroform and other items that Owens could not recall. In recalling the allegations against her uncle at that time, Owens now speculated that maybe Horton used the chloroform on Liz Wilson and accidentally killed her with it. Owens advised that she could not recall why she moved out of the Horton home, except that she was asked to move out by both Horton and Sharen.

Before Halvorsen and Wilson interviewed Owens, they had earlier that day interviewed her mother, Horton's sister, in Brookfield, Missouri. She had furnished the addresses for her daughters, Cindy and Christine, who lived in Purdin, Missouri. Her mother had told the agents that Cindy, following her eviction from the Hortons' home, had given birth to a baby boy on June 1, 1975, in Oklahoma. The mother explained that she understood the baby's father was the friend of a neighbor girl living across the street from the Hortons. The baby was given up for adoption. The agents had elected to not share their knowledge of the baby with Cindy.

Halvorsen and Wilson quickly tracked down Joy, the friend of Cindy Owens living across the street from the Hortons on July 7, 1974, to ask her about the chloroform incident on the golf course described by Cindy Owens. The interview took place on August 8, 2002 in the KBI's Overland Park office and lasted less than an hour. When Halvorsen and Wilson first mentioned John Horton to Joy, she immediately broke down, became emotional, and tearfully admitted that he had sexually molested her on a golf course near her childhood home in Independence, Missouri. She noted that she had not spoken of the incident since it happened. She recalled that in the summer of 1974 she was fourteen years old, living with her divorced mother. At that time, the Hortons moved into a house across the street with Cindy. She quickly became friends with Cindy, whom she described as a "tomboy" with no boyfriend and with whom she frequently smoked marijuana that summer. During one summer evening, probably in June 1974, Cindy and John Horton invited her to walk with them to a golf course near their neighborhood. On arrival, Horton produced a small, brown glass bottle containing, he said, chloroform. He also had two cloth rags. On one rag he poured chloroform, handed the rag to Joy, and told her to sniff it, explaining that it would make her feel good and get her "high." She sniffed it, didn't like the odor, and told Horton she didn't want to breathe it. He pushed it back toward her face and insisted. She sniffed the rag, reluctantly, and immediately passed out. When she first awoke, her jeans and panties were pulled down and Horton was molesting her with his hand. She tried to protest and move but passed out again. The next thing she knew she was sitting up, with her jeans and panties pulled up, and vomiting violently. When she was able to regain her composure and balance, the trio walked back to their respective homes in silence. She never spoke to Horton or Cindy again. And she reiterated that she never spoke of the incident to anyone, not even her mother. She felt humiliation, shame, and embarrassment ever since. She also said she did not know whether Cindy was a participant in the assault on her, another victim herself, or simply an observer.

Joy recalled the Liz Wilson case and stated she was positive the golf course incident occurred before Liz Wilson's disappearance. She also noted the golf course incident occurred quite late in the evening, after the course was closed for the day. Joy was interviewed again on January 14, 2003, by Cordts in a much longer, less emotional interview. Her powerful testimony would clearly be of tremendous value to the prosecution of John Henry Horton, if permitted in court.

Other potentially powerful evidence was obtained in KBI interviews of Christine, Cindy's sister, on August 7 and September 24, 2002. She confirmed Cindy's suggestion to Halvorsen and Wilson that when she was fifteen years old she had received unwanted and inappropriate sexual attention from her uncle. She explained that one night when the Hortons were visiting her family's home, she was awakened in her bed to find Horton kneeling next to her bed with his hand inside her panties. The room was dark and she was awakened by Sharen Horton's voice asking John Horton what he was doing. She said the Hortons left her room and she returned to sleep, never discussing the incident with anyone except her sister. While she always suspected Horton might have molested Cindy while her sister lived with the Hortons, Christine said she was fairly sure John Horton was not the father of Cindy's baby, born in June 1975, because "the baby looked nothing like John."

In addition to the productive KBI interview of August 7, Cindy Owens was again interviewed by Halvorsen and Wilson on August 8, and by Halvorsen and Cordts on August 22, 2002. Owens also telephoned Special Agent Wilson with additional information regarding her uncle on at least one occasion. The third and final interview, by Halvorsen and Cordts, was held at the Missouri State Highway Patrol's office in Macon and lasted four hours. It appeared Cindy Owens would be one of the prosecution's most important and most willing witnesses against her uncle, although she steadfastly denied any sexual impropriety by him toward her.

During the late evening of Wednesday, October 14, 2003, a year later, Cordts and Thomas confronted John Henry Horton once again. Cordts and Thomas, along with officers of the Prairie Village Police Department, the Lewis County (Missouri) Sheriff's Office, and the Missouri State Highway Patrol, served an arrest warrant on Horton at his rural mobile home residence in Lewis County outside Canton, where the Hortons had resided since

1995. Technically, the arrest warrant was served on him in his backyard after he had crawled out a rear window carrying his shoes and a cell phone, attempting to run from the residence as the uncooperative Sharen Horton argued with officers at the front door in a stalling tactic.

Later, at 10:30 P.M. on October 14, 2003, at the Lewis County Sheriff's Office in Monticello, Missouri, Sgt. David Hall of the Missouri State Highway Patrol, in the presence of Cordts and Thomas, read the Kansas charges to Horton and gave him a copy of the Kansas complaint. The complaint, filed October 14, 2003, charged that Horton, on or about July 7, 1974, in Johnson County, Kansas, kidnapped thirteen-year-old Liz Wilson to sexually assault her for his own sexual desires and, thereafter, feloniously killed her in the course of that kidnapping and sexual assault. Hall explained that it was first-degree murder and that Kansas had set a one million dollar bond on Horton. Cordts and Thomas noted that as Sgt. Hall read and explained the Kansas charges, Horton seemed neither surprised nor confused about any of it. The Missouri officer also explained the extradition process to Horton, whose only comments at that time related to his complaint that he had injured his back attempting to escape out his rear window and that he needed his medications.

Because he complained that his back was hurting too much to talk and because he said that he probably should talk to an attorney, Cordts and Thomas made no effort to interview Horton the evening of the arrest at the Missouri jail. Horton did volunteer that it had been stupid to jump out the window, having landed on his back on the cement patio beneath the window. He suggested he might want to talk to Cordts and Thomas the following morning, depending on how his back felt. The agents ensured that Lewis County Sheriff Dave Parrish was informed about Horton's claims of back pain and request for medications that evening.

The next morning, October 15, 2003, at approximately 8:45 A.M., Cordts met again with Horton at the Lewis County jail. Horton said his back was still hurting too much for an interview. He might like to talk later if the pain lessened, he said. Thereafter, Horton was taken before Missouri Circuit Court Judge Fred Westhoff. Judge Westhoff again read and explained the Kansas charges to Horton in the state district court in Monticello. Once again, Horton seemed neither surprised nor confused, and he readily waived extradition, agreeing to be returned to Kansas to face the charges filed against him.

Following the extradition hearing, deputy sheriffs took Horton to a Canton physician, who declared Horton fit to travel in an automobile to Kansas. Therefore, Cordts and Thomas proceeded toward Olathe, Kansas, and the Johnson County jail, with Horton in the backseat of a KBI car. They left Monticello a little before 1:00 P.M. on October 15, 2003. Shortly after pulling out of town, Cordts asked Horton if he felt well enough then to discuss the case. He agreed he felt better, but added that he had decided he probably should speak with an attorney prior to discussing the case with the agents. No questions relating to Liz Wilson were asked of Horton until about 4:00 P.M., as the KBI car pulled into the eastern outskirts of Kansas City, Missouri. Then, a final time, Thomas asked Horton if he wished to be taken directly to the Johnson County jail in Olathe for booking into jail, or if he would prefer to stop by the Prairie Village Police Department and speak to the agents about anything. Thomas reminded Horton of his rights to remain silent and to not speak to them without an attorney. Horton replied that he probably should speak to an attorney, so they might as well transport him directly to the jail. He was therefore taken to the county jail in Olathe. He was booked into jail on a charge of first-degree murder by Sgt. Craig Caster and Officer Kyle Shipps of the Prairie Village Police Department.

Less than two years after the official reopening of the unsolved Liz Wilson homicide case, the individual believed responsible was lodged securely in jail under a one million dollar bond. Chief of Police Chuck Grover, at a press conference on October 15, 2003, praised his own officers, the KBI Cold Case Squad, and the cooperation of Missouri authorities. Chief Grover reserved special praise for his own Kyle Shipps and the KBI's Brad Cordts, noting that their efforts since the case was reopened filled nine large volumes of information and witness interviews.

On Thursday, October 16, 2003, Horton made his first appearance in court before Kansas District Judge Steve Tatum in Olathe. Judge Tatum explained the charges and Horton's rights and appointed the public defender's office to defend the accused killer of Lizabeth Ann Wilson. No plea was requested by the court at that time and the next court appearance was scheduled for October 23, at which time the public defender's office formally entered a plea of not guilty in behalf of the bespectacled, balding Horton. His preliminary hearing was scheduled for February 17, 2004, and he was continued to be held in custody in lieu of the one million dollar bond.

The preliminary hearing, before Judge James Franklin Davis, began as scheduled on February 17 and ended two days later. When Johnson County Assistant District Attorney Rick Guinn had presented his last witness, Judge Davis ruled that the prosecution had established sufficient probable cause to try Horton for the first-degree murder of Liz Wilson on July 7, 1974.

Guinn's prosecutorial theory in the preliminary hearing, based primarily on the testimony of Shipps and Cordts, was that Horton had used physical force or deception to lure Liz Wilson into the school. He had intended to sexually assault her inside the school, but the chloroform he used to subdue her killed her instead, if he didn't actually strangle her during the assault. Guinn kept the witness stand full during the three-day preliminary hearing. Ten witnesses testified, including the young female tennis player, now forty-four years of age, who related the story she had told investigators about being confronted by Horton that Sunday evening outside the school, when he asked her if she had seen the nonexistent custodian and told her he needed help turning off an elevated water spigot. A former school administrator then testified there were no water spigots at the school that would have required a person to stand on the shoulders of another individual to operate it.

The young neighbor of Horton in Independence, now forty-three years of age, testified about going to the golf course with Horton and his niece, breathing chloroform at Horton's insistence, and waking up to find Horton sexually molesting her. She told the court she kept the incident a secret, out of embarrassment and humiliation, and especially because she didn't want her mother to know.

John Wilson, Liz's brother, testified about her strange, sudden disappearance and the events that he recalled from that tragic Sunday evening.

The public defender, Michael McCulloch, argued unsuccessfully that the prosecution's case was woefully circumstantial and based primarily on the single point that John Henry Horton was at Shawnee Mission East High School the evening Liz Wilson disappeared somewhere near the school. He complained, in vain, that there was no evidence of how she died, or that chloroform had even been used in her alleged abduction, or that she had been taken into the school, or that she had been sexually assaulted. After Judge Davis's ruling, McCulloch entered a plea of not guilty for Horton. Trial was scheduled for September 20, 2004.

On April 12, 2004, a suppression hearing was held before Judge Davis. Three witnesses testified, including Cordts, and Judge Davis ruled admissible all statements made by Horton to law enforcement officers in 1974, 2002, and 2003, as well as the evidence from the search of Horton's car on July 8, 1974. Another hearing for pretrial motions was scheduled for August 30, 2004, and the trial date was reconfirmed for September 20.

Despite last-minute defense motions for a continuance, the long-awaited trial began on schedule on Monday, September 20, 2004, in Olathe, the county seat of Johnson County, Kansas, in Johnson County District Court, Division 6, before District Judge James Franklin Davis. Assistant District Attorneys Rick Guinn and Brent Venneman of the Johnson County district attorney's office represented the state and Liz Wilson. Deputy District Public Defenders Michael McCulloch and Carol Cline represented the former high school custodian charged with first-degree murder in the abduction of Liz Wilson thirty years earlier.

Twelve jurors and three alternates were selected in a surprisingly short amount of time the first morning. Two rows of seats in the courtroom were reserved each day for the Wilson family. More than a dozen family members were in attendance daily, usually joined by several family friends and former Prairie Village neighbors. My wife and I were able to attend three of the trial's six days and heard much of the critical testimony on which the state's highly circumstantial case was based. We were pleased to meet Al and Kay Wilson, John Wilson, and most of their supportive family and friends, as well as Rick Guinn and Brent Venneman. Only Sharen Horton was present in support of the defendant, insofar as I could tell, at least on the days my wife and I were in the courtroom.

With a paucity of direct evidence and armed primarily with only obvious guilt and an impressive array of circumstantial evidence, the prosecution attempted to prove a pattern of behavior on the part of Horton: window peeping, inappropriate attention to young girls, sexual molestation, use of chloroform, lying, claiming car trouble, and so on. Such documentation of his modus operandi, it was hoped, would lead to the jury concluding that Horton had assaulted Liz Wilson using chloroform, after luring or forcing her into the school between 7:00 and 8:00 P.M. on the evening of July 7, 1974, thirty years and two months earlier. If convicted, Horton would be sentenced under the applicable Kansas law in 1974. Therefore, no death sentence could be imposed. The maximum sentence possible would be life imprisonment with no chance of parole for fifteen years. But first the state would have to prove its highly circumstantial case beyond a reasonable doubt to the jury, some of whom were not yet born when Liz was killed.

Al Wilson and John Wilson led off in an impressive roster of prosecution witnesses, as Guinn methodically and masterfully presented the state's case, ably assisted by Venneman. The prosecutorial witnesses included the famous Dr. Bill Bass of Tennessee (a former University of Kansas professor), who had corroborated identification of Liz's remains; retired FBI agents who had worked on the case in 1974; the retired FBI forensic hair examiner; KBI Agents Brad Cordts, Angie Wilson, and Bill Halvorsen; two of the cheerleaders and both female tennis players confronted by Horton at the school that fateful evening; retired Prairie Village officers; Joy, the golf course victim; Horton's nieces; his fellow custodians; and others. For five days there was a constant parade of prosecution witnesses to the witness stand.

The witnesses told of various incidents in which Horton had falsely claimed car trouble to approach young girls. The hair examiner was permitted to testify, based on his notes and the old FBI laboratory file, about his "microscopically . . . similar" finding years earlier, despite the inadvertent destruction of the hairs themselves, during a routine FBI clerical purge of closed files in Kansas City. Witnesses testified about Horton's apparent propensity to window peeping and an unnatural interest in young girls.

The only real setback for the state was that Cindy Owens retracted many of her incriminating statements to the KBI about her uncle; she seemed nervous and fearful throughout her testimony and ended up being more of a reluctant, hostile witness than a willing prosecution witness. She even accused her KBI interviewers of coercion, but then could not explain her voluntary telephone call to Agent Wilson to provide additional information or her willingness to be interviewed by the KBI on three occasions. The prosecution rested at midday on Friday, September 24. Judge Davis ruled that the defense could start its case on Monday.

On Monday morning, hoping that the jury agreed that the state had not made its case beyond a reasonable doubt, the defense put two witnesses on the stand and rested. Following his instructions, Judge Davis gave the case to the jury.

Justice for Liz Wilson, albeit woefully tardy, came at 4:30 P.M. on Monday, September 27, 2004. The jury, after less than two hours of deliberation, returned with the verdict for which the Wilsons and so many others had been hoping. John Henry Horton was declared guilty of first-degree murder in the abduction and death of thirteen-year-old Liz Wilson on July 7, 1974. The jury had agreed with the prosecution that the only logical conclusion, beyond a reasonable doubt, based on the totality of circumstances surrounding the abduction, was that Horton was responsible. Judge Davis scheduled posttrial motions for November 19.

The front-page headline of the *Kansas City Star* the next day proclaimed, "Jury Finds Horton Guilty." Veteran *Star* crime reporter Tony Rizzo perhaps summed up the situation best: "Technological advances such as DNA matches have allowed police to solve a number of 'cold cases' in recent years. But it was old-fashioned police work . . . that provided the break in this case."[2] Al Wilson and John Wilson emotionally embraced Shipps and Cordts in the courtroom following the verdict. "They never forgot about our sister," said John. "They're such good people."[3]

The Wilson family was not alone in its praise of Cordts and Shipps. The Kansas Association of Chiefs of Police, in its annual Kansas Law Enforcement Awards Banquet in Wichita on May 21, 2004, long before the trial and verdict, honored the pair "for their professional determination and dedication to Liz Wilson and Liz's family" and described their investigative efforts up to that point as a textbook example of how to reopen and investigate a cold case.

I commended the entire "KBI John Henry Horton team" in a communication dated September 30, 2004. To Larry Thomas, Brad Cordts, Ray Lundin, Bill Halvorsen, Angie Wilson, Jeff Muckenthaler, and Katie Schuetz, I wrote, "I wish to commend and thank each of you for your individual and collective contributions to the arrest and successful prosecution of Liz Wilson's abductor and killer. . . . I believe this case to be one of the KBI's most important investigations in the past ten years and I very much admire and appreciate what you did."

The Metropolitan Chiefs and Sheriffs Association, at its annual officer-awards luncheon in Kansas City, Missouri, on November 10, 2004, also presented awards to Shipps and Cordts for their investigative efforts.

In a letter to his local state legislators on January 4, 2005, Prairie Village Chief of Police Chuck Grover urged strong consideration of the KBI's budget concerns in their legislative deliberations. Chief Grover wrote of the Liz Wilson homicide case, "It is very clear to me that without the assistance of the KBI's Cold Case Squad this case would probably still be unsolved. I would ask that in your deliberations of granting resources to state agencies you keep in mind the valuable assistance this state agency provides to local and county government on an every day basis."[4]

Judge James Franklin Davis duly addressed all post-trial motions on November 19 and scheduled Horton's sentencing for Thursday, January 20, 2005. On that day, Judge Davis sentenced John Henry Horton to life imprisonment with no chance of parole for fifteen years for the first-degree murder of Liz Wilson. It was the maximum sentence available to the judge based on Kansas law applicable in 1974.

More honors for Cordts and Shipps followed on February 19, 2005, in Kansas City, Missouri, when the Kansas City chapter of The Sons of the American Revolution honored them for their investigative and prosecutorial efforts on behalf of Liz, and in September 2005 when Kansan Bill Kurtis and the A&E Television Network featured the two investigators and their work on the cold case in a special program telecast nationally.

John Henry Horton was serving a life sentence; a conditional life sentence, to be sure, but a minimum of fifteen years without parole and, hopefully, life. Those responsible for that investigative and prosecutorial success had been duly recognized and honored. The Wilson family felt better. All was well. The joy of Horton's conviction and incarceration was, however, short-lived. On, Friday, February 2, 2007, we received the disappointing news that the Kansas Supreme Court, in a unanimous decision, had reversed Horton's conviction, ruling that the Johnson County District Court had erred in permitting the jury to hear the testimony about the golf course sexual molestation incident. The prosecution, of course, had used that testimony, developed by KBI investigators, as evidence of a "prior bad act," similar in nature to what Horton had done to Liz, we believed. The court held, however, that the golf course incident should not have been admitted into evidence because the prosecution failed to demonstrate sufficient similarity between Liz's disappearance and the golf course witness's claim of sexual assault. The only similarity between the two scenarios, said the court's opinion, was the girls' ages. The one girl had gone willingly to the golf course, noted the court, and the prosecution presented no evidence that Liz had inhaled chloroform or was sexually molested, the court said.

Cordts immediately telephoned Al Wilson in Arizona and John Wilson in Florida to give them the bad news before a reporter could. Both were, of course, shocked and angry. Al Wilson described the decision as "disgusting." Both, at first, angrily vowed not to return to Kansas for any retrial. But they called Cordts back a day or two later and pledged their availability for a second trial whenever needed. Whatever final justice for Liz required, John Wilson told his friend, he would be there, although John's mother's poor health would not permit her attendance again.

There was a footnote of considerable irony to the disappointing judicial development in the John Henry Horton saga. In the attorney general election in Kansas in November 2006, former Johnson County District Attorney Paul Morrison, a recently converted Democrat, soundly defeated the Republican incumbent Phill Kline. Following Kline's defeat, the Republican County Committee of Johnson County appointed Kline to fill the Johnson County District Attorney's position vacated by none other than Morrison. Thus in defeat, Kline received a significant pay raise while the victorious Morrison incurred a substantial reduction in salary, as the two in effect simply swapped jobs following an exceptionally rancorous election campaign. Moreover, Morrison took Assistant District Attorney Rick Guinn, Horton's lead prosecutor, with him to the attorney general's office in Topeka. Any retrial of Horton would have to proceed without Guinn.

The new district attorney, of course, was very familiar with the Horton case, Liz Wilson's homicide, and the KBI's participation in that investigation. A native of Johnson County himself, Phill Kline, following his own election to the office of attorney general in November 2002, had followed that KBI investigation closely. Larry Thomas and I had briefed Kline often about the investigative progress and prosecutorial status, and he had attended the skeletal autopsy in Topeka following the Iowa exhumation of Liz Wilson's remains to confirm her identification. He was an admirer of both Thomas and Cordts.

In January 2007, I had announced my intention to retire on June 1. One of my final important official acts as KBI director was to telephone Kline in his role as Johnson County District Attorney on Monday, February 5, 2007, and commit Cordts and any and all KBI resources to another investigation, if required, and to the anticipated retrial of John Henry Horton. Kline graciously accepted the offer, promising there would indeed be a retrial. But first, he intended, as a formality, to ask the Kansas Supreme Court to reconsider its surprising ruling of February 2, he informed me.

On March 28, 2007, following the Kansas Supreme Court's refusal to reconsider its decision, District Attorney Phill Kline filed a charge of first-degree murder, or, in the alternative, felony murder, against Horton. His incarceration was continued at the Norton Correctional Facility with a one million dollar bond.

During a three-day preliminary hearing starting August 6, 2007, before Johnson County District Judge James Franklin Davis, the prosecution prevailed, and Horton was bound over for a second trial, scheduled for February 25, 2008.

The prosecutors for the second trial would be Kline as well as Stephen Maxwell, the former assistant attorney general under Kline and now his deputy district attorney in Olathe. Judge Davis would again preside and the defense team would again be Michael McCulloch and Carol Cline.

Coordinating the retrial's investigative needs would, of course, be Cordts and Shipps. From August 2007, following the preliminary hearing, until the start of the second trial, on February 25, 2008, the two investigators were occupied with locating the prosecution's witnesses from the first trial, reviewing the trial transcript and the original interview reports, keeping the Wilson family advised of preparation efforts for the retrial, and meeting with prosecutors in pretrial strategy conferences. Cordts and Shipps learned that one of the original FBI agents involved in the 1974 investigation of Horton had died after he had testified in the 2004 trial. But they found two other retired FBI agents who had testified in the first trial that Horton was the only suspect they had developed in 1974 who had the opportunity to abduct and murder Liz Wilson at or near the Shawnee Mission East High School. And they located the FBI chemist who had testified in the 2004 trial that the reddish hairs taken from Horton's car by police in 1974 and the reddish hairs found in a room at the high school during the initial crime scene search, a room Horton had admitted he had used that 1974 evening, were "microscopically very, very similar" to hairs removed by police from Liz Wilson's personal hairbrush. The two investigators also relocated the former tennis players and cheerleaders who had testified about John Henry Horton's bizarre actions at the school the evening Liz Wilson disappeared.

John Wilson would again be the lead witness, but his mother would be unable to attend the second trial due to her health. John would be accompanied by his father, both his younger brothers, and his uncles and aunts.

The star witness, the woman who had been sexually molested on the golf course after being drugged with chloroform, would again be available. Her testimony in the first trial had resulted in the Kansas Supreme Court's reversal of Horton's conviction. This time, however, Kline, Maxwell, Cordts, and Shipps were confident they had found proper legal foundation for her important testimony regarding "a prior similar bad act." Two of Horton's fellow inmates at the Norton Correctional Facility told Cordts and Shipps individually that Horton had confessed to Liz Wilson's abduction and murder during their mutual confinement, as imprisoned murderers often do. Both confessions involved details of chloroform use and sexual molestation.

Cordts and Shipps, of course, would testify again. So would all the other KBI agents who had taken the stand in the first trial. Dr. Bill Bass, who had confirmed the identification of Liz's remains, would return, and so would Major Dan Meyer of the Kansas Highway Patrol, who had reconstructed the timeframe of Liz's disappearance in the first trial, indicating that no one but Horton had the time and opportunity to commit the crime. Although retired, I would attend Mr. Horton's second trial as well.

The jury selection and opening statements started in Johnson County District Court on Monday, February 25, 2008. On Wednesday, March 5, 2008, a Johnson County jury once again returned a verdict of first-degree felony murder for John Henry Horton in the disappearance of Lizabeth Wilson. Prosecution witnesses and an overwhelming circumstantial case had once again carried the day.

On August 27, 2008, Judge Davis again sentenced Horton to the maximum prison term available to him, fifteen years to life, with parole eligibility in ten years, due to the five years already served by Horton. The defense again appealed. While not yet scheduled, there will be a final hearing in the courtroom of Judge Davis in July 2012. As this book went to press in June 2012, Cordts verified that Horton remained in the Kansas penal system, would be eligible for parole in 2018, and had almost exhausted all possibilities for appeal.

Lou P. Richter, first KBI director, 1939–1956. Photo courtesy of Margaret Sanford Symns from the Logan Sanford Collection.

Logan H. Sanford, sheriff of Stafford County, Kansas, during the Macksville bank robbery attempt, and second KBI director, 1957–1969. Photo courtesy of Margaret Sanford Symns from the Logan Sanford collection.

KBI
1944

C.C. MAUPIN   H.D. HENDERSON

C.E. BULLA   R.L. GRIFFITH   L.P. RICHTER   R.S. FOWKES   J.W. ANDERSON

L.P. RICHTER
Director

R.A. HUSE   R.E. DYER   H.A. NEAL

DIRECTOR AND SPECIAL AGENTS

Director Lou Richter and the original nine KBI special agents. Photo courtesy of Margaret Sanford Symns from the Logan Sanford collection.

OPPOSITE BELOW: The Macksville bank robbery investigation display case at KBI headquarters. Photo from the author's collection.

KBI agents Clarence Bulla, left, and Joe Anderson pose with the would-be bank robbers' automobile and Macksville townspeople following the attempted robbery on September 16, 1941. Photo courtesy of Margaret Sanford Symns from the Logan Sanford collection.

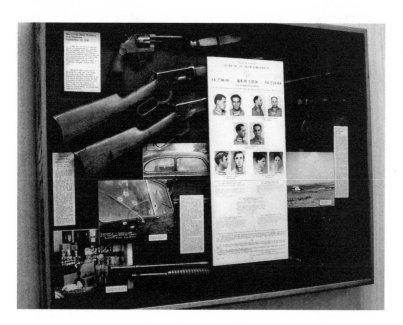

Perry Edward Smith, who, with Richard Hickock, murdered four members of the Clutter family near Holcomb, Kansas, on November 15, 1959. KBI photo.

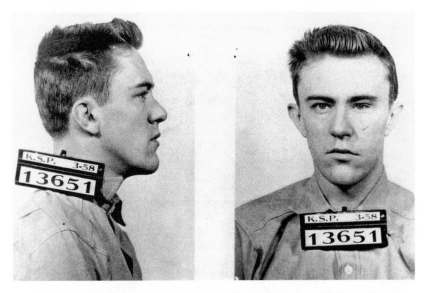

Richard Eugene Hickock, who died on the gallows in Lansing with Perry Smith on April 14, 1965, for the Clutter murders. KBI photo.

The four KBI agents primarily responsible for the investigation of the Clutter murders; left to right, Al Dewey, Harold Nye, Clarence Duntz, and Roy Church. Photo courtesy of Margaret Sanford Symns from the Logan Sanford collection.

The Clutter murder investigation display case at KBI headquarters. Photo from the author's collection.

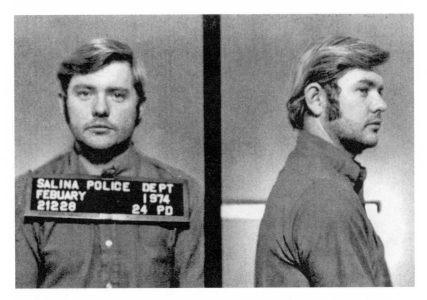

Francis Donald Nemechek, a Kansas serial killer who received five life sentences. Photo courtesy of Salina Police Department, Salina, Kansas.

Stephanie Schmidt, victim of Donald Ray Gideon. Photo courtesy of Gene and Peggy Schmidt.

The Stephanie Schmidt murder investigation display case at KBI headquarters. Photo from the author's collection.

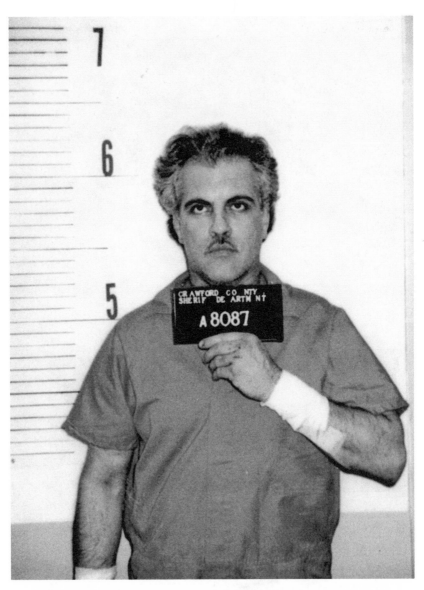

Gary Wayne Kleypas, killer of Carrie Arlene Williams. Photo courtesy of Crawford County, Kansas, Sheriff's Office.

The KBI's Brad Cordts, who twice helped bring John Henry Horton to justice for the murder of thirteen-year-old Liz Wilson. KBI photo.

Jeanette Stauffer testifies in Costa Rica in her daughter's murder trial. Photo courtesy of Jeanette Stauffer.

The KBI's Larry Thomas, left, advises prosecution attorney Juan Carlos Arce, right, through interpreter Jesse Ybarra during the trial of Shannon Martin's killers in Costa Rica. Photo courtesy of Jeanette Stauffer.

Shannon Martin and Brutus. Photo courtesy of Jeanette Stauffer.

Sheriff Matt Samuels, shot to death at the site of a meth lab in Greenwood County, Kansas, on January 19, 2005. Photo courtesy of Tammy Samuels.

Scott Cheever being escorted from Greenwood County District Court by KBI Agents Doug Younger, left, and Greg Skelton, January 23, 2008, after receiving the death sentence for the murder of Sheriff Matt Samuels. Photo by Bo Rader, courtesy of the *Wichita Eagle*.

Lt. Ken Landwehr of the Wichita Police Department, the guiding force of the BTK Task Force (second from right), and the author (second from left) with two members of the task force: KBI Assistant Director Larry Thomas, far left, and KBI Senior Special Agent Ray Lundin, far right. KBI Forensic Supervisor Sindey Schueler, who indirectly connected Dennis Rader's DNA to three of BTK's murders, is in the center. KBI photo.

Dennis Rader is escorted into the El Dorado Correctional Facility, August 19, 2005, to begin serving ten life sentences for the murders of ten Kansas citizens. Photo by Jeff Tuttle, courtesy of the *Wichita Eagle*.

Members of KBI Operation Katrina, better known as "Mississippi Mud 1," take a break from President George Bush's security detail in front of Air Force One. Left to right are KBI Agents Rod Page, Frank Papish, Tony Weingartner, Marc Perez (kneeling), Doug Younger, and Bill Roland. KBI photo.

Bob Stephan, who served as Kansas attorney general for sixteen years, provided KBI oversight longer than any other Kansas attorney general. Photo from the author's collection.

KBI Crime Scene van. KBI photo.

The author with two of the KBI's legendary gentlemen, Assistant Director Jack Ford, left, and Special Agent in Charge Bob Clester, center. Photo from the author's collection.

KBI Assistant Director Chuck Sexson was architect of the vital Kansas Criminal Justice Information System Improvement Project, 1994–2004, a model for the nation. KBI photo.

Kansas Attorney General Carla Stovall and local state legislators cut the ribbon (actually KBI crime scene tape) on the new KBI forensic laboratory in Pittsburg, Kansas, March 3, 2000. KBI photo.

Kansas Attorney General Carla Stovall and KBI Deputy Director Terry Knowles present the first accreditation achieved by the KBI forensic laboratories, July 1998. Photo by Steve Koch, KBI.

The author and PJ Adair, KBI executive secretary and assistant to the director, flanked by Deputy Director Terry Knowles, far left, and Associate Director Dale Finger, far right. Photo from the author's collection.

CHAPTER FOURTEEN

9/11: Priorities Change

I was sitting in a small witness room in the Reno County Courthouse in Hutchinson, Kansas, waiting to testify in Reno County District Court in a criminal proceeding. There was no telephone or television or radio in the room. It was the morning of Tuesday, September 11, 2001. Three KBI agents, Kyle Smith, Brad Cordts, and Scott Ferris, were also waiting to testify. As we visited, awaiting our individual summons to the witness stand, my KBI pager suddenly activated, indicating that my secretary, PJ, was sending me a message. I quickly read my pager's message: "Airplane crashed into World Trade Center, New York City, minutes ago. Many feared dead. PJ" It was a little after 8:00 A.M., Central Standard Time. I read the tragic message aloud to Kyle, Brad, and Scott. We were, of course, saddened by the news of the apparent accident, but soon, in more somber tones, we continued our casual conversation as we awaited our calls to testify in the KBI investigative proceeding.

Several minutes later PJ sent a second communication on my pager: "Second plane hit the WTC! What's going on?" As I read the second message aloud to my KBI companions we knew it was the work of terrorists. As we sat there, isolated, regretting that we each had left our cell phones in our cars, the only question we had was whether they were domestic or international terrorists. What was immediately clear to each of us was that our nation was being attacked by an enemy. But who?

Within days, of course, we learned that nineteen homicidal (I decline in such situations to term the individuals suicidal) al-Qaeda fanatics, each, presumably, dreaming of heavenly virgins, and apparently armed with box cutters, fierce religious determination, and an intense hatred for America, almost simultaneously hijacked four American commercial airliners, crashing three of the four into selected targets—the Twin Towers of the World Trade Center and the Pentagon in Virginia. The fourth plane's homicidal mission (later thought by many investigators to have been Washington, D.C.—possibly the U.S. Capitol or White House) was thwarted by heroes aboard, ordinary citizen-passengers. The attacks, closely concurrent with one another, had obviously been well coordinated and planned, and tragically effective.

We would eventually learn that nearly 3,000 men, women, and children died when the two hijacked jetliners, heavily laden with fuel, crashed into the World Trade Center, causing the towers to collapse into a smoldering pile of twisted steel and crushed concrete. Another 189 died when the third commandeered jetliner crashed into the Pentagon, causing considerable damage to that building. The fourth hijacked airliner crashed in a field in Pennsylvania, killing all 44 aboard. We would also learn of the heroism of countless law enforcement officers, rescue workers, and firefighters at the World Trade Center, as well as the names of some of the American heroes on the fourth jet who prevented the criminals on board from achieving success in their mission.

As a result of the worst foreign attack on American soil since Pearl Harbor on December 7, 1941, the post–September 11 era of new duties, new responsibilities, new challenges, and new concerns for American law enforcement had just dawned, especially for the FBI. And, as it turned out, for the KBI as well.

Although appointed director of the FBI by President George W. Bush on July 5, 2001, and confirmed by the U.S. Senate on August 2, Robert S. Mueller III took the oath of office on September 4, 2001, and therefore had actually been on the job only seven days when September 11 dawned. He inherited an agency whose national priority since 1998 was national and economic security, but whose priorities on September 10, 2001, as a practical matter, were as follows:

1. White Collar Crime
2. Violent Crimes—Major Offenders
3. National Foreign Intelligence Program
4. Organized Crime—Drugs
5. Domestic Terrorism
6. National Infrastructure Protection and Computer Intrusion Program
7. Civil Rights
8. Applicants
9. Training[1]

Within days of September 11, 2001, the new FBI priorities were (and continue to be) as follows:

1. Protect the U.S. from Terrorist Attack
2. Protect the U.S. against Foreign Intelligence Operations and Espionage

3. Protect the U.S. against Cyber-based Attacks and High-technology Crimes
4. Combat Public Corruption at All Levels
5. Protect Civil Rights
6. Combat Transnational and National Criminal Organizations and Enterprises
7. Combat Major White Collar Crime
8. Combat Significant Violent Crime
9. Support Federal, State, County, Municipal, and International Partners
10. Upgrade Technology.[2]

Of significant consequence to municipal, county, and state law enforcement, white collar crime fell from first to seventh on the list of FBI priorities. Violent crime fell from second to eighth. Drugs and training disappeared altogether from the FBI's top priorities. National columnist George Will later wrote of Director Mueller's priorities for the FBI: "He clearly expects the FBI to be central to Counterterrorism and Counterterrorism to be central to the FBI."[3]

The relationship between the FBI and the KBI had always been strong and important, dating back to KBI Director Lou Richter's friendship with FBI Director J. Edgar Hoover in 1939 and the subsequent selection of Logan Sanford to attend the prestigious FBI National Academy in Quantico, Virginia, in 1956, a rare invitation at the time. That relationship was just as firm on September 11, 2001. The head of the FBI's Counterterrorism Division in Washington, D.C., Assistant Director Dale Watson, had been a close friend since serving as assistant special agent in charge of the FBI office in Kansas City a few years earlier. In addition, the special agent in charge of the FBI office in Kansas City, Kevin Stafford, had already become a respected, good friend since his recent arrival to take over the Kansas City FBI operations. Fortunately, his wife, Debby, also an FBI supervisor, had been the FBI's expert on Osama bin Laden for Dale Watson at FBI headquarters prior to the Staffords' transfers to Kansas City in June 2001. Our strong liaison with their expertise soon helped the KBI better understand the events and aftermath of September 11, 2001, as the KBI and the FBI became even stronger partners in addressing the new challenges and new responsibilities ahead in the war on terror.

The KBI was, of course, a likely partner for the FBI and the U.S. Department of Justice, given the obvious developing need for confidentiality in future intelligence sharing. My associate director, Dale Finger, and all three assistant directors, Chuck Sexson, Bob Blecha, and Kirk Thompson, were graduates of the FBI National Academy at Quantico, Virginia, and had accordingly survived extensive FBI background investigations similar to those conducted on new FBI agents. Most of our nine special agents in charge, our first-line supervisors, were also FBINA graduates, and Terry Knowles, my deputy director, had retired from the FBI as deputy assistant director. Other KBI senior special agents were former FBI agents or FBINA graduates. And still other KBI agents in those early days underwent FBI background investigations to obtain the top-secret clearances necessary to work alongside FBI agents in confidential areas and to participate in confidential briefings. Some already enjoyed such clearances, due to having been assigned to various FBI task forces in the past. No KBI agent failed to pass those necessary FBI background inquiries, perhaps a reflection of the quality and rigor of the KBI applicant process.

During the late afternoon of September 11, after returning to Topeka, I informed Kansas Attorney General Carla Stovall of my intention to offer KBI resources, however thinly stretched, to the federal government. Her enthusiastic agreement came without hesitation or conditions. The requests for KBI help started coming from a variety of federal agencies almost immediately.

On September 14, Congress passed a resolution authorizing President George W. Bush to use "all necessary and appropriate force" against the terrorists of September 11 and/or those who assisted them. U.S. Attorney General John Ashcroft immediately called on each of his ninety-four U.S. attorneys to quickly form an Anti-Terrorism Task Force (ATTF) in each of the ninety-four federal districts across the country to help spearhead the national response to the challenges of September 11. Ashcroft explained to his U.S. attorneys that he wanted each such task force to include representatives of the FBI, the Immigration and Naturalization Service (INS), the U.S. Customs Department, the Secret Service, and the Bureau of Alcohol, Tobacco and Firearms (ATF), along with selected municipal, county, and state law enforcement agencies. The task forces would have three missions: (1) to gather and share information regarding suspected terrorists; (2) to implement an operations plan for the prevention of terrorism in each district; and (3) to serve as the base of response to any terrorist incidents occurring within the district.[4]

Acting U.S. Attorney Jim Flory at once named the chief of the criminal division for the district of Kansas as the coordinator of the Kansas U.S. attorney's Anti-Terrorism Task Force. In soliciting local law enforcement participants for the Kansas task force, the coordinator's first telephone call was to the KBI, requesting our active participation. I could not decline the invitation to join the effort. The coordinator was Assistant U.S. Attorney Lanny Welch, my second son. I promised my personal involvement, pledged the membership of at least a KBI assistant director and a KBI senior special agent and, at Lanny's request, suggested several Kansas police chiefs and sheriffs, as well as officials of the Kansas Highway Patrol, as good choices for active, dependable participants in the task force.

The first meeting of our ATTF was held in the U.S. Attorney's Office in Kansas City, Kansas, on September 20. Both KBI Assistant Director Bob Blecha and I attended that meeting. At first, and for several months, the U.S. attorney's task force, the Kansas ATTF, met weekly in Kansas City, Topeka, or Wichita, with many of the top law enforcement administrators in the state in attendance. The theme of each meeting was the prevention of terrorist activity in Kansas and the safety of our citizens. I attended many of the meetings, as did other KBI officials, but Assistant Director Blecha was our official representative.

Our KBI record section was also responding to requests from federal agencies to check the names of Middle Eastern suspects in our indices and criminal history records. In the first week, of 150 such names checked, we identified four as having had Kansas driver's licenses. We determined three had moved to Texas and one to Oklahoma. That information was promptly forwarded to the FBI and to Texas and Oklahoma authorities. None was ever determined to have a terrorist connection.

We were also routinely receiving tips and information from Kansas citizens and Kansas law enforcement, which we passed promptly on to appropriate federal agencies. We were, for a time, responding to more anthrax scares than we were to meth labs, which had been our top investigative priority for several years. No actual anthrax was ever identified in Kansas. Our agents were regularly responding to requests from the FBI, Customs, or INS to assist in locating and/or arresting aliens present in Kansas in violation of tourist, business, or student visas, mostly the latter and mostly involving those from the Middle East.

Forty-five days after September 11, at the request of President Bush and Attorney General Ashcroft, Congress overwhelmingly passed a 342-page antiterrorism bill, which provided law enforcement with unprecedented authority to search, seize, surveil, detain, and eavesdrop in pursuit of suspected terrorists. Entitled the USA PATRIOT Act, the bill was signed into law on October 26, 2001.

Inaccurately described by many, in my opinion, as a complete departure from police regulations and procedures based on the U.S. Constitution, the act's critics ignored the probable cause and judicial review requirements in its provisions, as well as its narrow, limited jurisdiction: terrorism. The greatest criticism of the proposed law enforcement counterterrorism measures came in November and December 2001 after Attorney General Ashcroft, on November 9, 2001, requested U.S. attorneys, through their respective Anti-Terrorism Task Forces, to coordinate the voluntary interviews of 5,000 Middle Eastern individuals across the nation who had entered the United States legally on nonimmigrant visas. The project was described to the ninety-four U.S. attorneys as nonadversarial and strictly intelligence-seeking, not custodial or confrontational. The interviewees were described as law-abiding legal visitors who might simply possess useful information. Kansas ATTF Coordinator Lanny Welch telephoned me sometime between November 9 and November 16, pointing out that the Kansas City FBI Office was stretched thin with regard to available agents; explaining Ashcroft's ambitious interview project; and asking whether the KBI could provide agents for such interviews across the state if needed. He noted that Ashcroft requested that the interviews be completed within thirty days. I replied affirmatively.

Bob Blecha and I attended a special ATTF meeting in Kansas City on November 16. By then, U.S. Attorney Jim Flory and Coordinator Welch had learned that approximately fifty of 5,000 Middle Eastern males slated for voluntary interview by the U.S. Department of Justice were believed to be residing in Kansas. Given the paucity of federal agents available for the interviews, it was quickly agreed that municipal police departments, including Lawrence, Topeka, Overland Park, Kansas City, and Wichita, would locate and interview those interviewees believed to be in their cities. The KBI would assume the responsibility for the remainder, which turned out to be more than half of the interviewees in Kansas. At the November 16 meeting, Flory shared with us copies of Ashcroft's eight-page memorandum. I was impressed with the detailed description of the interview project and further impressed with Jim Flory's explanation, legal justification, and suggested guidelines for the interviews, which he termed "chats," not interviews or interrogations.

In a letter dated November 20, Lanny Welch provided to the Kansas agencies participating in the interview project our official International Terrorism Interview Packets. The packets contained a list of all potential interviewees in our state and the agencies designated for the interviews. There were also copies of Attorney General Ashcroft's memorandum, a sample interview questionnaire, an personal history form for interviewees, a guideline to understanding Arab culture and how to avoid offending interviewees, a reward notice, a brief FBI summary of the events of September 11, identification of known suspects who had participated, and address verification forms and National Crime Information Center (NCIC) forms to ensure that the interviewees, when fully identified, were not the subjects of wanted notices or arrest warrants anywhere. (None of our Kansas interviewees was ever determined to be wanted anywhere or to have been involved in any manner in terrorist activities.)

We selected three KBI special agents in charge and five senior special agents, all experienced veterans, to handle our KBI interviews for the U.S. Department of Justice. I met with Special Agents in Charge Rick Sabel, Bill Delaney, and Larry Thomas, and Senior Special Agents Cathy Elser, Dana Moodie, Terry Morgan, Tom Williams, and Ezell Monts in my office on November 26, 2001. Each had already been deeply involved in KBI post–September 11 activities, and Sabel, Elser, and Moodie, on behalf of overworked and undermanned INS and U.S. Customs personnel, had already arrested several Middle Eastern males in Kansas in violation of tourist, business, or student visas. Also present at our briefing in my office were my associate director, Dale Finger; Assistant Directors Kirk Thompson and Bob Blecha; and KBI General Counsel Jane Nohr.

We provided all interviewers with their own Interview Packets and I explained the project to the group. I emphasized that the "chats" were voluntary, not custodial, confrontational, or adversarial. No *Miranda* warnings would be necessary. I explained that I didn't want the interviews to be conducted in any FBI or KBI office, sheriff's office, police station, or highway patrol facility. Middle Eastern males, rightfully so, were known to be wary and fearful of law enforcement facilities. The interviews, if and only if the subject agreed to an interview in the first place, would be held at a site of the subject's choosing, such as home, school, or workplace. No interviewee was to be identified to the media. In fact, no public comment about the assignment was to be made to anyone, except by the U.S. Attorney's Office or the FBI. We were to strive to avoid embarrassing any interviewee. A report regarding each interview was to be submitted in writing promptly to the U.S. attorney, the FBI, INS, and Assistant Director Blecha. Any indication during or following the interview that the individual might be in violation of INS regulations would be promptly reported to INS and Blecha. The agents were directed to be alert for international intelligence as well as domestic intelligence and to run each interviewee again through the NCIC computer immediately prior to the interview. The agents were also instructed to obtain complete and correct spellings of the individuals' names, not relying on the spelling of the names as reflected in their packets. And, given reports of some backlash against Middle Easterners in the United States following September 11, the agents were to ask each interviewee if he had been the victim of any hate crime or knew anyone who possibly had been.

The interview project went smoothly in Kansas. No one declined to be interviewed and, insofar as I know, there were no complaints or criticism by any of the interviewees. Our agents were later praised by the U.S. attorney and FBI for the promptness, thoroughness, and professionalism of their interview reports. While no one discovered a treasure trove of intelligence as a result of the interviews in Kansas, certain bits of information obtained in our KBI interviews were later deemed important by the FBI, resulting in investigative leads outside Kansas.

The project went smoothly in Kansas, but the same cannot be said of the effort's reception everywhere across the nation. Some media and a few Arab-American groups in other states complained about the constitutionality of such an interview project, and the American Civil Liberties Union (ACLU) was quick to label such interviews as racial profiling.

I was pleased the program received no such media criticism in Kansas, at least none that came to my attention. The *Wichita Eagle* and *Lawrence Journal-World* ran supporting and approving stories and/or editorials. Editor Dolph Simons in his *Journal-World* editorial on Sunday, November 25, 2001, commented:

> Some are displeased that federal authorities have been given names of young foreigners to interview as part of the Justice Department's efforts to blunt future terrorist acts and get new data about the September 11 tragedies in New York, Washington, D.C., and Pennsylvania. Officials and leaders would be remiss if they were not taking this action, considering how the guilty parties and their supporters used our free-flowing system to their advantage. Such questioning lists will contain the names of foreign students here on visas, as were at least three of those in the deadly airliner hijackings.[5]

Simons was right, it seemed to me. If we had learned nothing else in the early aftermath of September 11, surely we learned that, to better protect our own citizens, we should pay more attention to our visitors. Better tracking of those here on visas would likely translate to increased protection of our own citizens. No other nation permitted the free and easy, unchecked, unregulated, unmonitored travel of foreign visitors that we did prior to September 11, 2001. We quickly learned that many, perhaps hundreds, of Middle Eastern males were in the United States on student visas yet had never set foot on any school campus. As some of our KBI agents learned, in assisting INS and U.S. Customs even before the interview project, there were student-visitors who could not even correctly name the community in Kansas where the college he was ostensibly attending was actually located. Surely it would not be too much to ask school and immigration officials to keep better track of such visitors, in the name of national security.

I was not surprised by the considerable criticism of the interview effort outside Kansas in the media and by Arab-American groups and the ACLU. What did surprise and disappoint me was the opposition to the project from a few law enforcement agencies in other states. A quote attributed to Sheriff Don Horsley of San Mateo County, California, puzzled me: "We don't have any legal authority to question people. Unless they could articulate some suspicious activity, no, we wouldn't participate."[6] Surely the good sheriff was misquoted. No authority to question people? That's what we do, and can do, in law enforcement. The sheriff seemed to be confusing arrest or detention with interview. We most certainly are entitled to ask. No one is required to answer. These were not suspects of any crimes. These were intelligence-seeking "chats," to quote our own Jim Flory, not custodial interrogations, or involuntary detentions. They were voluntary interviews.

The overwhelming majority of law enforcement administrators, however, like Chief Michael Chitwood of Portland, Maine, dismissed any criticism of the project that described it as racial profiling and expressed puzzlement at the reluctance of any sheriff or police chief to permit officers to participate. "That's not racial profiling; that's good investigative work," said Chief Chitwood.[7] In Kansas we certainly agreed.

The criticism of the project outside Kansas prompted me to send out a report to all 165 Kansas legislators fully describing KBI participation on December 5, 2001.

The positive legislative response to my report reinforced my decision to assist the federal authorities in general and to participate in the national interview project in particular. Several legislators informed me they were pleased about our decision and proud of the KBI participation in efforts relating to national security. I did not receive a single legislative dissent. Questions about KBI involvement in post–September 11 activities became the most popular questions in my civic club appearances and other speeches around the state, and legislators frequently requested post–September 11 updates during my legislative appearances on other subjects. I was glad the KBI had not been one of the agencies that had demurred when help was requested by the federal government.

In November and December 2001, Special Agent in Charge Kevin Stafford of the Kansas City FBI office, began sharing with me his vision of an FBI Terrorism Task Force, involving numerous local, state, and federal law enforcement agencies across Kansas and western Missouri, engaged in intelligence and investigative counterterrorism efforts within those geographical boundaries. I was prepared to decline his manpower request since there seemed no need for a second federal counterterrorism task force, given the successful operation thus far of the U.S. attorney's Anti-Terrorism Task Force, and given my dire shortage of KBI special agents. (By 2004, eighteen of my authorized eighty-one special agent positions were vacant due to budgetary reasons.) Stafford explained that he had received tentative approval from FBI headquarters to form such a counterterrorism task force to operate in Kansas and western Missouri if he could obtain local law enforcement commitments to participate in the endeavor. It would be one of the first such investigative and intelligence-gathering joint federal-local law enforcement groups targeting terrorism created by the FBI since September 11. He emphasized that this federal task force would work closely with the U.S. attorney's more advisory-oriented task force. His would complement the other, not duplicate it, except that many of the players on the two task forces might be identical. He emphasized that an early KBI commitment would be a persuasive message to others he intended to ask to join. He pointed out that there were terrorist suspects, especially in the area of terrorism-related fundraising operations, across the two states. Prevention of future terrorism was the goal. Intelligence gathering and investigation would be the vehicles. The KBI would be on the inside from the start, enjoying top-secret FBI clearance and sharing vital intelligence and threat analysis. With the information from the FBI special agent in charge about definite terrorist threats already identified in our state, I acquiesced, despite my strong intention to resist any further assignment of precious agent resources to a federal task force. I agreed to serve on the executive board as my schedule permitted and to assign an agent to the endeavor full time. Joining the new task force would prove to be one of the wisest and most important commitments the KBI made in the two months following September 11. We knew what the FBI knew as soon as they knew it.

By December 16, Kevin Stafford's imagination and initiative were rewarded. The Heart of America Joint Terrorism Task Force (HOAJTTF) was officially formed, approved, and funded by FBI headquarters. Originally the effort included fourteen Kansas and western Missouri law enforcement agencies and seventeen full-time experienced investigators, including Senior Special Agent Terry Morgan of our Overland Park office. Morgan reported directly to the FBI office daily. (He retired in 2004 and was replaced by Senior Special Agent Tim Dennis.)

The original seventeen task force members had their hands full at the outset. The task force started its operation by considering, analyzing, and evaluating more than 200,000 terrorism-related leads that had been identified in Kansas (many by the KBI) and western Missouri in the aftermath of September 11. In the task force's early daunting pursuit of those leads, the KBI also regularly loaned post–September 11 veterans Rick Sabel, Cathy Elser, Dana Moodie, and Ezell Monts to the effort. New leads were being received and developed by the task force as the original leads were being explored. The task force eventually grew to eighty-eight investigators, fifty-six of them full time. They included FBI agents and municipal, county, and state officers from across Kansas and western Missouri. The unit was visited and lauded by many, including Senator Pat Roberts of Kansas, chairman of the Senate Select Committee on Intelligence; Attorney General John Ashcroft; and FBI Director Robert Mueller. Similar task forces were later created in the other fifty-six FBI divisions across our nation.

The *Kansas City Star* hailed Kevin Stafford's creation on the third anniversary of the September 11 attacks: "It may be the largest, most secretive law enforcement initiative in Kansas and western Missouri." The newspaper story explained that the goal of the task force was to "protect the United States from terrorist attack" and noted that the task force had "grown more robust since the Iraq War began in the spring of 2003, with more personnel and resources focused on terrorist fund raising and agro-terrorism." (The KBI had been a leader in the latter sphere of interest since 1999, thanks to the interest and leadership of Kansas Attorney General Carla Stovall, Senator Pat Roberts, Kansas State University officials, and KBI Deputy Director Terry Knowles.) The story also noted that one of the task force's most valuable assets was Kansas City FBI Supervisor Debby Stafford, aka Mrs. Kevin Stafford, "who once headed the bureau's Osama bin Laden desk in Washington."[8]

In testimony before a U.S. House subcommittee on August 20, 2002, Kevin Stafford had shared what he could with Congress in a public forum:

> There are numerous ongoing counterterrorism investigations being conducted by the HOAJTTF. Inasmuch as these are active investigations, I am unable to provide any specific details. However, it should be emphasized that terrorist related cells and threats are present within the "heartland" and are being addressed by the combined efforts of all law enforcement. . . . The "heartland" of America is also the "bread basket" of the nation. Therefore, the Kansas City Field Office with the help and support of the United States Department of Agriculture, and in conjunction with the HOAJTTF, has established close working relationships with the Kansas Bureau of Investigation, Kansas State University, the Ford County Sheriff's Office, and the Kansas Livestock Commissioner to develop and implement a response plan to a terrorist or weapons-of-

mass-destruction attack upon livestock and/or crops, such as through the release of diseases or biological agents.[9]

I was pleased that Kevin Stafford mentioned the KBI six times in the document he submitted to the committee in support of his testimony.

Between September 11, 2001, and March 2002, the KBI had handled a total of 258 terrorist-related calls. One hundred and sixteen were deemed important enough for referral to the FBI. During that period, forty-one KBI special agents and two support personnel logged 1,789 work hours in response to post–September 11 requests from federal authorities and local Kansas law enforcement.

KBI special agents, in support of the INS, which was seriously undermanned in Kansas, had participated in the arrests of seventeen Middle Easterners in those first five months. They were all found to be in violation of student, visitor, or business visas, and all were afforded formal hearings by INS prior to deportation. Some here on student visas were allegedly attending a nonexistent Kansas college or had not set foot on the campus of the legitimate school described in their visas. By March 1, 2002, the INS had given us another list of thirty Middle Easterners to locate and interview. By 2004 the number of KBI arrestees in support of INS approached sixty, in contrast with those interviewed in the voluntary program described above, none of whom was arrested.

During those first five months, we were not idle on the bioterrorism or agroterrorism fronts either. As noted, Deputy Director Terry Knowles had been involved with Senator Roberts, Kansas State University officials, and others since October 1999, at the request of Kansas Attorney General Stovall, in the analysis of the potential threat to our state's agriculture, crops, food security, livestock, and feedyards. September 11 energized that process or program of analysis, while providing it with instant credibility. To our KBI post–September 11 vocabulary of new words such as ground zero, Taliban, shoe bomb, homeland security, 9/11, heightened security, highest alert, Al-Qaeda or Al Qaida or al-Qaida, John Walker Lindh, and Osama bin Laden, we had added agroterrorism, anthrax, bioterrorism, Ebola, foot and mouth disease, mad cow disease, and foodborne pathogens, among others.

In my letter to the Kansas legislature on August 28, 2002, as the first anniversary of September 11 approached, I reiterated my belief that the primary lesson we had learned in that year was that if we could keep better track of our foreign visitors, we could better protect our own citizens. I also assured state legislators, Governor Bill Graves, and Attorney General Stovall in that communication that we remained mindful that there can be a delicate balance between individual civil liberties and national security. I told them that I remained confident we had not disturbed that balance. I also reported that the number of terrorist-related calls we had handled had increased to 317 and that we had assigned two KBI senior special agents, Cathy Elser and Dana Moodie, who together had made the majority of the previous INS arrests, to the new Topeka extension of the Kansas City HOAJTTF on a part-time basis.

Clearly, the KBI involvement in the aftermath of September 11 was not decreasing; indeed, despite budget constraints and limited resources, it continued to broaden and intensify throughout that first year. KBI agents were involved in assignments to contact all airports in Kansas to ensure that airport management and/or security officials would promptly report any stolen aircraft and attempts to steal aircraft, as well as stolen pilot and/or aircraft identification, stolen uniforms, or similar items. We were also involved in contacts with all prisons and correctional facilities in Kansas in an attempt to identify any inmates or recent releases suspected of connections to domestic and international terrorism as 2002 drew to a close.

In 2002, Kevin Stafford confided in me about FBI plans to create a regional computer forensic laboratory in Kansas City, with his encouragement. FBI Director Mueller had agreed with Stafford's recommendation to make the Kansas City facility the third such FBI laboratory in the country and one of only five new such facilities planned for the nation overall. Stafford envisioned the future Heart of America Regional Computer Forensic Laboratory (HARCFL), like the HOAJTTF, to be a partnership between the FBI and other federal, state, and local law enforcement agencies operating in Kansas and western Missouri. The primary purpose of HARCFL would be to provide forensic examinations of digital media, such as computers, in support of investigations and/or prosecutions of federal, state, or local computer crimes.

The forensic laboratory would be quickly followed and supported by a separate Cyber Crimes Task Force, and both the forensic HARCFL and the Cyber Crimes Task Force, the investigative part of the two-pronged endeavor, would be deeply involved in the investigation of terrorist activities and terrorist threats in the two states, as well as in the pursuit of more traditional computer criminal violations—child pornography, financial crimes, fraud, identity theft, and so on. Both entities would be extremely effective, Stafford predicted, in gathering evidence and intelligence relating to terrorism and homeland security. Naturally, he wanted a KBI agent assigned full-time to each of the two endeavors. Following appropriate selection processes, we assigned Senior Special Agent Cindy Smith to HARCFL and Special Agent Angie Wilson to the Cyber Crimes Task Force. Both proved to be excellent choices. Both endeavors were among Attorney General Phill Kline's favorite KBI efforts, and my own.

HARCFL officially opened its doors on July 9, 2003, funded by the federal government through the USA PATRIOT Act. Attorney General Kline was a keynote speaker at the grand opening. Located in an impressive, user-friendly facility north of downtown Kansas City, Missouri, the forensic laboratory serves all law enforcement in Kansas and western Missouri, concentrating on terrorism and child pornography, but assisting in all areas of computer-related crimes and investigations.

Meanwhile, we were pulling KBI special agents off everything except homicides, violent crimes, and major narcotic trafficking, especially methamphetamine, to accommodate our 9/11 responsibilities to our state and its citizens, and to prevent any acts of terrorism within our borders.

In a five-page report to the Kansas legislature on October 20, 2003, I summarized the first two years of the KBI's 9/11 activities.

September 11, 2001, and the resulting mandated shift in FBI investigative priorities had two primary impacts on the KBI. First, our participation in FBI task forces, always significant, increased. I was pleased that KBI agents were able to help bolster such important federal endeavors. There were 103 FBI Joint Terrorism Task Forces created across the nation. The task force we joined in Kansas City, immediately following September 11, was one of the first. FBI Director Mueller pointed to those task forces in June 2005 when he addressed the National Sheriffs Conference in Louisville, Kentucky. Shirley and I, with several Kansas sheriffs and their wives, were in the audience. The director said, "I think they [the task forces] are one of the main reasons why we haven't been attacked since September 11. It is the work we do now on the 103 joint terrorism task forces that is helping to keep our communities safe."[10]

Second, because of the FBI's shift to counterterrorism in investigative priorities, it is only investigating about half the general criminal violations it did prior to September 11. As Director Mueller told us at the National Sheriffs Conference in Louisville, "We're not doing as many drug cases. We're not doing as many white-collar criminal cases. We're not doing as many bank robberies."[11] The KBI, pursuant to custom and tradition, has attempted to fill as many of those voids as possible. It's what the KBI does.

CHAPTER FIFTEEN

Meth: Biggest Crime Scourge, 1996–2005

Nothing caused as much heartache and frustration during my tenure as KBI director as methamphetamine and what it did to Kansas communities, Kansas families, Kansas law enforcement, and the Kansas criminal justice system. The KBI fought that particular war, especially from 1994 until 2001, with extremely limited resources and few allies. Indeed, we fought the war with precious little support from anyone other than Kansas law enforcement and some appreciated financial assistance from our Kansas congressional delegation in Washington, D.C., especially Senator Pat Roberts, Congressman Jerry Moran, and Congressman Todd Tiahrt. We won skirmishes and even battles, often with fewer than thirty KBI narcotic agents for the entire state. Clearly, we did not win the war. But at least we eventually switched from defense to offense. The conflict continues today. The toll in lives, economic loss, quality of family life, and the exhaustion of the Kansas criminal justice system, has been heavy.

The 1963 *Webster's New Collegiate Dictionary* (seventh edition) contains no reference to methamphetamine.

The 1988 *Webster's New Collegiate Dictionary* (ninth edition) defines methamphetamine as "an amine, C-10 H-15 N, used in the form of its crystalline hydrochloride as a stimulant for the central nervous system and in the treatment of obesity."

Those who failed Chemistry 101 in high school but today consider themselves methamphetamine chemists and "cooks," as well as those who are addicted to the evil man-made drug, know it as crank, ice, glass, crystal, speed, crystal meth, or, most commonly, meth. Since 1996, the KBI has out of necessity been forced to focus a disproportionate percentage of scarce forensic and investigative resources on methamphetamine in general and meth labs in particular. Nothing has changed the face of crime in Kansas since 1996 as much as methamphetamine. Nothing has impacted so negatively the budgets of so many Kansas law enforcement agencies, especially the KBI, as has methamphetamine and meth labs.

Clandestine methamphetamine-manufacturing laboratories, or meth labs, are among the most dangerous assignments confronting American law enforcement officers today. In fact, one of the few law enforcement tasks more dangerous than entry into a known, operational meth lab site is entry into such a site unaware that meth cooks and an operational meth lab, with all its attendant dangers, are present therein.

Any Kansas physician or law enforcement officer with experience in dealing with meth users can attest that the drug is more addictive than cocaine, crack, or heroin. It can be smoked, snorted, taken orally, or injected. For the serious, helpless addict, the preferred manner of consumption is injection, for the quickest and most intense effect. No matter how the drug is consumed, high doses and/or chronic use can result in nervousness, irritability, extreme paranoia, aggressive behavior, delusions, psychosis, physical violence, hostility, dramatic mood swings, a yellow complexion, rotten teeth, severe weight loss, sexual dysfunction, serious skin disease, seizures, child abuse and endangerment, domestic violence, memory loss, heart failure, tremors, heart spasms, malnutrition, belligerence, poor hygiene, hair loss, insomnia, convulsions, permanent brain damage, schizophrenia, kidney damage, respiratory disorders, and auditory hallucinations. Users have been known to go without sleep for as many as three to five days, with sleepless binges that can last up to two weeks. Withdrawal invariably brings severe depression.

The three most popular manufacturing processes from 1994 to 2007 were the "Nazi method," the iodine-red phosphorous "Red P method," and the less common P2P-hydriodic acid method. The Nazi method depends on ephedrine or pseudoephedrine, sodium, lithium, and anhydrous ammonia (a common agriculture fertilizer) for its manufacture. This process was the most popular in Kansas because it was quick and inexpensive, required little overhead, and produced a relatively high yield of pure methamphetamine.

Both the process of meth manufacturing and the product itself are illegal. All the materials, ingredients, and equipment necessary for the manufacture of the toxic brew and its product are, however, legal to purchase and/or possess individually. They include anhydrous ammonia, ephedrine, pseudoephedrine, cold and allergy tablets, acetone, red phosphorous, aluminum foil, camping fuel, lighter fluid, paint thinner, iodine, drain cleaner, battery acid, kerosene, glassware and tubing, lithium batteries, coffee filters, denatured alcohol, engine starter fluid, gasoline additives, funnels, lye, matches, propane tanks, sodium hydroxide, and table or rock salt. The need for the various materials, equipment, and ingredients varies, depending on which one of the three most popular manufacturing processes is favored by the particular meth cooker.

I lamented to legislators, law enforcement, and the media that in law enforcement we seldom have the luxury of long-range planning. Five-year and ten-year plans are fantasies in law enforcement. We normally cannot select our targets of preference, our own goals and objectives. We are compelled to face what is in front of us at the time. We must confront the most serious threats, those challenging the safety and security of our citizens at the time. In short, we must address the beast in our face. From 1996 until 2007, the beast in our face was meth labs.

Meth labs exploded on the scene in California in 1989, in Missouri in 1993, Kansas in 1996, and throughout the Midwest, including Iowa, Nebraska, Oklahoma, and the Dakotas, in 1998. We declared meth labs the KBI's top investigative and forensic priority in 1996. By 2000 the labs were a national problem. And, as the *New York Times* reported, rural America was not exempt:

> Drugs and crime are unraveling rural America. . . . Crime, fueled by a methamphetamine epidemic that has turned fertilizer into a drug lab component and given some sparsely populated counties higher murder rates than New York City, has so strained small-town police budgets that many are begging the federal government for help. The rate of serious crime in Nebraska, Kansas, Oklahoma and Iowa is as much as 50 percent higher than the states of New York and New Jersey. . . . Drug-related homicides fell by 50 percent in urban areas, but they tripled over the last decade in the countryside. We have serious drug crime in places that never used to have it.[1]

I do not recall seizures of multiple operating meth labs in Kansas until 1994, when the KBI set a state record with the seizures of four meth labs across the state. We set another state record the next year with the seizures of seven such clandestine operations, and we were starting to become concerned. That concern changed to alarm with the explosion of seventy-one meth lab seizures in the state in 1996. The overwhelming majority were seized by KBI narcotics agents and KBI forensic scientists.

Based on what we were seeing in Missouri—authorities there were already seizing more meth labs than any state in the nation except California—I feared a crisis was developing in our own state. I didn't limit my warnings in 1996 and 1997 to only Kansas police chiefs, sheriffs, and legislators. In a letter to Governor Bill Graves on December 23, 1996, explaining why the Kansas application for a federal grant with which to join the meth-specific Midwest High Intensity Drug Trafficking Area program (Midwest HIDTA—Kansas, Iowa, Missouri, Nebraska, and South Dakota—later also North Dakota) was so important, I closed with this statement: "I respectfully suggest 'meth labs' now represent the single greatest narcotic problem facing Kansas law enforcement."

The governor later asked me to represent him at the National Methamphetamine Drug Conference in Omaha, Nebraska, on May 28–30, 1997. KBI Assistant Director Kirk Thompson accompanied me to the conference. We were both impressed with the organization, planning, and commitment that had gone into the first national conference on methamphetamine. Hundreds were in attendance and truly represented a cross-section of our nation: law enforcement, prosecutors, government officials, medical professionals, educators, and forensic scientists. National Drug Czar Barry McCaffrey, Nebraska Senator Bob Kerrey, DEA Administrator Tom Constantine, Attorney General Janet Reno, and numerous governors from around the country were in attendance. The Omaha conference remains the best conference on methamphetamine I ever attended, and I attended many thereafter.

In another letter to Governor Graves, dated June 16, 1997, reporting on our attendance at that conference, I reminded him of our own meth situation: "Sadly, our state now trails only Missouri and California in methamphetamine laboratory activity. . . . I have designated methamphetamine as our agency's top investigative priority."

The *Lawrence Journal-World*, October 10, 1997, reported that the previous day, at a Kiwanis Club luncheon, I had warned of an approaching epidemic of meth, noting Missouri was then first in the nation in meth lab seizures and we were third. The reporter quoted my description of the drug: "It is an evil, evil drug. It's cheaper than crack cocaine, it gives a more intense high, and it does incredible damage to your brain."[2]

Unfortunately, my predictions and fears proved prophetic. The number of meth labs seized in Kansas grew from under a hundred in 1997 to over seven hundred in 2000, with most of them seized by the KBI. I believe that during the years of 1998, 1999, and 2000, no single law enforcement unit anywhere in the nation seized more meth labs than the KBI narcotics division. Our undermanned and overworked KBI clandestine lab teams of agents and forensic scientists were scoring impressive statistics in lab seizures and in the arrests and convictions of methamphetamine manufacturers and dealers. But they were spending far too much time in their "moon suits" and respirators, the protective gear required for entry into a meth lab site. They were becoming physically and emotionally exhausted, and both agents and forensic scientists found it impossible to respond to all the prosecutors' subpoenas they were receiving in connection with the prosecutions of meth cooks and meth traffickers in state courts all across Kansas and in federal courts in Wichita, Topeka, and Kansas City. We seemed unable to bridle the escalating demands placed on us by the drug. In particular, we were not able to switch from a reactive mode to a proactive mode with meth labs until 2006, when the Kansas legislature enacted the Sheriff Matt Samuels Chemical Control Act of 2005.

The typical size of Kansas meth labs paled in comparison with the larger operations often found in Missouri, California, and Mexico; ours tended to produce grams and ounces of product rather than pounds. The typical Kansas operation was a small, mobile laboratory in a remote, rural area. We found such labs in garages, homes, sheds, barns, warehouses, trailers, businesses, hotel rooms, motel rooms, the trunks and backseats of automobiles, rural ditches, dry creek beds, groves of trees, the beds of pickup trucks, and in our state parks.

Only about 20 percent of the meth in Kansas was manufactured in Kansas, and most of that was for personal use by the manufacturer or for local consumption and distribution. The rest of the meth in our state, perhaps more than 80 percent, came from "super labs" in Mexico and California, mostly through Mexican drug-trafficking organizations. This continues to be the case today.

There are more dire consequences of meth labs than just the deadly, addictive product the operations deliver. There is always the potential for fire and explosion. The chemicals used in the process are highly toxic and unstable. The harmful exposure is not, of course, limited to just the cooks. The threat applies to emergency personnel, first responders, law enforcement, neighbors, and especially to children at meth lab-homes. Child abuse and child endangerment are common characteristics of meth labs in homes, especially if the cook is an addict and the primary consumer of his or her own product. In one case in Kansas, a neighbor watched meth lab operators repeatedly risk their lives to enter their burning home to recover the valuable methamphetamine product and manufacturing apparatus, while their children, an infant and two toddlers, remained inside. The children were saved last.

In addition, each meth lab represents a hazardous waste site. Typically, after a meth manufacturing process has been completed, the cook dumps the toxic chemicals on the ground, in street gutters, down waterlines, or in Kansas rivers, streams, and lakes. The average cost to law enforcement to clean up a typical small Kansas meth lab site was $3,000 in the 1990s. Costs to restore the sites of large meth labs could run many times the average $3,000 price tag. The contamination to our soil and groundwater cannot be estimated. It is commonly believed that the production of one pound of methamphetamine creates ten pounds of hazardous waste at that site. Hazardous waste is not the only collateral danger. Booby traps at meth labs are not rare, and meth cooks and dealers are invariably heavily armed, as many officers can attest. By 2000, the FBI was warning that "raiding a clandestine drug laboratory has become one of the most dangerous operations a law enforcement officer can undertake."[3]

Typical cooks (or cookers or manufacturers) are themselves not rocket scientists or experienced, educated chemists, of course. Often they are high school dropouts with little formal education or training in chemistry, lacking even an aptitude for the subject. They have typically learned the recipe for making meth from underground publications, the Internet, other cooks, or fellow inmates in jails and prisons. In contrast, law enforcement officers involved in meth lab seizures require certification from the KBI or the Drug Enforcement Administration (DEA), considerable special training, and expensive, sophisticated personal protective equipment.

From 1999 through 2002, Kansas was consistently in the top five states in the nation in the number of meth labs seized. From 2002 until 2005, we generally ranked in the top ten. California and occasionally Missouri usually led the nation.

In a letter to all Kansas legislators on March 28, 2001, I reported, "First, as I dictate this letter, Kansas law enforcement is averaging the seizure or discovery of two 'meth labs' a day this calendar year. Obviously, if that pace continues, we're on track to break last year's state record of 702, which broke 1999's record of 511 'meth labs' seized, which broke 1998's record of 189, which broke 1997's record of 99, which broke 1996's record of 71, etc., etc."

I was honest with state legislators through the years regarding the premise stated earlier that no more than 20 percent of the meth in Kansas was believed by the KBI to be locally manufactured. Approximately 80 percent of the meth in Kansas was manufactured by Mexican drug organizations in Mexico and transported into Kansas through the southwestern corner of the state or via Interstate 70, by Mexican criminal groups, usually wrapped in Mexican newspapers of recent vintage. I wrote that it was absolutely necessary that we achieve better control of our own Kansas meth labs and significantly decrease their number. We wanted to more effectively address the imported variety of meth and its traffickers, but we simply could not do so until we freed up much of our resources being directed toward Kansas meth labs.

The high numbers of meth labs that Kansas law enforcement seized annually demonstrated that we were addressing the problem, not simply looking away. As I pointed out to Kansas legislators in a letter on February 13, 2002,

"So the bad news is that Kansas law enforcement located 846 meth labs last year. The good news is that Kansas law enforcement located 846 meth labs last year." Kansas law enforcement seized 728 such operations in 2002, 649 in 2003, and 630 in 2004. After 2004, we hoped and believed that these figures reflected a decrease in the number of meth labs.

Although we had not yet experienced a turning point in the conflict, a significant fiscal development did occur in 2001 to bolster our effort on the meth front. Thanks to the efforts of Senator Pat Roberts and Congressmen Todd Tiahrt and Jerry Moran, the KBI received a federal appropriation of nearly two million dollars specifically to fight meth in Kansas. We were given wide latitude and broad discretion in how to use the desperately needed federal funding. Our only instruction from the senator and congressmen was to use it in such a way that best benefited all of Kansas law enforcement in our mutual battle against meth.

Long before the federal monies arrived, I met early and often with Associate Director Dale Finger; Deputy Director Terry Knowles, who had oversight responsibility over the beleaguered KBI forensic laboratories; Assistant Director Kirk Thompson, in charge of our exhausted narcotics division; KBI budget director Marsha Pappen; and Kyle Smith, one of my top advisors, to plan the wisest strategies for using the funds to best advantage for Kansas law enforcement.

One need was clear. From 1994 to 2000, KBI agents and KBI forensic scientists had responded to the majority of the hundreds of meth labs discovered in Kansas. That awesome self-imposed responsibility could not continue. We had to train, equip, and certify local law enforcement officers to help share that duty, even though that would be very expensive. Previously we did not have the means to undertake such a task. Now we did. With half of the huge grant, almost one million dollars, the KBI trained, equipped, and certified approximately 300 municipal, county, and state officers as meth lab responders and investigators within months. At the same time, we provided meth lab recertification training and new equipment to more than 200 officers previously certified by the KBI and/or DEA. We also provided methamphetamine- awareness training to 3,300 Kansas prosecutors and first responders—fire fighters, EMS personnel, and other officers. Those efforts enabled us to greatly reduce the number of KBI personnel being sent to meth labs. We would be able to send one KBI agent with a team of local officers, instead of a complete KBI team of agents and scientists. We could save our teams for the larger, most significant, or most dangerous meth labs. Eventually the KBI would be responding to fewer than half of all meth labs being reported across the state, rather than to the majority of the reports, as in earlier years.

A second need was also clear. In March 2001, our beleaguered KBI chemists had an unacceptable backlog of 299 meth lab cases awaiting forensic analysis. Kansas prosecutors were being forced to dismiss meth lab cases already charged, or forced to delay the filing of charges in other cases, because we were unable to provide them with the timely forensic reports they needed to go forward with prosecution. The explosion of meth labs across the state had completely inundated our chemistry sections and was severely crippling our forensic service to prosecutors and law enforcement in narcotic matters in general and in time-consuming methamphetamine cases in particular.

The chemistry sections of the KBI forensic laboratory, under Director Mike VanStratton and Supervisor Stan Heffley, in Topeka, Great Bend, and Pittsburg (opened in 2000) were doing yeoman work, but there was simply too much of that work for the size of our chemistry staff, the available drug-testing equipment, and our forensic resources in general. There had been no state money for more chemists or for additional expensive equipment. Accordingly, we used the remaining half of the sizeable federal appropriation to fund the hiring of additional chemists and agents, and for the purchase of needed forensic equipment. The nearly two million dollars helped level the playing field for us against methamphetamine. Chemistry backlogs and delays in our laboratories decreased sharply after 2001 and remained less serious through 2004, even though we were still awash in meth labs seized.

There were other key developments on the meth front in 2001. Deputy Director Knowles and Laboratory Director VanStratton created a secure, interactive website for the exclusive use of Kansas prosecutors to track progress of their meth lab evidence being analyzed at the KBI laboratories. It was an instant hit across the state.

Also, I teamed up with Secretary of Health and Environment Clyde Graeber, one of the finest gentlemen to ever work in Kansas state government, whose agency was conducting most of the meth lab cleanups in Kansas. At a news conference at the Kansas statehouse on May 14, 2001, we announced the creation of the Kansas Retailer Meth Watch Program. Secretary Graeber and I had decided to join our agencies in an effort to enlist the voluntary participation of Kansas retailers in a statewide program, wherein retailers would report to Kansas law enforcement suspicious sales of cold and allergy medicines, such as Sudafed and Actifed, which have ephedrine or pseudoephedrine as the active ingredient. It was hoped that, as a result of the innovative, voluntary program, these tablets, essential in the manufacture of meth, would be kept behind the pharmacy counter or, at least, kept only in limited amounts on retailers' open shelves for better monitoring and to reduce the rampant theft and shoplifting of the tablets. If the customer purchased large quantities of the cold and allergy tablets, we wanted to know. We wanted a name, a physical description of the buyer, and/or vehicle information. We had been involved in such a pilot program in Great Bend since 1999 and it was working well. Important meth cases and significant arrests and prosecutions had resulted from information and leads provided to the KBI, the Great Bend Police Department, and the Barton County Sheriff's Office by cooperative retailers in that community.

We preferred, of course, a law requiring such cooperation across the state. We needed an act to reinforce the 1999 Kansas Chemical Control Act, which ostensibly compelled distributors to report suspicious transactions of regulated chemicals to the KBI.

The Kansas Retailer Meth Watch, uniting retailers and investigators, never intended for retailers to take matters into their own hands by challenging meth cooks and traffickers when they purchased large quantities of cold and allergy tablets. Instead, they were only asked to report such suspicious activity promptly to Kansas law enforcement. Early on, thanks to the involvement of thirteen major Kansas retailers, including Dillons Food Stores, the Petroleum Marketers and Convenience Store Association of Kansas, Wal-Mart, IGA, Walgreen Drugs, and Kmart, more than 1,000 retail employees were trained as observers across the state. KDHE provided training videos to retail store managers and their employees. Large, colorful Meth Watch signs, identifying the particular retail store as a program member, were placed with hundreds of Kansas retailers, not only to publicize the program but also to discourage meth cooks and traffickers from buying their precursors there. As I said at the news conference on May 14, 2001, announcing Meth Watch, "For those methmakers who can still read, this will work."[4] Meth Watch enjoyed significant if not remarkable success. Many criminal investigations were launched as a result of the program.

Our efforts to combat methamphetamine were not limited to the utilization of Kansas retailers, or the ongoing partnership with KDHE and municipal, county, state, and federal law enforcement agencies, or broad media coverage. Nor were our efforts only characterized by the routine but impressive seizures of meth labs and methamphetamine itself or by the escalating numbers of arrests and convictions. We also held town hall meetings on meth awareness in Kansas communities large and small. We held such a meeting in my hometown, St. John, population 1,350, in July 2005. There were more than 200 concerned citizens from Macksville, St. John, Stafford, Hudson, Radium, and Seward, every community in the county. Sheriff Jeff Parr, St. John Police Chief Sonny Ralston, and I appreciated the turnout and understood the citizens' individual and collective concerns about meth and what it was doing to their families and communities. As director, I spoke on the subject at numerous other locations around the state, including Lansing, Salina, Leavenworth, Overland Park, Liberal, Garden City, Pittsburg, Wichita, Valley Center, Topeka, Hutchinson, Parsons, Eureka, and Lawrence. And the KBI's narcotics assistant director, Kirk Thompson, and narcotics Special Agents in Charge Kelly Ralston, Jeff Brandau, and Rod Page, and Kyle Smith, then director of governmental and public affairs, were all deeply involved in preaching about meth across Kansas as well. Enlistment of citizens to assist law enforcement as our eyes and ears is key in any such campaign.

Much of the new forensic equipment in our Great Bend and Topeka forensic laboratories in those years was purchased with federal dollars obtained for the KBI by Congressman Jerry Moran. Similarly, much of the equipment in our Kansas City forensic laboratory came to us through the efforts of Congressman Dennis Moore.

The positive impact of the almost two million dollar appropriation, exclusively for meth, obtained for us by Senator Roberts and Congressmen Moran and Tiahrt, was remarkable. Through this forensic support, the number of meth labs awaiting evidentiary analysis in KBI forensic laboratories for Kansas law enforcement and prosecutors decreased from the all-time high of 299 in March 2001 to 37 in November 1, 2003. Thanks to the extraordinary efforts of KBI chemists (some of whom were hired with the described federal funding) under the leadership of Supervisor Stan Heffley, drug analysis backlogs and delays were nearly eliminated in our forensic laboratories.

Congressman Moran had been one of the first Kansas public officials to support Kansas law enforcement's anti-meth campaign. He had expressed concern about meth in Kansas dating back to his days in the state senate. Later, he sponsored the Methamphetamine Anti-Proliferation Act of 1999, designed to fight meth trafficking by creating more HIDTAs across the nation. He called me occasionally to discuss the meth problem and we visited about the situation several times when he returned to Kansas.

At Congressman Moran's request, we set up a meeting of local sheriffs, police chiefs, and my KBI narcotics staff at our KBI field office in Great Bend on December 20, 1999. For more than two hours he listened as we described to him the increasing danger of meth. He asked many questions and took many notes. Then, in spring 2000, he discussed with me an idea he had on how to bring congressional attention to the meth problem in Kansas and the Midwest. He proposed to hold a meeting of the Subcommittee on Crime of the U.S. House of Representatives' Judiciary Committee in the state of Kansas. He told me he would provide the congressmen if I would provide relevant speakers to address the committee on meth's impact in Kansas. We agreed to hold the meeting in the large auditorium of the Kansas Highway

Patrol Academy at Salina, and we both hoped the public meeting would be the forerunner of federal anti-meth funds coming to Kansas. It proved to be.

We held the meeting on August 8, 2000. The official title given the committee meeting was "Oversight Forum before the Subcommittee on Crime on the Threat to Rural Communities from the Production, Trafficking, and Use of Methamphetamine." Congressman Asa Hutchinson of Arkansas presided over the Salina hearing.

Congressman Hutchinson, as he opened the hearing, informed the approximately 200 individuals in attendance of the reason for the congressional visit to Kansas:

> The purpose of this forum, of course, is to examine the trends in the production, trafficking and use of methamphetamine in the state of Kansas and how this applies to our nation. . . . Clandestine meth labs have been discovered in all 50 states, but the state of Kansas bears the dubious distinction of having one of the worst meth problems in the country, ranking third overall in per capita lab seizures in 1999, which is even a higher rate per capita than California.[5]

Jerry Moran then spoke, welcoming the committee and the hearing attendees, and explained his motivation for hosting the meeting:

> Methamphetamine is a serious problem for us. I think one of the hopes that I have that might come from this hearing is that Kansans will become aware of the problem we face. I think many of us believe that Kansas is a state kind of immune from the drug problem and clearly you will hear today that is not the case. . . . Kansas has become one of the hotbeds of methamphetamine manufacture and trafficking in our nation. And I hope that an awareness can be generated in our state that we can assist law enforcement, as well as the prevention activities, the treatment activities. . . . Through the testimony today we hope to develop a better understanding of the rising problems of methamphetamines and learn what resources and changes in federal law are needed to help combat the spread of meth. My interest in this issue was raised in large part by the director of the Kansas Bureau of Investigation, Larry Welch. And during my time in the state senate, I served on the committee that was responsible for appropriating dollars for the Kansas Bureau of Investigation. And because of that knowledge and because of that relationship with the Kansas Bureau of Investigation, Mr. Welch and others have made the case to me as of now as a member of Congress about the importance of this issue.[6]

I had assigned Assistant Director Thompson and Special Agent in Charge Ralston the responsibility of locating speakers to address the visiting congressmen. The ten selected speakers were divided into two panels for two separate presentations to the visiting members of the U.S. House of Representatives. The first panel included Bruce Swalley, originally from tiny Claflin in Barton County, a meth addict and convicted former dealer; DEA Special Agent in Charge Joe Corcoran of the DEA's St. Louis Division covering Kansas; Kirk Thompson; Chief of Police Dean Akings, Great Bend, already a veteran of many meth lab raids; and the down-to-earth and eloquent Dr. Pamela McCoy of the University of Kansas Medical Center in Kansas City, Kansas, who graphically spoke about what she had observed of meth users in emergency rooms the previous three years. The second panel consisted of Roxanne Dupre, another recovering addict, from Salina; Assistant County Attorney Tom Stanton, Saline County, today of Reno County; KBI forensic scientist Dwain Worley, one of our finest chemists and already a meth lab veteran; Sheriff Leon Shearrer of Pawnee County, at Larned, another meth lab veteran; and Kelly Ralston, who, at that time, had supervised more meth lab raids than anyone in our state. The candor of Mr. Swalley and Ms. Dupre was impressive and telling, but Dr. McCoy was the biggest star in the star-studded cast. None spared graphic details of the consequences of meth, ensuring the hearing's success.

There had been many Kansas prosecutors in the audience at Salina on August 8. One who was not in attendance was County Attorney J. Matthew Oleen of Morris County. He was kind enough to copy me on his letter of August 10, 2000, to Congressman Moran:

Dear Mr. Moran:

Due to an unusually busy docket, I was unable to be in Salina to attend the forum you held on August 8 regarding methamphetamine use, production, and trafficking. However, I would like to take the opportunity to let you know my thoughts on the situation. I have been a rural prosecutor for almost eight years. Based on my experiences with methamphetamine prosecutions, the single most important thing that can be done to combat methamphetamine use in Kansas is to adequately fund the Kansas Bureau of Investigation.

Within months of the Salina forum, Asa Hutchinson replaced the retiring Tom Constantine as director of the DEA, after which Jerry Moran again invited Hutchinson to Kansas, in his new capacity, as head of the federal drug agency. On February 18, 2002, Hutchinson and Moran spoke to a group of about 100 Kansas law enforcement officials and prosecutors on meth at the Kansas Law Enforcement Training Center, near Hutchinson.

The two addressed about 500 persons on October 17, 2002 at the Wichita Crime Commission's annual dinner. Once again, Hutchinson's topic was methamphetamine in Kansas.

Congressman Tiahrt hosted Hutchinson months later in Wichita at city hall for an informal discussion on meth with about fifty Kansas law enforcement officials, mostly sheriffs and police chiefs.

We had the attention of Congress and federal law enforcement. However, DEA did not and still does not have enough agents in Kansas, and since September 11, 2001, the FBI's new priorities, understandably, permit little interest in Kansas methamphetamine.

Meanwhile, the KBI continued the battle. From 1997 through 2004, the KBI made 2,362 meth-related arrests. Of those arrests, 1,859 were for manufacturing. From 1997 through 2004, the KBI obtained 1,326 meth-related convictions. Of those convictions, 1,013 were for manufacturing. During that period, 75 percent of all KBI arrests involved narcotics, primarily methamphetamine. Almost 80 percent of all KBI criminal convictions were related to narcotics, primarily methamphetamine, in the same period.

We kept the pressure on methamphetamine. Task forces of law enforcement officials, prosecutors, judges, and representatives of the medical treatment and prevention fields were formed by Attorney General Phill Kline in 2004 and Governor Kathleen Sebelius in 2005. The KBI was represented on both bodies and I served as co-chairman, with Colonel Bill Seck of the Kansas Highway Patrol, on the governor's task force.

On April 4, 2005, we again hosted Congressman Moran at our Great Bend KBI field office for a media gathering to announce his sponsorship of additional federal legislation aimed at meth. One proposed federal act would help restore farms and parks damaged by meth labs and would also promote anti-meth educational programs in schools. The second act sponsored by Jerry Moran would place common cold and allergy tablets containing pseudoephedrine behind pharmacists' counters, making them more difficult to buy or steal. A purchaser would be limited in quantity of tablets purchased and would have to register and provide identification. At Great Bend I again publicly commended Jerry Moran for caring about methamphetamine in Kansas: "Nobody in the state of Kansas has been a bigger ally in the fight against meth than Congressman Moran. He has been on the front lines with Kansas law enforcement officials since the beginning and has been with us, side by side, ever since. His efforts in obtaining funding for Kansas law enforcement and the KBI have benefited the state and the criminal justice system as a whole."

We definitely needed more Jerry Morans. And we needed state legislation similar to the federal legislation he was sponsoring in Washington to prevent meth cooks from having easy access to large quantities of cold and allergy tablets containing pseudoephedrine. Kansas law enforcement had encountered 630 meth labs in 2004. What we also needed was Kansas State Senator Derek Schmidt's Senate Bill 27, then being debated in the state capitol at Topeka, to combat the insanity of methamphetamine manufacture in our state.

CHAPTER SIXTEEN

Matt: Methamphetamine Costs
the Life of a Kansas Sheriff

January 19, 2005, was not a bad winter day for Kansas. It was a sunny, albeit cold, day. Fields and yards in Greenwood County, Kansas, in the southeast portion of the state, held isolated patches of snow, but it would be a shirt-sleeve day for many of the county's residents as those fields and yards turned soft and even muddy by midday.

Greenwood County, home to approximately 8,000 souls, is the second largest in area of all the state's 105 counties. Only Butler County, on Greenwood's west border, is larger. Some of Greenwood County's residents live in very small towns across the county. The population of Climax is 57, Virgil 86, Hamilton 320, and Madison 826. Eureka, the county's largest community, population 3,031, is a city, at least by Kansas standards. Like most of Kansas, Greenwood County, situated at the foot of the Flint Hills, is very rural.

At 9:00 A.M. on January 19, 2005, Matthew Hayden Samuels, the forty-two-year-old sheriff of Greenwood County, was having a late breakfast at his favorite café in Eureka, his hometown. Matt was born in Eureka and had spent all his life in that community, as had his father and grandfather before him. Matt was six foot three and, despite his adoring wife's best efforts, weighed about 300 pounds. He had been a football player and wrestler for Eureka High School. He was physically imposing, but everyone knew him to be the classic example of a gentle giant.

He was in the ninth day of his second four-year term as sheriff. He was first elected sheriff in November 2000 and had taken office in January 2001. He had started his law enforcement career in 1986, working as a deputy sheriff for Greenwood County Sheriff Charlie Samuels, his father. Matt represented the fourth generation of Samuels in Greenwood County law enforcement. His grandfather and great-grandfather had been city police officers in Eureka.

I have known three generations of Samuels. I first met Matt Samuels when he was a small boy and I was an FBI agent in Wichita, and I started hunting quail and prairie chicken with his father, uncles, and other relatives. I often hunted with Jim Fountain, then the sheriff of Reno County, and ten or twelve others in Greenwood County. Everyone else's last name in our hunting parties was usually Samuels. Later I watched Matt play high school football on Friday evenings prior to the weekends when the Samuels family went hunting, outings in which I was privileged to participate for so many years. I can attest that the name Samuels is synonymous with marksmanship and sportsmanship.

Sheriff Charlie Samuels was president of the Kansas Sheriffs' Association in 1983 and highly respected across the Kansas law enforcement community. Charlie and his wife, Cheryl, were good friends to Shirley and me. He died suddenly and prematurely at the age of fifty-six shortly after his retirement. I attended his funeral in February 1994 in Eureka along with Al Thimmesch, the retired Wichita Police Department deputy chief of police. There was standing room only at Charlie's funeral. The audience was large, but it turned out to not be the largest Samuels funeral Al and I ever attended.

Lowell Parker, Charlie's undersheriff, followed him as sheriff and named Matt his undersheriff before young Samuels was elected sheriff himself.

My relationship continued with Matt and Tammy, his wife, who was a correctional officer at the El Dorado Correctional Facility and a native of Climax. Like Matt's father, they were active in the Kansas Sheriffs' Association and the Kansas Peace Officers' Association.

Most important, the native-son sheriff was popular at home, too. He was president of the Eureka Kiwanis Club and director of Special Olympics for his county. He considered local schools his personal beat and the kids loved him. His daughter, Sharlee, age fifteen, a sophomore at Eureka High School in 2005, and his son, Heath, a junior at Washburn University, majoring in, of course, criminal justice, adored him. He was a frequent visitor at the Eureka Senior Center and never missed a charitable pancake breakfast or potluck supper anywhere in the county. He had, as they say, people skills.

And he hated methamphetamine and meth labs. He especially hated what meth labs were doing to his county and its communities.

Scott Dever Cheever was twenty-three years old. He was six foot three, weighed 205 pounds, and had brown hair, blue eyes, tattoos of teardrops under his right eye, and an addiction to methamphetamine. Except for periods of incarceration, primarily at Lansing but also in correctional facilities in Ellsworth, Winfield, and El Dorado, he was a lifelong resident of Greenwood County. He had been an exceptional athlete at Madison High School. He took third place in the high jump event at the state track meet in 1998 and played on the football team before graduating in 1999. He received several athletic scholarship offers from small colleges. He declined them all and went to work in the Kansas oil fields. It was there, his mother would later claim, that he became addicted to methamphetamine. Others are not so sure that the oil patch was actually the origin of his drug problems. They point to an early and continually unstable home. His biological father was not involved in his upbringing, and his mother admits that her son used meth and marijuana in high school. A high school coach, trying to help the troubled teenager, in whom he saw great potential, took the boy into his own home until he found Cheever one evening in another part of Madison sniffing paint to get high.

The same year Cheever graduated from high school, his mother pleaded guilty to marijuana possession. By January 19, 2005, her driver's license had been suspended as a result of a DUI conviction, and her sister, Cheever's aunt, was on probation in Madison following a marijuana conviction. Regardless of what influenced Cheever to use meth, it is clear that meth led him to serious crime. He had juvenile arrests for theft, fighting, criminal trespass, and underage drinking.

On May 24, 2000, he attempted an armed robbery of a Eureka convenience store. He severely beat the cooperative clerk, was quickly apprehended, pleaded guilty, and was sent first to Lansing. In prison he was disciplined for using drugs, possession of contraband, theft, lying to correctional officers, poor work performance, and disobeying orders. After release on parole in 2004, he bragged to his mother that while in prison he had learned seven different ways to make meth.

On December 27, 2004, Cheever broke into his former stepfather's residence in Virgil. He pried open a gun safe and stole the three handguns and ammunition therein: a Ruger .44-caliber Super Blackhawk revolver, a Ruger 9-mm semiautomatic pistol, and a Ruger .22-caliber semiautomatic pistol. He also stole an old Ford automobile and some of his sister's clothing for his girlfriend.

The burglary was immediately reported to the Greenwood County Sheriff's Office and Cheever's former stepfather found a handwritten note that Cheever had left behind, which he gave to the deputy sheriff who came to the scene. It read, "Sorry Dad—had to go—took 45 and 44. Won't shoot noone but I had to hit a bank. Will return everything in a couple of days. Paco." The family's occasional nickname for Cheever was "Paco."

When the deputy sheriff, Dean Piatt, finished his investigation and prepared to leave the home, the stepfather warned him, "Be careful. The Kevlar vest you're wearing won't stop what Scott will be using and he won't hesitate to shoot." The deputy thanked the gentleman, apologized for his loss, and promised everything possible would be done to apprehend Cheever and recover the stolen property.

Authorities were promptly alerted of the bank robbery threat and Cheever's armed and dangerous status, but no such robbery was ever identified in

Kansas or surrounding states. The abandoned stolen car was recovered the next day in Lyon County, adjacent to Greenwood County on the north. A can of starter fluid, a key meth ingredient, and some loose .22-caliber and .45-caliber rounds were found in the car.

On January 5, 2005, Cheever was declared a parole absconder. During the evening of January 10 he dropped by his aunt's residence in Madison, allegedly seeking help for his addiction. It appeared he had been on a methamphetamine binge and had gone without sleep for several days. The terms of his aunt's probation for her marijuana conviction prohibited her association with convicted felons such as her nephew. She, therefore, declined to help him. On January 14 he telephoned his mother. She later told law enforcement that he was crying, sounded desperate, and asked her to come and get him. But since her driver's license was suspended because of her DUI conviction, she told him she could not pick him up, but, if he would call back in a few minutes, she would arrange for a driver to come to him. She feared he had been on one of his frequent meth binges, going sleepless for days. He never called back.

State correctional officers and the Greenwood County Sheriff's Office were actively looking for Cheever. As a fugitive, he would be returned to prison. Sadly, all he would have had to do to stay free was report to his parole officer, stay off drugs, and get a job. He had failed at all three.

Cheever's girlfriend, her mother, and Cheever's methamphetamine associates in the area were not cooperating with the sheriff's office in searching for Cheever. But the grandmother of Cheever's girlfriend did cooperate. She liked Matt Samuels and did not like Cheever for a variety of reasons. She disliked how much time her granddaughter was spending with him. She blamed the ne'er-do-well parolee, rightly or wrongly, for her granddaughter being hooked on methamphetamine, and for the girl's complete disregard of her own health, personal hygiene, and appearance when in Cheever's company. It was her opinion that her twenty-three-year-old granddaughter did the best for herself and her baby (by another man) when Cheever was behind prison walls. She intended to help put Cheever behind those walls again—the sooner the better. She was quite brazen and persistent in her efforts to inform the sheriff's office of Cheever's whereabouts, often calling Matt Samuels or one of his deputies in the presence of her own daughter, Rhonda O'Brien, or the granddaughter when she obtained any information from either regarding the fugitive. Unfortunately, her information was usually a day old, and the officers were then a day or two behind Cheever, who never stayed in the same place very long—a night or two at most.

The grandmother continued being an informant, despite scoldings from her daughter and granddaughter, because she firmly believed Cheever was physically abusing the granddaughter whom she also feared would be in great danger in his company when Cheever was eventually apprehended. She had been especially concerned since hearing of Cheever's theft of three handguns. She was aware of his vow to never return to prison. Someone was going to get hurt because of Cheever. She did not want it to be her granddaughter, misguided though the young woman was, in her opinion.

On January 19, 2005, at approximately 9:00 A.M., the concerned grandmother made her final telephone call to the Greenwood County Sheriff's Office about Scott Cheever. She asked for Samuels, but he was having breakfast in a Eureka café. Her call was taken instead by Detective Mike Mullins. Cheever, she reported, was probably at that moment at the residence of Darrell and Belinda "Kay" Cooper in Hilltop. She believed he had been there most of the night. She explained that Billy Gene Nowell, who was the father of Rhonda O'Brien's youngest son, had just left her residence. He had come by to see O'Brien, who was staying with her parents temporarily due to frozen water pipes at her own home. Nowell had told O'Brien that he had just come from the Coopers' residence and had seen Cheever there. Cheever, he said, was in the presence of another unknown male whom he had claimed was a cousin. Nowell had added that Cheever was armed and still vowing to never go back to prison.

Detective Mullins knew the Coopers well, as did every officer in the department. He was also acquainted with their residence in Hilltop, an unincorporated community between Lamont and Virgil in the northeast corner of the county. Mullins went promptly to the café and interrupted his sheriff's breakfast. In separate vehicles they then headed toward Hilltop. En route, Sheriff Samuels called Deputy Sheriff Thomas Harm on his cell phone, advising the deputy of the new information about Cheever's whereabouts and asking him to drive to the Coopers' residence in his own vehicle. The sheriff then informed the dispatcher at the Greenwood County Sheriff's Office in Eureka of the trio's destination, some twenty-five miles away.

Unknown to the three lawmen, following the grandmother's phone call to Detective Mullins, Rhonda O'Brien, realizing her mother had once again informed on Cheever, tried twice, unsuccessfully, to reach Cheever on his cell phone. She then telephoned the Coopers. She learned that her daughter was not there, but that Cheever was indeed present. O'Brien informed Kay Cooper that her mother had told law enforcement of Cheever's location and that Sheriff Samuels was probably en route to the Coopers' residence to arrest him.

Because Cheever had failed to maintain contact with his parole officer following his release from prison, the state had issued a parole violation warrant for his arrest on January 5, 2005. However, that was not his only legal problem. The parole violator was also the subject of a bench warrant issued on December 2, 2004, by the district court of Woodson County, for the charge of forgery. The district court in Lyon County had issued an arrest warrant for him on December 21, 2004, charging felony theft. The district court in Greenwood County on January 12, 2005, had charged him with burglary, felony theft, possession of drugs, and criminal possession of firearms. Both the FBI and the Emporia Police Department wanted to talk to him. Cheever was giving new meaning to the term "fugitive."

As noted in Chapter 15, the only situation more dangerous for law enforcement officers than entry into a known meth lab site is entry into an unknown meth lab site while it is in operation. This is especially true when the operator of the meth lab is addicted to meth, is armed, and has vowed never to return to prison. Unbeknownst to Samuels, Mullins, and Harm, that's exactly what awaited them in Hilltop—an operational meth lab, four persons using meth, and one, Scott Cheever, an armed meth addict.

There had been a fifth user present, Billy Gene Nowell, but he had left earlier to visit O'Brien, his girlfriend, before heading to his native Missouri. He had been the first one to teach young Scott how to cook meth years earlier. Nowell, age thirty-five, was a large man with a lengthy arrest record in Kansas and Missouri for burglary, theft, forgery, assault, battery, escape, probation violation, and parole violation, among other charges, and had served sentences in Kansas correctional facilities in Topeka and Hutchinson. On January 19, 2005, he was on probation for domestic assault and called Bronson, Kansas, his home. He had spent much of the night at the Coopers' house using meth with them, and after the arrival of Cheever early that morning he had helped Cheever and Darrell Cooper set up the meth lab.

It was not the first time Cheever had cooked meth at the Coopers' residence. Both the Coopers used meth and Cheever's custom was to give them a small portion of what he manufactured on their premises. Darrell Cooper, age forty-three, could not read or write, had few teeth, was extremely skinny, and looked the part of a meth user. He had a minor arrest record for alcohol abuse, writing bad checks, and failure to appear in court. Kay Cooper, age thirty-seven, was about five feet tall and well over 200 pounds, strange dimensions for a meth user, and not a prizewinning housekeeper.

Matthew "Matt" Denny was another meth user in the Cooper residence that morning. He was twenty-three years old, six feet tall and 200 pounds, and called El Dorado home, but he was residing with his mother and stepfather in nearby Leon, Kansas, in January 2005. He had an arrest record for DUI, failure to appear, contempt of court, forgery, burglary, and theft. He had served little jail time, usually drawing probationary sentences. He was not Cheever's cousin or friend, having only met Cheever the previous evening in El Dorado. Denny's girlfriend and her sister were friends of Cheever's girlfriend. Three couples, Denny and his girlfriend, Denny's girlfriend's sister and her boyfriend, and Cheever and his girlfriend, had partied the previous evening at a residence in El Dorado. Cheever and Denny left there at about 3:30 A.M., picked up some meth lab materials and equipment that Cheever had previously concealed in a trailer home in rural Greenwood County, and arrived at the Coopers' residence about 5:00 A.M. There, Denny met the Coopers and Nowell for the first time and used meth with them and Cheever as the group set up a meth lab on the second floor of the less-than-modest house.

When Kay Cooper received the telephone warning from O'Brien, she promptly advised Cheever that law enforcement was en route to arrest him. Cheever replied with obscenities and reiterated his vow not to return to prison. He told the Coopers to simply inform any law enforcement officers who came that he was not there. The others later stated that Cheever appeared to place little credence in the warning. In any event, he had to protect his meth lab. First things first; his priority was methamphetamine.

Upon arrival at the Coopers' residence at 9:45 A.M., Sheriff Samuels positioned each of his officers on one side of the house in the event Cheever came out either side. Samuels went to the front door alone since he knew the Coopers and expected no trouble from them. Clearly, he also expected no difficulty with Cheever, whom he also knew and had arrested before. Cheever was a runner, to be sure, but Samuels had all doors of the small house adequately covered if that should occur.

Darrell Cooper admitted the sheriff into the house. When Samuels asked if Cheever was there, Cooper replied in the negative. Samuels, disbelieving him, directed the same question to Kay Cooper as the sheriff quickly examined the small downstairs area, but she did not respond. Samuels then went to his vehicle, retrieved a flashlight, and returned to the house. He proceeded to push past a hanging piece of carpeting which covered the staircase leading to the small, dark second floor. At that instant, he was shot twice by Scott Cheever, who had been waiting in ambush with the .44-caliber magnum handgun stolen from Cheever's former stepfather.

Within seconds, Mullins and Harm were inside the house beside their fallen sheriff, angrily ordering the Coopers out of their home. (Both officers later testified that it seemed to them the Coopers were more concerned about the welfare of a gaggle of dogs in their house than the well-being of Matt Samuels.) The two officers then courageously pulled their sheriff from the house as Cheever, still not visible downstairs, fired at them from the second floor. He fired at them again as they dragged Samuels's lifeless body to cover behind the sheriff's truck in the front yard. Meanwhile, the Coopers fled across the road to a vacant house owned by Darrell's family.

The two officers immediately commenced CPR on Matt while frantically calling for assistance on their cell phones; their police radios were not working well that day. Deputies Dean Piatt, Patrick Romans, J. J. Smith, Jim Oakley, Rusty Bitler, Chris Neal, Les Lumry, David Harris, and others from the Greenwood County Sheriff's Office, as well as John Bills of Kansas Wildlife and Parks, arrived quickly, surrounding the house and establishing an early perimeter. The CPR efforts continued, even though every deputy involved knew it was futile. CPR continued until emergency medical personnel were able to reach the beleaguered deputies and pronounce Sheriff Matt Samuels dead at the scene.

At approximately 9:48 A.M. on January 19, 2005, in a ramshackle, filthy house in rural Greenwood County, between the towns of Lamont and Virgil, in an unincorporated area known as Hilltop, and almost within view of the Verdigris River where he had hunted and fished all his life, Sheriff Matt Samuels was shot twice and died at the scene. He died in the middle of a meth lab he had not anticipated, sharing his last seconds of life with methamphetamine cooks, users, and traffickers. He had detested meth and what it was doing to his beloved county. He had detested meth cooks, users, and traffickers, but, ironically, he died in their midst, among people he had known—some of them anyway.

As troopers of the Kansas Highway Patrol and officers from law enforcement agencies in surrounding counties arrived, distraught, protesting deputies of the Greenwood County Sheriff's Office were pulled out of their positions and sent to the sheriff's office in Eureka or to their own homes. In most cases they were driven to those destinations by other law enforcement officers.

Among the first KBI agents to arrive early that morning were Senior Special Agents Bill Halvorsen and Bob Beckham. Halvorsen, stationed in Emporia, and Beckham, assigned to Fredonia, were both good friends of Matt Samuels and acquainted with the men and women of the Greenwood County Sheriff's Office. They were veteran KBI agents and fine investigators. Beckham was accompanied by KBI Agents Chad Commons and Tim Holsinger from our Pittsburg office. Commons and Holsinger were narcotic specialists, with considerable experience in the seizure of meth labs. Halvorsen became the case agent, with overall responsibility for the conduct of the subsequent investigation. Special Agents in Charge Randy Ewy and Rod Page would assume command of the scene and the developing situation involving a barricaded suspect on their arrival.

Few KBI cases have ever received such an immediate saturation of personnel as the murder of Sheriff Matt Samuels and its investigative aftermath. We had no fewer than a dozen special agents at the Greenwood County crime scene quickly, as we assumed investigative responsibility that tragic day. Within twenty-four hours, we had thirty-three KBI personnel—agents, forensic scientists, and crime analysts—involved in the investigation. It was instantly the KBI's top priority and, accordingly, we threw as much manpower into the effort as needed. After all, methamphetamine was our agency's number one investigative and forensic priority, and Matt Samuels, a Kansas sheriff, was our friend.

At precisely the same time Sheriff Samuels was shot and killed at the site of a meth lab in Greenwood County, several of us were at the state capitol in Topeka testifying before the Kansas Senate Judiciary Committee in support of Senate Bill 27, at the request of Senator Derek Schmidt. That scenario proved to be a cruel irony.

The proposed legislation replicated a law that had been enacted in Oklahoma in 2004 and that had been credited with dramatically decreasing the number of meth labs in that state. Senate Bill 27, like its Oklahoma predecessor, would limit the number of over-the-counter cold tablets containing ephedrine and/or pseudoephedrine, key ingredients in meth manufacture, that could be purchased at one time. Also, the customer would be required to show photo identification and to sign a register at the time of any purchase. In addition, as in the Oklahoma law, the tablets would be removed from open public shelves and placed behind a counter. Liquid and gel versions of the medications, not yet meth manufacture friendly, would not be affected. Sales would be restricted to three packages per customer a week, hardly an unconstitutional burden.

The legislation, brilliant in its simplicity, and so successful in our neighboring state to the south, was quite similar to legislation Kyle Smith and I had testified in support of during the 1999 Kansas legislative session. The effort on that occasion was so strongly opposed by pharmaceutical interests that we were unable to move that bill out of committee in that legislative session.

On January 19, 2005, however, Senate Bill 27's author, Senator Derek Schmidt, the senate majority leader and a strong law enforcement supporter and dedicated opponent of methamphetamine, had done his homework. He had consulted closely with Kyle Smith and with Kansas sheriffs. He understood the need and he had studied the Oklahoma law and the impressive results it had produced. Most important, he had not underestimated the strength of the opposition. Within the forty-member Kansas senate he persuaded twenty-two other senators, Republicans and Democrats, to join him in sponsorship of the bill. There are only forty senators in the Kansas Senate. Schmidt communicated with Governor Kathleen Sebelius and Attorney General Phill Kline, seeking and receiving their blessings as well. Moreover, among Senator Schmidt's twenty-two cosponsors was Senator John Vratil, the powerful chairman of the influential Senate Judiciary Committee. Kyle and I were cautiously optimistic about the bill's prospects, at least in the senate, despite our lack of success with similar legislation in 1999.

On January 19, 2005, Colonel Bill Seck of the Kansas Highway Patrol, representing the governor, testified in support of the bill. I testified on behalf of the KBI and the attorney general. Kyle Smith also testified, as did Sheriff Lamar Shoemaker of Brown County, representing the Kansas Sheriffs' Association. Following our testimony, we briefly visited with individual senators on the committee, thanking them for a warm reception, for their concern about meth, and for their apparent initial support for the legislation.

When I stepped out of the hearing room with my law enforcement colleagues, we were told by Lt. Colonel Terry Maple of the Kansas Highway Patrol that he had just been notified, via his pager, that the Greenwood County sheriff had been shot. At first I was stunned and then I was in disbelief. Given my relationship with Matt Samuels, I thought that I would have been notified immediately by PJ, my perfect secretary, or another KBI staff member if Matt had really been hurt. I suggested to the others that Maple's message actually meant that a deputy sheriff had been shot. While no less a tragedy, that would explain, perhaps, the absence of such a message on my pager. By then, however, others were receiving similar messages on their pagers or cell phones, although there was no indication in any of the messages of Matt's condition.

I borrowed a cell phone and called PJ, who reluctantly informed me that Matt had indeed been shot. His condition was not known. My staff was aware I was testifying before a legislative committee and had decided not to communicate such news to me in that situation. PJ had been in constant telephone contact with the Greenwood County Sheriff's Office, but communications from the barricaded-suspect location where Matt had been shot were ineffective thus far. I asked PJ to telephone Shirley and advise her that Matt had been shot and that I was headed to Greenwood County.

I learned that the site of interest was not near Eureka but actually between Lamont and Virgil in the northern part of the county. I was quite familiar with that area. I had sat with Charlie and Matt Samuels on many a chilly dawn awaiting flights of hungry prairie chickens into soybean fields in the area. As I passed by Madison, PJ called me on my car phone to give me what would be her final update regarding Matt Samuels. In a halting, emotional voice, she told me the young sheriff had not just been shot. The gentle giant had been shot and killed. I slowed down. Speed was no longer relevant. I was urged instead to go directly to Eureka to be with Tammy Samuels and the kids. I was told I wasn't needed at the crime scene. Special Agents in Charge Randy Ewy and Rod Page were now on the scene and had everything well under control. Matt's body had been moved to the Eureka hospital and the barricaded-suspect situation was then simply a waiting game. The KBI, Kansas Highway Patrol, sheriffs of every adjacent and nearby county, the FBI, and the ATF (U.S. Bureau of Alcohol, Tobacco, Firearms and Explosives) were doing everything that could be done. Some arrests had already been made. I proceeded to Eureka.

When I arrived at the Samuels home, Matt's son, Heath, was in the front yard embracing a friend. When I reached him, we too embraced. He thanked me for coming. I whispered something foolish to him that I cannot recall now. I have never felt so inadequate. Words are normally not difficult for me, but they were embarrassingly difficult for me in Eureka on January 19, 2005. First with young Heath and then minutes later with Tammy when she returned home from the hospital, having seen her husband's body. She and I embraced and she gave me words of comfort that I could not seem to reciprocate. I was four days short of my sixty-ninth birthday, had been in law enforcement forty-four years, and had experienced my share of tragedies and challenges. But I was a miserable failure as a comforter to Tammy and Heath. Instead, despite their incredible burdens, they comforted me throughout that afternoon and the following day when I returned. Although devastated themselves emotionally, I received more comfort and support from Heath and Tammy the first day, and additionally from Matt's other child, Sharlee, on the second day, than I was ever able to reciprocate.

Any description of the events of that awful day in Greenwood County must include the incredible, spontaneous support extended by Kansas law enforcement to the KBI as we quickly assumed investigative responsibility that morning at the request of Matt's department and the county attorney.

Foremost was the Greenwood County Sheriff's Office itself. No law enforcement agency ever responded more professionally to such a tragedy than did Matt's own department, despite its own unprecedented agony and despair. The small department (eleven deputies) struggled with its grief, to be sure, but Undersheriff Kendel Bartholomew and his officers and staff performed admirably that day and in the days that followed.

Sharon Shaw, the matriarch of the Greenwood County Sheriff's Office, and who was strongly devoted to generations of Samuels, was a pillar of strength, assisting everyone, and ensuring that the office continued to operate as smoothly as possible in support of the KBI and constantly arriving law enforcement colleagues.

The immediate outpouring of assistance from the Kansas sheriffs of the region and their staffs, as well as from municipal departments in the surrounding area, was impressive. Kansas has always been a model of law enforcement cooperation.

Chief of Police Lyle Kee, from nearby Yates Center, and Officer Ken Leedy were among the first arrivals at the scene. They escorted Matt Samuels's ambulance to Eureka. At the hospital they took custody of the sheriff's bloody clothing and gear and protected the chain of custody in delivering that evidence to the KBI.

Sheriffs Dan Bath of Wilson County, Gary Eichorn of Lyon County, Gerald Ingalls of Chase County, Tom Williams (retired KBI) of Allen County, Doug Hanks of Elk County, Jim Keath of Neosho County, Dave Waddell of Woodson County, Craig Murphy of Butler County, Randy Rogers of Coffey County, and Undersheriff Bill Miles of Osage County were also among the first to arrive to support the original Greenwood County deputies at the scene. The sheriffs also brought their undersheriffs and/or deputies. They helped secure and then protect the scene. They transported and housed arrestees; brought food to the countless officers at the scene; helped establish a crime scene perimeter; controlled traffic in the area around the homicide scene; and assisted in many investigative interviews, as requested by the KBI supervisors. Sheriff Randy Rogers, who arrived on crutches with a leg in a cast, brought his well-equipped command bus. The vehicle proved to be a welcome respite from falling temperatures and north winds for many officers, and Sheriff Rogers served as an inspiration to all.

There were also investigators from the Kansas Department of Corrections, who had been hunting Cheever for weeks, and who were professional colleagues of Tammy Samuels. Police Chief Scott Blackburn of Howard, Kansas, was at the scene quickly, as were federal agents from Wichita, both FBI and ATF. Supervisor Tom Atteberry of the ATF and his agents were involved for several days in the subsequent investigation, pursuing various leads out of state for the KBI, at our request. The largest law enforcement contingent in Greenwood County on January 19, of course, consisted of representatives of the KBI and the Kansas Highway Patrol.

Following the homicide of Matt Samuels, District Court Judge John Sanders closed down much of the normal operations of the Greenwood County Courthouse and made available to the KBI the many resources of that facility as our overall operational command post in Eureka. Everything we needed was provided to us—everything from coffee and the invaluable stenographic skills of Greenwood County Court Reporter Mary Gaffey, another close friend of the Samuels family, to the district courtroom itself for use as our briefing room. And, as quickly as we developed probable cause for arrest and search warrants in those first days, Judge Sanders just as quickly became our personal provider of those necessary warrants.

Certain facts became quite evident very early at the crime scene. First, Samuels, Mullins, and Harm had not discharged their weapons on January 19. Matt's Glock .40-caliber pistol was still strapped in its holster when the two courageous deputies dragged his body from the house. Two of the entering team of troopers later that day fired their weapons in self-defense as the parole violator-turned-killer was finally captured. But the gunfire that day was woefully one-sided. The Greenwood County trio of officers had clearly been ambushed. Second, the homicide scene was also the site of an operational meth lab—a previously unknown meth lab.

The KBI investigation of the homicide of a Kansas law enforcement officer and the operation of a meth lab at 2612 310th Street, Hilltop, Greenwood County, the residence of Darrell and Kay Cooper, began hours before the last shots were fired at that site, before Scott Cheever was taken into custody, and before that crime scene was finally secured. As they presided over the barricaded-suspect ordeal, attempting to contact and negotiate with that suspect (presumed throughout the day to be Scott Cheever), Special Agents in Charge Page and Ewy, the on-site commanders, and case agent Bill Halvorsen were relaying investigative assignments via cell phones to other KBI agents. The assignments were based on information being gathered from the arrestees at the scene and also from information about Cheever, his family, and associates, provided by the deputies of the Greenwood County Sheriff's Office and others.

Matt Denny was arrested at the scene by Sheriff Dave Waddell of Woodson County and Greenwood County deputies after he was found hiding in the brush near the Coopers' house. He had jumped from the structure's second floor following the initial gunfire. In the understatement of the day, he told the arresting officers, "I think I need an attorney." He was transported to Eureka by Senior Special Agent David Klamm and lodged in the Greenwood County Jail that day at about noon. He was advised of his rights to remain silent and to be represented by an attorney. He waived those rights and spoke freely to Klamm en route to jail and at the jail. He quickly volunteered what he knew about Cheever, the Coopers, the meth lab, and the shooting of Matt Samuels. He repeatedly lamented to the KBI agent that it was the worst day of his life, detailing what had already happened at the crime scene. He would be interviewed again the next day at the Butler County Jail in El Dorado, where he had been moved, by Special Agent in Charge Randy Ewy and Special Agent Robert Jacobs. He again waived his rights to silence and legal representation and answered questions for more than two hours. A third interview, on January 21, was conducted by Ewy and Butler County investigator Tony Wilhite. Denny again waived his rights and answered questions for about an hour, furnishing a sworn statement reflecting his version of the events of January 19. Mary Gaffey recorded and transcribed the sworn statement.

Following her arrest at the scene, Kay Cooper was also initially lodged in the county jail in Eureka. At about 2:45 P.M., she was interviewed by KBI Senior Special Agent Jeff Hupp after waiving her rights. Hupp interviewed her again on January 20 in the Lyon County Jail in Emporia, after again waiving her rights.

Darrell Cooper was placed under arrest at the scene a little after noon by Senior Special Agent Ron Hagen, who transported him to the Greenwood County Jail. Like his wife and Matt Denny, he also freely waived his *Miranda* rights and consented to the interview by Hagen and Butler County Sheriff Craig Murphy. He was also moved to the Lyon County Jail in Emporia and reinterviewed by Hagen on January 20 after waiving his rights again. At the outset of both interviews, he was able to sign his name on the rights waivers, despite his claimed inability to read and write. And, like his wife and Denny, he blamed Cheever for everything from global warming to Matt's murder.

Billy Gene Nowell, who had departed the scene prior to the arrival of law enforcement but who was indirectly responsible for the subsequent arrival of Matt and his deputies, was arrested by Special Agents John Durastanti and Wes Williamson of the ATF on January 21 in Nevada, Missouri, at the request of the KBI. Nowell waived his *Miranda* rights as well as extradition back to Kansas. On January 22, he was transported from the Vernon County Jail in Nevada, Missouri, to the Wilson County Jail in Fredonia, Kansas, by KBI Senior Special Agents Rick Atteberry and Ron Hagen.

By 2:00 P.M., the KBI's Tim Holsinger and Chase County Sheriff Gerald Ingalls were in Virgil, Kansas, at the residence of the distraught grandmother of Cheever's girlfriend. She had already heard that her worst fears had been realized: Cheever had hurt someone. She told these officers of her ongoing efforts to turn Cheever into law enforcement. She reiterated the information she had relayed earlier that morning to Mike Mullins, which she had obtained from Nowell. She knew Matt Samuels well and deeply regretted his loss, especially at the hands of one she detested so much. She tearfully told all that she knew about Cheever and his associates, including Nowell's claim that very morning that Cheever had two guns in his waistband and was vowing not to be taken alive.

KBI Agents Chad Commons and Chris Bumgarner had been given the assignment to find and interview Rhonda O'Brien, the person who had called the Coopers that morning with the information that law enforcement was en route to their home to arrest Cheever. In addition to that information from the Coopers, the KBI had already traced phone calls that date to the Coopers' residence, confirming O'Brien's cell phone call to them.

Commons and Bumgarner were told that O'Brien could be found in Virgil at her parents' home. They arrived to find Holsinger and Sheriff Ingalls interviewing the girlfriend's grandmother, O'Brien's mother. O'Brien agreed to be interviewed in another room of the house while the grandmother's interview continued under the same roof.

O'Brien, aware of Sheriff Samuels's murder four hours earlier, admitted her telephone call to the Coopers' residence after unsuccessful calls to the cell phones of her daughter and Cheever. She described Nowell's visit that morning at her parents' home, and she told them of her mother's telephone call to the Greenwood County Sheriff's Office with the information Nowell had provided about Cheever and the Coopers. She confessed that her phone call to the Coopers was poor judgment, born of the desire to ensure the safety of her daughter and the Coopers. She insisted that she did not call to warn Cheever that law enforcement was on its way in order to assist him in eluding the authorities, and, indeed, she did not tell the Coopers that law enforcement was en route at all. Instead, she wanted to ensure that her daughter would not be present when the law arrived. She claimed that the phone call was really to warn her daughter, if present, and the Coopers, not Cheever.

While O'Brien was being interviewed by KBI agents, her daughter telephoned her from El Dorado on O'Brien's cell phone. Bumgarner, knowing that KBI supervisors also desired an interview with Cheever's girlfriend, spoke briefly with her by telephone and requested that the young woman proceed to the El Dorado Police Department to await them. She agreed. Before the interview with O'Brien concluded, she admitted that she and her daughter used drugs, including methamphetamine, and admitted knowing Cheever used and cooked meth. She also admitted that she was well aware Cheever was a parole violator and was wanted by several law enforcement agencies prior to killing Sheriff Samuels.

Commons and Bumgarner picked up Cheever's girlfriend at the El Dorado Police Department and transported her to the Greenwood County

Sheriff's Office, interviewing her about her relationship with Scott Cheever as they traveled. She admitted she had been Cheever's girlfriend about a year. They had stayed together at a friend's home in El Dorado the previous evening. She last saw him at 2:00 A.M. on January 19 when he awakened her, said he loved her, and left with Matt Denny. She also admitted during the ride in the KBI car that she had known he was a parole violator, but she volunteered little else.

At the Greenwood County Sheriff's Office that evening, in an extension of the interview in the car, the girlfriend was interviewed by Bumgarner and Klamm for an additional thirty-two minutes. That interview was recorded by audio equipment and later transcribed by a KBI stenographer. Of all the people interviewed by the KBI that first day and during the days that immediately followed, Cheever's girlfriend, not surprisingly, was the least forthcoming. She denied receiving any physical abuse from Cheever, contrary to claims by her grandmother. She denied any recent use of meth and denied knowing that Cheever was addicted to meth or manufactured it. She did admit she had heard Cheever's well-known vow to not be taken alive and not to return to prison but denied ever seeing him in possession of a gun.

At 4:39 P.M. on January 19, when a Kansas Highway Patrol team entered the Coopers' house under fire and captured and removed the lone occupant, Scott Cheever, Rod Page, Randy Ewy, Bill Halvorsen, and Senior Special Agent Bruce Adams were planning the searches of the Cooper residence. Separate search warrants for the site would be necessary. It was not only a homicide scene, but also a meth lab, requiring two separate and distinct sets of probable cause. It was also decided in advance to secure the site for the night and to initiate the searches the next morning, Thursday, January 20, when daylight would provide a more accommodating search environment.

The highway patrol team had deployed several canisters of tear gas into the Coopers' house prior to entry, without apparent effect. However, because of his exposure to the heavy tear gas and because of the suspected normal meth lab fumes to which he had been exposed all day, firefighters decontaminated Cheever at the scene with water following his arrest as Tim Holsinger and others guarded him. Bill Halvorsen then rode with Cheever in an ambulance to the Eureka hospital where doctors examined the suspect. Although two troopers had returned Cheever's gunfire, and although he had been exposed to gas and chemicals and had physically resisted the arresting troopers for a brief moment, Cheever, remarkably, was uninjured.

At about 5:00 P.M. at the command post near the Cooper house, as Cheever was being decontaminated and prepared for transportation to the hospital, the KBI's Bruce Adams, charged with responsibility for crime scene security, spoke with six law enforcement officials present. He asked Butler County Sheriff Craig Murphy, Chase County Sheriff Gerald Ingalls, Coffey County Sheriff Randy Rogers, Lyon County Sheriff Gary Eichorn, Osage County Undersheriff Bill Miles, and Captain Rick Wilson of the Kansas Highway Patrol if they and their personnel could provide around-the-clock security, starting immediately, with checkpoints on the road running by the house, in both east and west directions and surrounding the dwelling as well. As one put it, "We'll stay until hell freezes over or the KBI tells us to stand down." As it turned out, it was bitterly cold the night of January 19 in Hilltop, and continued that way the nights of January 20–22. The integrity of the crime scene was never violated, however. The around-the-clock security continued until 11:28 A.M. on Sunday, January 23, the day of Matt's funeral, when the searches in Hilltop ended.

The first KBI search warrant, later referred to as the capital murder search warrant, was issued by Judge Sanders the afternoon of January 19 on the affidavit of Bob Beckham while the barricaded-suspect situation was still in progress. That warrant provided the authority for the highway patrol entry and also for the first KBI investigative entry later that first evening after the premises were secured. The initial warrant targeted weapons, ammunition, live rounds, and shell casings alike, any notes, and the person known as Scott Cheever.

During the evening of January 19, in appropriate "moon suit" meth lab attire, Senior Special Agents Holsinger and Adams, joined by Special Agent Jim Lane, entered the house to ventilate it of any hazardous fumes and to assess the potential danger of the operational meth lab. The agents opened every window and door that would open, dismantled the meth lab, and agreed with the earlier decision to delay the search until the next day, after a second search warrant, specific to the meth lab, could also be obtained, and the light of day could assist the searchers.

I attended the briefing early the next morning in the Greenwood County Courthouse, held at the invitation of Judge Sanders in the district courtroom. Bill Halvorsen presided. The meeting was attended by a host of KBI personnel, ATF agents, Greenwood County deputies, and other local officers. Agents who had interviewed the Coopers, Denny, and others the previous day reported on the results of those interviews. Additional interview assignments were made and Holsinger was asked to prepare an affidavit for the second search warrant. Ewy, Page, and Halvorsen assigned search duties and responsibilities.

Judge Sanders issued the second search warrant, on Holsinger's affidavit in the early afternoon of January 20, and that search began at 2:34 P.M. the same day. The processing of the house, outbuildings, an abandoned mobile home, and vehicles at the Cooper residence continued throughout the daylight hours and late into the evenings of January 20, 21, and 22. The search team consisted of Special Agent in Charge Rod Page; Agents David Klamm, Tim Holsinger, Chris Bumgarner, Marc Perez, Jim Lane, and Robert Jacobs; and Forensic Scientists Brad Crow, Susan Lee, Bruce Coffman, and John Horn; Laboratory Supervisor T. L. Price; and ATF Agent Neal Tierney, the only non-KBI member.

The processing ended the evening of January 22. Attorney General Phill Kline, Assistant Attorney General Steve Maxwell, Assistant U.S. Attorney Lanny Welch, Assistant U.S. Attorney David Lind, and others were provided a walk-through briefing at the Cooper residence the morning of January 23 before their attendance at Sheriff Samuels's funeral in Eureka.

More than 250 items of evidence were seized, including 5 firearms; 120 ounces of anhydrous ammonia; 64 ounces of ether; 16 lithium batteries; 64 ounces of liquid methamphetamine; 5 grams of solid methamphetamine; 19 empty packages of pseudoephedrine cold tablets; numerous plastic bottles and glass jars with clear liquid and/or white residue; a cell phone belonging to Scott Cheever; numerous syringes; a bloody sheet; 20 swabs of blood spatter; and a Kansas Highway Patrol ballistic shield, with one bullet hole and two spent rounds lodged in it. One of the firearms recovered was a Ruger .44-caliber revolver. It held six fired shell casings in its cylinder and there was blood on the gun's barrel.

During the morning of Thursday, January 20, at the Shawnee County Coroner's Office in Topeka, Dr. Erik Mitchell conducted an autopsy of the body of Matt Samuels. Senior Special Agent John Kite attended the autopsy. During the procedure, Bob Beckham arrived, bringing the sheriff's bloodstained clothing for examination by Dr. Mitchell.

It was noted that the sheriff had not been wearing his protective vest. It mattered not. He had been shot once in the right armpit—undoubtedly while his arm was raised in a defensive move—and a second time in the neck, as he lay prone on his back. The vest would not have protected him.

As the autopsy report noted, "The palm of the right hand and fingers bore small wounds consistent with an object having sharp protrusions being dragged through the tight grasp of the hand around it." It was recalled that there had been blood on the Ruger's barrel. Had the sheriff been able to grab his assailant's gun?

Rhonda O'Brien was interviewed again on the afternoon of January 20 at her parents' residence in Virgil for more than an hour by Senior Special Agent Frank Papish of the KBI and Special Agent Wes Williamson of the ATF. She agreed to meet them that evening at the Greenwood County Courthouse to provide a sworn statement. That final interview of O'Brien began at 6:05 P.M. and ended at 7:14 P.M. Court Reporter Mary Gaffey again recorded the statement under oath for the KBI.

At both interviews that day, O'Brien was informed by her interviewers that she was not under arrest and was free to terminate the interview and depart if and when she chose to do so. In both statements, she reiterated her story to KBI agents of the previous day regarding Nowell's visit to her parents' home and his observations about events and persons at the Coopers' residence in Hilltop that morning. She reiterated her presumption that her mother, during Nowell's visit, had telephoned the Greenwood County Sheriff's Office about Cheever's presence in Hilltop. She reiterated as well her admission that she had telephoned the Coopers not to alert Cheever, she still insisted, but to check on the welfare of her daughter and the Coopers. She had been relieved, she noted, to learn her daughter was not with Cheever at the Coopers' residence. She continued to attribute her telephone call to the Coopers to "poor judgment," not to any desire to assist Cheever in eluding law enforcement. She admitted knowing Cheever was wanted for parole violation, and she finally admitted, in the sworn statement, that she had in fact told Kay Cooper that law enforcement was en route and that the Coopers should warn Cheever. She confessed she had not been honest on that point in previous interviews; again, it was simply poor judgment, she pleaded. When that interview was terminated at 7:14 P.M., O'Brien departed.

The day of Gaffey, Papish, and Williamson, however, was not over. From 7:25 P.M. until 8:33 P.M., Papish and Williamson interviewed, again, this time under oath, Cheever's nemesis, his girlfriend's grandmother, at the Greenwood County Courthouse. The tireless and professional Mary Gaffey again recorded the sworn statement for the agents. The interviewee's candor and cooperation never wavered in any of her three KBI interviews, nor did her disdain for Scott Cheever.

The sixth and final defendant in this case was arrested on January 23, the day of Matt Samuels's funeral. Rhonda Lisa O'Brien, age forty-three, of Toronto, Kansas, who had warned the Coopers and Cheever that law enforcement was en route on January 19, was arrested by Ron Hagen and Rick Atteberry of the KBI and Chase County Sheriff Gerald Ingalls at her parents' home in Virgil. The arrest warrant charged her with aiding a felon. She was transported by Hagen and Atteberry to the Allen County Jail in Iola. No questions were asked of her.

Ron Hagen interviewed Cheever's former stepfather at the sheriff's office in Eureka on January 24. He and Cheever's mother, Brenda Freisner, had been divorced in June 2004. He described the burglary of his residence in which Cheever had stolen three handguns, including a Ruger .44-caliber revolver.

The next day, January 25, Hagen and Jacobs interviewed Cheever's mother in the county courthouse in Eureka. Freisner acknowledged her son's criminal record and drug use, primarily marijuana and methamphetamine. She noted that when he was on drugs she always called her son Paco instead of Scott. The logic for the nickname was lost on the agents.

On the same day, Greenwood County Deputy Sheriff Chris Neal gave Jacobs a letter that Tammy Samuels had provided to him and that she had received from Cheever's grandmother, Freisner's mother, and written by Freisner. Jacobs went to Tammy's residence to confirm it was the same letter. Tammy identified the letter as the one given to her the previous day by Cheever's grandmother, who had explained that Cheever had been "strung out" on drugs when he killed Sheriff Samuels. In a fine example of "Felony Stupid," Cheever's mother, in the letter to Tammy, wrote: "I know you won't believe me, but that wasn't Scott who pulled that trigger. It was Paco. Scott is a terrific guy like Matt. Paco'd been strung out on meth for 25 days. He knew the law had a shoot to kill order on him. He was a scared 23 year old kid, that had spent all of his adult life in prison." In addition to alleging that there was a "shoot to kill order," the killer's mother also blamed much of her son's problems on the fact that "the cops had suspended my driver's license,"[1] preventing her from picking him up when he tearfully called her for help with his meth addiction five days before he shot the Greenwood County sheriff.

The only thing stranger than her ill-advised letter to Tammy was Freisner's interview with Stan Finger of the *Wichita Eagle*, published Tuesday, February 1, on the front page of the newspaper, with photographs of Freisner and her son. The headline told the story: "Mother details life of slaying suspect. Years of drug abuse led up to night sheriff was killed, Scott Cheever's mother says."[2]

In the two-page story, which no doubt discouraged Cheever's defense attorneys, she claimed meth and her son's meth addiction killed Matt Samuels, not her son. "Scott didn't do this. Meth did." Indeed, when her son was convicted of the attempted armed robbery of a convenience store in Eureka in 2000, he was attempting to get money with which to pay his large debt to his meth dealer, she explained. She acknowledged that she had pleaded guilty to a marijuana charge in 1999 and had a recent DUI conviction as well. Moreover, her sister was currently on probation for a marijuana conviction, she said. Then there were Scott Cheever's juvenile arrests for theft, battery, underage drinking, and criminal trespass, followed by the three years in Kansas prisons in Lansing, Ellsworth, El Dorado, and Winfield for the attempted armed robbery.

Interviewed for the story, Cheever's high school football coach recalled the young man as a gifted athlete who lacked confidence and a stable home life. The coach recalled their high school game-day dress code required a dress shirt and tie. Scott had neither until the coach purchased them for him, at a time when the young man lived with the coach and his family several weeks during his junior year. Cheever's mother, however, had profanely criticized the coach's kindness and generosity at the time in a strange "mind your own business" response.

On Sunday, January 23, 2005, Sheriff Matt Samuels was buried in Eureka, with more than 3,000 in attendance. The services were held at Eureka High School, the only site in Greenwood County almost large enough for the funeral. Mourners filled the gymnasium and hallways and overflowed into the parking lot. At least 1,000 of those in attendance were law enforcement officers from Kansas, Arkansas, Oklahoma, Nebraska, Missouri, Iowa, and Illinois.

On Monday, January 24, 2005, the day following Matt's funeral, charges drawn by Attorney General Kline were filed in Greenwood County District Court before District Judge John Sanders, charging six defendants in connection with the murder of Sheriff Matt Samuels.

The official court docket reflected that Scott D. Cheever, age twenty-three, was charged with seven felony counts, including the capital murder of the sheriff, the attempted capital murder of a deputy and two troopers, the manufacture of methamphetamine, conspiracy to manufacture meth, and criminal possession of a firearm. Matthew Denny, age twenty-three, of El Dorado; Darrell Cooper, age forty-three, and Belinda K. Cooper, age thirty-seven, of rural Madison; and Billy Gene Nowell, age thirty-five, of Bronson, were each charged with one count of conspiracy to manufacture methamphetamine. Rhonda O'Brien, age forty-three, of Toronto, was charged with aiding a felon and obstructing official duty.

The initial hearing for all six defendants was held later that afternoon in the Eureka court, amid unprecedented security measures. A metal detector was brought in from Emporia to check attendees for weapons prior to their admission into the courtroom. Hand-held wand detectors were also used by officers. Snipers were posted on the roofs of nearby buildings and KBI agents checked out vacant buildings and mingled with the crowd inside and outside the courthouse. Happily, there were no incidents and no threats to any of the defendants.

Cheever, wearing a protective vest under his orange jail jumpsuit, merely nodded or responded to Judge Sanders's questions with one-word answers during the brief proceeding. The other five defendants were also attired in protective vests and were equally reticent.

The judge ordered Cheever held without bond and set a $500,000 bond for each of the other five defendants. Judge Sanders tentatively scheduled preliminary hearings for all six for February 3, but he acknowledged to the defense attorneys that that date would probably be changed to permit more time for all concerned to prepare. He also knew that, if the prosecution continued in his district court, he would have to recuse himself. Sheriff Samuels had been a friend, as were most members of that large Greenwood County family.

Steve Maxwell knew there would be revised or additional charges. Attorney General Kline wanted the death penalty for Cheever, as did Tammy Samuels and her family, most if not all of Greenwood County, and most if not all of the Kansas law enforcement community.

The problem was that in December 2004 the Kansas Supreme Court, in a 4–3 decision in *State of Kansas v. Michael Marsh,* had ruled the Kansas death penalty law unconstitutional because it required jurors to impose the death sentence if they found the aggravating evidence of the crime's brutality in equal balance to any mitigating factors. In other words, any equal balance should be resolved in the defendant's favor and a life sentence imposed instead, according to the highest court in Kansas.

Attorney General Kline had quickly appealed the *Marsh* decision, but there was no guarantee the U.S. Supreme Court would agree to hear the appeal, let alone reverse the Kansas ruling, nor any guarantee as to when it would hear the case if it even agreed to accept the appeal.

Thus, the attorney general wanted very much to prosecute the killer of Matt Samuels, but the uncertainty of the Kansas death penalty law worried him greatly. Attorney General Kline, knowing the U.S. Attorney's Office had a federal death penalty available to it, struck a deal with U.S. Attorney Eric Melgren to pursue justice for all the defendants in U.S. District Court in Wichita, including the death penalty for Cheever. The methamphetamine manufacturing and Cheever's use of firearms in defense of his manufacturing operation in the Coopers' home provided federal jurisdiction.

As Kline would later explain to the media, "There is a cloud over the Kansas death penalty. It is a matter of seeking justice where justice is deserved."

U.S. Attorney Melgren added, "We believe that we owe that [the death penalty] to Sheriff Samuels, that we owe that to his family, that we owe that to all law enforcement officials in the state of Kansas."[3]

Therefore, the initial filing of state charges in Eureka's state district court was, at that time, just the means of getting all six defendants officially charged and bound over. Kline and Melgren had already jointly selected their prosecutorial team the day after the murder, and Lanny Welch and David Lind would accordingly be cross-designated for appropriate jurisdiction in state court, and Steve Maxwell likewise for federal court.

Despite Kline's decision, which surrendered his opportunity to personally pursue the prosecution of a Kansas sheriff's killer in Kansas courts in an election year, there was still no certainty of federal prosecution, conviction, and, especially, execution. Moreover, it was not Melgren's decision that would determine whether the federal death penalty could even be sought for Cheever. That discretion belonged only to U.S. Attorney General John Ashcroft. Melgren filed the appropriate papers quickly with the U.S. Department of Justice, commencing the application process for the highest federal penalty.

Meanwhile, Senator Derek Schmidt and his fellow state senators wisely entitled Senate Bill 27 "The Sheriff Matt Samuels Chemical Control Act." Opposition to the legislation melted as the Kansas Association of Chiefs of Police, the Kansas Peace Officers' Association, the Kansas Sheriffs' Association, and the Kansas County and District Attorneys' Association urged Kansas legislators to approve the act.

Several of us spoke before legislative committees in support of the bill. None of us spoke more eloquently, however, than the soft-spoken Tammy Samuels, whom we persuaded to address the important Corrections and Juvenile Justice Committee of the Kansas House of Representatives on March 14, 2005, to convince that group to approve the proposed legislation. Her opening paragraph was probably enough oratory: "Thank you for allowing me to address you today. I stand before you as the voice of my deceased husband, Matt Samuels, Greenwood County Sheriff, whose voice was tragically, senselessly and abruptly silenced on January 19, 2005, by Scott Cheever, a methamphetamine user." Others followed her, but the issue was pretty much decided after Tammy's reluctant, brief, tearfully eloquent speech to the committee. Thereafter, the legislation, in a rare, completely bipartisan effort, raced to approval in the Kansas legislature without a single dissenting vote. Shirley and I joined Tammy and many others in Wichita at a special ceremony on April 15, 2005, when the act bearing her husband's name was signed into law by Governor Kathleen Sebelius.

The KBI investigation relating to Scott Cheever's actions on January 19, 2005, in Greenwood County, continued well into 2007. Justice for the other defendants, however, was settled before the end of 2006.

In August and September 2005, Billy Gene Nowell, Belinda Kay Cooper, Darrell Cooper, and Rhonda O'Brien entered guilty pleas to their respective federal charges in U.S. District Court, Wichita, before U.S. District Judge Monti Belot, who sentenced them over September, October, and November 2006. Nowell, charged with conspiracy to manufacture methamphetamine and aiding in the possession of a firearm during a drug-trafficking crime, drew a sentence of thirteen years in federal prison, the harshest sentence of those pleading guilty. Belinda Cooper and Darrell Cooper, charged with drug-related violations, received sentences of twenty-four months and forty-six months, respectively. Rhonda O'Brien, for charges related to obstruction of justice, was sentenced to nineteen months in federal custody. One could say that O'Brien received nineteen months for an ill-advised phone call.

Meanwhile, Matthew Denny was prosecuted in state court by Assistant U.S. Attorneys Welch and Lind, and Assistant Attorney General Maxwell in September 2005. The jury trial was held in Butler County District Court in El Dorado with District Judge Mike Ward presiding. Most of the prosecution's witnesses carried KBI badges. Agents Ewy, Holsinger, Jacobs, Bumgarner, and Halvorsen testified, as did three KBI forensic scientists, David Wright, Brad Crow, and Bruce Coffman. Following the return of a guilty verdict by the jury, Judge Ward sentenced Denny to thirteen years and six months in state prison for his part in the manufacture of methamphetamine in Hilltop on January 19, 2005, which he had already called the worst day of his life.

The judicial path to justice for Scott Dever Cheever was more circuitous and considerably slower than that traveled by Nowell, O'Brien, Denny, and the Coopers.

Following his arrest, Cheever was initially lodged in the Lyon County jail in Emporia. There, in a move as ill advised as his mother's front-page pronouncements explaining his guilt in the *Wichita Eagle*, he attempted to smuggle a letter to a fellow inmate boasting of his killing of a Kansas sheriff. The letter, seized by jail officials, was turned over to Bill Halvorsen, who immediately provided it to the prosecutors. The letter, later ruled to be admissible evidence in the murder trial, read in part, "I'd do it again in a heartbeat. . . . I'm still an outlaw until they bury me. . . . I gotta get out of here. Either I do the hostage thing or the wall gets blown out . . . pick one!"[4] Laced with obscenities, the letter bragged of exceptional marksmanship at the murder scene. It omitted the fact, however, that Matt Samuels was shot from ambush at close range with his own gun still holstered. It also omitted any description of the writer's subsequent whimpering, tearful surrender to officers, with pleas of "I give, I give," as he threw down his second empty gun.

There would be other foolish and incriminating notes and letters authored by Cheever and seized by officials. Most had an escape theme. Cheever was soon moved to the Sedgwick County jail in Wichita after threatening another inmate in Emporia. When he was later found in possession of a homemade shiv fashioned from a toothbrush at Wichita, he was moved to a detention facility in Leavenworth.

In due course, Attorney General John Ashcroft and the U.S. Department of Justice approved the pursuit of the federal death penalty for Scott Cheever. Accordingly, the Welch-Lind-Maxwell prosecution team began to call U.S. District Court in Wichita home. Judge Belot was assigned the capital murder case.

Because Bill Halvorsen's assigned station in Emporia was eighty-five miles from the prosecutors' headquarters in the U.S. Attorney's Office in Wichita, the prosecutors also relied heavily on young KBI agent Robert Jacobs of the Wichita KBI office and Special Agent Neal Tierney of the Wichita ATF in the coordination of the Cheever investigative and prosecutorial efforts and in support of the veteran Halvorsen.

The federal prosecution of Cheever began well enough. On May 9, 2006, Judge Belot heard pretrial motions, ruling in the government's favor on nine of ten issues. The major victory for the prosecution was the judge's decision that Cheever's ill-advised and incriminating letters and notes, previously seized in jail, would be admissible at trial, which was scheduled in September.

When jury selection started, progress became less discernible. I attended two days of jury selection, September 21 and 22, 2006, with Tammy Samuels. That selection process had begun the previous week, but there was still no jury sitting in the box ready to hear the capital case. The potential of the death sentence, if Cheever were convicted, slowed matters. The prosecution sought jurors who could vote to execute Cheever if the capital murder case were proven to their satisfaction. Cheever's two public defenders slowly explained to every potential juror, individually and collectively, that the case they would hear was "not a whodunnit." Their objective was not acquittal.

Their goal was a verdict of first-degree murder and a life sentence without the possibility of parole, or, better yet, second-degree murder and life with the possibility of parole, but certainly not capital murder and lethal injection.

Tammy Samuels strongly desired the death penalty for Cheever and her wishes guided the prosecution. Accordingly, the prosecutors never entertained any notion of a plea bargain. In any event, federal prosecution of Scott Cheever, for all practical purposes, ended Friday, September 22, 2006, suddenly and unexpectedly. Following a surprise defense motion, Judge Belot, in a sealed order and without public explanation, granted a defense request for a continued trial date and appointment of a new public defender. The judge announced he would set a date, within thirty days, to review the status of the case. Tammy Samuels and the prosecutors were crestfallen. Significant delay appeared inevitable. The jurors were released.

But a new strategy, actually an old strategy, was available again, and the prosecutors, with Tammy Samuels's blessing, elected to follow that original course of prosecution. The U.S. Supreme Court favorably resolved the question about the constitutionality of the Kansas capital sentencing statute during the summer of 2006. Attorney General Kline had argued *State of Kansas v. Michael Marsh* before the Supreme Court on December 7, 2005, and April 25, 2006. On June 26, 2006, the U.S. Supreme Court reversed the Kansas Supreme Court's *Marsh* decision, ruling the Kansas death penalty statute constitutional.

Thus, on October 25, 2006, U.S. Attorney Eric Melgren and Attorney General Phill Kline announced they were collaborating once again to pursue prosecution of Scott Cheever and justice for Sheriff Matt Samuels. Melgren advised he would request dismissal of federal charges against Cheever. Kline stated he would join with Greenwood County Attorney Ross McIlvain to file capital murder charges against Cheever in state district court in Eureka. The death sentence would be pursued in state court rather than federal court. Tammy was pleased when Melgren and Kline added that Welch, Lind, and Maxwell would join McIlvain as the prosecution team. She was acquainted and comfortable with all four. Thus the original state charges were refiled by the attorney general's office in Eureka's state district court on October 25, 2006, and *U.S. v. Scott Cheever*, again, became *State of Kansas v. Scott Cheever.*

Judge Mike Ward, who had presided over the Matthew Denny trial in September 2005 in El Dorado, was assigned the Cheever capital murder trial. I had known Judge Ward when he was Butler County's very able and respected prosecutor years earlier. The trial was in good hands.

Ron Evans, perhaps the state's best-known public defender, of the Kansas Death Penalty Defense Unit, and colleague Tim Frieden, another veteran, were assigned to the defense of Cheever.

The KBI's Bill Halvorsen and Robert Jacobs, with ATF's Neal Tierney, would continue in their support roles as part of the prosecution team in the new venue.

Meanwhile, one event and one nonevent affected the course of prosecutorial action. The event was the election of November 7, 2006, in which Attorney General Kline was defeated in his reelection bid by Johnson County District Attorney Paul Morrison. Assistant Attorney General Barry Disney—hero of the Gary Wayne Kleypas prosecution with John Bork—would eventually replace Steve Maxwell as the new attorney general's representative on the Cheever prosecutorial team.

The nonevent was Cheever's apparent personal decision not to pursue a change of venue for his trial. He elected to take his chances with the citizens of Greenwood County, where he had been born and raised. The nonevent puzzled and surprised some observers.

Judge Ward set the trial for October 2007 in Greenwood County District Court in Eureka, after agreeing with Judge Belot's earlier opinion that the foolish, incriminating letters and notes that Cheever had authored in jail would be admissible in trial.

On October 19, 2007, two years and nine months after Sheriff Matt Samuels was killed in the line of duty, following seven days of jury selection, the capital murder trial of his alleged killer finally began in state court in Eureka. Shirley and I were able to attend almost every day of the trial. We sat in the section of the courtroom reserved for the large Samuels family and friends, usually next to Mary Gaffey.

On Cheever's side, only his aunt was present at the outset of the trial. His mother, Brenda Freisner, in continuation of "Felony Stupid," was unable to attend the trial's opening days because she was lodged in the Butler County jail, charged with two counts of threatening prospective jurors.

It was clear from the opening statements, offered by Lanny Welch for the prosecution and Tim Frieden for the defense, that the key issue in the trial would be premeditation. Indeed, it would not be an oversimplification to say that the theory of Cheever's defense was never innocence, but rather that he had been so high on methamphetamine he had been incapable of forming premeditation, a prerequisite for capital murder and the death penalty. In other words, he had been so intoxicated on the drug he had made that he lacked that highest level of criminal intent, premeditation, when he shot and killed Sheriff Samuels. He could be convicted of first-degree or second-degree murder, the defense reasoned, making him eligible for a life sentence, with or without the possibility of parole, but not capital murder, which required premeditation and could earn him a lethal injection. Known in legal circles as the "Voluntary Intoxication" defense, the strategy has saved the lives of others who faced the ultimate penalty.

Welch's opening statement for the prosecution at the beginning of the trial made it clear that the prosecution intended to rebut at every opportunity the defense strategy of intoxication and absence of premeditation. In prose approaching alliteration, Welch set the stage for the government's rebuttal of the defense theory with the rhythmic reiteration of the words "And Scott Cheever waited," describing the ambush that awaited Samuels, Mullins, and Harm following O'Brien's ill-fated telephone call to the Coopers warning Cheever of the approaching lawmen. "And he waited" preceded the prosecutor's description of Cheever's actions at every step, until the two fatal shots that signaled the end of Cheever's premeditation.

Following the prosecution's opening statement to the jury, Frieden outlined the "Voluntary Intoxication" defense and emphasized the inability to premeditate as claimed by Scott Cheever.

Then the trial began in earnest, as the tag team of prosecutors McIlvain, Disney, Lind, and Welch presented a litany of witnesses who described the events, circumstances, environment, and participants in the tragedy of January 19, 2005. Much of the drama, however, came on the first day as Welch examined Detective Mullins and Disney questioned Deputy Harm. The heartbreaking, emotional testimony by the two courageous officers provided the graphic details of Samuels's senseless murder. On the second day alone, twelve prosecution witnesses took turns answering the four prosecutors' questions and undergoing cross-examination from Evans and Frieden.

Among other early prosecution witnesses were the KBI's Halvorsen, Jacobs, Bumgarner, Page, Wright, and Crow; Trooper Travis Stoppel; and ATF Agent Neal Tierney.

No toxicology examination of Cheever had been ordered following his arrest, emergency room treatment, and confinement because no law enforcement officer or medical official had detected such a need or made such a request. At the time of his capture, Cheever had appeared arrogant, defiant, calm, coherent, and remorseless, but not intoxicated. And a parade of prosecution witnesses testified accordingly, from Belinda Cooper, who was with him at the start of the fateful day; officers who arrested and decontaminated Cheever; Halvorsen, who escorted him into the ambulance and interviewed him during that journey; and the three medical personnel who treated him that evening, two at the homicide scene, and one later at the hospital. Witness testimony established what urine and blood analysis undoubtedly would have shown. The prosecution argued that during the morning of January 19, 2005, Scott Cheever had the necessary mens rea or requisite criminal intent to commit murder.

When the prosecution rested, Cheever took the witness stand in an attempt to save his own life. He was, of course, limited in his response to questions from both prosecution and defense by the constraints of the defense strategy. That strategy required his admission that he shot and killed Sheriff Samuels, albeit sans premeditation. The strategy received a setback, however, when, during Disney's masterful cross-examination the defendant was asked, "You didn't want to go back to jail and that's why you shot the sheriff?" The accused, without any evidence of remorse, replied, "Yes."

Cheever's mother and aunt testified that the defendant was raised in a household where drugs and drug use were common. The family routinely smoked marijuana in his presence, starting at age six, and Cheever was given his own stash of pot at fourteen. Later, the mother and son made and used methamphetamine together. Blame the family, not Cheever, seemed to be the argument.

The trial that started on October 19, 2007 ended on October 30 when Judge Ward gave the case to the jury at 12:30 P.M. The jury took a fifteen-minute break before beginning deliberations. It was announced at 3:52 P.M. that the jury had reached a unanimous verdict. At 4:30 P.M. Judge Mike Ward announced the jury had found Cheever guilty of capital murder of Greenwood County sheriff Matt Samuels, guilty of attempted capital murder of Deputies Mike Mullins and Tom Harm, guilty of attempted capital murder of Troopers Robert Keener and Travis Stoppel, guilty of possession of a firearm by a felon, and guilty of manufacturing methamphetamine.

On November 1, 2007, the sentencing phase of the trial began. The jury of his peers that had found the defendant guilty of all charges two days earlier was called on to decide his fate—a life sentence in prison or execution by lethal injection.

Cheever again took the stand in an attempt to save his own life. Again his attempt at remorse fell short of obvious sincerity and believability.

In his closing argument, prosecutor Welch dismissed Cheever's attempt at remorse as "empty." He reminded the jury that Cheever, on January 19, 2005, in addition to killing Sheriff Samuels, had also fired at and attempted to kill two of Samuels's deputies and two state troopers. "He has never responded remorsefully for attempting to kill four other men that day," Welch said. "Consider that when you consider his remorse for Sheriff Samuels." Then, in one of the dramatic moments of the trial, the young prosecutor referred to Cheever's tattooed teardrops beneath his right eye and closed his remarks with this: "His only tears are the tattoos under his eye."

Less than two hours later the jury returned with a recommendation of death for the defendant. Judge Ward scheduled a hearing for January 23, 2008, to announce his approval or disapproval of the jury's recommendation, pursuant to Kansas law.

On January 23, 2008, exactly three years to the day since the funeral of Matt Samuels, Shirley and I sat in Eureka's Greenwood County District Court with Tammy Samuels and many of her family and friends. We were there to witness the sentencing of Scott Cheever, and we sat between the heroic Mike Mullins, who, during Cheever's trial less than three months earlier, had delivered with such professionalism dramatic testimony regarding the tragic events of January 19, 2005, and, on our other side, Mary Gaffey, who had transcribed so much of that story in KBI interviews, gaining intimate knowledge of the sad and senseless circumstances surrounding Matt Samuels's murder.

A little over two months earlier the jury of his Greenwood County peers had found the remorseless Cheever guilty of all seven charges against him, including the capital murder of Sheriff Samuels. Then, requiring less than two more hours of deliberation, that jury of eight women and four men voted unanimously to put Cheever to death.

Under Kansas law, however, even if a jury imposes the death penalty, the presiding judge must approve that penalty before the automatic review by the Kansas Supreme Court. Thus, we were present with Tammy, Sharlee, and Heath Samuels and their extended family; KBI agents; Greenwood County deputies; ATF agents; a gaggle of news reporters, photographers, and television cameramen; four prosecutors; two defense attorneys; Cheever's mother and aunt; and the shackled Cheever, to hear Judge Ward's decision regarding the death penalty for Cheever as recommended by the jury.

The four gentlemen who successfully prosecuted the case, McIlvain, Lind, Welch, and Disney, were seated together again at the prosecution table. Public defenders Evans and Frieden of the Kansas Death Penalty Defense Unit were seated at the defense table, flanking the defendant, as they had during the trial in October 2007.

Disney and Welch spoke briefly for the prosecution. Disney urged imposition of the jury's death sentence. He also requested just under 600 months of custody for the other six counts of criminal violations for which Cheever had also been convicted. Welch responded to various evidentiary questions posed by Judge Ward, in support of the jury's guilty verdict and sentencing recommendation.

Tammy Samuels, at Judge Ward's invitation, spoke for the family, quietly and respectfully asking the judge to approve the jury's recommendation

to impose the ultimate penalty. Her soft eloquence reminded me of her remarks before a committee of the Kansas House of Representatives at the
state capitol on March 14, 2005, in support of the proposed legislation that
would eventually be titled "The Sheriff Matt Samuels Chemical Control
Act." She was as effective in support of the death penalty for Cheever as she
had been in support of the proposed legislation earlier. Tammy described her
husband's killer as a coward who deserved no mercy. She lamented that Matt
did not have the opportunity to watch their daughter leave their home for her
high school prom, or attend Sharlee's high school graduation. She regretted
that Matt would never again take Heath hunting or fishing. There were few
dry eyes in the courtroom when Tammy ended her comments—none in our
row.

Cheever declined Judge Ward's invitation to speak and only Frieden spoke
for the defendant. Frieden suggested that the evidence presented at the trial
had not justified either the jury's guilty verdict or their imposition of the
death sentence. He requested that the judge set aside the death penalty and
reconsider life without parole for Cheever.

In the end, Judge Ward was unmoved and unpersuaded by the defense
attorney's words. The judge chose his words carefully, and spoke slowly,
clearly, and deliberately in respectfully rejecting the defense arguments and
approving the jury's decision to impose the ultimate sentence on Cheever.
More surprisingly, the judge exceeded the prosecution's recommendations
for sentencing on the four counts of attempted murders of the two Greenwood County deputies and the two state troopers, and also the sentencing
recommendations on the counts of methamphetamine manufacturing and
being a felon in possession of a firearm. Disney had asked for slightly less
than 600 months of custody for those six counts. Instead, Judge Ward sentenced Cheever to the maximum sentence of 737 months, more than 61 years,
for the six lesser charges. Death and more than 61 years.

Following the sentencing, thirty or so of the Samuels's family and support
group gathered for lunch at a local Eureka restaurant. Always the thought-
ful and considerate lady, Tammy surprised me with her knowledge that it
was my birthday and presented two birthday cakes to me. As the group sang
"Happy Birthday" to me, a warm feeling of satisfaction came over me. The
sense of contentment I experienced was not only inspired by the realization
I had reached the important milestone of seventy-two years of life that day,
but because I also realized that, at that approximate moment, Scott Cheever
was being transported from the Greenwood County Courthouse by Doug
Younger and his KBI security detail out of Eureka en route to a Kansas penitentiary. Younger had confided in me earlier that morning that the destination would not be the nearby El Dorado Correctional Facility that Cheever

had requested and anticipated, but another Kansas prison—Lansing. I shared the news with an amused and pleased Tammy Samuels, as she cut the first birthday cake. After all, Lansing was built to hold the worst of Kansas.

In May 2008, Halvorsen, Jacobs, and Tierney were honored by U.S. Attorney Eric Melgren for their individual and collective investigative efforts in the Cheever case. Each received the prestigious "Guardian of Justice Award" from Melgren and the U.S. Department of Justice.

As noted, the peak year for the seizure of meth labs by Kansas law enforcement was 2001, with 846 meth lab incidents across the state reported to the KBI and the DEA. And meth lab seizures continued to stretch KBI and other Kansas law enforcement resources in 2002 (728 seizures); 2003 (649); and 2004 (583).

The Sheriff Matt Samuels Chemical Control Act went into effect on July 1, 2005. In 2006, the first full-year of the law's effect, 168 meth labs were seized, the fewest since 1997. The number of vile sites confronted by Kansas officers plummeted to 97 in 2007, the fewest since 1996. The new law appeared to be working, although not to perfection. Almost 100 meth lab seizures were recorded in the first seven months of 2008 in Kansas.

Scott Cheever remains confined in Lansing under a death sentence, which has been appealed by his defense.

CHAPTER SEVENTEEN

BTK: The KBI Helps Pursue
the Infamous Killer

On the morning of January 15, 1974, four members of a family were brutally murdered at 803 North Edgemoor in Wichita. The victims, a husband and wife and their two youngest children, had been bound with window blind cord, gagged, and strangled to death for no apparent reason. A few days later, I had lunch in downtown Wichita with Bill Cornwell, the Wichita Police Department homicide chief, later Deputy Chief of Police, and Senior Resident Agent Elmer "Reid" Fletcher of the FBI. At the time, I was a special agent with the FBI and Fletcher was my boss. During lunch, Cornwell briefed us on the quadruple murder case.

Cornwell explained that these recent homicides seemed premeditated and yet without any clear motive. He asked if Fletcher and I would like to visit the homicide scene, which by then had been released, following three or four days of intense examination by Wichita detectives and forensic investigators. We quickly agreed and I drove us to 803 North Edgemoor. I recall, before we entered through the front door of the home and crossed the yellow "Police—Do Not Cross" tape left by the crime scene crew, that Cornwell showed us the back door, pointing out the absence of any sign of forced entry. He also directed our attention to the cut telephone line at the rear of the home, and then he walked us around the outside of the small, modest, one-story wood-frame home, indicating that the windows, like both doors, front and back, revealed no indication of physical disturbance. Then, as we walked through every room of the house, the homicide chief reiterated the lack of any obvious motive for the crime and the lack of any evidence of forcible entry. Nothing of value had apparently been taken, although the thirty-eight-year-old husband's wristwatch, and maybe a radio, were possibly missing, according to the three surviving children, who were in school when the deadly assault occurred. Cash and jewelry in the home were untouched.

The father, Joseph Otero, was recently retired from the U.S. Air Force with an honorable discharge. He and his thirty-four-year-old wife, Julie, had been born in Puerto Rico but raised in Spanish Harlem in New York City.

Julie Otero, who had loved being a military wife and had thoroughly enjoyed their last military posting in Panama prior to retiring to Wichita, had found a job she liked with the Coleman Company. She was a devout Catholic and the driving force behind the family's faithful church attendance. She was also passionate about the family's Puerto Rican heritage. Although weighing only one hundred pounds, the petite Julie, like all seven members of her family, was expert in judo. She possessed the brown belt. A pretty lady, she was excited about the family's new life, new home, and future in Wichita, although not yet fond of winter in Kansas. Indeed, on January 15, 1974, Wichita and much of Kansas were covered with snow.

Joseph Otero, who had enlisted in the U.S. Air Force as a New York teenager, had been a champion boxer, an expert in judo, an avid pilot, an exceptional flight instructor, and a master aircraft mechanic. Airplanes and his family were his great loves. He had retired from the air force with more than twenty-one years' service in August 1973 to accept a position as flight instructor and aircraft mechanic at a small airport near Wichita.

Mr. and Mrs. Otero were found dead on their bed in the master bedroom, lying side by side and fully clothed. Both had tape on their mouths, with their wrists bound behind them, and their ankles tied together. Mrs. Otero had not been sexually assaulted. Both had been strangled. Cords were still around their necks when they were found. In addition, Julie had a pillow atop her face and Joseph had a pillow case over his head, both removed by one of the surviving children when he discovered the bodies.

Bill Cornwell wondered aloud how the Oteros could have made such an enemy, or enemies, in such a short period of time in Wichita. They had arrived in Wichita barely five months earlier. Investigators had already learned that the Oteros were admired at their respective jobs and popular at their children's schools and at the family's church.

The nine-year-old son, Joseph, called Joey or Joe Jr., was the baby of the family. He had been found by his surviving siblings on the floor, dressed for school, next to his bed. He was also strangled. He was bound and gagged, his ankles were tied and his hands bound behind his back, and a T-shirt and plastic bag had been placed over his head, similar to his parents.

The strangest revelation at the homicide scene had been the discovery of the Oteros' pretty eleven-year-old daughter, Josephine, known as Josie, hanging by her neck from a sewer pipe in the basement. The thin girl, with long black hair, was wearing only a knit top and socks, with her panties pulled down around her bound ankles. Her hands, like those of the other victims, were tied behind her back. Her bra had been cut in two in front. Her slacks and boots lay nearby. Josie's toes did not quite reach the floor.

Dr. Bill Eckert, a Wichita pathologist, had handled the four autopsies. He had ruled that Josie, like her mother, had not been raped or sexually assaulted, although, bizarrely, semen had been found on the floor under her lifeless, hanging body and on her body, but not in her—and not a small amount, but an inordinate amount of semen. Indeed, Cornwell told us that some of the crime scene investigators were of the opinion that there were multiple offenders, at least two. Perhaps in some evil, strange ritual, they had both, or all, ejaculated toward the little girl; either that, some reasoned, or a lone killer had spent considerable time in the presence of Josie as she died by hanging. Dr. Eckert suggested the sexual attention directed at Josie Otero was postmortem or, perhaps, had occurred as the little girl died. Dr. Eckert was certain of one thing: the Oteros had died as a result of strangulation. Slow, intermittent strangulation, in fact, insisted Eckert.

There seemed no reason to suspect the Oteros of any criminal activity. Early indications from the U.S. Air Force were that Joseph Otero's military service was distinguished and without any indication of discipline. Neither Otero had ever been arrested, according to preliminary criminal history checks.

Josie was popular with her sixth grade classmates and teachers. She was artistic and loved to paint. She was also fond of reading and writing poetry. She liked Barbie dolls, and, like all Oteros, she enjoyed judo as well. She possessed a yellow belt in judo and coveted her mother's brown belt.

Little Joe was also popular with his fourth grade classmates and teachers. He was a handsome boy, athletic and, naturally, skilled in judo. Teachers advised detectives that Joey was already attracting attention from the girls in his class.

The surviving Otero children discovered the four victims on their return from school that afternoon. Charlie, age fifteen, Danny, fourteen, and Carmen, thirteen, had departed for school that morning prior to their father's scheduled departure for work; normal routine was for him to drop Joey and Josie off at their school en route to his work. Whoever had intruded into the Otero home that morning had done so after the three older children departed for school and before Joseph Otero could leave with the two younger children. The kitchen gave indications that Mr. and Mrs. Otero, Joey, and Josie were finishing their breakfast at the kitchen table when the intruder, or intruders, interrupted them.

How, speculated Bill Cornwell, could a lone intruder physically dominate a family of judo experts, including the athletic, strong Joseph Otero? Investigators learned later that Joseph Otero, a few days before the murders, had been involved in an automobile accident. On January 15, he was suffering with very sore ribs. Although police never established a connection between the accident and the motivation for the homicides, it is plausible that Otero's injuries made it possible for the perpetrator to overpower him.

Not only had the telephone line been cut, with no sign of forced entry anywhere, but the Oteros' home's thermostat had been turned up to full heat. The three surviving children all agreed that their parents never had the temperature so high. A professional killer or, at least, a well-read killer would know that such manipulation of the thermostat could accelerate body decomposition.

Indeed, the murders did seem premeditated, almost professional, and definitely organized, but without motive, unless, of course, the semen under and on pretty little Josie was evidence of a motive. No semen had been found anywhere near, or on, Julie Otero, or elsewhere in the home. It seemed to many of the investigators that Josie had been singled out for special attention. It was difficult to imagine, however, that the Otero tragedy could have been orchestrated by an impotent pedophile, especially a lone, impotent pedophile.

The final mystery within the mystery was why the Oteros' automobile was found later that evening blocks away in the parking lot of a Dillons grocery store. Had the killer, or killers, been afoot?

The few leads developed early in the investigation went nowhere. Theories abounded among the investigators, but none bore fruit or could be confirmed. Closer examination of the Oteros' history revealed only a close-knit, God-fearing, law-abiding family who, five months prior to the murders, had never been in Kansas. A more thorough review of Joe Otero's military service records only confirmed the preliminary conclusions. He had been a good and honorable airman and a respected noncommissioned officer. His record was without blemish and all inquiries indicated Joe and Julie were devoted to each other. Their children's futures had been their priorities.

Soon, Charlie, Danny, and Carmen Otero were taken in by an air force family in New Mexico. The two families had grown close in the military service. The surviving Otero children lived thereafter in New Mexico and would not return to Kansas for more than thirty years.

The motive for the murders of Joe, Julie, Josie, and Joey Otero remained obscure, and more murders would follow.

By October 1974, hundreds of people had been interviewed by the Otero investigators, and hundreds of leads had been pursued to exhaustion. An Otero case tip line was set up by the Wichita Police Department and manned twenty-four hours a day. The *Wichita Eagle* provided a reward of $2,500 for any information about the murders.[1]

Among the hundreds interviewed were three young men, ages nineteen to thirty, two brothers and a cousin, all of questionable mental stability and one a psychiatric patient. One had been arrested after attempting to molest a small girl and a duck. The trio confessed to responsibility for the Otero murders. Their implausible confessions, however, were quickly disproved, but not before the news of their detentions and their possible involvement in Wichita's quadruple murder case had leaked to the media. The story of the three confessions was carried on all three Wichita television stations, on local radio stations, and in the morning *Wichita Eagle* and the afternoon *Wichita Beacon* newspapers.

As it turned out, the actual killer of the Oteros read the news of the trio's confession and was offended and angry over the apparent attempts of others to claim credit for his work. On October 22, 1974, he telephoned Don Granger of the *Wichita Eagle* and directed him to a two-page typewritten letter to be found inside an engineering textbook, *Applied Engineering Mechanics,* third edition, by Jensen and Chenowith, at the public library across the street from the Wichita Police Department. Granger telephoned Chief of Police Floyd Hannon, who dispatched Detective Bernie Drowatzky to retrieve the described letter.

That telephone call to Granger and the letter found by Drowatzky changed Wichita and the Wichita Police Department forever, launching a thirty-one-year cat-and-mouse, adversarial, ongoing relationship between the city and the police department, on one hand, and the serial killer who became known as BTK, on the other.

The typewritten letter was entitled "OTERO CASE" atop the first page and read as follows (errors and misspellings as in the original):

I write this letter to you for the sake of the tax payer as well as your time. Those three dude you have in custody are just talking to get publicity for the Otero murders. They know nothing at all. I did it by myself and with no oneshelp. There has been no talk either. Lets put it straight . . . .
. . . . .

Joe:
Position: Southwest bedroom, feet tie to the bed. Head pointed in a southerly direction.
Bondage: Window Blind cord.
Garrote: Blind cord, brown belt.
Death: The old bag trick, and strangulation with clothes line rope.
Clothes;   White sweat shirt, green pants.
Comment: he threw up at one time. Had rib injury from wreck few week before. Laying on coat.

Julie:
Position: Laying on her black crosswise on the bed pointed ina southwestern direction. Face cover with a pillow.
Bondage: Blind cord.

Garrote: Clothes line cord tie in a clove-hitch.
Death: Strangulation twice.
Clothes: Blue house coat, black slack, white sock.
Comments: Blood on face from too much pressure on the neck, bed
              unmade.
Josephine:
Position: Hanging by the neck in the northwest part of the basement.
              Dryer or freezer north of her body.
Bondage: Hand tie with blind cord. Feet and lower knees, upper
              knees and waist with clothes line cord. All one lenght.
Garrote: Rough hemp rope ¼ dia., noose with four or five turns.
              New.
Clothes: Dark greatshirtntrt stripe, bra cut in the middle, sock.
Death: Strangulation once, hung.
Comments: Rest of her clothes t the bottom of the stairs, green pants,
              and panties. her glasses in the southwest bedroom.
Joseph:
Position: In the east bedroom laying on his back pointed in eastern
              direction.
Bondage: Blind cord.
Garrote: Three hoods; white T-shirt, white plastic bag, anther
              T-shirt. Clothes line cord with clove-hitch.
Death: Suffocation once, stranglation—suffocation with the old
              bag trick.
Clothes: Brown pants, yellow-brown stripe T-shirt.
Comments: his radio is missing.

All victims had their hand s tie behind their backs. Gags of pillow
case material. Slip knotts on Joe and Joseph neck to hold bag down or
was at one time. Purse contents south of the table. Spilled drink in that
area also, kids making lunches. Door shade in red chair in the living
room. Otero's watch missing. I needed one so I took it. Runsgood.
Themostast turn down. Car was dirty inside, out of gas.

    over

I'm sorry this happen to the society. They are the oneswho suffer
the most. It hard to control myself. You probably call me "psychotic
with sexual perversion hang-up." Where this monster enter my brain I
will never know. But, it here to stay. how does one cure himself? If you
ask for help, that you have killed four people they will laugh or hit the

panic button and call the cops. I can't stop so, the monster goes on, and hurtme as well as society. Society can be thankfull that there are ways for people like me to relieve myself at time by day dreamsofssmevictim being torture and being mind. It a big compicated game my friend of the monster play putting victims number down, follow them, checking up onthem waiting in the dark, waiting, waiting. . . . the pressure is great and some times he run the game to his liking. Maybe you can stop him. I can't. He has aready chosen his next victim or victims I don't who they are yet. The next day after I read the paper, I will know, but it to late. Good luck hunting.

YOURS, TRULY GUILTLY

P.S. Since sex criminals do not change their M.O. or by nature cannot do so, I will not change mine. The code words for me will be . . . Bind them, toture them, kill them, B.T.K., you see he at it again. They will be on the next victim.[2]

The detailed descriptions in the letter left no doubt. The author of the document, B.T.K., whoever that was, had murdered the Oteros. The specific positions and locations of the bodies had not been released by the police, and neither had the information about the victims' clothing, Mr. Otero's wrist-watch, Joey's radio, or the precise manner of death. B.T.K., or BTK, as the reference would evolve, had most certainly been present at the Otero homi-cide scene.

Hannon, Cornwell, and their investigators were excited about the receipt of the letter. The decision to keep the letter secret was made easily and imme-diately. Initially, they tried to communicate with the letter's author through subtle classified ads and editorials in the *Wichita Eagle* and the *Wichita Bea-con*. Those efforts were unsuccessful. The letter was provided to more than thirty psychiatrists and psychologists, seeking suggested profiles of the killer. The resulting profiles provided no immediate breakthrough for the investi-gators.

To complicate the investigation even more, the imposed cloak of secrecy surrounding the letter was involuntarily lifted when a reporter from a new weekly newspaper, the *Wichita Sun*, visited Hannon in early December 1974. The reporter possessed a copy of the BTK letter, and she warned the Wichita police chief that she and her editor intended to run portions of the letter on December 11. She declined to identify the contributor of the letter. Chief Hannon asked only one question: Was there any chance that the person who provided the letter to her was actually the killer? She assured him that was not possible, and she added that she had consulted some psychologists about the consequences of publishing the letter. They had actually recommended such action, explaining that without such publicity, obviously craved by BTK, he might kill again. Despite the chief's wishes to the contrary, portions of the letter were published on December 11 in *The Sun*.

On December 12, 1974, Chief Hannon held a news conference and confirmed the letter's authenticity and the likelihood that the letter writer was the Oteros' killer, or, at least, one who had intimate knowledge of the crime.

The Otero investigators could not know that the man they pursued would eventually become known as one of America's most prolific killers—an arrogant, egotistical, psychopathic, incredibly lucky serial murderer, who would kill ten persons over three decades. He was a serial killer whose downfall would eventually come, in part, from the professional collection and preservation of evidence at the Otero homicide scene by those same investigators, and, in part, from his own arrogance and bottomless ego.

Following the brutal murders of the Oteros, the killer would graduate from neophyte status and murder again in April 1974, less than three months after killing the Oteros. He would also commit two murders in 1977 and one each in 1985, 1986, and 1991. All ten murders were committed in or near Wichita. He would not again murder a child or a male, and he apparently tried to avoid any home with an adult male therein. He would strangle, cut, stab, and shoot, and he would often confess to murder in taunting, anonymous letters to the Wichita police, primarily through the U.S. mail and Wichita television and newspaper media. The taunting, however, would grow to arrogant mockery and lead to his downfall.

On April 4, 1974, Kathryn Bright, an attractive twenty-one-year-old former University of Kansas student employed by the Coleman Company, as had been Julie Otero, was stabbed repeatedly in her home at 3217 E. 13th Street in Wichita. She had lived with her sister Karen but was accompanied home that day by her nineteen-year-old brother, Kevin. Together they were confronted by an intruder armed with two handguns and a large hunting knife who had been waiting that afternoon for Kathryn's return after breaking the back door's window, unlocking the door, and entering the house.

At gunpoint, the intruder compelled Kevin Bright to tie up his sister before doing the same to Kevin in another room. The assailant returned to Kathryn, now tied to a chair, and attempted to strangle her. Meanwhile, Kevin loosened his own bindings and physically struggled with their assailant in an attempt to save his sister and himself. He was shot twice in the head in two separate physical encounters, collapsing after each struggle, before the intruder presumed him dead. Kevin, however, recovered a third time and fled the house for help, flagging down a passing motorist. Harried and distracted by Kevin's resistance and escape, the intruder ceased his efforts to strangle Kathryn and instead stabbed her eleven times, primarily in the abdomen. He then fled, leaving Kathryn seminude and unconscious. She died hours later at a Wichita hospital, never having regained consciousness. She had not been sexually assaulted. Incredibly, the brave, determined Kevin Bright survived the two gunshots to his face and head. He would be the only survivor of the serial killer's assaults.

On March 17, 1977, a divorced mother, Shirley Vian, was suffering from influenza at her home at 1311 S. Hydraulic in Wichita with her three children: Bud, age eight, Steven, five, and her toddler, Stephanie. Due to her illness, Vian, age twenty-six, a mainstay of her church choir, had permitted her two older children to miss school that day.

Shortly before noon, a man carrying a gun in one hand and a briefcase in the other followed Steven through the front door of the Vian home after Steven's playtime in the front yard. The distraught mother pleaded repeatedly with the intruder to not hurt her children or her. He promised he would not as he herded the children into a bathroom adjacent to Shirley's bedroom. He tied the defective bathroom door closed with a rope and positioned a bed against the door as well.

By the time the frightened children were able to escape from their confinement, the man was gone and their mother was lifeless, almost nude, and face down on her bed. She had been bound by her hands and feet and had a plastic bag over her head. She had been strangled to death with a cord that remained around her neck. The only items missing from the home were articles of Shirley Vian's underwear. She had not been sexually assaulted.

Shirley Vian's children would be raised by her parents in Oklahoma.

Shortly after 8:00 A.M. on December 9, 1977, a Wichita police dispatcher received a telephone call that she answered with the simple greeting, "Dispatcher." The male caller, calmly and without a trace of emotion, responded, "Yes, you will find a homicide at 843 South Pershing, Nancy Fox." The dispatcher replied, "I am sorry sir, I can't understand you. What is the address?" Actually, she had heard the address well enough, and already had traced the location of the phone booth the caller was using. She was simply attempting, as she had been trained, to keep the caller on the line as long as possible. Unfortunately, the listening telephone operator intervened and volunteered, "He gave 843 South Pershing." The male caller quickly added, "That is correct," and then terminated his call.

Officers responding to the telephone booth to which the call had been traced found no latent fingerprint impressions or anything else of evidentiary value. On the other hand, officers responding to the duplex apartment at 843 South Pershing, where the attractive twenty-five-year-old Nancy Fox resided alone, found a window broken out in the rear bedroom, the telephone line cut, and the thermostat turned up to the maximum 90 degrees inside the house. They also found Nancy Fox lying on her stomach on her bed wearing only a sweater and a bra, with her panties down around her ankles, strangled to death. Her hands were bound behind her with her own panty hose. Her gag was also created from her own panty hose. Furthermore, there was panty hose around her neck, as well, giving the indication she had been strangled with them. Medical examiners later thought a belt had also been used as a strangulation tool. Although she had not been sexually assaulted, semen was present on a nightgown found next to her head.

The popular young lady, known for an exceptional work ethic, was a full-time secretary at a Wichita construction company and also worked part-time two or more evenings weekly at a Wichita jewelry store. She had worked at the jewelry store the previous evening until 9:00 P.M. It was estimated that she had been murdered shortly before midnight.

Based on the evidence of a fierce struggle, investigators were sure that had the other side of the duplex not been vacant at the time, neighbors would have heard the assault taking place. Missing from Nancy Fox's residence were jewelry, including a particular necklace, and the victim's driver's license.

The tape of the telephone call was later enhanced and played for months on all local Wichita radio and television stations. Hundreds of suggestions about the male caller's identity were received by the Wichita Police Department. None of those leads proved productive. Yet years later, another generation of investigators would quickly agree that the telephone caller's voice was clearly that of the apprehended killer, BTK. Why had not someone earlier recognized that voice when it was telecast and broadcast frequently on Wichita stations? Such good fortune would continue unabated for the killer until 2005.

On January 31, 1978, an envelope arrived at the offices of the *Wichita Eagle-Beacon* newspapers addressed simply, "EAGLE BEACON 25 E. DOUGLAS CITY." The envelope contained an index card on which was printed, apparently with a child's print set, a poem of sorts, entitled "SHIRLEY LOCKS." The seven-line rambling attempt at imitation of the "Curly Locks" nursery rhyme, started with, "SHIRLEY LOCKS SHIRLEY LOCKS WILT THOU BE MINE?" It was signed "B.T.K." and closed with, "POEM FOR FOX NEXT."

It was intended by BTK to be his clever way to claim credit for the murders of Shirley Vian and Nancy Fox, as he had earlier for the Oteros. Instead, it was misunderstood by an *Eagle-Beacon* employee to be a valentine for someone's sweetheart, to be printed on the upcoming holiday, and was mistakenly routed to the classified advertisement section.

This misunderstanding and the failure to route the card to police and/or print it on the front page of a newspaper obviously angered BTK. It would become frighteningly clear that BTK did not merely crave publicity. He demanded publicity and recognition. It would also become evident that BTK closely monitored the media until 2005.

The proof for this was revealed when, on February 10, 1978, KAKE-TV in Wichita received an envelope postmarked Wichita, February 9, 1978. Inside the envelope were a two-page typewritten letter signed "B.T.K.," the promised poem to Nancy Fox, also signed "B.T.K.," and a drawing of a bound and gagged, almost nude woman on a bed, accurately depicting the position, attire, and bindings of Nancy Fox.[3]

BTK's anger was immediately evident in the typed letter's opening lines (again quoted here with the original grammatical errors and misspellings):

> I find the newspaper not wirting about the poem on Vain unamusing. A little paragraph would have enought. Iknom it not the news media fault. The Police Cheif he keep things quiet, and doesn't let the pubbic know there a psycho running lose strangling mostly women, there 7 in the ground; who will be next? How many do I have to Kill before I get a name in the paper or some national attention. Do the cop think that all those deaths are not related?

The police chief referred to was Richard LaMunyon, who had succeeded the retired Floyd Hannon in 1976. He would serve as Wichita police chief until his own retirement in 1989. That reference was clear, but what puzzled the investigators was the reference "there 7 in the ground." There were the four Oteros in 1974 and Shirley Vian and Nancy Fox in 1977. Who, when, and where was the seventh victim? (Police had not yet connected Kathryn Bright to the Oteros, Vian, and Fox.)

The rambling, pouting letter continued:

> Golly-gee, yes the M.O. is different in each, but look a pattern is developing. The victims are tie up-most have been women-phone cut—bring

some bondage mater sadist tendencies—no struggle, outside the death spot—no wintness except the Vain's Kids. They were very lucky; a phone call save them. I was go-ng to tape the boys and put plastics bag over there head like I did Joseph, and Shirley. And then hang the girl. God-oh God what a beautiful sexnal relief that would been. Josephine, when I hung her really turn me on; her pleading for mercy then the rope took whole, she helpless; staring at me with wide terror fill eyes the rope getting tighter-tighter. You don't understand these things because your not underthe influence of factor x. The same thing that made Son of Sam, Jack The Ripper, Havery Glatman, Boston Strangler, Dr. H.H. Holmes Panty Hose Strangler OF Florida, Hillside Strangler, Ted of the West Coast and many more infamous character kill. Which seem s senseless, but we cannot help it. There is no help, no cure, except death or being caught and put away It a terrible nightmarebut, you see I don't lose any sleep over it. After a thing like Fox I ccome home and go about life like anyone else. And I will be like that until the urge hit me again. It not continuous and I don't have a lot of time. It take time to set a kill, one mistake and it all over. Since I about blew it on the phone—hand-writting is out—letter guide is to long and typewriter can be traced too,. My short poem of death and maybe a drawing; later on real picture and maybe a tape of the sound will come your way. How will you know it me. Before a murder or murders Y you will receive a copy of the initials B.T.K., you keep that copy the original will show up some day on guess who? May you not be the unluck one!

At the bottom of page 1 he added, "7 down and many moreto go"--another reference to the unknown seventh victim and the threat of more. On the second typewritten page, he referred to victim #5 by saying, "You guess motive and victim." In reference to victim #6, he identified her as "Shir-ley Vain," but he accurately described her homicide scene and bondage. He closed that paragraph with, "Chose at random with some pre-planning. Mo-tive Factor X." In the next paragraph he identified victim #7 as Nancy Fox and, again, accurately and vividly, described that homicide victim and scene, including the "seminal stain" found on the nightgown next to her head. He also admitted, as had been surmised by the medical examiner, that he actu-ally strangled Nancy Fox with his belt, even though panty hose were found around her neck. He closed that paragraph with the following: "Chose at random with little pre-planning, Motive Factor X." In the final paragraph he promised there would be victim #8 and explained, graphically, what he intended to do to her. He closed with this: "Will be chosen at random. Some pre-planning—Motive Factor X." He signed the letter, "B.T.K."

His poem to Nancy Fox was entitled, "OH! DEATH TO NANCY." The "poetry" closed with these lines:

"I'll stuff your jaws till you can't talk
I'll blind your leg's till you can't walk
I'll tie your hands till you can't make a stand.
And finally I'll close your eyes so you can't see
I'll bring sexual death unto you for me."

It was signed "B.T.K."

Investigators traced the "OH! DEATH TO NANCY" poem to a photocopier in the basement of the Life Sciences building at Wichita State University by tracing the toolmarks left on the paper by the rollers of the copier. Professor P. J. Wyatt at the university identified for the police the basis of the Nancy Fox poem: an Appalachian folk song entitled "Oh Death," used in her English classes in the 1970s. On the theory that the killer might have become familiar with the folk song as one of her students, BTK investigators paid close attention to her past class rosters, but they never developed a solid lead there.

Some things were clear in this most recent communication from the individual who called himself "B.T.K.," because he liked to "bind them, torture them, kill them." Certainly the author was the murderer of the Oteros, Shirley Vian, Nancy Fox, and apparently one other. Also, the motives for his dreadful crimes were "sexual fantasy" and "Factor X," whatever those influences were.

Chief of Police LaMunyon and his Deputy Chief Cornwell wasted no time. In a hastily called news conference, Chief LaMunyon announced what many already realized. Wichita was being stalked by a serial killer who had killed six or seven times already and was threatening to kill again. The police, the chief said, believed the threat to be credible. LaMunyon identified the known victims as the Oteros, Shirley Vian, and Nancy Fox. He told the city, state, and nation that BTK had admitted killing those six people and had also claimed an additional unknown victim as well. The chief told of the victims' cut phone lines, and he warned women to immediately check for a dial tone on their telephones when returning to their residences. He told them to leave their homes immediately if they heard no dial tone. The police chief asked for the public's help and announced a new telephone tip line that would be manned twenty-four hours daily.

Although Kathryn Bright's homicide had not fit neatly with those of the Oteros, Shirley Vian, and Nancy Fox, the police had already been looking at her murder as possibly the work of BTK. They proceeded now under that premise; their suspicion was later corroborated.

In the days, months, and years that followed during LaMunyon's tenure as police chief of Wichita, he spared no effort in attempting to identify and apprehend BTK. His investigators used every tactic and strategy known to law enforcement of the day. They directed subtle messages and pleas to BTK in local editorials, letters to the editor, and classified advertisements. They used subliminal messages on television. They continued to consult with psychiatrists and psychologists for advice and counsel. Although there was a paucity of witnesses, they used artists' conceptions whenever available. They repeatedly played BTK's voice on local television and radio stations. They used the best criminal profilers available, including the FBI's famous Roy Hazelwood, Bob Ressler, and John Douglas.

On Saturday night, April 28, 1979, Wichita police responded to 615 South Pinecrest on the report of a burglary. The lady, whom we will simply call Anna, age sixty-three, lived there alone. She advised the officers that she had arrived home from a dance about 11:00 P.M. and discovered the apparent burglary. Someone had gained entry by breaking a basement window. Several items of jewelry, some scarves, various items of lingerie, and about thirty-five dollars in cash were missing. The lady's underwear and hosiery drawers were in disarray, and the telephone line had been cut.

Little significance was attached to the burglary on Pinecrest until June 15, 1979, when the lady received a large manila envelope in the mail.[4] The envelope contained a drawing of a woman in bondage similar to Nancy Fox and a poem entitled, "Oh Anna, why Didn't You Appear," wherein the author expressed regret that Anna had returned home too late on the evening of her burglary to become his victim "number eight." The poem was signed "B.T.K." That signature was followed by a strange symbol that became the killer's unofficial logo in subsequent communications to the police. The logo consisted of the letters B, T, and K transposed atop each other with the B drawn on its side, rotated ninety degrees to the right, which the early investigators and profilers concluded was intended to depict a woman's breasts. The police decided not to make the logo public.

The envelope also contained some pieces of Anna's jewelry and items of her lingerie. Anna promptly surrendered the envelope to the Wichita Police Department. A similar envelope arrived at KAKE-TV the next day, also including some of Anna's jewelry and lingerie.[5] Chief LaMunyon's other deputy police chief, Bobby Stout, announced that the department was convinced BTK had burglarized Anna's home and sent both envelopes.

BTK would not communicate with Wichita again for more than twenty-five years. Anna moved from Wichita.

As Chief LaMunyon would later say, they had tried everything except a psychic. He drew the line there. As a last resort and without fanfare, in 1984, LaMunyon formed a special squad of eight detectives dedicated to one mission and one mission only: to catch BTK. The youngest of the eight detectives was Kenny Landwehr, fresh from the patrol division. The others were Gary Fulton, Al Stewart, Paul Dotson, Mark Richardson, Jerry Harper, Paul Holmes, and Erwin Naasz. The squad's members were exceptional investigators, and they took new, exhaustive looks at the Otero, Bright, Vian, and Fox murders, and at the burglary on Pinecrest. They diagrammed every sentence in BTK's communications, reviewed every report written in every investigation, reinterviewed Shirley Vian's children and Kevin Bright, and interviewed hundreds of suggested and developed suspects. They recontacted profilers, psychiatrists, and psychologists.

The consensus was that the arrogant serial killer was a white male in his thirties or forties who had some Wichita State University connection and lived in somewhat close proximity to his victims. It was theorized that he might also have a military or law enforcement background and that he was still killing or would likely kill again. Despite its best efforts, however, the special squad was disbanded less than three years after its creation without accomplishing its mission. The BTK investigation went cold, and even BTK's taunts fell silent.

On January 17, 2004, in recognition of the thirtieth anniversary of the Otero murders, the *Wichita Eagle* published a feature story about BTK and the unsolved homicides.[6] The story reminded readers of the serial killer's seven known victims, that he had referred to an eighth unknown victim in a communication twenty-five years earlier, and pointed out that some were considering writing books about the mysterious unidentified killer who had remained silent so long. Prompted by the story, many Wichitans speculated that BTK had died, moved, been incarcerated, or been institutionalized. All such speculation would end two months later when BTK ended his twenty-five years of silence and confirmed the fears of many. He was alive and well, and, apparently, in Wichita. Painful memories and fears returned to the community.

On March 19, 2004, an envelope arrived at the *Wichita Eagle* postmarked Wichita, March 17.[7] It was addressed to the newspaper and bore the return address "Bill Thomas Killman, 1684 S. Oldmanor, Wichita, Ks. 67218." (That address would prove to be a long-vacant apartment.) Inside the envelope was a single sheet of paper on which appeared a photocopy of the Kansas driver's license of one Vicki Wegerle, 2404 W. 13th Street, Wichita, and copies of three Polaroid photographs of what appeared to be a dead female in three slightly different poses, lying on a floor beneath the photographer. The photographs seemed to be of a homicide scene, yet did not appear to be official homicide-scene photographs. The woman depicted was clothed but bound, lying on her back between a television set and a bed. In the bottom right corner of the sheet of paper, below the driver's license, was the hand-drawn logo BTK had used faithfully long ago to authenticate his correspondence for police.

The envelope and its contents meant nothing to those who first observed them at the newspaper's offices. Then the new evidence made its way to the desk of Hurst Laviana, a veteran crime reporter who immediately recognized the name of Vicki Wegerle as that of a victim of an unsolved murder almost twenty years earlier. He made a copy of the single sheet of paper for himself and then delivered the original envelope and sheet to the Wichita Police Department. It would be three more days, however, before the correspondence actually reached the Wichita Police Department's homicide squad, prompted by an inquiry from Laviana. Lt. Ken Landwehr, veteran of Chief LaMunyon's (now retired) special BTK squad, and now commander of Wichita's homicide squad, was on leave that day. First to view the mailing was one of Landwehr's detectives, Dana Gouge. Detective Gouge, with another detective, Kelly Otis, had been assigned the Wegerle homicide in 2000 as a cold case. Because of his intimate knowledge of the facts of that case, Gouge recalled immediately that Vicki Wegerle's driver's license had been taken during her homicide. He also knew that Wichita investigators had never used Polaroid cameras at crime scenes and that no official photographs were taken of Wegerle at the scene. Wegerle, strangled and unconscious but still clinging to life, had been moved by EMS to the hospital before Wichita police arrived that day. EMS personnel found her lying on the floor between a bed and a television set. She died at the hospital. Gouge had no doubt the mailing was from Wegerle's killer. Given the sender's name on the envelope, and, most important, the personal logo-signature of BTK, not yet made public, he also knew Wegerle's killer was BTK.

Gouge telephoned Landwehr and described in detail the envelope and its contents. Gouge's commander at once shared his excitement and his belief that BTK had finally resurfaced. It was Monday, March 22, 2004, and Hurst Laviana, Dana Gouge, and Ken Landwehr were the first to know that BTK was back, after twenty-five years. Landwehr thanked the gods for a second chance at Wichita's nemesis and vowed to catch BTK this time. He requested permission from his police chief, Norman Williams, to quickly form yet another special squad of homicide investigators, including the KBI and the

FBI, with which to track down, capture, and prosecute the serial killer of eight Wichitans. Chief Williams's approval was promptly forthcoming.

Despite the fact that eighteen of our authorized eighty-one special agent positions were then vacant for budgetary reasons, and that I was continually asking for funding from the Kansas legislature with which to fill some of those positions, I quickly accepted the invitation of Chief Norman Williams and Lt. Kenny Landwehr to join the BTK Task Force.

On March 24, 2004, I officially committed Special Agent in Charge Larry Thomas, commander of the KBI Cold Case Squad, and two of our best homicide investigators, Senior Special Agents Ray Lundin and Brad Cordts, to the BTK Task Force.

Almost immediately, however, we had to pull Cordts off the BTK assignment. Johnson County District Attorney Paul Morrison, in Olathe, requested that Cordts, because of his important work on the Liz Wilson homicide, be assigned to Olathe to help Morrison's staff prepare for the trial of John Henry Horton, who had murdered the thirteen-year-old girl in 1974. I, of course, honored that request.

Thus, on March 25, 2004, the roster of the initial BTK Task Force was Lt. Ken Landwehr, Detective Dana Gouge, Detective Cheryl James, Detective Kelly Otis, Detective Tim Relph, Detective Clint Snyder, and Detective Randy Stone, all of the Wichita Police Department; Special Agent in Charge Larry Thomas and Senior Special Agent Ray Lundin of the KBI; and Special Agent Chuck Pritchett and Special Agent John Sullivan of the FBI.

Thomas and Lundin would live in Wichita hotels for the duration. My budget director, Marsha Pappen, assured me we could afford the expense for a few months, and our agents cooperated by moving from hotel to hotel, always seeking less-expensive lodgings, not wishing for their BTK assignment to end for budgetary reasons. When possible, they returned to their Topeka homes and families on the weekends. Later, through the efforts of Congressman Todd Tiahrt, federal funds were appropriated for Wichita and the KBI was reimbursed for its BTK expenditures at the insistence of Chief Norman Williams.

I was pleased the KBI had been asked to join the BTK effort, and I promised Williams, Landwehr, Thomas, and Lundin that the two KBI agents would be on the case until BTK was identified, apprehended, and prosecuted. I was convinced that he would, in fact, be captured this time. I was certain his arrogance in resurfacing after all those years would be his downfall and I was determined to have the KBI involved in that noble cause. With my serious agent shortage, however, I hoped the mission would require only months of that determination and not years.

In my 2004 report to the Kansas legislature, I shared my confidence with our legislators, Governor Kathleen Sebelius, and Attorney General Phill Kline: "The KBI, since March 2004, has had two agents of our popular KBI Cold Case Squad assigned to the Wichita Police Department's BTK Task Force to assist in the eventual identification and apprehension of that nationally infamous serial killer. Our forensic laboratory has assisted Wichita authorities, as well. In fact, seventeen KBI employees have contributed to the BTK effort this year. He *will* be captured and prosecuted."[8]

On March 23 and 24, 2004, FBI profilers recommended that only one individual, Ken Landwehr, henceforth, handle all BTK media releases and conferences. The strategy, designed to build rapport between Landwehr and BTK, was followed faithfully thereafter. In subsequent vital exchanges between BTK and the police, Landwehr was always the face and voice of Wichita.

On March 25 and 26, Landwehr announced to the media that BTK had communicated with the Wichita police again, after twenty-five years of silence. He explained that the police were convinced of the mailing's authenticity and believed BTK's implied claim to be responsible for the murder of Vicki Wegerle on September 16, 1986. He also formally announced the creation of the BTK Task Force, comprising investigators from the Wichita Police Department, the KBI, and the FBI.

The *Wichita Eagle's* thirtieth anniversary story, January 17, 2004, BTK's response two months later, and Kenny Landwehr's media releases on March 25 and 26, 2004, not only ended twenty-five years of silence on that front, but those developments also resumed the cat-and-mouse saga between BTK and police, with added intensity twenty-five years after the killer's last contact with the police and media. The process would become a furious scavenger hunt for law enforcement and would lead eventually to an international media frenzy in Wichita.

Vicki Wegerle, a pretty, blonde, twenty-eight-year-old homemaker and gifted pianist, had been found on September 16, 1986, by her husband when he returned home for lunch. The couple's two-year-old son was in the home unharmed (their daughter was at school) and a family car, one normally driven by the young wife, was found two blocks away. She was fully clothed when discovered by her husband and the telephone line had not been cut. Both circumstances were contrary to typical BTK crime scenes. On the other hand, as at other BTK scenes, there was no evidence of actual sexual assault.

Evidence at the scene and from the autopsy indicated that she had fought fiercely with her attacker before he was finally able to subdue and strangle her with nylon hose in the presence of her toddler son. Skin, presumably that of her killer, had been recovered from her fingernails. DNA procedures in 1986 were ineffective with such evidence, however. Not so, however, in 2004, and DNA from the semen at the Otero and Fox homicide scenes and from the fingernail scrapings from Wegerle would soon be connected forensically, linking BTK to three of his eight victims—six of his eight victims, if Josie Otero's parents and brother were included by implication from the evidence near Josie's body.

Although the media and the public always called it the BTK Task Force, that was not the multiagency investigative body's official name. It was agreed that Chief of Police Norman Williams, Special Agent in Charge Kevin Stafford, head of the Kansas City division of the FBI, and I would formalize our joint effort to catch BTK with a Memorandum of Understanding (MOU) entitled "Memorandum of Understanding between the Wichita, Kansas Police Department, Kansas Bureau of Investigation and the Federal Bureau of Investigation Establishing the Bind, Torture and Kill (BTK) Serial Killer Violent Crimes Task Force."[9] The first paragraph read, "This MOU has been established based upon a formal request from the Chief of the WPD soliciting assistance in investigating serial killings which have and continue to occur in the Wichita, Kansas metropolitan area." The objective of the effort was to outline the mission of the Bind, Torture and Kill (BTK) Serial Killer Violent Crimes Task Force, hereinafter, "Task Force." This MOU will formalize relationships between the participating agencies for guidance and planning, in order to maximize interagency cooperation and create a close knit cohesive unit capable of analyzing and processing all information and investigative leads regarding an unknown serial killer believed to be located in the Wichita, Kansas area and commonly referred to as the "BTK Killer."

With this commitment we pledged our resources, our time, and our manpower, to each other. The signed MOU was actually not necessary. We had already shaken hands. Though the printed words did not make it so, "a close knit cohesive unit" was indeed created. To this day, when Kenny Landwehr, one of the most modest, unassuming people I have ever known, speaks of the original BTK Task Force members, he speaks in hushed tones and with deep respect.

Detective Kelly Otis, a tough, experienced, no-nonsense investigator, once attempted to explain to me his feelings about the experience of working closely with Larry Thomas and Ray Lundin, among others. He looked away after describing them forevermore as "brothers," for whom he would do anything. The group's *esprit de corps* was simply remarkable.

I know that Detective Cheryl James, the lone woman in the initial group of eleven veteran investigators, and who always held her own, would not be offended but honored if I describe that original BTK Task Force as a brotherhood. It became more than just a team of investigators under Landwehr's masterful direction and Chief Williams's wise discretion. The unit, from the beginning, exhibited professionalism, confidence, and determination. Egos were left at the door and an uncommonly strong work ethic became commonplace.

At first, the task force worked in a very small, cramped underground-like space adjacent to Wichita's city hall and police department. In those days, the task force's briefings that I attended were held in a conference room at the Sedgwick County Jail. Later, the FBI obtained nicer, more spacious workspace for the group in the Epic Center building in downtown Wichita.

I visited the BTK Task Force and attended its briefings in Wichita when my schedule in Topeka permitted. Chief Williams was exceptionally faithful in briefing me by telephone almost weekly on the task force's progress. Actually, Larry Thomas and Ray Lundin kept me advised of task force activities and Chief Williams was well aware of that fact. Nonetheless, he continued to personally ensure that I was advised of all key developments.

Not only was the task force occupied with elimination of hundreds of suggested suspects identified on a BTK tip line in those early months following the group's formation, but Landwehr also made other special, wise assignments. He assigned every BTK homicide to a task force member, or, in a couple of cases to two investigators, with the request that they quickly become experts on that particular homicide. They were asked to read every word in that homicide file, analyze every report and every interview, and know all forensic aspects of the case. In addition, he asked that they reinterview every possible witness, neighbor, family member, and all available former investigators of the particular case, and then interview people even indirectly connected to the case who had not been previously interviewed, such as victims' classmates, relatives, employers, and fellow employees.

I was pleased that Thomas and Lundin were assigned as a team to the Otero case. Those four murders became their special responsibilities. They became experts in every aspect of that case, familiar with every detail of BTK's first homicidal efforts. Then they traveled to New Mexico and located and interviewed the three surviving Otero children, developing lasting rapport with them. Given KBI jurisdiction and authority, Larry and Ray were also assigned most of the leads and suspects developed outside Sedgwick County, across the state, and outside the state during the life of the task force.

Detective Clint Snyder was assigned the Kathryn Bright investigation. Detective Dana Gouge was given the responsibility for Shirley Vian and Detective Kelly Otis for Vicki Wegerle. FBI Special Agent Chuck Pritchett and Detective Tim Relph drew Nancy Fox and also the "Oh Anna" burglary, where the intended victim's late arrival apparently thwarted BTK's deadly plans.

Although Thomas, Lundin, and later Sindey Schueler, biology section supervisor of the KBI's Forensic Laboratory Division and one of the nation's foremost DNA specialists, would carry the heaviest KBI loads for the task force, every agent assigned to the Wichita KBI Division would eventually cover BTK leads for the task force, and three KBI criminal analysts would assist the investigation as well. Ten agents, with the three analysts and Schueler, would log 6,695 BTK hours in the next eleven months. Next to Thomas and Lundin, KBI Special Agents Robert Jacobs and Angie Wilson worked more BTK hours than any other agents.

When the task force was organized, the case files were stored in approximately forty large boxes. KBI Crime Analysts Katie Schuetz, Fran Sheddan, and Jeff Muckenthaler, at the request of the task force, sorted, copied, and organized the case files into sixty-nine three-ring binders. They scanned 1,100 photographs of the homicide scenes, autopsies, composite drawings, BTK correspondence, and victims' photographs into the computer. They entered 15,900 names of individuals from those forty boxes of case files into the KBI's Cold Case Index System. They also indexed 2,300 business names and gathered complete background information (residences, employments, vehicles, criminal histories, and driver's licenses) on 199 suspects requested by the investigators. Later, when it was learned that BTK might be driving a Jeep, model year 1997–2004, they identified 6,253 such Jeeps in Sedgwick County and the seven surrounding counties to be eliminated by the investigators.

Lured from his hibernation of twenty-five years by the *Wichita Eagle's* thirtieth anniversary issue, and thereafter obviously pleased with the reaction and response to his Wegerle mailing—especially Landwehr's public acknowledgment that BTK was alive, well, and still a threat, and the newspaper's bold headline of March 25, 2004, "BTK resurfaces after 25 years"—BTK changed from an infrequent correspondent to the Wichita Police Department's most avid pen pal.

Following the Wegerle mailing of March 2004, BTK would communicate in writing with the Wichita Police ten more times in the next eleven months. Landwehr publicly acknowledged every BTK submission, often guided and counseled by the profilers of the FBI's Behavioral Science Unit in Quantico, Virginia. Landwehr, always the sole spokesperson and responder, occasionally replied more than once to each BTK communication. Landwehr's responses clearly delighted BTK and encouraged more communications.

The creation of the task force named for him also pleased him, as he would indicate in subsequent communications. It would become clear, too, that BTK was anxious to tell his own story rather than leave such an important biography to less-qualified authors who were apparently planning to write BTK books, as indicated in the newspaper's BTK anniversary issue.

The BTK Task Force, on the other hand, was excited and encouraged by the killer's brazen communications of increasing frequency. The squad's morale was the highest following the receipt of each BTK taunt. The group's goal was to catch him before he killed again, as he threatened and/or predicted in some communications. In the increased frequency and growing boldness of his reports, the squad saw increased potential for carelessness that could lead to identification and capture. He was overdue to commit a major mistake. Surely his supply of good luck was not inexhaustible.

No leads were developed from the Wegerle mailing itself—no latent fingerprint impressions or DNA. With its sad contents—copies of three photographs of Vicki Wegerle in different, apparently near-death poses, and the missing driver's license—and the official BTK logo-signature, the mailing did confirm that BTK had killed Wegerle. That confirmation was the primary value of the mailing to investigators.

BTK's next post-hibernation communication arrived, again via U.S. mail, at KAKE-TV on May 5, 2004. Postmarked May 4, it bore a return address of "Thomas V. King, 408 Clayton St., Wichita, Ks. 67203," a nonexistent address.[10] The envelope's contents were three sheets of paper. One sheet contained a strange word-search puzzle with "Chapter 8" atop it. The second sheet contained photocopies of two identification cards. One card was labeled "Wichita Public Schools" and the other "Southwestern Bell Telephone Company." On the second sheet was also a photocopy of what appeared to be a badge with a star and the words "Special Officer." The third sheet was the most interesting. Across its top was printed "THE BTK STORY." Below that title were thirteen apparent chapter headings:

1. a serial killer is born
2. dawn
3. fetish
4. fantasy world
5. the search begins
6. btk's haunts
7. pj's
8. mo–id–ruse
9. hits
10. treasured memories
11. final curtain call
12. dusk
13. will there more?

On May 10, Landwehr displayed all three enclosures of "THE BTK STORY" mailing in another media release.[11] This mailing lacked the usual BTK logo-signature of authenticity, permitting Landwehr to publicly display all three complete sheets. Despite the absence of the BTK logo, the FBI quickly confirmed what every task force member had known immediately. The author was definitely BTK.

One result of Landwehr's public disclosure of the latest BTK mailing was the quick recovery of the actual "Special Officer" badge depicted on one of the enclosures. Postal authorities following the media release recognized the badge as a recent addition to their lost and found box. The badge had apparently fallen out of BTK's envelope as it passed through the post office. As with all BTK communications, no forensic evidence was retrieved from the badge, the three sheets of paper, or the envelope—no fingerprints, DNA, or anything else useful. It was evident early on that BTK had a fondness for gloves. Investigative efforts to trace or identify the unimpressive, cheap, generic badge and the two depicted identification cards were unsuccessful as well. The two different names on the two identification cards proved irrelevant. Hours spent by task force members at the executive offices of Wichita Public Schools and Southwestern Bell Telephone Company failed to identify any similar cards ever used by either organization. The badge and the cards were displayed on television and in newspapers, without any recognition reported by any citizen.

Regarding the strange word-search puzzle depicted on one of the three sheets, similar to an anagram, task force members, KBI analysts, and especially the FBI's Behavioral Science Unit at the FBI Academy collectively identified twenty-nine words and five number sequences hidden therein. None of the words or number sequences were ever determined to have significance, other than the likelihood that BTK seemed to be implying that Chapter 8 of his promised book could be found within the anagram.

Landwehr's handling and coordination of the Wichita media on one hand and BTK on the other, while directing the day-to-day operations of the BTK Task Force, can only be described as masterful. He developed exceptional liaison and rapport on all three of those fronts and effectively maintained it for eleven long, stressful months.

One of his strong sources of support was Janet Johnson, assistant to Police Chief Norman Williams. Chief Williams loaned Johnson to Landwehr and the task force at the outset. She was the squad's girl Friday, morale officer, and sole administrative assistant. She organized Landwehr's media events and staff briefings and assisted everyone on the task force, while continuing to serve her police chief. She was also the primary police liaison to the city's three network television stations, sole major newspaper, numerous local radio stations, and the growing number of interested national and international news media. I was especially fond of Johnson because of her wonderful treatment of our agents Larry Thomas and Ray Lundin, and also because she and I share the same hometown of St. John, Kansas, generations apart.

Following the initial public disclosures by Landwehr, the public suggested hundreds of BTK suspects. It became clear that a strategy for suspect elimination was desperately needed. The sheer volume of information being provided to the task force by citizens, despite the squad's complete computerization of the data by KBI analysts, was overwhelming the investigators.

Landwehr's March 25, 2004, news conference alone resulted in almost 400 tips in the first twenty-four hours. After his May 10, 2004, media event, the total number of tips received grew to 2,000. Between March 2004 and February 2005, the squad recorded nearly 6,000 tips. Efficient elimination of suspects became a priority.

Age (those too young or too old to have committed the murders) and race (DNA told us that BTK was Caucasian) were the earliest and most common eliminators. But age and race were not enough. Another criterion for elimination would be needed, one that could be employed quietly and privately and without embarrassment to the suspect.

The best, most efficient eliminator of BTK suspects in 2004 and 2005 turned out to be DNA, thanks to the evidence professionally collected and preserved in the Josephine Otero (semen), Nancy Fox (semen), and Vicki

Wegerle (fingernail scrapings) homicide investigations of 1974,1977, and 1986, respectively. A DNA swab is brilliant in its simplicity as well as minimally invasive—an important constitutional detail. Gently rubbing a small cotton swab for two seconds inside the mouth along both cheeks of an individual who has given an agent or officer his permission to do so does not violate a potential suspect's constitutional rights.

During the task force's eleven months of operation, 1,300 men voluntarily agreed to be swabbed for their DNA, and, accordingly, those 1,300 possible suspects were each quickly and quietly eliminated from suspect consideration. Only forty men declined the request of a BTK Task Force member to provide a DNA sample in such a manner. Each dissenter was also subsequently eliminated as a suspect through more traditional and more time-consuming investigative measures.

I considered the DNA swabbing procedure to be an unintrusive, logical, practical, legal, and a very private elimination tactic. Jane Nohr, our agency general counsel, and Attorney General Phill Kline shared my legal opinion, given the strategy's dependence on voluntariness. There was, however, considerable criticism of the procedure, most of which did not surprise me, but some of it did.

For instance, I was not surprised when the *Wichita Eagle* on Sunday, August 15, 2004, quoted the executive director of the Kansas and western Missouri chapter of the American Civil Liberties Union (ACLU) on his opinion of our DNA swabbing program: "I think the whole idea is offensive from a civil liberties standpoint. Is it in keeping with the basic American values of privacy and being left alone by the government? To me, it runs afoul of that value."[12]

I was also not surprised when a Wichita attorney, who was then in the process of writing a book about the uncaptured BTK, was quoted in the same story, calling the process a "swabathon." Nor was I offended or surprised by media characterizations of the swabs as "DNA sweeps," nor by the *Wichita Eagle's* editorial criticism of September 15, 2004, which urged that the BTK Task Force "should rethink that broad-swabbed approach, which is probably ineffective, possibly unconstitutional, and risks smearing innocent people."[13]

The criticism of the BTK DNA elimination procedure that did disappoint and surprise me came from an instructor in a college criminal justice program. He was quoted in the *Eagle* in the August 15, 2004: "He said he advises his students not to consent if a police officer asks to search a car. He said he'd probably give the same advice about requests for DNA samples. 'That is a search, and it is an invasive search because they have to enter the body to get the sample.'"[14]

Despite such criticism, 1,300 men voluntarily consented to be swabbed by task force members and were expeditiously eliminated from the investigation, saving precious time. No DNA specimen collected by the task force's "swabathon" was ever used for any other purpose, and all such DNA specimens were destroyed, as promised when obtained, in 2006.

Thomas and Lundin swabbed their share of BTK suspects in Wichita and handled most of the swabbing assignments outside Wichita across the state—approximately seventy-five. They also handled swabbing assignments in Oklahoma, Texas, Missouri, Colorado, and Arkansas. DNA swabs were analyzed and compared to BTK's DNA by Lisa Burdett, a KBI biologist and supervisor of the KBI's Forensic Laboratory in Great Bend, and by Sindey Schueler, then the KBI's biology and DNA supervisor, headquartered at our Topeka laboratory.

The third post-hibernation communication, unlike the Wegerle and "THE BTK STORY" submissions, did not travel in the U.S. mail or in a normal-size envelope. It was found by a Wichita citizen in a large manila envelope taped to a stop sign at the intersection of First and Kansas Streets, immediately east of the central downtown section of Wichita, on June 13, 2004.[15] Landwehr responded to the scene himself and took personal possession of the package, on which was typewritten "BTK's Field Gram."

The manila envelope contained three sheets of photocopied paper. The first sheet was another copy of "THE BTK STORY" and the thirteen chapter headings previously submitted with the second communication. Chapter heading #8 (MO-ID-RUSE), however, on this version was blacked out. The familiar BTK logo-signature appeared on the bottom right corner of this sheet. The next two sheets (with the usual misspellings) were entitled "Death on a Cold January Moring" and "C1" (Chapter 1 of his book?). The narrative on those two sheets reflected a rambling, disjointed, but detailed description of the Otero murders and homicide scene. The message closed with a hand-drawn depiction of the hanging Josie Otero, captioned "THE SEXUAL THRILL IS MY BILL." Below the drawing was the BTK logo-signature. The Otero information contained specific details relating to the four victims and the scene known but to the investigators: heads encased in plastic bags, location of bodies, victims' attire, furniture arrangement, cause of death, and so on. BTK seemed to especially enjoy taunting his pursuers with graphic details of the fright, torture, and indignities he claimed to have inflicted on his victims, especially Josie. Landwehr then issued another headline-making media release on June 24, but withholding the graphic details.[16]

Communication #4 was found by a staff member in the book-return box of the downtown Wichita Public Library on Saturday, July 17, 2004.[17] The Wichita Police Department was promptly called because the package was labeled "BTK FLASH GRAM." Detective Kelly Otis retrieved it, and he and Ken Landwehr inspected the package's contents at the task force's office. Inside were photocopies of four photographs of what appeared to be individual men in various stages of bondage. In one photograph the subject was hanging by his ankles, upside down and nude, from a tree. The individuals and scenes depicted were unidentifiable, due to the poor quality of the photocopies and/or photographs. (Later, following his apprehension, the photographs were determined to be of BTK, taken by BTK, one in an autoerotic pose.) This communication bore the official logo-signature of BTK, closed with a threat to kill again, and contained the usual misspellings:

I have spotted a female that I think lives alone and/or is a spotted latch key kid. Just got to work out the details. I'm much older (not feeble) now and have to conditions myself carefully. Also my thinking process is not as sharp as it uses to be. Details-Details-Details!!! I think fall or winter would be just about right for the HIT. Got to do it this year or next! Number X, as time is running out for me.

Chapter Two will tell my interest in RR and the mighty power it instilled upon me.

Now back to Chapter Two. May not made the July deadline, be patient.
Attached: Picture of us doing
Bondage Games
Cc: BTK FILES

The task force was especially intrigued by the references to "Number X" and "Cc: BTK FILES." Did "Number X" refer to a tenth victim? If so, what happened to victim #9? As to the carbon-copy reference, it would be learned after his capture that BTK had indeed maintained his own BTK file, retaining copies of everything sent to the task force, and even more. He later referred to the file as his "treasure trove." It would become the prosecutors' treasure trove.

In response to communication #4, and because of the threat to kill again, Landwehr held four media events after the July 17 message from BTK. Those four releases, July 22, August 20, August 23, and August 26, covered public acknowledgment of the fourth communication found at the library; general information regarding Professor P. J. Wyatt, the folk song taught in her English classes, and the "OH! DEATH" poetry; general tips and advice about anti-BTK safety precautions at home; and some details of the "Oh Anna" burglary.[18]

On October 22, 2004, another large envelope, labeled "BTK FIELD GRAMS," was found in a United Parcel Service drop box at an office building at Second and Kansas Streets, only one block north of where communication #3 had been found taped to a stop sign.[19] Detective Otis responded to that call and claimed the fifth communication from BTK since the Wegerle mailing. Following communication #3, which had contained the first chapter of BTK's promised book, "A SERIAL KILLER IS BORN," his version of the Otero murders, this latest submission contained the second chapter, "DAWN," as well as a copy of a photograph montage of children, with bindings hand-drawn on their bodies. Two of BTK's logo-signatures were on the enclosures.

The second chapter of his "book" described recollections of his childhood and adolescence. In six typewritten pages, BTK wrote about his youth and background in a disjointed, strange, cryptic style: "Mother gone all day and days at time. Grandparents took care of me. I missed Mother a lot. . . . Smells of tobacco, coal and kerosene. Oh Grandfather, they played the song, a haunting song; it was a cool damp evening on the porch. They told me you died of lung disease. I will miss you forever!!!"

He went on to make many rambling claims, including the following:

He was born in 1939.

His father was killed in World War II.

His mother was promiscuous and his grandparents raised him.

His mother worked nearby and they lived near a railroad.

His mother dated, among others, a railroad detective for several years.

He had a cousin named Susan who moved to Missouri.

As a youth, he hunted, fished, camped, and attended church.

He had a female Hispanic friend named Petra, who had a younger sister named Tina.

He attended a military school in 1960.

He later entered the active military and was discharged in 1966.

He often solicited prostitutes.

He has had a fascination with trains all his life.

Lt. Landwehr held a brief news conference four days later, on October 26, generally acknowledging, though without specific details, the receipt of the latest BTK communication.

The question within the BTK Task Force was how much, if anything, could be believed in the serial killer's description of his early years. What if the arrogant, boastful, brazen jerk was actually being truthful about his background? If the facts and circumstances he described were accurate and Landwehr released them, perhaps someone could identify him from those clues. Accordingly, on November 30, 2004, after considerable discussion within the task force, a hesitant, disbelieving Landwehr repeated to the world approximately twenty of BTK's alleged background circumstances selected by the task force, with the following plea: "Based on these BTK-provided clues about his own background, do you recognize him, please?" Although more than 350 tips were called in during the first week following the release of these details, none proved productive.

Had BTK's claims been truthful, there might have been probable cause to arrest several of the nominees. One suspect in particular, suggested by an ex-wife, had the railroad history claimed by BTK, as well as an errant mother who dated, among others, a railroad detective. His father had been killed in World War II, and there was also a Missouri connection. Most important, according to the ex-wife, her nominee had the same unusual sexual practices and preferences that BTK apparently possessed. Her ex-husband had preferred to ejaculate on her rather than engage in actual intercourse. A DNA swab, however, quickly eliminated that suspect and greatly disappointed both the BTK Task Force and the ex-wife.

Because of BTK's apparent sexual proclivities, and because his fifth communication had boasted that he regularly availed himself of prostitutes, the task force reviewed all Wichita Police Department's prostitution investigations, arrests, and convictions (of both johns and prostitutes) for the previous ten years. They also interviewed many of those johns and prostitutes and many active prostitutes as well. They advised the prostitutes of BTK's suspected sexual abnormalities, hoping to identify BTK within their clientele. Every prostitute they interviewed was cooperative, but no significant leads were developed in those interviews.

On December 2, Landwehr thanked the public for past BTK referrals and invited more. He followed with another media release on December 7 about BTK in general.[20] As always, distasteful though he found it, the task force leader was professionally respectful to and about BTK, hoping to continue building rapport with the serial killer and encourage more communications. The strategy's success continued and communication #6, the last of 2004, followed promptly, reconfirming that BTK appreciated the attention and craved more.

On December 13, 2004, in Wichita's Murdock Park, near Murdock Street and Interstate 135, a citizen found a package that he believed was related to BTK.[21] The package made its way to the task force through the KAKE television station the next day. The package contained no authenticating BTK logo-signature, but such validation was not necessary. Among the contents was chapter 9, "HITS," subtitled "PJ Fox Tail 12/8/1977." Those two pages described in graphic detail the murder of Nancy Fox. BTK told of leaving his semen on blue lingerie near the victim's head after he strangled her with his belt. He told of replacing his belt with her panty hose postmortem. He also described turning the thermostat up to the maximum temperature "for quicker post mode on her body" and told of carrying lingerie, jewelry, including a necklace, and her driver's license from the homicide scene. To further confirm his claim, he also included in the package a bound, cheap imitation of a Barbie doll. Tied to the doll's ankles was Nancy Fox's driver's license. The doll, unclothed, was bound with hands behind her and a ligature around her neck.

Communication #6 was clearly from BTK, logo-signature or no logo-signature. His arrogance and excitement appeared to have reached new heights. The same day Landwehr received the package, December 15, the task force commander issued a media release acknowledging its receipt.[22] He withheld the graphic details of Nancy Fox's death and the information relating to the doll and Fox's driver's license.

No connections among any of the eight homicides, other than the similar modus operandi and the commonality of the perpetrator, were ever identified. Accordingly, the task force was convinced that BTK's awful deeds were random in nature—organized and planned—but random.

BTK's apparent typing deficiencies, spelling mistakes, and poor grammar in his communications provided hours of debate and discussion for the task force. The investigators again turned to the advice and counsel of respected profilers, psychiatrists, and psychologists. Some of those experts suggested that the apparent academic deficiencies were actually veiled attempts by the deviant author to mask a high IQ or at least to conceal above-average intelligence and extensive education. Others predicted that the poor spelling, grammar, and syntax were simply the best the author could do and accurately represented BTK's literary limitations. The latter theory would prove to be the more accurate.

By late December, the eleven members of the BTK Task Force had cautiously formed a consensus of certain beliefs about their adversary. Collectively, they believed him to be a sexual psychopath with pedophilic tendencies. They believed he had a connection or relationship, directly or indirectly, with Wichita State University in the early 1970s. They believed he was acquainted with or possibly had studied under Professor Wyatt (now deceased) at Wichita State University. They believed he actively wrote poetry and considered himself a gifted poet. They believed he had used fraudulent identification and/or an official-looking uniform to gain entry into some victims' homes. They believed he had conducted surveillance or stalked potential victims before committing most or all of the murders. They believed there was at least a quasi-law enforcement connection or relationship in BTK's past. They continued to cling to the belief that BTK's increasing arrogance would lead to a mistake and his apprehension in the near future. Of these collective beliefs, only one, that relating to Professor Wyatt, would prove to be erroneous.

As 2004 ended, the task force was not yet aware that the squad's fortunes were about to improve dramatically and that the uncommon good luck of the man whose self-declared mission in life was to bind, torture, and kill was about to run its course. Within fifty-six days the task force would run its prey to ground, following a dizzying flurry of boasting, taunting communications from BTK.

Landwehr issued another media release on January 5, 2005.[23] This one concentrated on Nancy Fox's necklace that BTK had mentioned in the sixth communication. It included a photograph of the necklace that the task force, based on contacts with Nancy's family and her previous jeweler-employer, believed to be the one that was missing. The hope was that someone might recognize that necklace and know its current whereabouts.

The beginning of the end revealed itself that month. BTK's communications #7, #8, and #9, all in January, included, among their collective enclosures, one chart labeled "BOOM."[24] Perhaps sensing that his days were numbered and that the Wichita Police Department, FBI, and KBI would soon be knocking on his door, BTK wrote at the top of the page: "If you get to [sic] close to BTK's LAIR or upon Capture and time unchecked this house will go—BOOM." Exposing the first chink in BTK's armor of self-confidence, the chart warned that his home was booby-trapped with explosive devices. He wrote of propane bottles from old grills filled with gasoline, and heavy locked and alarmed doors throughout a house with two stories, a basement, an elevator, bondage room, garage, and hidden stairway. Nothing could have been further from the truth. Modest would be an exaggeration in describing the real home from which he periodically sallied forth to do his evil.

Perhaps finally exposing his real IQ or, at least, his lack of computer expertise, BTK made the inevitable error the BTK Task Force had anticipated. The most important part of the serial killer's January 2005 trinity of communications was the brief insert within the "BOOM" package entitled, appropriately, "COMMICATION." It read, "Can I communicate with Floppy and not be traced to a computer. Be honest. Under Miscellaneous Section, 494, (Rex, it will be OK), run it for a few days in case I'm out of town-etc. I will try a floppy for a test run some time in the near future-February or March. 3216912." The task force members were immediately excited. It seemed that BTK wished to do away with paper and henceforth communicate solely via floppy disks. The task force couldn't believe that he did not realize a floppy disk could indeed be traced to a particular computer. They understood that "Section 494" meant a section in the classified ads in the *Wichita Eagle. He* was giving instructions to communicate with him through a classified ad in order to assure him—with the message "Rex, it will be OK"—that it would be safe for him to contact them via a message saved to a floppy disk. The number 3216912 was how he was now signing his communications, rather than using his traditional BTK logo-signature; no explanation was given for the change.

Landwehr wasted no time in responding to communication #7, the "BOOM" package. The next day Detective Cheryl James ran the requested response in the *Wichita Eagle:* "Rex, it will be ok, Contact me PO box 1st four ref. Number at 67202."[25] The last part was intended as a coded reference for BTK to use in his reply so that the task force could easily find his next communication among hundreds of classified ads. James's ad ran seven days. BTK's reply was received on the seventh day, though not, as it turned out, through the *Eagle.*

Investigators soon realized that BTK's three January communications did not find their way to the BTK Task Force in the order in which they had been transmitted. The "BOOM" package—including the booby trap chart; the "COMMICATION" insert; BTK's claim of a relationship with the late Professor Wyatt; a letter revisiting the Josie Otero and Nancy Fox homicides; the enclosure of a necklace attributed to Nancy Fox—was actually communication #7. BTK had deposited it in a Kellogg's Special K cereal box on January 8, 2005, in the back of an employee's pickup truck in the parking lot of a Wichita Home Depot store.[26] It did not reach the task force, however, until January 27 following the task force's receipt of BTK's communication #9—a postcard mailed to KAKE-TV on January 25. The postcard bore the Oteros' return address of 803 N. Edgemoor in Wichita and indicated that the missing communication #7 could be found at a Home Depot—"Home Depot Drop, Site 1-8-05."[27] With that lead, the task force had been contacting Home Depots across the city and studying parking lot security videos from each one. That led to the recovery of the cereal box from a Home Depot employee, who thought it was simply trash tossed into his pickup truck while it was parked in the store lot. He put the box in his trash bin at home, and it was still there with BTK's "Rex" inquiry inside when investigators arrived three weeks later.

Communication #9 also told investigators where and when communication #8 had been deposited ("Week of 1-17-2005 Between 69th N and 77th N on Seneca St. . . . Post Tosties [sic] Box").[28] Communication #8 turned out to include miscellaneous jewelry; a nude doll bound and gagged and with its neck tied to a piece of plastic pipe (clearly depicting Josie Otero); another copy of the chapter headings of "THE BTK STORY"; another report detailing the Otero homicides, reflecting, again, BTK's obsession with little Josie; and another strange word-search puzzle entitled "BTK's Acronym List." In other words, it was more of the same; there was nothing new, unlike #7.

BTK was clearly puzzled about the lack of response from the task force regarding the two missing communications. He was correct in his assumption that the task force had not yet received either. Thanks to communication #9, #8 was finally tracked down and retrieved on January 25 and #7 was located on January 27. Landwehr issued media releases on January 27 and February 3, respectively, telling BTK that what was lost was found.[29]

BTK's response to the task force's "Rex, it will be ok," classified ad in the *Wichita Eagle* was another postcard to KAKE-TV, this one postmarked February 2 from Wichita and received at the station February 3. Communication #10 read, in part, "Thank you for your quick response on #7 and 8. . . . Tell WPD that I receive the Newspaper Tip for a go. Test run soon. Thanks."[30]

Spirits within the BTK Task Force were sky-high on February 3, 2005. They held their collective breath awaiting the possibility that a floppy disk from the serial killer might lead them to his computer.

After the task force had identified the correct Home Depot and then found the employee in whose pickup truck communication #7 had been deposited, investigators continued to spend hours reviewing videotape from the store's security cameras, focusing on the employee's vehicle while it was in the parking lot on January 8. The time-consuming effort paid off. The investigators concentrated on a suspicious vehicle driving around the parking lot for several minutes before parking near the pickup truck. The driver of the suspicious vehicle could then be seen exiting his vehicle and tossing an object in the back of the employee's truck before reentering his own vehicle and driving away.

The grainy quality of the tape did not permit an identifiable picture of the suspect or his vehicle, nor a reading of the vehicle's license plate. Following additional hours of viewing the tape, however, the consensus of the task force members was that the grainy figure was indeed BTK and that his vehicle was a dark-colored 1997–2004 Jeep Grand Cherokee. KBI analysts determined there were 2,500 Jeep Cherokees registered in Sedgwick County, Kansas.

On February 8, the BTK Task Force moved into a very nice working space acquired by the FBI in the Epic Center office building in downtown Wichita. Eight days later, Landwehr received BTK's eleventh and final communication via mail sent to a different Wichita television station, KSAS.[31] "P. J. Fox" was the name on the return address of the bulky package, which contained some index cards, a gold chain, a pendant, and, incredibly, BTK's promised floppy disk. Perhaps the villain's evil-minded lady luck was finally running out.

With most of the task force crowding around him, Detective Randy Stone, the squad's computer whiz, inserted the purple disk into his computer and opened the only file number listed there: "Test A.rtf." Further exploration identified the file's creator as "Dennis" and found that the purple disk had been used on a computer at the Christ Lutheran Church, and was last used at Park City Community Public Library. On another computer Stone quickly located Christ Lutheran Church in Wichita, finding that the congregation's president was one Dennis Rader. And then he located a Dennis Rader at 6220 Independence Street, Park City, a northern suburb of Wichita.

Stone's cyber efforts required slightly less than an hour and seemed more like a mere twenty minutes. When he pushed himself away from his computer, pleased and proud, and rightfully so, he found himself alone. Some of his comrades were already racing to 6220 Independence Street in Park City, and others had retreated to their own computers to learn more about someone named Dennis Rader, his family, and Wichita's Christ Lutheran Church. Cheryl James had already reported that there was no local arrest record for anyone named Dennis Rader and, worse, no Jeep Cherokee registered to anyone by that name. It was determined, however, that the Dennis Rader of that address in Park City was a compliance and animal control officer in that municipality.

Detectives Tim Relph and Clint Snyder in one car and Detectives Dana Gouge and Kelly Otis in another reached Rader's neighborhood in Park City, a suburb north of Wichita. At first sight it was clear to those investigators discreetly observing the small structure at 6220 Independence Street that the residence obviously lacked a garage, two stories, an elevator, and a hidden stairway, as BTK had described his home. Rader's home still might have booby traps with explosives and incendiary devices, and perhaps a basement and bondage room, but certainly not the other features that BTK had claimed in the "BOOM" communication. Our officers were not immediately confident the residence was really that of BTK.

What that modest residence did have on February 16, 2005, was a black 1997 Jeep Grand Cherokee parked in its driveway. Detective James had not been mistaken about there being no vehicle registration tying Dennis Rader to the ownership of a Jeep. A check of the vehicle's license plate, however, revealed that the Jeep in Rader's driveway was actually registered to his absent son, a sailor in the U.S. Navy stationed at submarine school in Connecticut. Therefore, Dennis Rader did in fact have access to a dark-colored Jeep.

Both Chief Williams and Larry Thomas telephoned me with the news of a new BTK suspect named Dennis Rader. The excited BTK Task Force met for a briefing in its spacious new Epic Center offices on February 16 to plan strategy for determining how to eliminate or validate Dennis Rader as a BTK suspect. The easiest and first decision Landwehr and his colleagues made was to not yet confront Rader. The squad did not wish to prematurely alert Rader or the media of their interest in him. Some even felt that there was a possibility BTK was setting up Rader, given the ease with which Stone had traced the origin of the purple floppy disk. Perhaps BTK was watching for any demonstration of law enforcement interest in Dennis Rader of Park City that would reveal the floppy disk had been traced, despite Landwehr's advance assurances to "Rex" to the contrary.

It was decided that the most expeditious avenue to eliminating or validating Rader as a suspect was through DNA—not a swabbing, of course, but a more discreet, covert collection of his DNA to compare with the DNA evidence from the Josie Otero, Nancy Fox, and Vicki Wegerle homicides. Physical surveillance of Rader might eventually lead to picking up a cigarette butt (though it would be learned that he did not smoke) or a drinking or eating utensil (though it would also be learned he seldom ate away from home), but time was of the essence, and such a tactic could prove time-consuming, as it had with the forty dissenters of the "swabathon."

Initial inquiries determined that Rader lived at the Park City residence with his wife, Paula. In addition to their sailor son in Connecticut, they also had a married daughter in Michigan. Those inquiries further ascertained that the daughter had attended Kansas State University in Manhattan. The KBI's Ray Lundin, a proud K-State alumnus, suggested at the task force briefing that the daughter might have availed herself of the student health center facilities during her student days. If so, perhaps samples of her DNA might still be available at that college campus. The KBI Cold Case Squad veteran was well aware of the potential of familial DNA. If a sample of her DNA could be located and obtained, the KBI forensic laboratory could tell us whether BTK was her father and the contributor of DNA evidence in three of the BTK's homicides. Sindey Schueler had performed countless such DNA analyses in homicide and rape cases.

Landwehr and the rest of the task force liked Lundin's idea. They all agreed it was certainly worth a try. Lundin was well acquainted with the university and the city of Manhattan. He volunteered to handle that assignment if I would give approval for such KBI action. First, Landwehr sought the legal opinion and approval of Sedgwick County District Attorney Nola Foulston. Initially uneasy about the situation, the veteran prosecutor eventually approved Landwehr's impassioned request to covertly pursue the daughter's DNA. Larry Thomas then quickly telephoned me for my approval to deploy Lundin to Manhattan to see if he could find a sample of the daughter's DNA at the K-State medical facility. And, if successful in obtaining such forensic evidence, they also wanted my consent to have our KBI forensic laboratory standing by to conduct the DNA analysis. I happily agreed to both requests.

I briefed Attorney General Phill Kline, my laboratory director, Mike VanStratton, Supervisor Sindey Schueler, and the rest of my executive staff. I encountered some misgivings about the tactic's propriety, but not from the attorney general, VanStratton, or Schueler. I remained comfortable with my decision.

On February 17, 2005—armed with two subpoenas, a Wichita judge's court order, and considerable optimism—Lundin departed Wichita and headed to Manhattan.

On the same day, Landwehr issued what would be his final media release to BTK, acknowledging in general the recent reception of more BTK communications and expressing pleasure in the continuing dialogue between the task force and its adversary. He said nothing that would have betrayed the new development afoot, Lundin's covert mission, or Stone's apparent cracking of the BTK floppy disk so as not to make BTK suspicious or angry.[32]

Lundin's trip to Manhattan bore fruit within days. At the student health center he learned that Rader's daughter had indeed availed herself of that facility's services during her student days having gone there for a Pap smear. The tissue from that examination was stored at a local medical laboratory. By February 22 Lundin had the potential evidence in his possession and his car pointed toward Topeka. He presented the material to Sindey Schueler in the laboratory's biology section at KBI headquarters. Realizing the importance of the material they held, both later admitted they had never been so nervous.

I was in Wichita on February 23 and 24 to visit the new task force quarters on the third floor of the beautiful Epic Center building and to attend the task force briefing on Dennis Rader and his potential arrest, if warranted. I had hoped Schueler would call the task force with great news before I had to leave, but that did not occur. Shortly after my arrival home in Lawrence, however, at about 9:00 P.M. on February 24, 2005, I received a telephone call from a happy Larry Thomas in Wichita. I will always remember his first words: "Director Welch, this is the call you've been waiting for a long time. He's BTK. Sindey Schueler confirmed the family connection minutes ago."[33] BTK was Dennis Rader. Thomas then advised me of the task force's plan to arrest Rader the next day. Rader would be stopped and arrested as he drove home from his city office for lunch, pursuant to his custom. Both Lundin and Thomas were on the arrest team. Thomas, Landwehr, and Relph would transport Rader to the Epic Center for interrogation. The primary interrogation team would be Landwehr, Thomas, and FBI Special Agent Bob Morton. There would be constant physical surveillance of Rader prior to the noon arrest and, with the proper search warrants secured, searches of Rader's home, a rented storage unit, all his family's vehicles, and his office at city hall, contemporaneous with and following the arrest.

I called members of my top staff and Attorney General Kline with the good news. Then I telephoned the exhausted, happy Sindey Schueler, still at KBI headquarters, where she had labored at her forensic bench for most of two days and two nights. I praised, congratulated, and thanked her, and then ordered her home to her family. (I learned later that Sindey returned to her office before midnight to send out a confirming forensic analysis report on the DNA examination to Lundin and Thomas on their KBI laptop computers in Wichita at 12:12 A.M. Her subsequent sheepish confession to me was simple: "Director, I couldn't sleep anyway until BTK was in custody.")[34]

At 7:00 A.M. on Friday, February 25, 2005, I received a telephone call from a very satisfied and gracious Wichita police chief. Chief Norman Williams thanked me again for the KBI commitment to the BTK Task Force and praised Lundin, Thomas, and Schueler in particular. The chief reiterated the arrest plans Thomas had described to me and also extended an invitation to participate in the events of BTK's last day of freedom. I declined but, at Chief Williams's insistence, agreed to be in Wichita the next day to attend a news conference acknowledging BTK's identity and custody.

First, of course, we had to actually arrest BTK and end his reign of terror before we could tell the world about him. We knew BTK was Dennis Rader. The unanswered question was now, "Who is Dennis Rader?"

Dennis Lynn Rader was born in Columbus, Kansas, on March 9, 1945, the eldest of four sons. His parents, William and Dorothea Rader, were natives of southeastern Kansas. His mother's hometown was Columbus and his father was from Pittsburg. The family eventually moved to Wichita. The parents, middle class and blue collar, were respected in their north Wichita neighborhood. Rader's father, a World War II marine, spent his career with the Kansas Gas and Electric Company, and his mother was a bookkeeper for a neighborhood grocery store.

Academics were never Dennis Rader's thing. Neither were athletics. He did, however, greatly enjoy the Boy Scouts, hunting, fishing, target shooting, and model airplanes. His family considered him artistic and an above-average painter.

There would be no evidence that Rader was physically, sexually, or emotionally abused as a child. His father was considered strict but fair by all his sons, and all the brothers remained close to their mother and their grandparents on both sides. The family was active in the nearby Christ Lutheran Church, and Rader served as an altar boy. Rader never had any apparent difficulties with school officials or law enforcement. His brothers could not recall him dating any girls other than the woman who would become his wife. He graduated from Wichita Heights High School in May 1963 and entered the U.S. Air Force in June 1966. He was first sent to Lackland Air Force Base outside San Antonio, Texas, for basic training. Additional electronic training followed at Sheppard Air Force Base, near Wichita Falls, Texas, and Brookley Air Force Base in Mobile, Alabama. Overseas assignments then took him to Kadena Air Base on Okinawa (six months) and Tachikawa Air Base, near Tokyo (almost two years). Contacts in 2005 with law enforcement authorities in Texas, Alabama, Okinawa, and Japan failed to connect Dennis Rader to any unsolved homicides within those jurisdictions. Rader was honorably discharged with the rank of sergeant on August 12, 1970, in Denver, Colorado. He was credited with receipt of the Air Force Good Conduct Medal, the National Defense Service Medal, and the Small Arms Expert Marksmanship Ribbon. His tenure in the U.S. Air Force generally involved various uneventful electronic assignments. He helped install antennae and various electronic systems. He climbed lots of towers.

Rader returned to Wichita following his military service. On March 22, 1971, at age twenty-six, he married Paula Dietz, age twenty-three, and they settled in Park City, a small suburb north of Wichita. Rader began taking community college courses and from June 1972 until July 1973 he worked on the assembly line at the Coleman Company in Wichita. He received a two-year associate's degree from Butler County Community College in spring 1973 and began classes at Wichita State University in fall 1973.

From 1974 until 1988, Rader worked for ADT Security Services in Wichita, installing residential security alarms. A son was born in 1975 and a daughter in 1978. Never a gifted student, Rader finally received his bachelor's degree from Wichita State in spring 1979. He majored in criminal justice and was a part-time student from 1973 to 1979.[35] During that same period, from

1974 to 1988, as he installed residential security alarms in Wichita homes, he committed his nine murders in or near Wichita and the other later, in 1991. None of his victims was an ADT customer. In 1989 Rader started working for the Census Bureau and, for the first time in connection with employment, worked outside Wichita, traveling primarily across northern Kansas. (He would later admit some burglaries during those travels, but denied any murders and was never connected to any killings.)

From May 1991 until February 25, 2005, Dennis Rader held the last job he would ever have. He was hired as the compliance and animal control officer by the municipality of Park City. He daily sought unleashed dogs, cluttered yards, and unmowed lawns, and he also trapped offending varmints for complaining citizens. As he chased dogs and measured the height of uncut grass in Park City's yards, he wore a brown uniform of his own styling that he apparently thought made him look like a member of law enforcement. Offending dog owners and property owners were fined in Park City Municipal Court, where "Officer" Rader had a reputation as an officious bully. Throughout their more than thirty years of residence in Park City, twenty-five of those years in the same small unpretentious house at 6220 Independence, Dennis and Paula Rader were faithful in their attendance at services at Christ Lutheran Church. He was elected president of the church's governing council in January 2005.

Contemporaneous with Schueler's telephone call to Lundin confirming the DNA connection, a loose and discreet surveillance was placed on Dennis Rader. Non-task force officers were brought in to tail Rader home from his city office on February 24 and to watch his Park City residence throughout that night—assuring his presence there—to follow him to work the next morning, and to stay with him if he left his city office during the morning. The officers' instructions were simple: "Do not tip him off and do not lose him."

At 11:00 A.M. on Friday, February 25, at a Kansas Highway Patrol station north of Wichita, near Park City, the BTK Task Force gathered briefly to brainstorm a final time about BTK in general and BTK's arrest in particular. The arrest warrant and several search warrants obtained during the night were reviewed. Assignments for the arrest, searches, prisoner transport, and interrogation were revisited. The initial stop of Rader's municipal pickup truck would be made by uniformed Wichita patrolmen Dan Harty and Scott Moon, whom Landwehr had selected personally. Harty and Moon would be the tip of the spear and the only non-task force officers on the arrest team. A Wichita police swat team and additional Wichita police officers, FBI agents, and KBI agents would be available in and around Park City to reinforce the task force before, during, and after the arrest. Wichita police helicopters would be in the air, and Chief Norman Williams would be on the scene with top staff as well.

Four cars and nine task force officers composed the designated arrest team. Ray Lundin and Kelly Otis, an imposing pair, would be in the primary arrest car. Detectives Dana Gouge and Clint Snyder would be in another car and FBI Special Agents Chuck Pritchett and John Sullivan in the third vehicle. Detective Tim Relph would drive the fourth car, the BTK transportation car, occupied also by Ken Landwehr and Larry Thomas flanking the suspect in the backseat for the postarrest travel to the Epic Center building. Cheryl James and Randy Stone would also be nearby. Every task force member anticipated a violent response from Rader. It had been determined he was probably in possession of shotguns and handguns. Armed resistance seemed likely. Suicide, or "suicide by cop," where the subject points a gun toward officers, forcing one or more to fire at him in response to the threat, also seemed a possible outcome of the confrontation.

All assigned units were in position at Park City by 11:20 A.M. for the lunchtime arrest. Forty minutes later, a member of the surveillance team radioed that Dennis Rader was headed home for lunch in his city truck. More than one member of the task force was probably thinking about all the officers since January 15, 1974, who should have been there with them. Let it end here and now, they undoubtedly prayed.

The scheduled felony car stop occurred at precisely 12:15 P.M., with Harty and Moon, as planned, making the initial traffic stop. The only deviation from task force planning was that Lundin, driving arrest team car #1, in his haste, inadvertently braked his KBI car so close to the patrolmen's that his partner, Otis, was temporarily trapped inside their car unable to exit, and Harty was blocked momentarily between the two cars. Only later was the humor of that situation appreciated.

Many guns were pointed at the surprised Rader, who had stepped from his truck after being stopped by the two uniformed officers in the unmarked Wichita police car. The first officer to actually reach him was Lundin, running, who repeatedly yelled, "Get on the ground" to Rader as he raced toward the serial killer. Slow to comply, Rader was forcibly placed on the ground by Lundin and quickly handcuffed by Gouge, using Snyder's personal handcuffs as Gouge and Snyder had planned. The beast was finally in its cage.

Rader's first words to law enforcement were "Would you please call my wife? She was expecting me for lunch. I assume you know where I live?"[36] Lundin gave him his assurances that Mrs. Rader would be informed.

Detective Relph assumed custody of BTK from Lundin and Snyder and escorted him to the transport vehicle, where he was turned over to Larry

Thomas. The KBI agent opened the car's back door on the driver's side and helped the prisoner into the middle of the back seat. It was then that Rader first saw Landwehr in person and that the task force commander first saw BTK. The two former altar boys stared into each other's faces as Rader spoke first: "Hello, Mr. Landwehr." The ever-pleasant Landwehr replied, "Hello, Mr. Rader." Thomas and Landwehr later noted that at that moment, due to Rader's demeanor, they were convinced their prisoner was going to confess. They anticipated eight confessions. There would be ten.

Following the arrest of Dennis Rader at 12:15 P.M. on February 25, 2005, the BTK Task Force and its cohorts did not dawdle. Their infamous prisoner was quickly transported out of Park City.

At 12:38 P.M., Detective Gouge, in an office on the fourth floor of the Epic Center in downtown Wichita, pursuant to one of many BTK-related search warrants obtained previously by the task force, took four oral swabs of Rader. He placed two of the swabs in an envelope and gave it to Lundin, who in turn gave it to KBI Special Agent Robert Jacobs for transportation to Sindey Schueler at KBI headquarters in Topeka. The purpose of the swabbing was final, positive DNA confirmation of Dennis Lynn Rader as BTK. Gouge carried the other envelope with the remaining swabs to the local Sedgwick County forensic laboratory for the same analysis, as Jacobs raced north on the Kansas Turnpike with his important envelope.

At 12:43 P.M., Ken Landwehr and Bob Morton, in the same Epic Center office, advised Rader of his rights to remain silent and to have an attorney present. Rader signed the requisite accompanying waiver of those rights at 12:45 P.M., thereby launching forty-two hours of close custody in the Epic Center offices and thirty-one hours, eighteen minutes, and four seconds of confessions to ten homicides recorded on video, punctuated by frequent meals, restroom breaks, refreshments, reminders of his legal rights, and naps—a cot was placed in the Epic Center interview room for him, although he declined long sleeps, awaking from brief naps to summon interviewers for continued discussion of his crimes.

As Thomas monitored the first interrogation, Landwehr and Morton started the discussion by presenting Rader with his slightly delayed lunch, a McDonald's hamburger, French fries, and Coke. Rader chided them about the unhealthy lunch; accordingly, the next meal brought to him included a large salad, which greatly pleased the serial killer.

Meanwhile, task force members and others were executing search warrants at Rader's city hall office, at his home, in a storage unit he utilized, and in various vehicles he used. Some of the searches continued over the weekend. Also, while Rader was being interrogated, Otis and Snyder were interviewing Rader's mother; Relph and Pritchett were speaking with Rader's wife; Sullivan and James were interviewing Rader's brothers; FBI agents in Michigan were advising a shocked, disbelieving daughter of BTK's arrest in Wichita; and other FBI agents in Connecticut performed the same task with Rader's submariner son. The son would be more fully interviewed at his naval base on March 2 by Otis and Lundin.

Landwehr and Morton sparred gently with Rader for three hours before the latter asked if the death penalty was a possibility for BTK's crimes. When assured that lethal injection would not be legally applicable to BTK's homicides, Rader paused and announced, rather proudly, "I'm BTK," confirming what his interrogators already believed. Then, Rader expressed disappointment in Landwehr for lying to him about the floppy disk, admitted the eight known BTK murder victims, and claimed credit for two more: Marine Hedge and Dolores Davis.

Marine Hedge, a petite fifty-three-year-old widow and grandmother, not Vicki Wegerle, was actually BTK's eighth victim. Wegerle was the ninth. The error in chronology was due in part to the fact that BTK did not call attention to the Hedge homicide as he had with his other victims, and in part because the Hedge investigators, in 1985, although suspicious of BTK involvement, were unable to connect that killing to him or his modus operandi. The little lady lived alone in Park City, just north of Wichita. She loved to dress nicely, play bingo, attend her Baptist church, and work in her yard and garden. She also loved her job in a Wichita hospital coffee shop.

During the night of April 27, 1985, Hedge returned home from a date about 11:00 P.M. She and her date visited about an hour before he departed. She went to bed and was suddenly confronted by BTK, who earlier in the evening had cut her phone line and broken in through the back door. He had mistakenly believed she had returned home some time earlier because her automobile was parked in her carport, so he waited in a closet for her. After handcuffing the frightened woman, Rader first strangled Hedge with his hands and then with panty hose he had found in her lingerie drawer before her return home. He wrapped her nude body in a blanket and placed her in the trunk of her automobile. He then drove to Christ Lutheran Church in north Wichita about 1:00 A.M., and, using a key he possessed, opened a door to the church and carried Hedge's body to the church basement. There he spent considerable time taking Polaroid photographs of her nude body in various lewd and suggestive poses, as he ejaculated on her. Just before dawn he carried her defiled body from the church, replaced it in her automobile's trunk, and drove to a water-filled culvert in the country northeast of Wichita. He tossed her body in the culvert and covered it with brush, weeds, and tree limbs. Marine Hedge's badly decomposed body was found nine days later. Her car was found in a Wichita shopping center, and her empty purse was discovered about six miles from her body in a rural roadside ditch. In addition to her nude, lifeless body, Rader also carried from Marine Hedge's home her driver's license, jewelry, and several items of lingerie and underwear. From the church, besides her nude, lifeless body, he also carried a large collection of Polaroid photographs of Hedge in bondage and sexually suggestive positions.

Rader, following his apprehension years later, would describe the Marine Hedge murder to his interrogators as his "most complicated hit." Indeed, it was not a typical BTK killing. For starters, Rader and Hedge were neighbors in Park City. They were acquainted. Her murder was the most premeditated homicide of all BTK's "hits," as he later classified his crimes. And, in 1985, she was the oldest of his victims. Hedge's homicide marked the first time he had removed a victim's body from the original crime scene. Incredibly, he traveled to the vicinity of Hedge's home by taxicab—another first. And he never wrote about that murder to the police—yet another first. Some suggest that he did not later boast to the task force about Marine Hedge in any of his communications because his conscience bothered him about desecrating his own church when he violated her there with the lewd photography. But BTK had no conscience. He later gleefully directed his interrogators to that collection of victim photographs. Furthermore, during his interrogation he explained with pride and excitement his use of his own church as the venue for the lewd photography. The selection of that site was neither spur-of-the-moment nor impulsive. He had taped black plastic to all the church basement windows several days before he photographed Hedge's body there, evidence of premeditation. And he later admitted that he stalked and surveilled Hedge longer than any other victim. Only Rader knows why he remained silent, until his capture, about this particular homicide. Whatever the reason, it certainly was not related to conscience. Seventeen months later he killed Vicki Wegerle.

Rader's tenth, final, and oldest victim was pretty Dolores "Dee" Davis, who lived alone in the country north of Wichita near Park City. The sixty-three-year-old divorced grandmother was a retired oil and gas company secretary. Rader took her life on the cold, snowy night of January 19, 1991. As in the Marine Hedge homicide, Rader cut Davis's telephone line and handcuffed her after rousing her from bed by throwing a large concrete block through her sliding glass patio door late at night. In addition to the cut phone line and breaking and entering, there were other similarities to BTK homicides. Dee Davis was killed in her own home. Her wrists and ankles were bound with panty hose. She was first strangled manually and then with panty hose that he left tied around her neck. Trophies—jewelry, a jewelry box, and lingerie—were taken from the home. And, of course, there was no evidence of rape.

There were, however, more dissimilarities to BTK's work than similarities: Davis, like Hedge but unlike other BTK victims, resided outside Wichita. She, like Hedge, was older than the other victims. Her body, like Hedge's, was wrapped in her bedding, moved from her home, the actual homicide scene, in her own car's trunk, and placed under a rural bridge north of Wichita. Almost two weeks after her disappearance from her home was discovered, her nude, frozen body was found, badly decomposed, under the bridge. The most significant dissimilarity, as with Hedge, was that BTK never referred to the Davis killing in any of his communications years later to the task force. But as with the Hedge case, Wichita city detectives and Sedgwick County investigators early on harbored strong suspicions that BTK was responsible for Dee Davis's death.

Years later, following his apprehension, Rader would quickly and enthusiastically claim credit for the Hedge and Davis murders and would direct his interrogators to nude and lewd Polaroid photographs of Hedge (taken in his church) and Davis (taken during several visits to the body on different days under the bridge).[37] Strangely, in an attempt to delay Davis's decomposition, he would also admit after his capture that, during his returns to the body, he would apply cosmetics and/or a mask to the victim's face, as he put it during interrogation, "to pretty her up." As with Hedge, while he photographed Davis he ejaculated on or near the body. One plastic mask was recovered at that site, next to the body. In one final striking similarity between the Hedge and Davis homicides, on both those occasions Rader, a popular Boy Scout leader, slipped away from area Boy Scout camps to commit the murders, returning to the camps early each morning following the two homicides.

Pleased with Rader's willingness, even eagerness, to speak of his crimes, Landwehr turned the verbose, remorseless serial killer over to designated interview teams to obtain the specific details of each homicide: Thomas and Lundin (Oteros); Snyder and Gouge (Bright and Vian); Relph and Pritchett (Fox); and Otis and Gouge (Wegerle).

In addition, Landwehr asked Thomas to interview Rader about where in his home and office he was keeping his "treasures," his word for homicide trophies, which he admittedly used to relive his personal excitement of each "project," his word for each murder. Wishing to avoid disarray at his home and office as a result of the searches, Rader volunteered to provide information to assist the respective quests. Thus, the searchers easily located victims' wrist watches, lingerie, underwear, jewelry, driver's licenses, panty hose, and other items. Also found were the originals of BTK's communications; his detailed, revealing journals; BTK's knife; photographs of victims at the actual homicide scenes; bondage materials; and self-photographs of Rader in autoerotic poses, many showing him dressed in his victims' lingerie.

Relph and Pritchett were assigned to interrogate Rader about every communication he directed to the task force, seeking his explanation of each. Rader delighted in that task, although he continually mispronounced the word "ruse," one of his favorites, as "russ."

Lastly, Landwehr summoned Captain Sam Houston and Sergeant Thomas Lee of the Sedgwick County Sheriff's Office to accept Rader's confessions to the Hedge and Davis murders.

At 11:00 P.M. on February 25, 2005, Sindey Schueler telephoned me with the news that her analysis of Rader oral swabs, received earlier that day from KBI Special Agent Robert Jacobs, had forensically confirmed that Rader was BTK. I telephoned Larry Thomas with the expected news and he shared the confirmation with Landwehr and their colleagues. Then I called Attorney General Kline, making his day.

Pursuant to the invitation extended to me by Chief Williams, I drove to Wichita early Saturday morning from Lawrence to attend the first of several media events—the news conference scheduled at 10:00 A.M. in city hall to announce BTK's apprehension. This was preceded by a 9:00 A.M. briefing of BTK victims' families from task force members and others who were to speak at the news conference in another private meeting room in city hall. Chief Williams and Ken Landwehr had decided to tell the victims' families about BTK's identity and arrest prior to the official public announcement in the city hall auditorium, where, in another appropriate gesture, the chief and his task force commander had arranged priority seating for those families. Attorney General Kline, Congressman Todd Tiahrt, Sedgwick County District Attorney Nola Foulston, Sedgwick County Sheriff Gary Steed, Special Agent in Charge Kevin Stafford of the FBI, Wichita Mayor Carlos Mayans, several other local politicians, and I joined Chief Williams, Ken Landwehr, and the task force members in visiting with the families of the Oteros, Kathryn Bright, Shirley Vian, Nancy Fox, Marine Hedge, Vicki Wegerle, and Dolores Davis. Ray Lundin and Larry Thomas ensured that I met the surviving

Otero children, Charlie, Carmen, and Danny. I enjoyed meeting them and quickly developed an admiration for the individual and collective strength of those three determined individuals, an admiration also held by Lundin and Thomas, who were the first to witness the tragic evidence of BTK's evildoing. I was also privileged to visit with Kevin Bright, the only BTK survivor.

After nearly an hour with the victims' families, we moved to the city hall auditorium for the news conference. There we found a packed auditorium—more than two hundred persons. The crowd consisted of interested Wichita citizens and scores of national and international media representatives, including every organization from CNN, MSNBC, and Fox News to the Associated Press and the local ABC, CBS, and NBC network affiliates. Satellite trucks filled the city hall parking lot.

The news conference highlight was Chief Williams's simple declaration, "The bottom line: BTK is arrested." Landwehr then told the audience that BTK had been arrested by the Wichita Police Department, the FBI, and the KBI, and that the killer was Dennis Rader, age fifty-nine, of nearby Park City, charged with ten counts of first-degree homicide and currently lodged in Sedgwick County jail.

I recall nine speakers at the unprecedented (in Wichita) media event. I was the briefest. My comments required less than a minute and concluded, "It has been the KBI's pleasure and privilege to have had agents of our Cold Case Squad and also KBI forensic scientists involved in this effort since March of 2004. The KBI is delighted with the predicted outcome."[38]

The next day, Sunday, February 27, the Wichita *Eagle* featured a large photograph of Dennis Rader on its front page.[39] Wichitans finally saw the face of BTK. Throughout the newspaper was a complete rundown on the previous day's news conference and the first interviews of victims' families and Rader's neighbors, relatives, and former classmates and coworkers by eager reporters. The most stunned interviewees were members of Christ Lutheran Church in north Wichita. Many of his neighbors and coworkers found it difficult to believe Dennis Rader could be the clever BTK who had avoided capture for more than thirty years.

Rader's first court appearance, before Sedgwick County District Judge Greg Waller on March 1, 2005, provided the next media event. A solemn Rader, clad in a red prison jumpsuit—denoting maximum security—appeared via closed-circuit television from the county jail. Judge Waller ordered Rader held in lieu of a $10 million bond.

From the day of the arrest, February 25, 2005, the most popular media speculation concerned how Rader's DNA was obtained prior to his arrest, which

then confirmed his identity as BTK. I was amused by the variety of erroneous explanations in the media relating to the source of Rader's DNA sample.
Some of the media speculation accurately suggested that the DNA sample
had been obtained from Rader's twenty-six-year-old daughter, who resided
in Michigan. The first such reports, however, indicated that the daughter
had approached law enforcement, turned in her father, and voluntarily submitted her DNA to prove she was the offspring of BTK. Other mistaken
reports speculated that the FBI had obtained the DNA in some brilliant
fashion directly, but discreetly, from Rader.

On Wednesday evening, March 2, 2005, shortly before 8:00 P.M., my wife,
Shirley, our daughter, Laurie, and I were preparing to enter Allen Fieldhouse
on the University of Kansas campus in Lawrence for the KU-Kansas State
basketball game. I was then paged by the KBI Communications Center at
KBI Headquarters in Topeka, advising me that Tim Potter of the *Wichita
Eagle* urgently needed to speak with me. I told my wife and daughter to go
ahead and I would follow.

Tim Potter was, and is, a reporter I respect and trust. Like all my reporter-
friends (most of whom had my home phone number), Tim was well aware
that I would not comment on the BTK investigation. Prior to Rader's arrest, I had referred all BTK media inquiries to Chief Williams and Ken
Landwehr. Following Rader's arrest, I referred all such calls to District Attorney Foulston, who would be handling Rader's prosecution. I always confirmed KBI involvement in the BTK Task Force but nothing more. When
I reached Tim Potter on Shirley's cell phone, he thanked me for returning
his call and apologized for interrupting my entry into Allen Fieldhouse. He
then explained that he wanted to advise me that his newspaper was running
a story the following morning identifying the KBI as the real collector of
Rader's daughter's DNA sample. I dutifully referred Tim to Nola Foulston,
reminding him I would not comment on the BTK investigation. The veteran reporter said he understood, but felt he owed me the opportunity to
make a comment. He didn't want to run the story without alerting me first.
I thanked him for the courtesy but declined any comment on the ongoing
investigation. (I then entered Allen Fieldhouse and watched the Jayhawks
defeat K-State 72–65.)

The *Wichita Eagle*'s front-page headline on Thursday, March 3, 2005,
read, "DNA Came from Medical File—Source: Daughter's Records Were
Subpoenaed," heralding a lengthy story that continued inside the newspaper.
In the article, Potter admitted it was not known where the KBI found the
daughter's DNA sample that had confirmed she was the offspring of BTK.
The story read in part:

The KBI agents' strategy was to use a DNA sample from the daughter to see whether it would link her father to DNA left at BTK's crime scenes.

Over the years, authorities had collected DNA evidence from at least three killings.

The KBI agents went to prosecutors in the Sedgwick County district attorney's office, and a judge in Sedgwick County issued a subpoena for the 26-year-old daughter's medical records in Kansas, a source said.

It wasn't clear where in Kansas the records and the tissue sample had been held.

DNA was extracted from the daughter's tissue sample, and it was processed within the week before Rader's arrest, the source said.

District Attorney Nola Foulston and KBI Director Larry Welch declined to comment on any reports of a DNA sample taken in Kansas.

Further investigative confidentiality soon became unnecessary. The cloak of secrecy started falling from the investigative details in the next few days as the prosecution's court filings began to reveal the probable cause for the BTK arrest, searches, and prosecution. The real facts of the acquisition of the daughter's DNA and even details of Rader's ten confessions became well known.

Prosecutors and many task force members feared that the public defenders appointed to defend Rader would be overwhelmed by the government's case facing them and would encourage Rader to plead guilty rather than go to trial. After all, how could defense counsel successfully challenge DNA and more than thirty-one hours of properly recorded confessions? Foulston and Landwehr, however, wanted the intimate facts of the serial killer's guilt and atrocities to be public knowledge, so no one could ever claim the wrong man was charged as BTK. The BTK saga required a final and absolutely unambiguous ending, leaving no skeptic.

In the end, everyone, the public defenders, Foulston and Landwehr, and Rader himself, had their wishes fulfilled on June 27, in one of the most extraordinary arraignments ever held in any court. Having pleaded guilty to the ten homicides, thereby eliminating the need for a trial by jury, Rader finally had the stage and audience he craved. The hearing, more than an hour in duration, was televised live and sent across the nation and around the world, to Rader's delight. And, most important, due to Judge Greg Waller's masterful prodding and probing of the remorseless, contented Rader, the intimate details that Foulston and Landwehr wanted public poured from the serial killer's own lips, shocking much of his courtroom and television audiences.

Inspired by the judge's invitation and encouragement, Rader methodically described in cruel detail how he had managed to "bind, torture, and kill" ten victims. Judge Waller accepted Rader's ten guilty pleas and scheduled the sentencing for August 17.

The sentencing hearing proved as unusual as the arraignment. Rader's sentencing, with a packed courtroom and live television again, required two days, August 17 and 18. The families of Rader's victims had reserved seating in front, and media representatives filled the other seats. Again, Rader was in the national and international spotlight.

The prosecution saw the sentencing hearing as the final opportunity to present the prosecution's case, since there would be no public trial following the defendant's guilty plea. The arraignment had provided some of the horror of Rader's deeds, but Foulston wanted more. She wanted the interrogators to tell the court and world exactly what Rader had said to them in his confessions. The task force agreed with the strategy. So did I. It would eliminate any remaining disbelievers.

Therefore, the first day consisted of hours of graphic testimony from the interrogators, repeating the details of each homicide as told to them by BTK. Lundin testified about Rader's claimed preference for Hispanic females and how Rader mimicked Josie Otero's little girl voice as he described how she pleaded with her killer for her family's life. Lundin also told of Rader's admission that he had pulled up a chair next to little Joey to watch the little boy in his death throes. Larry Thomas displayed to the court the T-shirt placed around little Joey's head by Rader and told of Rader's excitement in describing his ejaculation on the dying Josie. Dana Gouge showed the judge and courtroom spectators some of the toys Rader used to entertain Shirley Vian's children in the bathroom as he killed their mother in her bedroom. Kelly Otis testified about Rader's admission that Vicki Wegerle had fought him like a "hellcat" and that he had listened to her playing the piano before he entered her home. Tim Relph told of Rader's amusement in describing how he had whispered to Nancy Fox that he was BTK as she died. Clint Snyder told of Rader's description of how he had "hunted, stalked, and trolled" for victims and of his "hit kits," which consisted of knives, firearms, cord, rope, and other bindings. Deputy Sheriff Thomas Lee held up the panty hose Rader had used to secure and strangle Marine Hedge and repeated the killer's description of Hedge's last minutes of life.

So it went, as each of the interrogators took a turn on the witness stand to repeat Rader's graphic admissions—all day on the first day of the sentencing hearing. Family members alternately grimaced in disgust and/or wept at the candid testimony. Each word they heard came from Rader, through his interrogators. Despite the fact that each interrogator was a veteran, professional law enforcement officer, none could disguise his personal scorn for the confessor. Strangely, that seemed to unsettle Rader as he listened, clearly reluctantly, to each interrogator's testimony. He was taken aback by their individual and collective disgust. He stopped looking at their faces as they testified and instead looked down at the defense counsel table where he sat. His swagger had disappeared. Apparently he had considered his interviewers to have been his buddies.

Finally, that afternoon, before sentencing, Judge Waller invited Rader to speak in his own behalf. Suddenly, as Rader arose to address the court, the victims' families, en masse, stood and silently walked from the courtroom. This remarkable action greatly distracted Rader. He looked puzzled and asked the judge if he should continue. The judge nodded affirmatively and Rader, haltingly, started to speak. He spoke for a bit more than fifteen minutes, strangely expressing his gratitude to everyone, including his captors and jailers. But he really never regained his composure. The families' united departure had drained him of his last trace of arrogance and he had become surprisingly docile. He appeared quite rattled and indecisive in his irrelevant remarks. He recovered enough, however, to make my day. He paused at one point in his brief thanks to the world to tell Judge Waller that the only "sore spot" he felt in the investigation of the killings was the use of his daughter's DNA. That had been unfair, in his opinion. Judge Waller made no response to that observation. Then, with the death sentence not available to him for crimes committed between 1974 and 1991 in Kansas, the judge sentenced Rader to ten consecutive life sentences, ensuring that the serial killer will die in prison with no chance for parole.

A week before Rader's sentencing, Chief Williams and Lt. Landwehr had invited Special Agent in Charge Stafford, Sheriff Steed, and me to join them on August 19, 2005, in Wichita City Hall for a final news conference to answer any remaining questions about the BTK Task Force operation and Dennis Rader. We all accepted the invitation. The most popular questions were "Did Paula Rader suspect her husband was BTK?" and "If not, should Paula Rader have suspected her husband was BTK?" Also, "Did Rader kill more than ten people?" The unequivocal answers to those three questions were "no," "no," and "no," respectively. Williams, Landwehr, and Stafford primarily handled those questions and those three answers accurately reflected the strong opinions of task force members.

Why were we confident that Rader had not killed more than ten people? Once he started speaking to his interrogators, he didn't want to stop talking about his exploits. He himself had added the homicides of Marine Hedge and Dolores Davis to his litany of evildoings, initially surprising his interrogators. If he had killed twenty people, he would have enthusiastically volunteered those details, his questioners believed. As it was, they couldn't shut him up during interrogations. He would have helped himself more by keeping quiet.[40]

Several reporters asked me my thoughts about Rader's lament during sentencing that his only "sore spot" about the investigation of the killings was the use of his daughter's DNA. On August 20, the Kansas newspapers also quoted part of my response to that inquiry: "Welch said he wants Rader to know that he was proud of obtaining that DNA. 'I'm glad we contributed to his sore spot,'" the KBI director said.

Rader was twenty-eight years of age when he strangled the Oteros in 1974. He was forty-five in 1991 when he killed his last victim, Dolores Davis. He was fifty-nine when he was arrested and sixty when convicted and sentenced in 2005.

The who, what, when, and where of BTK have been revealed. What is less apparent is the why of it all. Why did Dennis Lynn Rader become BTK? Rader said he killed to satisfy sexual fantasies, blaming the claimed uncontrollable urges within him on the mysterious "monster" he termed "Factor X." In his communications to his pursuers, and later in the interviews with his captors, he seemed to fancy himself a sex criminal and, in describing himself and his activities, he used the words "rape," "sodomy," "sexual thrill," "sexual perversion," "sexual fetish," "sex criminal," "sexual fantasies," "sexual death," "sadist tendencies," "sexual relief," "seminal stain," "sexual sadist," and "sexual bondage."

The truth is, however, that Rader did not rape or sodomize any of his ten victims. He was actually an impotent, pedophilic transvestite with autoerotic tendencies who became a serial killer, not a serial rapist. Nor was he legally insane. Few serial killers are legally insane. They understand very well the difference between right and wrong, the legal standard for insanity in Kansas and most other states. Dennis Lynn Rader is no exception. The Jekyll and Hyde church leader was simply bad, not mad. He was a narcissistic, remorseless coward without a conscience. He was fond of his own thoughts and voice. Rader was also fond of wearing women's clothing, especially the trophy lingerie taken from his victims' homes. His own admissions to his interrogators and his collection of photographs and other materials in his office and home confirmed his occasional preference for female attire. The cross-dressing enabled him to revisit his crimes and relive the excitement of those homicide scenes.

If, indeed, Rader had ever been a Christian and faithful to his religion, he had lost his moral compass and veered sharply from the paths of righteousness somewhere along life's journey, long before he defiled Marine Hedge's body in his own Christ Lutheran Church in 1985. Consider the agony of the twisting, turning, tightly bound, incredibly frightened, dying little Josie Otero in 1974. Her plight excited her executioner. In her final, tortured seconds of life, he ejaculated on her. Surely that approached the depth of human depravity.

Rader's own reckless arrogance and foolish overconfidence, coupled with a highly successful law enforcement stratagem designed to fuel that arrogance and overconfidence, led to his capture. Other factors also contributed to his downfall. His misjudgment about the floppy disk was significant and pointed the investigation toward him. The daughter's DNA confirmed Dennis Rader was BTK. And generations of Wichita officers, with their professionalism, investigative reports, and interviews, laid the foundation for the success of the BTK Task Force. The evidence collection and preservation by Wichita officers, from January 15, 1974, to January 19, 1991, especially those who labored on the Otero investigation (1974), the Fox investigation (1977), and the Wegerle investigation (1986), made it possible to confirm Rader's identity as BTK in 2005.

> *"If you do evil, be afraid, for we do not bear the sword in vain."*
> —BTK Task Force
> 2004–2005

CHAPTER EIGHTEEN

Expansion: Special Agents Repositioned and the Creation of a Cold Case Squad

"I, Larry Welch, solemnly swear that I will support the Constitution of the United States and the Constitution of the state of Kansas, and will faithfully discharge the duties of director of the Kansas Bureau of Investigation. So help me God."

I repeated those words and that oath to Kansas Attorney General Bob Stephan on July 18, 1994, in the crowded auditorium at KBI headquarters, filled with active and retired KBI employees, family members, friends, and Kansas law enforcement officials. Former KBI directors Logan Sanford, Jim Malson, Tom Kelly, and Dave Johnson honored me with their presence, and Bob Davenport telephoned his best wishes from his home in Kentucky minutes before the ceremony.

Weeks before he administered the oath of office to me, Attorney General Stephan and I had a few conversations in his Topeka office. The only request my old friend and future boss made of me in those discussions was to work on the relationship between the KBI and the Kansas legislature. The attorney general was aware that we had enjoyed an excellent liaison with the state legislature and governors at the Kansas Law Enforcement Training Center (KLETC), the state's central law enforcement academy and headquarters for training and central repository for Kansas law enforcement records.

One of the liaison strategies we had employed at KLETC was an informal periodic letter that I sent to each legislator, the attorney general, and the governor, keeping each abreast of law enforcement training matters in Kansas. Each year we labeled one such letter as the "KLETC Annual Report," eliminating the traditional expensive, bound, boring annual report, full of meaningless facts, figures, and statistics, and devoid of much narrative. The new version of the annual report became quite popular with the legislators. Therefore, we added the same innovation at the KBI, eliminating the usual expensive annual report, which was often placed, unread, on legislators' bookshelves. Our annual letter to the legislators, governor, and attorney general summarized KBI developments and accomplishments of the previous year and identified current needs, punctuated with bits of humor where appropriate.

PJ Adair, the KBI's executive secretary, served as editor for the annual reports and ensured that those communications never exceeded ten pages in length after I dictated them to her. Legislators thanked and complimented us for the unusual annual reports. Some confessed that it was the only state agency annual report they read each year. In addition to the governor and attorney general, PJ also sent copies of that annual legislative letter to law enforcement administrators and prosecutors, and I annually shared the document with selected media friends, who published selected portions of interest to their areas of the state.

Before assuming KBI leadership reins in July 1994, I had been a close observer and unabashed admirer of the KBI for many years. Despite my familiarity with KBI operations, a few discoveries surprised me. Budget woes were more oppressive than I had anticipated, and the agency was more understaffed than I had realized. The shortages within the ranks of forensic scientists and agency support personnel were even more troublesome than that of special agents.

Also, I learned that there was some laboratory staff sentiment for closing the forensic laboratory at Great Bend. That disappointed me, inasmuch as I had promised central and western Kansas police chiefs, sheriffs, and prosecutors that I would significantly reinforce, not close, that forensic facility. There were only three forensic scientists assigned to Great Bend in 1994, with no supervisor. Each scientist there reported to a different supervisor in Topeka. I intended to triple the number of scientists and add an on-site forensic supervisor. There were, however, warnings from laboratory staff critics of such lofty objectives. They explained to me that the legislature would never adequately support two KBI laboratories and, furthermore, any unlikely enhancement of the Great Bend forensic facility would come at the expense of the vital Topeka forensic laboratory. I disagreed, and, more important, so did Kansas legislators. Such fears and dire predictions proved to be unfounded. Before too long, with proper laboratory direction, the KBI would have nine scientists and a forensic supervisor in Great Bend serving central and western Kansas law enforcement and prosecutors.

I was surprised in July 1994 to learn that the KBI Forensic Laboratory charged Kansas law enforcement agencies and prosecutors for the cost of forensic DNA analysis of evidence. We were the only state crime laboratory in the nation to do so. Granted, the fee we then charged our clientele for DNA analysis, $375, was a bargain, given much higher DNA charges by private laboratories across the country in 1994 and 1995. Nonetheless, it was not a paltry sum for budget-challenged law enforcement agencies and prosecutors, and the expense was discouraging the use of the powerful forensic ally in criminal investigation and prosecution of rape and homicide. No urgent pleas to end the DNA fee were needed, but I received them from prominent Kansas prosecutors, including District Attorney Nola Foulston (Sedgwick County), County Attorney Tim Chambers (Reno County), County Attorney Chris Biggs (Geary County), and District Attorney Nick Tomasic (Wyandotte County).

Accordingly, in 1995, I ordered that the practice of charging for DNA services be discontinued. The decision had little to commend it, except for the grateful response that followed. That response was appreciated, but it remained to be seen whether my decision was wise or practical, given already serious forensic backlogs throughout the laboratory, especially in the biology and chemistry sections.

I was also disappointed to learn that eastern Kansas investigators and prosecutors, especially those in southeastern Kansas, because of those KBI forensic backlogs, often sent forensic evidence to private laboratories in Missouri and Oklahoma for expensive but timely analysis. Again, I was embarrassed that Kansas law enforcement agencies had to pay for forensic services in the investigation of Kansas crimes, and I was determined to end that particular nonsense as well. The Kansas law enforcement community deserved no less from the KBI.

Not all my initial surprises originated in the forensic science division. I learned that almost two-thirds of all our KBI special agents in general, and three-fourths of our narcotic agents in particular, were assigned to KBI headquarters in Topeka. We were authorized to employ eighty-one special agents. Even that modest complement, due to budgetary constraints, had seldom been achieved. It made no sense to me, especially understaffed as we were, to have two-thirds of that vital investigative resource assigned to our headquarters city rather than positioned strategically around the state.

The easiest of the early dilemmas to resolve were the DNA examination fee being charged law enforcement, which required only a simple executive decision to remedy, and the geographic imbalance of agents, which simply required time. With thirty-eight new agents added between 1996 and 2001, we were able to reverse the two-thirds ratio of agents assigned to Topeka fairly soon.

Soon after my arrival at KBI headquarters, I encouraged our executive staff and personnel division to change the qualifications for the position of special agent. Previous law enforcement experience had always been the primary requisite for becoming a KBI special agent. I wanted to change the primary qualification to a preference for a college degree, plus law enforcement experience—a minimum of three to five years of investigative experience. Certainly, if an applicant had impressive law enforcement experience or a particular, important expertise, but no higher education on his or her resume, we would welcome that person aboard. Conversely, if the right applicant had a bachelor's degree and law degree, or a master's degree in an important discipline or expertise, we would ignore the absence of law enforcement experience in their resume—as we already did with our forensic scientists. But, we would prefer a healthy combination of experience and education.

The hiring philosophy of many federal law enforcement agencies, in particular the FBI, has been that education and intelligence can sometimes trump law enforcement experience. The theory is that the well-educated, intelligent candidate can be trained for whatever mission and duties would be required of the special agent. Law enforcement experience would, of course, be icing on the cake.

During the 1980s and 1990s many local law enforcement agencies—municipal, county, and state—adopted the philosophy of our federal cousins and made higher education a requirement for internal promotions. Even more agencies made higher education a preference, at least, for hiring. After all, a college degree is often but not always an indicator of maturity if not intelligence. Coupled with experience, it can produce an impressive employee.

I firmly believe that Directors Richter and Sanford would highly approve the preference we adopted for the hiring of special agents. They both respected and pursued a college education in a day when few others in the profession thought such a course of action necessary or even advisable.

Our first opportunity to hire a new class of KBI special agents came in July 1996. We had ten agent vacancies, and the legislature earlier that year provided the funding to hire and equip the agents needed to fill those vacant positions. It would be the only time—a woefully brief period—that we enjoyed a full complement of agents during my tenure (1994–2007).

Our first class of new special agents began with an applicant pool of 300 qualified men and women. I formed two selection-interview teams. My second-in-command, Dale Finger, served as overall coordinator and chairman of one team. He had our agency human resource manager and three veteran agents, including an African American male, on his team. Deputy Director Terry Knowles chaired the second group. He had four veteran special agents, including one of our female agents, on his team. Those two teams spent many hours over two days reviewing the applications of the 300 candidates; together, they selected about sixty applicants for interview. Following a full week of interviews by the two teams, they recommended thirty finalists for consideration. Finger; Knowles; our human resource manager, Anne Brunt; and I then spent much of two weeks making final hiring decisions, after background investigations, polygraph examinations, psychological and intelligence tests, and some reinterviews trimmed the final pool of candidates.

The ten new hires were sworn in as KBI agents on July 29, 1996, by Attorney General Carla Stovall. They included one female, a Kansas sheriff, one county detective, one deputy sheriff, five police officers, a graduate of the FBI National Academy, a law school graduate, a certified firearms instructor and armorer, and a border patrolman fluent in Spanish. Collectively, they had almost seventy years of law enforcement experience, three associate degrees, six bachelor's degrees, one master's degree, and one law degree. Three were assigned to Great Bend, two to Wichita, one to Liberal, one to Overland Park, one to Garden City, one to Concordia, and one to Junction City. None were assigned to Topeka.

Between 1996 and 2007 we hired forty-four new agents and reassigned five KBI employees (criminal analysts and/or forensic scientists) to the special agent position. I still have my personal notes regarding the appointments of forty-one of the forty-nine agents—all except eight brought aboard in 1999. These notes reflect that, collectively, the forty-one new agents held forty-three college degrees. Those forty-three diplomas included thirty-five bachelor's degrees, four master's degrees, one law degree, and three associate degrees. The forty-one agents included eight women, one Hispanic male, and one African American male. We wanted more of all three of those categories but were unsuccessful in that quest. Also included were two graduates of the FBI National Academy in Quantico, Virginia; three Kansas sheriffs and two Kansas undersheriffs; and one U.S. Secret Service agent who was a West Point graduate.

Only four of those forty-one new agents did not have prior law enforcement or investigative experience. Those four, collectively, had earned six college degrees, including a law degree, a master's degree, and four bachelor's degrees. Three of the four possessed special computer expertise and the fourth was an attorney. Despite the missing notes about the new agents of 1999, I recall that all of the eight had previous law enforcement experience, and I believe that all but one were college graduates.

The majority of those forty-nine special agents were assigned to Kansas communities like Pittsburg, Wichita, Great Bend, Liberal, Garden City, Scott City, Clay Center, Kansas City, Manhattan, Emporia, Winfield, Meade, and Cimarron—but not Topeka.

The original headquarters of the KBI consisted of a 920-square-foot area on the first floor of the south wing of the state capitol building in Topeka. The space accommodated well enough Director Lou Richter and the agency's sole secretary, Mary Collins, inasmuch as the nine special agents of the day were usually elsewhere in 1939 and throughout World War II.

In the late 1940s, however, Director Richter was able to persuade a legislature worried about the escalating crime of postwar Kansas to double the number of KBI agents. That trend continued in 1957, when Director Logan Sanford significantly increased KBI services to Kansas law enforcement and prosecutors, especially forensically, and added more agents, scientists, and support staff. By the late 1960s the KBI space in the state capitol had been increased to nearly 3,000 square feet but was still inadequate.

I visited Director Sanford at KBI headquarters in 1960 while a student at KU Law School and again in 1969 when the FBI transferred me from Texas to Kansas City. Although more spacious than the original 1939 space, I recall how crowded the KBI office was during both my visits.

In July 1970, under Director Harold Nye, KBI headquarters were finally moved from the crowded, inconvenient state capitol building—with its attendant space limitations, parking problems, and lack of accessibility to the KBI by law enforcement and the public—to an office building at 3420 Van Buren in Topeka, where the bureau would eventually have 23,000 square feet of space to better accommodate the physical needs of the growing agency. The legislature, which had coveted the KBI space in the state capitol building almost since they gave it to the original KBI in 1939, happily approved Director Nye's request to move from the capitol building, needing that space for legislators and staffs in 1970.

A field office and a small satellite forensic laboratory were opened by Director Fred Howard in Great Bend in 1973 to serve central and western Kansas. Director Howard also obtained office space in suburban Kansas City for agents working in that region. A similar office followed in Wichita later.

In October 1984, Director Tom Kelly moved KBI headquarters to 1620 Tyler, close to downtown Topeka, near 17th and Topeka Boulevard. The ancient building, constructed as a Topeka junior high school in 1929, provided a welcome 48,820 square feet of space in its three stories, not including 6,000 square feet in the attic, later used for storage and offices for narcotic agents. In 1984, however, it was impossible to anticipate the eventual space demands of the Automated Fingerprint Identification System (AFIS); Deoxyribonucleic acid (DNA); the Combined DNA Indexing System (CODIS); the Integrated Ballistics Identification System (IBIS); national forensic accreditation; computers; cybercrime; evidence storage; methamphetamine; meth labs; and so many other law enforcement forensic and investigative technologies and practices of the 1980s, 1990s, and early twenty-first century. The old junior high school building was simply not designed for the uses to which the KBI was later forced to put it. In addition, the building, because of its age and/or location, lacked many amenities and had many problems: inadequate parking; a paucity of rest rooms, meeting rooms, interview rooms, offices, and squad rooms; antiquated and frustrating heating and cooling systems; insufficient bench space for scientists; a tiny auditorium; and a leaky roof.

Finally, in 2006, a grateful legislature addressed the space problems at 1620 Tyler in Topeka. They purchased for us the IMA Insurance Company building, located across a narrow alley from KBI headquarters. Built in 1986, it was a beautiful, spacious building. Literally overnight, we added sixty parking spaces and 12,000 square feet of space. We soon moved sixty-six employees of the KBI Information Services Division, with the division's Assistant Director Dave Sim and Special Agent in Charge Dave Hutchings, into the new facility, creating additional space for agents and scientists inside the KBI headquarters building. That same legislative session also approved and funded extensive renovations for KBI headquarters and long-awaited remodeling of office and laboratory space in our KBI building at Great Bend. Both renovations, in Topeka and Great Bend, began in 2006 and were completed in 2007. Our cup was the closest to full in KBI history.

Kirk Thompson and Kyle Smith led the legislative campaign for the purchase of the IMA building and the subsequent remodeling of the headquarters building. Sim and Hutchings coordinated the challenging logistics of the move of an entire KBI division. The two Davids, assisted by their enthusiastic top staff, quietly and efficiently moved almost seventy employees across the alley, with all the accompanying equipment, supplies, materials, files, records, and computers, without an interruption in the operations of the KBI Information Services Division.

In the first recorded homicide, Cain, elder son of Adam, slew his brother Abel. Ever since, homicide has invited, and investigators have pursued, solution, resolution, and punishment. Like killers who came after him, Cain lied about his evildoing when first questioned. When asked about his brother's whereabouts, Cain replied to the Lord, "I know not. Am I my brother's keeper?" For his homicide, Cain was expelled from Eden and sentenced by the Lord to a life of exile, as "a fugitive and vagabond." Like killers who came later, Cain, at his sentencing, whined and complained about the discipline he received: "My punishment is greater than I can bear." Cain was quite fortunate that the electric chair, gas chamber, gallows, guillotine, firing squad, and lethal injection were still in the distant future and not available in the fourth chapter of Genesis.

The history of the KBI cannot be traced to Genesis 4—only to July 1939—but, throughout its proud history, one KBI pursuit has remained constant: a consistent primary investigative and forensic priority has been the solution of homicides. Working with local law enforcement and prosecutors to help clear unsolved homicides has always been what the KBI is primarily about. A KBI agent who has not attended the autopsy of a homicide victim is a rarity. Rarer still, regardless of primary investigative assignment, is the KBI agent who has not labored at homicide scenes, conducted interviews, or assisted with other leads in homicide investigations.

Much of the motivation across the nation in the early 1990s for formation of cold case squads to address the plethora of unsolved murders came from the plummeting homicide solution rate. The national homicide clearance rate dropped from 91 percent in 1963—the first year such records were kept—to 65 percent in 1992 and 61 percent in 2007.[1] Grades of 65 percent and 61 percent are considered failing grades in most arenas of life. Those dramatic reductions in homicide-solution success came despite greatly improved law enforcement training; better law enforcement equipment; computers and automation; national crime databases like the National Crime Information Center (NCIC), the Combined DNA Indexing System (CODIS) for Deoxyribonucleic Acid (DNA), the Automated Fingerprint Identification System (AFIS), and the Integrated Ballistics Identification System (IBIS); improved ballistics; enhanced communications; Crime Scene Investigation (CSI) wizardry; and national forensic laboratory accreditation.

So why was there a decrease in homicide solution? Primarily because of the increase in gangs and drugs from 1963 to 2007 and the accompanying drug-related homicides and drive-by shootings, with the resulting impersonal and anonymous nature of American murder. Homicide solution was simply easier in the 1960s because the killer then was often a family member, friend, or an acquaintance, not a stranger as is frequently the case today. Another factor today is the availability of firearms. When I entered law enforcement in 1961, burglars and other so-called nonviolent criminals did not typically carry guns to their crimes. Armed robbers and determined murderers carried guns. Today, shoplifters, pickpockets, purse snatchers, drunk drivers, and drug dealers may be in possession of firearms.

Always willing to borrow successful crime-solving tactics and strategies from other agencies, I was eager to create such a KBI resource for the Kansas law enforcement community, despite the omnipresent significant budgetary vacancies within our special agent ranks. The first opportunity to move toward the creation of the first KBI Cold Case Squad and fulfill one of my earliest KBI priorities did not present itself until 1998. It was then that the

Kansas legislature finally grew tired of my pleas to relieve the KBI of the responsibility for the conduct of background and applicant investigations in the state gaming industry and to provide the state gaming agency with its own investigators to conduct such inquiries. My frustrated staff had grown weary of pulling KBI special agents off major criminal investigations to meet deadlines on these applicant background investigations. We welcomed that legislative action and quickly ended the KBI Gaming Unit, redirecting its resources to form the special homicide squad envisioned in its place.

By July 1998, the initial membership of the KBI Cold Case Squad had been selected: Agents Ray Lundin, Tim Dennis, and Ezell Monts and Office Assistant Cynthia Roberts, under the supervision of Special Agent in Charge Larry Thomas. Collectively, the group possessed a wealth of expertise and experience. Lundin, Dennis, Monts, Roberts, and Thomas had a combined total of fifty-one years in the KBI and eighty-three years in law enforcement. In addition, the four agents, especially Lundin and Thomas, had extensive homicide investigation experience.

The next order of business was to establish the operating protocol for the squad. How would they select the unsolved cases to pursue? How many would they address at one time? How old would be too old? How recent a case would be too recent? Early on, at their invitation, I met with the new team frequently and sat in on their preliminary discussions. I mostly listened. The protocol decisions had to be theirs. My participation consisted mostly of my agreement to send the entire squad anywhere in the nation to observe the existing cold case squad they most wished to visit and to send the entire squad to one of Vernon Geberth's advanced homicide investigation seminars. Larry Thomas and I were alumni of both the basic and advanced Vernon Geberth "Practical Homicide Investigation" seminars. Additionally, we were both close friends of the former commander of the New York Police Department's famous Bronx Homicide Task Force. We considered the retired Geberth to be one of the foremost authorities in the world on the investigation of homicides and an excellent resource for our new squad.

After evaluating several cold case squads from afar, the team informed me that the unit they would prefer to visit was that of our counterparts in Minnesota, the Minnesota Bureau of Criminal Apprehension's Unsolved Homicide Unit. Accordingly, all five members traveled to St. Paul, Minnesota, in August 1998, where they were hosted and assisted by Larry Thomas's Minnesota counterpart, Special Agent Everett Doolittle, commander of Minnesota's Unsolved Homicide Unit. The Minnesota cold case squad had begun in 1991 with Doolittle alone. When the Kansans visited in 1998, the Minnesota unit consisted of three agents and was averaging two cases solved a year. The oldest case solved was thirty-two years old. Two others were twenty and fifteen years old, respectively. The KBI team spent three days in Minnesota before returning home with copies of the Minnesota protocol, many solved and unsolved case summaries, the unit's policies and procedures, and considerable advice and counsel from Doolittle and his colleagues. Also, in August 1998, all five members attended Vernon Geberth's homicide training seminar hosted by the Lawrence Police Department in Lawrence, Kansas.

Based on input from other KBI homicide agents, Kansas law enforcement investigators, Kansas prosecutors, other cold case squads across the nation, their Minnesota and Geberth experiences, and their own ideas, the KBI Cold Case Squad established their guidelines for selection of the cold cases to be pursued and for operation of the squad:

> KBI Cold Case Squad assistance must be officially requested by the local case agency;
> Any case selected must be at least five years old and preferably at least fifteen years old;
> The local case agency must be actively involved in the cold case reinvestigation;
> There must be no apparent legal obstruction to successful prosecution, and the local prosecutor (or the office of the state attorney general) must officially agree to pursue prosecution, if warranted, when the cold case reinvestigation is completed;
> The cold case's original investigators must be consulted and thoroughly interviewed at the outset;
> Surviving members of the victim's family must be consulted at the outset and their support for the reinvestigation solicited, although that support would not be a prerequisite for case selection;
> A minimum of two unsolved cold cases would be pursued at the same time, but no more than six such cases would be investigated simultaneously. [Three or four became the norm.]

The squad adopted other factors to also be considered in the selection of unsolved homicides to be pursued. Those factors included the following:

> Existence of physical evidence? If so, is that evidence conducive to analysis by modern technology, for example, DNA, AFIS, ballistics, latent fingerprint impressions, national databases?
> Availability of original witnesses?
> Any identifiable living suspect?
> Availability of original investigative reports, interview reports, and crime scene and victim photographs;

Motive of the homicide identified;

Quality of collection and preservation of original trace evidence?

Availability of original forensic laboratory results?

Availability of original medical examiner's report and/or autopsy report?

Known cause of death?

Availability of a suspect profile?

Clearance potential: excellent, good, or poor? [Poor potential did not preclude adoption of a cold case.]

The special homicide squad proved to be one of the KBI's most popular innovations with Kansas media, law enforcement, and prosecutors. The 1998 summer issue of the *Kansas Sheriff,* official publication of the Kansas Sheriffs' Association, hailed the squad's creation: "The creation of the first ever KBI Cold Case Squad was announced in July by Director Larry Welch. . . . The creation of the squad, which has been a longtime goal of Welch, was made possible by legislative changes this year allowing a redirection of the former KBI Gaming Unit."[2]

Typical of letters of support we received from Kansas prosecutors was one dated September 11, 1998, from veteran prosecutor Nick Tomasic, district attorney of Wyandotte County, Kansas City, Kansas:

RE: Unsolved Homicides—Cold Case Squad

Dear Mr. Welch:

The formation of the Cold Case Squad by the Kansas Bureau of Investigation has my support, 100 percent. This past week my office filed first-degree murder charges against two (2) men arising out of a 1976 homicide. Agents from your newly formed Cold Case Squad actively pursued the investigation after receiving information about the possible suspects. Their work directly contributed to the charges being filed.

In Wyandotte County since 1976, we have 141 unsolved homicides. I'm sure the statewide number would be staggering. Many of the cases could be solved if only someone had the time to work the cases. In our area, the homicide detectives are jumping from one new case to another, and they don't have the time to work the old cases.

Larry, my office offers its unconditional support to the program. If there is anything you need to support the program, let me know.

Yours truly,

Nick A. Tomasic

District Attorney[3]

Due to personnel reassignments and promotions, the squad's complement soon changed to Thomas and Lundin, with Senior Special Agent Brad
Cordts, KBI Analyst Jeff Muckenthaler (an exceptional criminal analyst and
researcher), and KBI Intern Katie Schuetz (later an analyst and a fine special
agent).

The involvement of the KBI Cold Case Squad in the Shannon Martin,
Liz Wilson, and BTK homicides—twelve cold cases in all—has been described in previous chapters. Between 1998 and 2007, the KBI cold case
closers helped local Kansas law enforcement agencies reopen, reinvestigate,
solve, and successfully prosecute another dozen unsolved murders.

The squad's first success came in a twenty-two-year-old cold case in Wyandotte County, Kansas. On August 31, 1976, the body of a young white
male, later identified as George Wayne "Frankie" Tiller, age thirty-one, was
found by three young fishermen on the Kansas bank of the Kaw River, separating Wyandotte County, Kansas, and Jackson County, Missouri. Tiller, a
recent Missouri parolee with an arrest record for armed robbery and parole
violation, had been beaten to death. A bloody tire iron and two bloody boards
were found near the body. Human hair, red in color like that of Tiller, was
found on all three of those items. The blood was determined to be human
and of the same blood type as that of Tiller. The case went cold.

In July 1998, about a week after the cold case squad's formal beginning,
Larry Thomas received a telephone call from Iowa authorities. They advised
that a man just arrested for a recent rape there wanted to speak to a Kansas
officer about a murder he and his brother allegedly committed in the Kansas
City area approximately twenty years earlier.

Ray Lundin drove to Iowa and interviewed the jail inmate, Kenneth Levy.
The prisoner told Lundin that during the late summer of 1976 or 1977 he
and his half-brother, Huel Pennington, with Pennington's girlfriend, Beverly
Cordrey, were in a Kansas City bar and met a redheaded man who called
himself Frankie. As Levy recalled, that man was a recent arrival in Kansas
City and might have been an ex-con. During the evening in the bar, the man
allegedly made advances to Cordrey. The two brothers decided to teach him
a lesson and, with Cordrey, they drove him to a river. They intended to hurt
him, not kill him, but the subsequent beating, in front of Cordrey, with a
tire iron and heavy pieces of wood went too far. The stranger was killed on
the riverbank. Lundin returned to Kansas City and spent a couple days with
detectives of the Kansas City, Kansas, Police Department, sharing with them
the homicide information Levy furnished him in the Iowa interview. The
good news was that they identified the Tiller homicide as likely being the
murder Levy described. Things seemed to match. The bad news, however,

was that most of the investigative reports, physical evidence, and all the crime scene photographs from the Tiller case were destroyed in the flooding of the police department's storage facility several years earlier.

A few of the investigative reports and all of the medical examiner's reports and autopsy reports were available, but none of the photographs of the crime scene or victim could be found. The prosecutor wanted more than just Levy's confession.

Accordingly, I made an appeal to Kansas City area media on August 24, 1998:

> Dear Kansas City Area News Media:
> On August 31, 1976, fishermen observed a body in the Kansas (Kaw) River near the I-635 bridge in Kansas City, Kansas.
> The body was soon identified as that of Frank W. Tiller, age thirty-one, a parolee from the Missouri State Prison and a recent arrival in Kansas City, Missouri.
> Investigation determined that Tiller had been beaten to death with a tire tool and a piece of lumber.
> New information has been developed and the Kansas Bureau of Investigation and Kansas City, Kansas, Police Department are seeking copies of any print photographs, film, video, etc., possibly still in possession of any Kansas City area news media, which might assist the KBI and Kansas City Police Department in reconstructing the events and that crime scene of almost twenty-two years ago.
> We respectfully request that your files and archives be reviewed in an effort to identify such materials.
> Please contact Special Agent in Charge Larry Thomas, KBI Cold Case Squad, Topeka, 785-296-8200, if any such materials are located.
> Sincerely,
> Larry Welch
> Director[4]

The media response was prompt and impressive. Television stations and newspapers in the Kansas City metropolitan area provided us with excellent photographs, considerable video film, and complete print coverage about the Tiller case from their respective archives.

Meanwhile, Kansas City detectives and KBI Cold Case Squad agents located Beverly Cordrey in an area rest home. She corroborated in detail Levy's confession and agreed to testify against the two brothers in a Kansas City district court.

Levy soon recanted his confession, but he and Pennington were arrested by Lundin and local detectives on September 2, 1998. Pennington, ironically, died of natural causes three days later in an Iowa jail, prior to extradition to Kansas.

We proceeded to trial against Levy in Wyandotte County District Court in June 1999, with District Attorney Nick Tomasic handling the prosecution. Beverly Cordrey, in failing health, was escorted to the trial each day by a nurse. Following her strong, emotional testimony against Levy, the defendant's attorney requested a brief recess. Then, on resumption of the trial, Levy withdrew his plea of not guilty and entered a plea of guilty to voluntary manslaughter. His guilty plea was accepted and Levy was found guilty of killing Tiller.

The second of the first three cold cases adopted by the new KBI squad in July 1998 also resulted in arrest and conviction. That case involved the murders of a young mother and her infant daughter in their Junction City apartment in Geary County, Kansas.

On July 24, 1994, Private First Class Jade Blount, after one week of field maneuvers with the U.S. Army at Fort Riley, Kansas, returned home to find his young wife, Kasey Marie, and his daughter, Alannah, dead. His wife had been raped and strangled. The specific cause of death, however, was one of her baby's socks being forced down her throat. Alannah, less than one year of age, was found in an upstairs bedroom in her crib. She had died of extreme dehydration and two or three days of neglect following her mother's murder. In another case highlighted by the investigative skills and patience of Ray Lundin, the new KBI squad, working closely with Junction City Police Department detectives and Geary County Sheriff Bill Deppish, scored the second and third clearances of cold cases. Almost five years to the day of the discovery of the Blount bodies in Junction City, Kansas, Lundin and Florida authorities arrested Artis Tremain Cobb in Suwannee County, Florida, for those murders. Cobb had been a soldier stationed at Fort Riley at the time of the homicides. He was identified as the killer through an exhaustive series of interviews of former Fort Riley soldiers, and former neighbors, friends, and associates of the Blounts by Lundin across Kansas, Georgia, and Florida. Cobb was convicted of the crimes in a three-week jury trial in March and April 2000 in Geary County District Court, with District Attorney Chris Biggs the prosecutor.

Not every cold case selected for reinvestigation ended with arrest. For example, on May 11, 1992, attractive twenty-year-old Jennifer Judd was found by her husband in their Baxter Springs home stabbed to death. The murder occurred only nine days after the couple's wedding. The local homicide investigation went cold and the Judd murder case became one of the first three cold cases adopted by the KBI Cold Case Squad in 1998 at the request of local authorities. Weeks into the reinvestigation, Larry Thomas and Ray Lundin were confident they knew who had murdered Jennifer. Despite extensive investigative efforts and the offer of a $10,000 reward, the veteran homicide investigators were unable to prove their mutual belief.

In criminal investigation and prosecution, knowing something and being able to prove that premise in a court of law are, of course, two quite different propositions. The burden of prosecution is to persuade all twelve jurors of the defendant's guilt beyond a reasonable doubt. The burden of the defense is simply to confuse one juror.

Ironically, Thomas and Lundin were able to disprove the confession of an inmate on Alabama's death row claiming responsibility for the Judd homicide. The career criminal had ties to Cherokee County and Baxter Springs, Kansas, and, for some undetermined reason—probably the massive media coverage attracted by the homicide—wanted credit for Jennifer's murder. Many in Alabama, Kansas, and the confessor's native Oklahoma believed his story; however, extensive efforts by the two KBI investigators, including a lengthy interview on Alabama's death row, disproved his confession.

At any rate, the cold case solution rate achieved by the KBI Cold Case Squad, while not perfect, approached perfection and was much appreciated by Kansas prosecutors, local law enforcement, victims' families, and media.

Forensics: Murder in a Soccer Field, National Accreditation, and New Laboratories

In July 1998, the KBI formed a small squad of agents to help address the dramatic increase in computer crimes that Kansas law enforcement was experiencing. The squad's charter members were Dave Schroeder, Richard Marchewka, John McElroy, and Richard Vick, under the command of Special Agent in Charge Kevan Pfeifer. Schroeder and Marchewka, each blessed with special computer expertise, had already been assisting local authorities for more than a year with all types of computer crimes, ranging from complex fraud cases to child pornography. The two agents, however, were swamped with calls for their computer expertise. We hoped the special squad's creation would significantly bolster the KBI's support of local law enforcement in such critical matters. As with the KBI Cold Case Squad's creation, the formation of the KBI's High Technology Crime Unit (HTCU) was made possible only by the redirection of the former KBI Gaming Unit's resources and membership. We soon lost Kevan Pfeifer and his wife, Melanie, our agency's general counsel, to a new life in Montana. Special Agent in Charge Rick Sabel took over the squad and Agents Marchewka and McElroy retired in 2000 and Vick in 2002. Agents John Kite and Steve Elsen were added as replacements.

HTCU was basically the brainchild of Senior Special Agent Dave Schroeder, and he remained the heart and soul of the KBI's response to cybercrime. Early on, he led the bureau's involvement in an international investigation by the U.S. Customs Service that, in turn, led to numerous arrests of child pornographers using the Internet. We were learning, however, that there was more to cybercrime than Internet fraud and child pornography. As Schroeder told the *Lawrence Journal-World* in a story about the HTCU on October 21, 2002, "Any type of crime you can think of, there has probably been a case that involved a computer."[1] Schroeder did not exaggerate. A woman in southwestern Kansas shot and killed her husband. Minutes before law enforcement arrived at their home, the new widow had e-mailed a confession to her parents in another state. We were also finding that drug traffickers were increasingly using their computers to record and maintain the names, addresses, and contact numbers of customers, associates, and suppliers, as well as their inventories of product. Accordingly, KBI search warrants authorizing the seizures of drugs were often accompanied by KBI search warrants authorizing the seizures of computers on those premises. There were, of course, other varieties of cybercrime to occupy our investigators, including identity theft, extortion, investment scams, threatening e-mails, an Internet-fueled array of sexual perversion and exploitation, and other lewd and lascivious behavior, too often involving children. Despite the expertise and dedication of our cybercrime investigators, we were never able to adequately address the unending requests from Kansas law enforcement for KBI assistance in computer-related crimes.

The KBI, Kansas law enforcement, and the state greatly benefitted from the FBI's creation of the Heart of America Regional Computer Forensic Laboratory (HARCFL) in Kansas City in 2003 in the fight against cybercrime. The decision early on to assign KBI Agents Cindy Smith and Angie Wilson to HARCFL and to the companion FBI Cybercrime Task Force, respectively, proved to be a wise one. The emphasis in that two-pronged FBI effort was child exploitation and pornography in Kansas and western Missouri. Smith and Wilson were commended by the FBI, the Kansas attorney general, and the KBI director for their contributions to those two important KBI allies, HARCFL and its supportive task force.

In addition, Smith and Schroeder were each named Certified Forensic Computer Examiners in 2004 by the International Association of Computer Investigative Specialists, a coveted distinction in law enforcement investigation of cybercrime. They were not geeks with guns, but solid investigators. Neither the KBI's HTCU nor the FBI's HARCFL could stay abreast of the Internet crimes referred to them. Backlogs persisted and requests for help soared.

The BTK serial murder investigation was not the first time that the KBI's Sindey Schueler assisted the Wichita Police Department with her DNA expertise in a major multiple-homicides case. On December 5, 2000, Reginald Carr was inadvertently released from jail in Dodge City because of an error in paperwork. He and his younger brother, Jonathan, both in their early twenties, made their way to Wichita and launched a brutal nine-day crime spree, targeting and stalking people, primarily women, simply because the victims were operating newer automobiles in east Wichita. The senseless rampage of robbery, carjacking, auto theft, kidnapping, murder, and rape began on December 7, 2000, with the carjacking, abduction, and ATM robbery of a lone Wichita male. That first victim, fortunately, survived his encounter with the out-of-control duo. The brutality, however, quickly escalated thereafter. During the nine days of mindless cruelty that followed, five of the Carr brothers' next six victims did not survive—and the sixth barely did.

Ann Walenta, age fifty-five, was a gifted cellist with the Wichita Symphony. During the cold winter evening of December 11, at approximately 9:30 P.M., Walenta was returning from a late evening symphony rehearsal for a concert the next night. As she drove into her driveway in her sport utility vehicle, she was immediately followed by another vehicle occupied by two African American males. One of them suddenly jumped out and stood beside her driver's door, then demanded at gunpoint that she exit her vehicle. Walenta's response to that demand was to place her vehicle in reverse and start to back out of her driveway. She paid dearly for her disobedience. The assailant fired three rounds with a .380 semiautomatic pistol, blowing out the driver's window and covering the driver with glass. Worse, the three rounds struck the victim once in her left arm and twice in her back as she turned away from the shooter. One round pierced her left lung. Another one severed her spinal cord, leaving her paralyzed from the waist down for the few remaining days of her life.

As the would-be carjackers fled, Ann Walenta turned on her vehicle's flashing hazard lights and began honking the horn. In the minutes that followed, she described her primary assailant to the first person who responded to her calls for help—a neighbor lady and friend—and later to her husband, emergency medical responders, and Wichita police officers. Four days later, still clinging to life, she would select a photograph of Reginald Carr from a photo array shown her by police in the hospital. She was, however, unable to select a photograph of Jonathan Carr from a second photo assortment as the other assailant. The courageous woman succumbed to her wounds on January 2, 2001.

During the evening of December 14, the Dodge City brothers were again cruising east Wichita looking for a likely victim. They spotted an attractive blonde woman leaving the restaurant where she was employed and followed her as she drove her BMW automobile to her apartment in a triplex on Birchwood Drive. The intended victim resided with her two children in one of the three units. Probably because of the poor visibility that snowy, dark night, the pair did not see which of the three doors the lady entered. Fortunately for the single mother and her children, and tragically for five unsuspecting people, the brothers guessed wrong and knocked on the door next to that of the intended victim.

The door selected by Reginald or Jonathan Carr that evening led to a three-bedroom apartment shared by three friends. Jason Befort, age twenty-six, was a popular science teacher and coach at Augusta High School, nineteen miles east of Wichita. Brad Heyka, age twenty-seven, was employed by

Koch Industries, and twenty-nine-year-old Aaron Sander was preparing to enter the seminary, hoping to become a Catholic priest. Also present were Heather Muller, age twenty-five, a preschool teacher at a Wichita Catholic church, and Befort's visiting twenty-five-year-old fiancée, whose identity I withhold to protect. Muller was helping her friend Sander pack his belongings for the move. The group's individual and collective plans for a quiet, uneventful evening went terribly awry when either Muller or Sander responded to the knocks on the door and the two intruders burst into the home brandishing handguns and seeking the attractive blonde they had seen outside. A three-hour ordeal of assault, battery, repeated rape, sodomy, and forced trips to the victims' ATMs followed.

Out of respect for the victims, the disturbing details of the unspeakable degradation suffered by the five friends at the hands of the two intruders will not be described here. Suffice it to say that few examples of man's inhumanity to man throughout Kansas history approach the depths of depravity suffered by the five young men and women in the barbaric treatment they received that night at the hands of Reginald and Jonathan Carr.

The terror and torment did not end for the five victims within the walls of the apartment. The three men were eventually placed in the trunk of one of the victim's Honda automobile, and the two young terrified women were placed in the Dodge truck of another victim. They were driven to a soccer field in a rural area of northeast Wichita where the five friends, mostly unclothed, were forced to kneel in the snow in a line together, and then each was shot in the back of the head, execution-style. The lives of Heather Muller, Jason Befort, Aaron Sander, and Brad Heyka ended on that soccer field that dark night in six inches of new snow. Incredibly, and mercifully, a plastic hair clip deflected the bullet that struck Befort's fiancée, and, following the departure of the two killers and rapists—in a final indignity, they drove over her in the Dodge truck—the courageous young lady, bleeding and naked, ran one mile in snow and across frozen fields to the nearest home to call for help. She survived and provided invaluable, detailed descriptions of the assailants' physical descriptions, criminal conduct, conversations, and vehicle. By 4:00 A.M., December 15, Deputy Chief of Police Coy Lee was sharing the survivor's information that he could properly share with the Wichita media. Almost immediately, calls came in regarding the brothers and their vehicle and continued throughout the day.

Since the original carjacking of the lone Wichita male on December 7 and the attack on cellist Ann Walenta December 11, Lt. Ken Landwehr and his detectives had been tracking the heretofore unidentified invaders from Dodge City. On December 15, thanks to the lone survivor of the soccer field massacre and the Wichita Police Department's typical wise use of Wichita media as a resource and ally, the three different crimes and the two perpetrators were connected. The police were even receiving telephone calls from recent Wichita acquaintances of the two Dodge City brothers, providing the names of Reginald and Jonathan Carr.

From the same photograph arrays shown to Ann Walenta, the carjacking victim identified Reginald Carr as his assailant, and that same day the soccer field survivor identified photographs of both Carrs as the killers and rapists of the previous night. Not as tough with armed officers as with helpless, frightened victims, both brothers were arrested later in the day, December 15, without incident. They would spend the rest of their Wichita visit in the Sedgwick County jail awaiting trial.

Very soon, Landwehr's homicide squad was sending evidence from the crime spree to KBI Forensic Laboratory Supervisor Sindey Schueler in Topeka for her expert analysis. Schueler spent countless hours processing the clothing of the two suspects. She identified Heather Muller's blood and DNA on the undershorts of both Reginald and Jonathan Carr, and on Reginald Carr's shirt and other outer garments as well. She also identified the surviving woman's blood and DNA on Jonathan Carr's underwear. In addition, Schueler found Jonathan Carr's DNA in semen that was recovered on carpeting from the Birchwood Drive apartment, where both female victims had endured repeated rapes. DNA from both Carrs' semen was identified by Schueler in rape kits administered on both women victims, deceased and living, confirming the sexual abuse and rapes of Heather Muller and Jason Befort's fiancée by both brothers.

Additional evidence was provided by Joe House of the KBI Forensic Laboratory. House received and entered the evidence received from the Wichita Police Department at KBI headquarters in the Carr case prior to Schueler's forensic analysis of it. House found Heather Muller's ring in a pocket of Jonathan Carr's trousers and would later testify in the trial about that evidentiary discovery.

Judge Paul Clark presided over the trial. The Carr brothers were defended by two separate teams of state public defenders, attorneys experienced in capital murder trials. The prosecution was handled by Sedgwick County District Attorney Nola Foulston with two of her assistants, Kim Parker and Kevin O'Connor, all veteran, successful prosecutors. The preliminary hearing was held April 16–18, 2001, and initially the brothers were charged with 113 felony counts. Those charges were later trimmed to ninety-seven counts, fifty against Reginald Carr and forty-seven against Jonathan, including five counts of murder and multiple counts of kidnapping, rape, sodomy, and robbery against each Carr. For the remainder of 2001 and for most of 2002, Judge Clark addressed numerous pretrial motions. Most were defense motions.

Jury selection started September 9, 2002, and was completed on October 2. The trial started on October 7 and the prosecution presented more than 800 exhibits and more than ninety witnesses. The trial ended November 4 with ninety-three verdicts of guilty. The jury found Reginald Carr guilty of all fifty charges and his younger brother guilty of forty-three of forty-seven, including all major counts.

Schueler provided the key testimony as she simplified and explained the complex concept of DNA. The KBI biologist especially impressed the jury and courtroom with her explanation of the fact that the odds of the DNA in the blood on some of Reginald Carr's clothing belonging to anyone other than Heather Muller were one in six quadrillion. Only 110 billion humans, Schueler emphasized, were estimated to have ever walked the earth. Following two days of direct testimony for the prosecution, Schueler was cross-examined by Reginald Carr's increasingly frustrated attorneys for two more days. Jonathan Carr's attorneys listened intently and then elected to not ask the KBI forensic scientist a single question. The front page of the *Wichita Eagle* on October 24, 2002, featured a photograph of Sindey Schueler on the witness stand pointing out the location of DNA on the shorts of Reginald Carr. The headline over the photograph and accompanying story was "DNA ties Carrs to victim." Ron Sylvester, the story's reporter, described Schueler's presentation as "powerful testimony."[2] The "smoking gun" testimony was, of course, the heartbreaking, graphic story told from the witness stand by the beautiful, courageous survivor of the night of December 14–15, 2000.

On November 14, 2002, Reginald Carr's twenty-fifth birthday, the same jury that had convicted him and his twenty-two-year-old brother returned to the Wichita courtroom with a unanimous recommendation of the death penalty for both defendants. Judge Clark, in final sentencing in December, approved and imposed the recommended death sentences.

The Carr brothers' trial was not the first time Sindey Schueler had delivered "powerful testimony" in support of the police department and criminal justice in Wichita. Earlier, in 2000, another jury heard critical DNA testimony from the KBI biology supervisor in the Riverside Rapist trial. Leon McClennon Jr., age forty-six, dubbed the Riverside Rapist by the media prior to his identification and capture, was eventually charged with thirty-one criminal counts, including eleven counts of rape and twenty counts of assault, sexual battery, aggravated sodomy, and kidnapping. The charges stemmed from early morning home invasions in Wichita by McClennon, in which the victims were brutally battered and raped by the unknown intruder.

On May 25, 2000, following two weeks of trial and five hours of deliberation, the jury found McClennon guilty of twenty-nine of the thirty-one original criminal counts, including all eleven rape counts.

Reporter Ron Sylvester's story the next day in the *Wichita Eagle* indicated that DNA and Sindey Schueler contributed heavily to the prosecution's success. In the words of the jury foreman, "Obviously DNA was the big deal. . . . They didn't have a lot of other physical evidence. . . . She [Schueler] was the state's strongest witness." Even the defendant's public defender was impressed with the forensic team: "The state put on a very formidable case. It's hard to argue with science."[3]

On June 29, 2000, Judge Rebecca Pilshaw sentenced the serial rapist to 257 years, the maximum prison sentence then permitted under Kansas law.

I was blessed with outstanding assistants in the KBI. I was fortunate to have exceptional back-to-back associate directors, one I inherited and his successor whom I helped to groom. I inherited my initial second-in-command, Dale Finger, from KBI Directors Jim Malson, who promoted him to that position, and Bob Davenport, who retained him there. Meticulous in all things, Finger was exactly the second-in-command I needed. Unlike me, he was a detail-oriented person, a master of budget, and blessed with endless patience. He was my closest advisor until his retirement. Dale Finger and Marsha Pappen, our KBI budget director, another wonderful administrative inheritance, formed a perfect budget team, especially for a budget-challenged director. Masterful overseers of the fragile KBI budget, their most common response to my purchase questions was a simple "no." Just as important, they always had me well prepared for our budget presentations to the legislative committees and regularly accompanied me to those hearings.

I depended on Pappen's fiscal counsel and held no executive staff meeting without her. I made it a rule for all KBI supervisors that, if they wished to meet with me regarding any issue that might have a fiscal impact on the agency, they should bring Marsha Pappen to our meeting. She was to be present at any meeting where budget and/or expenditures would be discussed. Because of Dale Finger and Marsha Pappen and, later, other top staffers, including Terry Knowles, Kyle Smith, and Kirk Thompson, my presentations to the legislature were usually productive experiences.

Associate Director Finger held a bachelor's degree in criminal justice from Washburn University in Topeka and a master's degree in public administration from the University of Kansas. He was also a graduate of the FBI National Academy in Quantico, Virginia. He started his KBI career in 1973 in the narcotics division and advanced steadily through the ranks. In 1994, Dale Finger was serving as second-in-command of the KBI, with primary responsibility for oversight of the Investigations Division, supervising all KBI special agents, two assistant directors, and the KBI budget process. The Investigations Division was then the smoothest-running division of the three KBI divisions. My initial administrative concerns, therefore, were reserved for the Forensic Laboratory Division and the Information Services Division.

With the challenges facing the KBI forensic laboratories, it was clear to me we needed another Dale Finger to assume oversight of that important area of the KBI. The forensic division was in critical need of strong leadership; bright lines of supervisory responsibility; more funding; several physical enhancements, especially more working space for the forensic scientists; more forensic scientists; and national forensic accreditation, a top forensic science priority of mine.

I knew whom I wanted. There were, however, a few problems. First, the person in mind was not then a KBI employee. Second, he was not even in the state, and, third, he already held a prestigious law enforcement position elsewhere. He was director of the Missouri Department of Public Safety, presiding over all Missouri state law enforcement agencies, and very content in that office. He was, however, a native Kansan.

Terry Knowles, a native of Great Bend, entered the U.S. Marine Corps after his graduation from Kansas State University and, four years later, in 1965, resigned his commission as captain to enter the FBI as special agent. He eventually retired from the FBI in 1989, after having served as special agent in charge of the FBI's Salt Lake City and Sacramento divisions, and also as deputy assistant director of the FBI at headquarters in Washington, D.C. He then served as chief of police in Springfield, Missouri, from 1989 to 1993 before being appointed director of the Missouri Department of Public Safety by the governor in 1993. It was during his tenure as Springfield police chief, while I was director of the Kansas Law Enforcement Training Center, that our paths first crossed at law enforcement conferences in Missouri and Kansas. I was aware that both Terry and Marcia Knowles still had family in their Kansas hometowns, Great Bend and Glasco. I thought I had an excellent chance of luring the Knowles family back home, so Terry could serve as my deputy director—third-in-command of the KBI—and oversee all KBI laboratory services.

The deputy director position in the KBI had actually been an attorney general slot in the KBI organizational chart. Before 1994, it had been called a liaison position between the attorney general and the KBI. The attorney general, not the KBI director, had always determined who served as KBI deputy director. Soon after my arrival, I asked Attorney General Bob Stephan to give the position to the KBI. I explained to the attorney general that I had plans for that position. I would need it for Terry Knowles, if I could persuade the veteran lawman to accept my invitation to join me at KBI headquarters. The gracious and trusting Stephan, who had been quite satisfied with my nomination of Bob Davenport to become KBI director in 1992, and was interested in my idea of bringing aboard another former FBI administrator, honored my request, and his successors, Carla Stovall and Phill Kline, later respected his judgment. They each permitted me to retain the position during their tenures the next twelve years.

Terry Knowles accepted my invitation and, on March 18, 1995, Carla Stovall administered the KBI oath of office to him in one of her first official acts as state attorney general, having replaced the retiring Bob Stephan in January. I had made two promises to Knowles: a significant reduction in salary from that of his position in Missouri and the opportunity to attend all the Kansas State ball games he wished. I would keep both my promises. On the other hand, I made three requests of him: be a strong advocate and cheerleader for the men and women of the KBI laboratories, improve the KBI's forensic support of the Kansas law enforcement community and the Kansas criminal justice system, and strongly consider the pursuit of national forensic accreditation.

The retention of Dale Finger as second-in-command and the hiring of Terry Knowles as deputy director proved to be among my wisest decisions as KBI director. Being flanked by two top assistants like Dale and Terry for my first ten years in the KBI lightened any burden of KBI directorship and was one of the greatest privileges of my law enforcement career. Thanks to those two gentlemen, I was comfortably encircled by integrity, loyalty, and professionalism. They both retired in 2005, Knowles in July and Finger in December.

When Dale Finger first discussed with me, in late 2004 or early 2005, his plans to retire from the KBI in late 2005, after thirty-two years of distinguished service, I requested his recommendation for a successor. Without hesitation, he advised me that his choice to succeed him as KBI associate director would be Assistant Director Kirk Thompson. His response pleased me. I already knew Thompson was my preference. Dale's recommendation sealed it. I did not wish to lose the only associate director with whom I had served in the KBI, but Dale's loss would be considerably easier to bear knowing Kirk Thompson was available to replace him.

In Thompson, I had another Dale Finger, insofar as budget expertise, attention to details, work ethic, integrity, loyalty, and professionalism were concerned. The similarities between the two did not end with the special administrative abilities they shared. Thompson also held a bachelor's degree from Washburn University and was a graduate of the FBI National Academy in Quantico, Virginia. He became a KBI special agent in 1979. I promoted him to special agent in charge in 1994 in one of my first official acts, to assistant director in 1996, and to associate director in 2005. He had commanded KBI narcotic investigations and then the Information Services Division prior to being elevated to second-in-command as replacement of Finger. In other similarities, when Finger retired from the KBI, he accepted a top executive position with the Leawood Police Department, and when Thompson retired from the KBI, he accepted a top executive position with the Topeka Police Department. Their final similarity was that no KBI director ever had, or will ever have, a more qualified second-in-command than either Dale Finger or Kirk Thompson or the legendary Jack Ford, "Mr. KBI," who served the longest in that position from 1975 until his retirement in 1987.

During the ten years that Terry Knowles gave the KBI, the KBI Forensic Laboratory Division experienced unparalleled growth, and morale in that division improved dramatically with his oversight. The extraordinary increase in square footage of forensic space and in numbers of forensic scientists orchestrated by Deputy Director Knowles may never be equaled.

The initial significant laboratory hurdle that the new deputy director cleared in his program of expansion and growth for the laboratory division was the selection of the first on-site supervisor in Great Bend that I had promised. His second, more daunting mission was the pursuit of the prestigious national forensic accreditation by the American Society of Criminal Laboratory Directors (ASCLD), a goal I considered to be critical for the laboratory division's professionalism.

The foundation for selection of the Great Bend forensic supervisor was laid in 1996 when we persuaded the legislature to permit us to hire eleven new forensic scientists. We then increased the number of scientists at the Great Bend lab from the original three to nine. One of the forensic scientists hired for Great Bend in 1996 was Mike VanStratton (latent fingerprints), who held a bachelor of science degree from Western Michigan University. VanStratton, a commissioned police officer with the Battle Creek, Michigan, Police Department from 1970 to 1993, had supervised the forensic science unit of that department from 1993 until 1996, when he accepted the KBI's invitation. He brought with him the experience of hundreds of homicide crime scenes. With strong recommendations from Knowles and Special Agent in Charge John Green, commander of the Great Bend region, one of our finest supervisors in the KBI, we promoted Mike VanStratton to forensic supervisor of the Great Bend laboratory in 1997.

Meanwhile, we had begun the study of the challenging process of national accreditation. We had learned from Terry Knowles's preparatory meetings with ASCLD and other forensic officials that accreditation application was a difficult, complicated, and expensive procedure. (The nonrefundable application fees alone were $14,400 in 1998 and $23,725 in 2003.)

To evaluate our chances of achieving ASCLD accreditation, Deputy Director Knowles arranged a preliminary audit of our laboratory division by the highly respected Dr. Bill Tilston and David Epstein of the National Forensic Science Training Center in July 1997. Their findings included recommendations that we completely overhaul our laboratory policies, rewrite our laboratory policy manual, formalize testing protocols, and establish clearer lines of supervision of forensic scientists. Terry immediately started the process to implement their helpful recommendations.

In September 1997, Knowles, VanStratton, Carl Anderson (chemistry), and L. J. Stephenson (firearms and ballistics) attended a week-long ASCLD conference in San Antonio, Texas, interviewing attendees regarding their experiences, good and bad, with ASCLD inspections. Our KBI crew returned with helpful recommendations and observations and some serious reservations as well. We were learning that, when we thought we were ready to be forensically tested in Topeka and Great Bend, ASCLD inspectors would descend upon us to thoroughly examine, evaluate, and challenge our forensic procedures, policies, practices, rules, and regulations. The exhaustive process would last several days at both sites and involve interviews and observations of most laboratory personnel. There would be probing audits of each section or unit within the division: biology, DNA, chemistry, firearms and toolmarks, toxicology, questioned documents, and latent fingerprints, with special attention to all aspects of evidence collection, handling, analysis, and storage.

If accreditation were achieved, it then became an unending process. An accredited laboratory was required to be reaccredited every five years, and most officials who had been through the process claimed reaccreditation was more difficult than accreditation. If those forensic obstacles were not daunting enough, there was another significant impediment threatening the success of our accreditation attempt. A national search for a KBI laboratory director had not produced the desired result. We had not yet identified the person we needed to lighten the deputy director's leadership burden in the laboratory and guide the division into the twenty-first century. Therefore, to help coordinate the KBI pursuit of national accreditation, Knowles selected Carl Anderson, one of the three original forensic scientists in Great Bend. Anderson, a forensic chemist, was another one of those meticulous KBI employees who thrived on details and welcomed challenges. He was also exceptionally candid in his opinions and not given to sugarcoating prospects. Knowles sent Anderson to Springfield, Illinois, in January 1998 to observe the work of ASCLD inspectors during the Illinois State Police's successful pursuit of reaccreditation. He returned with doubts about our chances of receiving accreditation ever, let alone on the first attempt, given available resources and the crowded forensic working conditions and circumstances then prevailing. Our scientists averaged half the workspace recommended by ASCLD and the U.S. Justice Department and were battling daunting backlogs in almost every section of the laboratory.

Even after Anderson briefed us on his Illinois observations and shared his personal misgivings about our own prospects, my deputy director and I remained undeterred and were more convinced than ever that national accreditation was imperative for our bureau's well-being.

Strongly supported by Attorney General Stovall and Associate Director Finger, we agreed to proceed with the accreditation process. In Anderson we knew we had the perfect project coordinator. Knowles went a step further and named Anderson as the KBI's first laboratory quality-assurance manager as we plunged into the ASCLD process.

After Anderson's return from Springfield, Illinois, in January 1998, he probably spent as much time in Topeka as he did in Great Bend, helping Terry Knowles guide our accreditation effort in the final months of our forensic campaign. We had been informed by ASCLD that our forensic inspection would occur in May 1998. Terry added L. J. Stephenson and Larry Mann (toxicology) as additional coordinators for the accreditation effort.

In another wise preparatory move, Terry Knowles, at Anderson's suggestion, invited Dr. Keith Coonrod of the New York State Crime Laboratory to come to Topeka and conduct a preliminary inspection for us. Dr. Coonrod had been the chief inspector in charge of the Illinois ASCLD inspection observed by Anderson. Invited in January 1998, Dr. Coonrod juggled his schedule and accepted the KBI invitation to evaluate our Topeka laboratory. He promised to come to Topeka on March 18, stay with us two days, and provide us with candid observations and appropriate suggestions. Before he departed Topeka on March 20, he identified several deficiencies that he feared would preclude the achievement of accreditation. His most serious criticisms concerned general handling of evidence and evidence storage procedures. Those criticisms surprised Deputy Director Knowles. He had placed a section chief in charge of those specific inspection responsibilities months earlier and had anticipated that area would be a strength, not a weakness, in our accreditation effort. On March 20, 1998, Knowles relieved that section chief of any further ASCLD inspection responsibilities and replaced him with Larry Mann. Knowles asked Mann and Anderson to quickly focus on the Topeka laboratory's evidence control center, as the dedicated forensic staffs in Great Bend and Topeka continued other essential efforts throughout both laboratories, in what was becoming a race against time.

By April 25, the Topeka evidence control center's policies and procedures had been completely rewritten and that area of the laboratory physically renovated. All evidence had been removed, labeled anew, and temporarily stored elsewhere in the laboratory during the renovation. The area had been painted, new evidence storage shelves installed, a new electrical system added, and the air-conditioning system replaced, improving airflow and employee safety throughout the evidence storage section, as recommended by the Occupational Safety and Health Administration (OSHA) and the local fire marshal's office, following on-site inspections the KBI deputy director requested of those agencies. He and his colleagues had made dramatic changes and improvements in both laboratories, but especially in Topeka, given the seventy-year-old building that housed that laboratory.

When the ASCLD inspection team arrived in Topeka on May 17, 1998, only twenty-one other state crime laboratories enjoyed ASCLD accreditation, and none had achieved that prestigious distinction on the first application, we were told. The chief inspector in charge of the ASCLD inspection team was Dr. Don Plautz of the Illinois State Police. Like Tilston, Epstein, and Coonrod, Plautz enjoyed an excellent reputation within the forensic science circles of the American law enforcement community.

In 1998, ASCLD had three categories of criteria, 137 different criteria in all, to be evaluated in accreditation inspections: first, "essential" criteria (71 criteria, and failure to pass even one was fatal); second, "important" criteria (46); and third, "desirable" criteria (20).[4] Dr. Plautz's team hit the ground running. The ASCLD forensic experts assessed KBI laboratory operations at Topeka and Great Bend for five days, interviewing forensic personnel, monitoring procedures, observing working conditions, and reviewing facilities, equipment, policy manuals, organizational and supervisory charts, and safety rules and regulations.

On May 21, 1998, Dr. Plautz sat down with Dale Finger, Terry Knowles, and me to inform us of the inspection findings his team would be sharing with ASCLD officials, and to share with us the recommendation of either pass or fail that he would deliver to those officials.

Regarding the least-critical category of criteria, "desirable," Dr. Plautz advised us that both laboratories had scored an impressive 93 percent. With the category of "important" criteria, the chief inspector explained that Topeka had scored 87 percent and Great Bend 97 percent. Such compliance figures were unheard of in that day, but the real stunner came with his announcement that, in the live-or-die "essential" criteria category, both Topeka and

Great Bend had scored 100 percent! His recommendation to ASCLD would be to grant national accreditation to both KBI forensic laboratories!

He congratulated us, complimented our people, and pointed out that his recommendation was just that, a recommendation. The final decision would come from the ASCLD national board after their review of Dr. Plautz's report and that board's conference with Plautz and his team. We would have to appear before the ASCLD board in Denver to receive the final decision. Then, Dr. Plautz said to me, "Director Welch, the KBI achieved this distinction despite your facilities, not because of your facilities." In the years that followed, during many appearances before legislative committees, I took advantage of every opportunity to remind Kansas legislators of his words. The lawmakers later approved major renovations at both Great Bend and Topeka.

On July 11, 1998, Terry Knowles flew to Denver to appear before the AS-CLD Laboratory Accreditation Board to answer any remaining questions that board might have after reviewing the Plautz report and conferring with the Plautz inspection team, and, thereafter, to receive the board's final decision regarding KBI forensic accreditation. We hoped that decision would concur with the Plautz recommendation.

As Knowles waited to appear before the eight-member board, he saw Dr. Don Kerr, director of the FBI Laboratory, exit that chamber. Dr. Kerr, acquainted with Knowles, approached Knowles and said, "That is a tough group. I hope you are ready. We didn't make it and we will have to try again in six months."

Within an hour Terry Knowles was on the telephone to me. His first words were: "Mission accomplished." He then explained to a very happy KBI director that our laboratories were now accredited. The vote of the eight-member board had been unanimous. With that vote, the two KBI forensic laboratories had become the only accredited forensic crime laboratories then in Kansas and it placed them among the few accredited crime laboratories in the Midwest. We also became the twenty-second accredited state crime laboratory in the nation and the first to achieve that distinction on the first attempt.

We, of course, did not keep the important accomplishment a secret. Typical of the Kansas media response to the subsequent announcement from an elated Attorney General Stovall was a congratulatory editorial by the *Topeka Capital-Journal* on August 19, 1998, entitled "KBI Labs Accredited," which read, in part:

> The board of the American Society of Crime Laboratory Directors certified accreditation for the Kansas Bureau of Investigation laboratories in Topeka and Great Bend. Kansas is only the 22nd state to earn the

national accreditation. ASCLD has recognized only 174 labs across the country. . . . That is extremely important, especially now as forensic science gets even more technical and detailed and has the awesome power to prove someone's guilt or innocence. . . . The accreditation assures Kansans that they can count on the labs for quality work.[5]

It is difficult to exaggerate the significance of July 21, 1998, and its importance in KBI history or the accomplishment of Deputy Director Knowles, his staff, and all the men and women of the KBI laboratories—a team effort if ever there was one—and the challenging obstacles that dedicated group overcame. The achievement of forensic accreditation, against incredible odds, and the importance of the accomplishment to the professional integrity of the forensic wing of the KBI, in a day when criminal justice, criminal courtrooms, judges, prosecutors, defense attorneys, and juries were starting to demand that standard of forensic excellence, provide additional examples of ordinary KBI men and women doing extraordinary things—a persistent theme throughout the bureau's history.

When one considers historical milestones in the story of the KBI, I submit that forensic accreditation in 1998 (and retention of that prestigious recognition five years later with reaccreditation in 2003) ranks with the Macksville bank robbery resolution and the Clutter investigation in overall importance to the KBI's well-being.

In a subsequent critique of our accreditation effort, Knowles was effusive in his praise of the contributions of Carl Anderson, L. J. Stephenson, and Larry Mann, giving that trio considerable credit for our success in our first attempt. In further deflection of credit for himself, Knowles complimented the supervisory leadership within the different forensic sections by Stan Heffley (chemistry), Carl Carlson (latent fingerprints), Eileen Burnau (biology-DNA), T. L. Price (firearms and toolmarks), and Mike VanStratton in Great Bend. He emphasized that every laboratory employee contributed significantly to the achievement.

As early as February 1997, when the meth lab surge was beginning across the state, especially in southeastern Kansas, Knowles and I were advising legislative committees that a KBI forensic facility was needed in southeastern Kansas. No part of the state was being ravaged more severely by methamphetamine and meth labs than the twelve counties in the Missouri-Oklahoma corner of Kansas.

Pittsburg, county seat of Crawford County, seemed a logical site for a regional office and a satellite forensic laboratory. Pittsburg Police Chief Mike

Hall, Crawford County Sheriff Sandy Horton, and Pittsburg State University Police Chief Darrell Masoner were early and enthusiastic proponents. Prosecutors and law enforcement officials throughout southeastern Kansas quickly joined the campaign, as did area state legislators, especially Senator Jim Barone and Representatives Ed McKechnie, Mary Compton, Doug Gatewood, and Bob Grant. There was no stronger advocate, however, than Attorney General Stovall. Her undergraduate degree was from Pittsburg State University, and, after receiving her law degree from the University of Kansas, she had been elected county attorney of Crawford County, the first woman county attorney of that county. She had strong ties to that part of the state and agreed that a stronger KBI presence was needed there, especially given the explosion of meth labs in that area. Her popularity there helped ensure the project's success.

The most critical need was for chemists on-site to combat narcotics in general and methamphetamine in particular, but we had also decided we wanted more than a forensic laboratory in Pittsburg. In addition to that urgent need, we also wanted a regional KBI office to accommodate KBI special agents and to serve as headquarters for a multiagency drug task force in Pittsburg then on our drawing board. Thanks to the lobbying efforts of many, we received legislative approval for a third forensic laboratory and a stronger KBI presence in what I considered a neglected part of our state.

Reporter Mike Berry broke the news in his story in the *Wichita Eagle* on November 2, 1997, headlined "KBI Adding Mini-Lab in Southeast Kansas: Pittsburg Will Be Home to Third Forensics Facility, with Emphasis on Fighting Methamphetamine Producers."[6]

Terry Knowles designated L. J. Stephenson, the accreditation veteran, as coordinator for the forensic laboratory portion of the Pittsburg project. Chemistry supervisor Stan Heffley, Stephenson, and Knowles soon became frequent travelers between Topeka and Pittsburg, as did Assistant Director Kirk Thompson, to whom I assigned responsibility for the regional office and task force portions of the Pittsburg project.

Realizing how anxious we were to position two of Stan Heffley's chemists in Pittsburg to begin analyzing narcotics evidence—especially evidence from seized meth labs—for area law enforcement investigators and prosecutors, Dean Tom Baldwin, on behalf of Pittsburg State University, offered us free, temporary space in the university's chemistry department. We quickly accepted that invitation and, during the following eighteen months, KBI forensic chemists Sara Anderson and Jennifer Miller conducted 1,500 drug examinations for area law enforcement.

On March 3, 2000, 100 local and area government and law enforcement officials watched Attorney General Stovall, Senator Barone, and Representative McKechnie cut the ribbon (KBI crime scene tape) at the new KBI facility at 821 N. Broadway in Pittsburg. The 4,000-square-foot former retail establishment had undergone extensive renovation, converting half the building into offices, a forensic laboratory, and reception area. Two chemists, a latent fingerprint examiner, a combination secretary-evidence technician, and the veteran local KBI resident agent Bruce Adams had moved into the facility prior to the grand opening and dedication. The official name of the new KBI property was the Southeast Kansas KBI Regional Office and Laboratory. The gracious, supportive folks of the Pittsburg Area Chamber of Commerce were prominent in attendance at the ceremony, as were legislators and law enforcement officials from at least nine southeastern Kansas counties. I took advantage of the occasion to present a plaque of appreciation to L. J. Stephenson, coordinator for the forensic side of the project. As I told that audience, in speaking of the new facility and L. J.'s involvement, "His DNA and fingerprints are all over this place." Stephenson was retiring on April 1, 2000, ending a twenty-year distinguished career as a KBI forensic scientist. The Pittsburg project was his final achievement in a long series of forensic accomplishments, primarily in the firearms and ballistics arenas, as well as our national accreditation campaign. Attorney General Stovall, Dale Finger, Terry Knowles, Kirk Thompson, and I also presented a plaque to Dean Tom Baldwin of Pittsburg State University as a token of our gratitude for the hospitality extended to our chemists the previous eighteen months, and another plaque of appreciation to Chief of Police Mike Hall, a driving force in the establishment of the new KBI facility in Pittsburg.

A few weeks later, when the remodeling of the other half of the large building was completed, the original complement of KBI personnel at 821 N. Broadway in Pittsburg was joined by the Southeast Kansas Drug Enforcement Task Force (SEKDETF), created in 1999 by the KBI, eleven police chiefs, six sheriffs, and six Kansas county attorneys in Allen, Bourbon, Cherokee, Crawford, Labette, and Neosho counties. The KBI-led task force originally consisted of an assistant attorney general, who would handle prosecution of cases developed; a crime analyst; several local officers selected from participating departments; and KBI agents Dave Hutchings, Gary Smith, Frank Papish, Tim Holsinger, and Tim Botts. Other KBI agents, including Steve Rosebrough, Shawn Campiti, and Chris Farris, were later assigned to the new KBI regional office and/or the task force. The KBI, for the first time in its history, had a strong presence in southeastern Kansas.

Assistant Director Kirk Thompson, Crawford County Sheriff Sandy Horton, Senior Special Agent Dave Hutchings, and Special Agent in Charge Rod Page (Wichita) provided oversight and leadership for the task force, which was uniquely funded by federal grants, state money, and matching funds from municipalities and counties in the six-county region. The federal grants came from the Byrne Program in Washington, D.C., through the Kansas Criminal Justice Coordinating Council, and from the Midwest High Intensity Drug Trafficking Area (HIDTA) program in Kansas City, Missouri.

SEKDETF, which became a model for multiagency drug task forces, drew praise and commendations from U.S. Attorney General Janet Reno; the Kansas Association of Chiefs of Police; Midwest HIDTA (representing law enforcement officials and prosecutors—municipal, county, state, and federal—in Kansas, Missouri, Iowa, Nebraska, South Dakota, and North Dakota); the Kansas U.S. Attorney's Office; and regional media. From July 1, 2000, through December 31, 2004, SEKDETF launched 820 drug investigations; made 717 drug arrests; achieved felony drug convictions in 399 state cases and 95 federal cases; seized 430 firearms; executed 427 search warrants; raided 410 meth labs; and seized 714 pounds of marijuana, 2,000 marijuana plants, 60 pounds of methamphetamine, and 5 pounds of cocaine. The elite unit was still going strong when I retired in 2007, and southeastern Kansas was the better for it.

Following success with accreditation in 1998, Deputy Director Knowles had not spent all his time in Pittsburg plotting the new forensic laboratory in that city. He had also logged considerable highway mileage to and from Great Bend, planning a major renovation project in that regional KBI office to eventually double the forensic space there. In addition, he had spent much time in travel to and from Kansas City, Kansas, a possible site for the fourth KBI forensic laboratory we envisioned.

If Chief of Police Mike Hall was the local driving force behind the opening of a KBI laboratory in Pittsburg, his counterpart in Kansas City, Kansas, was Wyandotte County District Attorney Nick Tomasic. The veteran, respected prosecutor depended on KBI forensic services, and he wanted that resource closer at hand. Local Kansas City police officials, area state legislators, including Representatives Tom Burroughs and Bill Reardon, and U.S. Congressman Dennis Moore were also strong advocates of the new KBI laboratory, but Tomasic was the leading local proponent and ally.

The primary purpose of the Pittsburg laboratory was to assist area law enforcement and prosecutors in their fight against narcotics in general and methamphetamine—especially meth labs—in particular. Therefore, the forensic disciplines placed in the Pittsburg laboratory were chemistry and latent fingerprints, with two chemists, a fingerprint examiner, and an evidence technician.

The needs in Kansas City and in northeastern Kansas, on the other hand, related to homicides, rapes, gangs, and drive-by shootings. Thus, the forensic disciplines required there were biology-DNA, firearms, and ballistics. Two biologists, two firearms examiners, and an evidence technician would be assigned to that facility.

Following the requisite approval and funding by the legislature for a Kansas City KBI laboratory, the only remaining question was where it would be housed. Dr. Tom Burke, president of the Kansas City Kansas Community College and one of the most gracious, hospitable, accommodating gentlemen I have ever met, answered that question with an invitation to place the laboratory on that college campus. At the dollar-a-year lease price Dr. Burke demanded, we did not dawdle in our acceptance of his kind invitation. We shook hands and I gave him a five-dollar bill, paying the rent five years in advance.

Unlike Pittsburg, where we combined a forensic laboratory with a regional office in the new facility, there was no need for anything but the forensic laboratory and forensic scientists in Kansas City. We had a regional office with special agents and a secretary nearby in Overland Park, under the leadership of Special Agent in Charge Bill Delaney. The beleaguered Kansas City Police Department, in its struggle with rising violent crime statistics, needed forensic biologists, DNA specialists, firearms and ballistics examiners, and an evidence technician. That's what we intended to provide them.

Following weeks of remodeling the space that Dr. Burke had made available to us, we held a dedication ceremony for what was being called the KBI Satellite Laboratory at Kansas City Kansas Community College, on August 18, 2000. Deputy Director Knowles presided as master of ceremonies, and the featured speakers were Dr. Burke and Attorney General Stovall. Moore, Tomasic, Burroughs, Wyandotte County Commissioner Tom Bruns, and I also made comments. Then Attorney General Stovall and Dr. Burke cut the traditional ribbon (KBI crime scene tape again), and we provided tours of the new facility to the attendees.

Approximately one year later, on August 29, 2001, the *Kansas City Star* ran a feature story evaluating the new KBI forensic laboratory. Reporter Anne Lamoy's story was headlined "KBI Lab Curtails Police Waiting Game: Year-Old Facility Draws Praise from Officials."[7] In the story Lt. Vince Davenport of the Kansas City Police Department advised that his department was solving cases faster because of the new KBI forensic support. Tomasic echoed Davenport's praise of the laboratory, adding, "We are using it and it has worked well so far." Mary Koch, KBI biologist, in answer to a Lamoy question, explained that she, in the first year of operation, had analyzed twenty different DNA cases, and that each of those twenty cases had ended with a guilty plea and no trial due to DNA's formidability.

Knowles, who was also interviewed for the story, pointed out that, in the first year, the two KBI on-site biologists had worked 269 criminal cases from Kansas City, Bonner Springs, and Leavenworth—mostly Kansas City, of course. And he added that, overall, the new laboratories in Pittsburg and Kansas City together had helped reduce the forensic backlog in Topeka from 2,453 cases to fewer than 900. Both labs were already earning high marks and proving their worth.

Terry Knowles and his dedicated professionals of the laboratory division did not rest on their laurels of 1998 (accreditation) or 2000 (the two new forensic laboratories). Individually and collectively, they scored countless more successes and, together, continued on an ascendant path.

Most of those forensic science successes in the late 1990s and in the new twenty-first century came from KBI scientists' workbench analysis of physical evidence recovered at Kansas crime scenes. For example, the prosecution of Gary Wayne Kleypas in July 1997 for the 1996 murder of Carrie Arlene Williams was discussed in Chapter 14. Much of the credit for Kleypas's residency today on Kansas's death row in El Dorado can be attributed to KBI forensic scientists. Individual contributions of Lisa Villalobos were described in that chapter. Steve Koch also connected a footprint impression found at the murder scene to a particular size 12 Reebok tennis shoe purchased by Kleypas at a Sears store in Joplin, Missouri. Kleypas was in possession of the Sears credit card used for that purchase at the time of his arrest. The shoes were also recovered. Other forensic efforts in the Kleypas case came from KBI scientists Carl Carlson, John Horn, Gretchen Paxton, Dennis McPhail, and Dwain Worley.

In 1998, in the town of Lebo (population 911) in Coffey County, two unknown suspects invaded a home and held a couple hostage all night, forcing a bank withdrawal the next morning. From the only evidence at the crime scene (a discarded cigarette butt), Lisa Burdett of the KBI's Great Bend laboratory developed a DNA profile that was entered in the national DNA database (CODIS). The case remained unsolved for six years, until a DNA "hit" connected a Georgia prison inmate to the crime. Senior Special Agent Bill Halvorsen and Coffey County Sheriff Randy Rogers traveled to Georgia and obtained a confession from the inmate, who then identified his partner in the Kansas home intrusion. Both were convicted, thanks to KBI DNA, and each received a sentence of fifteen years in the Kansas prison system.

In 2000, at a golf course just outside Syracuse (population 1,545) in Hamilton County, a sixteen-year-old female was assaulted, shot three times, and then ran for her life. The courageous victim survived. KBI forensic scientist James Newman of our Great Bend laboratory developed a DNA profile from a cigarette butt discarded by the unknown suspect. Thanks to DNA, the criminal was identified, arrested, and convicted.

In 2003, following a bank robbery in Hanston (population 289) in Hodgeman County, the fleeing bandit tossed a latex glove and a baseball cap after departing the bank. Great Bend KBI forensic scientist Eric Moore developed a latent fingerprint impression inside the latex glove, and Lisa Burdett developed DNA profiles from both the glove and the cap's sweatband. Subsequent "hits" in both the computerized fingerprint database (AFIS) and the computerized DNA database (CODIS) led to the robber's identification, arrest, and conviction.

In the years following our 1998 accreditation, ASCLD honored the KBI and seven of our KBI forensic scientists by inviting them to serve as national inspectors for ASCLD forensic inspections across the nation. The seven KBI scientists—Mike VanStratton, Carl Anderson, Lisa Burdett, Steve Koch, Larry Mann, T. L. Price, and Sindey Schueler—expressed their willingness to serve as ASCLD inspectors, subject to their respective KBI commitments and schedules. The deputy director and I quickly agreed to share our seven scientists' individual and collective forensic expertise with ASCLD and America's other crime laboratories—an impressive distinction for our scientists and for the KBI as an agency.

In 1999, Mike VanStratton, Great Bend's forensic supervisor, was honored by the International Association for Identification (IAI), the world's oldest and largest forensic science organization, by being named one of only nineteen certified bloodstain pattern examiners in the world.

By late 2000, we realized that, within our own ranks, we had the logical person to fill our vacant laboratory director position. Accordingly, in January 2001, we promoted Mike VanStratton to KBI laboratory director, equivalent to an assistant director, and transferred him to headquarters to direct all KBI laboratory operations in Great Bend, Kansas City, Pittsburg, and Topeka. That promotion proved to be another excellent decision, as did our September 2001 promotion of Great Bend biologist Lisa Burdett to Great Bend forensic supervisor, succeeding VanStratton.

During the peak meth lab years of 2000–2004, I doubt that any pair of drug chemists anywhere in the nation analyzed evidence from more clandestine labs than Dwain Worley and Jim Schieferecke, under supervisor Stan Heffley. Nearly overwhelmed by the sheer numbers of meth labs seized and the evidence submitted by Kansas investigators, and inundated with the resulting subpoenas requiring expert courtroom testimony—as were all KBI chemists during that period—the Schieferecke-Worley team still found time for methamphetamine research. The KBI forensic duo published several important papers, sharing their research results with the nation's forensic scientists, as reported by Worley's hometown newspaper, the *Rawlins County Square Deal* of Atwood, Kansas, in a feature story on September 9, 2004.[8] The pair's research focused on a new way to detect red phosphorous, a key component in methamphetamine manufacture, and turn it into white phosphorous by using existing equipment designed to analyze paint and fibers. The studies by Worley, a graduate of Colby Community College and Kansas State University, and his close friend Schieferecke, a native of Selden and Hoxie, Kansas, and a graduate of Colby Community College and Fort Hays State University, also resulted in the development of a technique to lessen the dangers of handling white phosphorous, and a less expensive strategy to detect lithium, another essential methamphetamine ingredient. Much of the pair's research was published in the prestigious *Journal of Analytical and Applied Pyrolysis* in 2004 and brought the two KBI chemists considerable national acclaim.[9] Their research efforts were strongly supported by Knowles, VanStratton, and Heffley.

In 2004, another KBI forensic scientist was honored by the prestigious International Association for Identification (IAI). Steve Koch, supervisor of the latent fingerprints section (actually, crime scene latent prints, tire tracks, and footprints), was named one of only forty-six certified footwear examiners in the world. Dubbed the "sole-searcher" by his colleagues, Koch is considered one of the world's top experts on impressions of shoe and boot soles at crime scenes.

In June 2006, our biology-DNA supervisor, Sindey Schueler, was elected by her national peers to serve on the National DNA Index System (NDIS) Procedures Board, which sets and oversees national DNA policies and procedures.

In July 2006, blood spatter specialist Holly Wasinger of the Great Bend KBI laboratory joined Mike VanStratton as IAI-certified bloodstain pattern examiner. VanStratton and Wasinger were two of only twenty-eight forensic scientists in the world receiving such certification. Wasinger also served as an adjunct instructor of bloodstain pattern analysis at the prestigious National Forensic Academy in Tennessee.

When Terry Knowles stepped down as deputy director and third-in-command of the KBI in July 2005, he had achieved the goals I had assigned him in 1995. He had significantly increased the quality and extent of KBI forensic support of Kansas law enforcement and the Kansas criminal justice system. In 2005 fifty-six forensic scientists labored in four accredited KBI forensic laboratories across the state, instead of the thirty-three beleaguered scientists working in two unaccredited KBI laboratories in 1995. He had become the strong advocate and cheerleader the men and women of the KBI forensic division deserved. When he left the building in 2005, turning over the forensic leadership to Mike VanStratton, not only had morale improved and internal confidence increased, but there was also a pronounced swagger throughout the corridors of KBI laboratories. No better example of KBI forensic improvement under Knowles existed than that in evidence at 625 Washington Street in Great Bend in 2005. There we had not only nine forensic scientists (chemistry, latent fingerprints, biology, and DNA) and an exceptional on-site forensic supervisor, Lisa Burdett, we also had Knowles's legislature-approved plan to convert the building's attic into an additional 4,300 square feet of working space.

A grateful 2006 Kansas legislature gave $1 million for the Great Bend facility improvements, and U.S. Congressman Jerry Moran helped obtain a grant of nearly $150,000, with which to upgrade Great Bend's DNA computer systems, purchase analytical equipment used in forensic drug analysis, and enhance laboratory security at the Great Bend facility.

The renovation planned years earlier by Terry Knowles began in October 2006 and was completed during the summer of 2007. I was proud of the Great Bend improvements. My earlier promises to central and western Kansas police chiefs, sheriffs, and prosecutors regarding the future of the KBI at Great Bend, our western outpost, had been fulfilled. Thanks were due many, including the legislature and, in Great Bend, Special Agents in Charge Bruce Mellor and Kelly Ralston, and especially Terry Knowles and all his dedicated laboratory people, led by Mike VanStratton and Lisa Burdett.

If there had been a director's annual MVP award for the laboratory division, I would have been tempted to present that recognition, year in and year out, to that division's matriarch, Kathy Orr—secretary, stenographer, receptionist, scheduler, chief clerk, chief support person, girl Friday, morale officer, and unsung heroine. Her professionalism, candor, cheerfulness, and unwavering devotion to the employees of the laboratory division endeared her to one and all.

Reflections: The Project;
Mississippi Mud; Technology

What Terry Knowles and his dedicated people were accomplishing within the forensic chambers of the KBI was similar to what Special Agent in Charge (and later Assistant Director) Chuck Sexson, Special Agent in Charge Dave Sim, Information Resource Manager Ron Rohrer, and the equally dedicated men and women of the KBI's Information Services Division (ISD) were concurrently accomplishing on the third floor of KBI headquarters, two floors above Knowles's forensic scientists.

The realization that changes were also needed within ISD came contemporaneously with the conclusion that I needed Terry Knowles to serve as the laboratory division's rudder. With ISD it was a simple matter of division oversight. Tighter supervision was needed from above. There was nothing wrong with the caliber of the employees of that division or with the quality of its unit supervisors. People like Vicky Harris, Jack Steele, Mary Ann Howerton, Tammy Sisk, Stan Pfeifer, Ely Meza, Barbie Berggren, Helen Ohlsson, Tonya Thoman, Judy Ashbaugh, Shawn Brown, Tim Turner, Norma Jean Schaefer, Leslie Moore, and many others were certainly equals of their impressive counterparts in the other KBI divisions. Indeed, three of the first six KBI employees of the year, in that special personnel recognition program we implemented in 1998, came from ISD: Mary Ann Howerton, 1998; Tim Turner, 2000; and Stan Pfeifer, 2003. As with the forensic division, I already knew the right person to place in charge of the KBI's ISD. Unlike the laboratory division scenario, the person I wanted was already drawing a KBI paycheck.

I knew Chuck Sexson by reputation and also through our mutual involvement in FBI National Academy activities. He was one of the KBI's finest supervisors. Both Attorney General Bob Stephan and Director Bob Davenport had expressed this opinion in our previous informal discussions about KBI personnel.

Chuck Sexson received a bachelor's degree from Fort Hays State University in 1972, the same year KBI Director Fred Howard hired him as a special agent. In 1978, he added a master's degree in criminal justice from Wichita State University, and in 1980 he graduated from the FBI National Academy

in Quantico, Virginia. Director Jim Malson, a man with a proven eye for successful future supervisors, promoted him to special agent in charge in 1990.

In July 1994, Sexson was supervising the bureau's narcotics division, officially entitled the Special Operations Division. He loved his work and was
respected by his agents. A natural leader, he demonstrated fidelity, integrity, patience, common sense, courtesy, and wisdom. I needed him to leave
his beloved narcotics division—with all its excitement of arrest warrants,
search warrants, drug raids, surveillances, apprehensions, and courtroom
successes—and assume command of approximately seventy professional civilians.

When I advised Chuck that I believed ISD was in dire need of stronger
supervision and that I intended to reassign him to that division to take control of matters, he was disappointed. The narcotics division was operating
well. ISD was in need of his personnel skills and administrative abilities.
After all, ISD was, arguably, the most important division in the KBI, I told
him, not just to a majority of the participants of the Kansas criminal justice
system but perhaps even to the KBI itself. That case could easily be made,
because almost every function, mission, responsibility, duty, and obligation
of that division was a legislative command, mandated by the state legislature
by statute. Much more was expected of the KBI's ISD in the next few years.
I told him that he was one of the KBI's finest supervisors and admired by
the entire agency. It was a critical period for ISD and, therefore, for the KBI.
The division's people were exceptional KBI employees and their first line
of supervision was outstanding. I reiterated to him that the division simply
needed stronger overall oversight. Chuck Sexson, I insisted, was the answer.
Sexson, always a gentleman, was respectful and professional during my comments, but also, it appeared, unmoved, still disappointed, and not yet persuaded. Accordingly, I changed my strategy just a bit, relying on his professionalism and his dedication to the KBI as a whole. I promised him that, after
one year at the helm of the Information Services Division of the KBI, if he
wished, I would then transfer him to any other position in the KBI he might
covet. I also promised him I would immediately transfer any KBI employee
he wanted as his top assistant as he took over the reins of that division. The
two promises may have given him pause, but I believe the real reasons Chuck
Sexson reluctantly, yet "voluntarily," assumed supervision of the approximately seventy civilian employees of ISD were his own professionalism, his
dedication to the KBI, and his knowledge that the KBI's ISD was about to be
sorely tested by the state of Kansas. Those dedicated, skilled civilians of the
KBI's Information Services Division were responsible for most of the state
resources important to Kansas investigators, prosecutors, and courts—more

than even the KBI laboratory or investigations divisions, because most of that division's functions were mandated by statute.

Extremely goals- and mission-oriented, the popular Sexson was typecast for his new role. He spent the next several weeks in long, full days learning what his new division did and how it was doing it. He spent considerable time in each unit of the ISD with that unit's employees and supervisors, asking questions and observing operations.

The new division head was learning the ins and outs of the new units under his supervision. This included the Criminal Justice Records Unit, which serves as the state's central repository for adult and juvenile criminal history records and also maintains the state's fingerprint identification services, including the day-to-day operations of AFIS, in which personnel classify fingerprints received from criminal justice contributors and identify subjects of criminal history checks on the basis of fingerprints, with approximately 158,000 fingerprint records processed, 624,000 record checks conducted, and 1,200,000 computerized criminal history records available in 2007. Another unit was the Kansas Offender Registry, which was originally created to contain only convicted sex offender information—name, aliases, address, city, county, zip code, photograph, physical description, and criminal convictions, later amended to include all violent crime offenders; we were the first in the nation (1997) to place our registry on the Internet, readily available to the public, and the registry reached 5,600 offender registrations by 2007. Then there was the Data Processing and Communications Unit; the Kansas Incident-Based Reporting System; the Kansas Missing Persons Program; the Crime Data Information Center, which serves as the state's central clearinghouse for criminal justice system statistical data; the Telecommunications Unit, which provides service to the state's criminal justice agencies that have access to the Automated Statewide Telecommunications and Records Access (ASTRA) network, allowing the agencies to communicate with other criminal justice agencies within Kansas and across the nation; and the Information Technology Unit, which maintains computer hardware, software systems, and the security systems used by the KBI, as well as the KBI's Internet, e-mails, document imaging, digital photographs, mug shots, and desktop video conferencing.

As daunting as the duties cited above were, that list was not inclusive. The list did not even include the most important and challenging of all the tasks then assigned to the KBI's ISD by Kansas legislators and by a 1994 legislative creation called the Kansas Criminal Justice Coordinating Council. In 1994, the state's criminal justice information system was archaic and inefficient. It still resembled the old teletype model rather than a system based on modern computer technology, as existed in many states. Kansas courts, local and state law enforcement agencies, state prosecutors' offices, and corrections were still paper-driven. Manual searches of computers, rather than searches of broad databases, poor communications, paper files, and other antiquated practices, were commonplace throughout our criminal justice information system. The officer in the field was not being adequately supported.

The Kansas legislature, therefore, established in 1994 the Kansas Criminal Justice Coordinating Council to study numerous criminal justice issues and to oversee the development and management of a state-of-the-art criminal justice information system, based on automated databases rather than paper. The council was also charged with oversight and coordination of essential federal funding then available to states for improvement of state criminal justice information systems, primarily from federal Byrne Grants.

The council's original statutory membership consisted of the governor, or designee; the attorney general, or designee; the chief justice of the Kansas Supreme Court, or designee; the secretary of corrections; the secretary of social and rehabilitation services; and the director of the KBI. In 1996, the commissioner of juvenile justice was added to the membership and, years later, the superintendent of the Kansas Highway Patrol replaced the secretary of social and rehabilitation services. I served on the council from its creation in 1994 until my retirement in 2007, usually as vice-chairman.

The council's first major official action was to adopt the document "Criminal Justice Information System Criminal History Record Improvement Plan" in April 1995. That led to the Kansas Criminal Justice Information System Needs Analysis-Implementation Plan, which resulted in the contracting of Steve Davis of ECG (later MTG) Management Consultants of Seattle. Steve Davis became the architect for the Kansas Criminal Justice Information System Improvement Project, known as "The Project."

By 1997, Steve Davis and the council had identified ten strategic initiatives and twenty-five interconnecting specific projects, most involving or dependent on the KBI, for improving the state's core criminal justice information technology infrastructure, and created a number of task forces and subcommittees operating under an umbrella advisory board of twenty members, including prosecutors, judges, law enforcement officers and officials. Those task forces and subcommittees, consisting of representatives of the criminal justice community from across the state, reported to the advisory board, which reported to the council, which reported regularly to the legislature.

The Kansas Criminal Justice Coordinating Council operated originally with a budget of approximately $10 million. In 1999, it was increased to $12 million. Approximately 70 percent of the funding came from federal grants and 30 percent came from state funds.

Because of their individual and collective efforts during the most critical years of 1995–2002, the major credit for the successes of "The Project" belongs to Attorney General Carla Stovall, council chairperson during those years; Steve Davis, the program's original consultant and architect; Secretary of Corrections Chuck Simmons of the Council; Neil Woerman of the attorney general's office, a drafted advisor especially important in overseeing budget matters; Gordon Lansford, hired as the second project director in November 2000; and the KBI's Chuck Sexson and Ron Rohrer.

None were more important to the effort's success than Sexson, who directed all aspects of the KBI's broad involvement in "The Project." The KBI was the hub and centerpiece of the overall effort. Since the KBI was directly responsible for the majority of the technology improvement goals, the council assigned Chuck Sexson as manager of all the vendor contracts for "The Project," except the AFIS contract, which was assigned to Ron Rohrer, the computer whiz Sexson asked me to hire as the KBI's first information resource manager in 1996. Sexson and Rohrer excelled in those roles assigned to them by the council, as did Rohrer in his additional critical assignment as leader for the introduction of all new information technology implemented by "The Project."

The improvements targeted by this ambitious statewide program came quickly and constantly, thanks to the leadership cited above; the Kansas Criminal Justice Coordinating Council, with its various task forces and subcommittees; countless unsung employees of the KBI; and federal money.

Six years and $12 million after its inception, the core objectives of "The Project" had been completed and the overall goals of the program's strategic plan achieved, as reflected in the Kansas Criminal Justice Information System Project Summary, authorized by the Kansas Criminal Justice Coordinating Council, dated November 25, 2002.

Highlights of those accomplishments included:

The quality of criminal justice records in the state, especially the KBI
    criminal history computerized system, the KBI juvenile justice
    information system, the state's incident-based reporting system,
    AFIS, and the ASTRA network, were dramatically improved by
    2002.
The number of authorized users of the new criminal justice information
    system increased from 4,000 in 1998 to 7,000 in 2002.
Authorized users of ASTRA and the National Crime Information
    Center (NCIC) increased from 1,316 in 1997 to 4,346 in 2002.
ASTRA transactions rose in number from 176 million in 1999 to more
    than 404 million by 2001.

KBI criminal files were completely automated and paper files eliminated
by 2002.

In 2002 the Center for Digital Government and The Progress and
Freedom Foundation ranked Kansas in a tie for first place with
Colorado and Wisconsin, among all fifty states, for most effective use
of modern technology in criminal justice information systems.[1]

In 2004, Kansas joined fewer than ten other states in making criminal
records available to the general public via the Internet, after having already
been the first state to place information about sex offenders on the Internet.[2]

We had gone from the back of the pack to a national leadership role in
the quality of our overall criminal justice information system. We could
use a two-word summation to describe the improvements: automation and
computerization. Perhaps the best proof of the impressive improvements
achieved by "The Project" is a practical example. The KBI's "help desk"
of the ISD received a telephone call in January 2001 from an investigator in
another state. He explained that he was in the process of taking a statement
from an armed robbery suspect. The suspect had volunteered that he had
also robbed an unrecalled convenience store in an unrecalled location while
traveling across Kansas weeks earlier. The KBI, via the new criminal justice
information system, broadcast the information. Within minutes, a response
confirmed the unsolved Kansas robbery and also the suspect's two traffic
violations near the robbery site, which the suspect had also volunteered.
Prior to "The Project," that statewide inquiry would have been possible only
through FBI channels and would have required days, if not weeks.

Dubbed "Mr. CJIS" by Kansas law enforcement for his leadership role
in "The Project" and the modernization of our criminal justice information
system, Chuck Sexson was honored in 2003 by the Kansas Association of
Chiefs of Police for those efforts, and, in 2004, he received the nation's highest award for achievements in criminal justice information systems from the
National Consortium for Justice and Statistics in Sacramento, California.

Sexson had agreed to stay one year in the ISD position. He never asked for
that transfer or reassignment I had promised in 1994, and he remained ten
years in that critical position, with no complaints and exceptional success.
His only request was that I assign his friend Special Agent Dave Sim from
narcotics to him as the assistant I had promised. I did so, promoting Sim to
special agent in charge as Sexson's top aide.

When the soft-spoken Sexson retired on January 1, 2005, he was the first
of three outstanding KBI leaders we lost to retirement that year. The retirements of Deputy Director Terry Knowles on July 15, 2005 and Associate Director Dale Finger on December 17, 2005 were noted above. All three

gentlemen were men of exceptional character, as were their replacements, Dave Sim, Kyle Smith, and Kirk Thompson, respectively.

Following his KBI retirement, Sexson was appointed director of the attorney general's new concealed-carry firearms division by Attorney General Phill Kline. As of this writing, he remains in that position, continuing his long career of public service to Kansas citizens.

Only "The Project" challenged the state's meth lab menace and forensic accreditation as the top KBI priority during my tenure. I remain proud of the KBI's response to all three challenges. Bold agendas require bold staffs. Fortunately for the KBI, our leadership in addressing those three bold agendas and priorities was provided by a bold staff: Dale Finger, Kirk Thompson, Terry Knowles, Mike VanStratton, Chuck Sexson, Dave Sim, Ron Rohrer, and Kyle Smith, boldness aplenty. No person ever shared command with a better lot.

On August 23, 2005, the National Hurricane Center reported the formation of Tropical Depression #12 over the southeastern Bahamas. That system became Tropical Storm Katrina on August 24 and then Hurricane Katrina on August 25, making landfall between Hallandale Beach and Aventura, Florida, that day. On August 26, it crossed the Florida panhandle and entered the Gulf of Mexico, heading west. It soon became a Category Five hurricane, with maximum sustained winds of 175 miles per hour (gusts to 215), before dropping to a Category Four, with sustained winds of 145 miles per hour, on August 29, when it struck Louisiana and Mississippi in savage, unprecedented fashion, and Alabama to a lesser extent.

Hurricane Katrina would be declared the most destructive and costliest natural disaster in our nation's history. Total damages were estimated at approximately $80 billion, with coastal Mississippi and Louisiana the primary victims. Hard hit were Gulfport, Waveland, Bay St. Louis, Pass Christian, Long Beach, Biloxi, Ocean Springs, and Pascagoula in Mississippi, and all of coastal Louisiana, but especially the city of New Orleans. Katrina spawned at least thirty-six tornadoes, eleven in Mississippi alone. The official death toll on the Gulf Coast eventually reached more than 1,800. More than one million people in the Gulf Coast area were displaced. The subsequent migration of people, due to Katrina, was the largest migration of Americans since the Great Depression of the 1930s, when 3 million plains people, Dakotans, Nebraskans, Oklahomans, and Kansans, left the "Dust Bowl" and headed west, mostly to California.[3]

Katrina had barely departed the Gulf Coast, heading north into the Midwest, before pleas for assistance started coming from law enforcement agencies in the ravaged, almost destroyed, portions of coastal Mississippi and

Louisiana. The thought of sending volunteer special agents to assist had already entered my mind. Attorney General Phill Kline and my top staff were all in strong agreement.

I received a call for assistance from Louisiana quite early and I would have most certainly dispatched agents there, if necessary. I was well aware, however, that coastal Mississippi had been hit as hard as coastal Louisiana. Although New Orleans was receiving most of the nation's attention, I knew that Gulfport and Biloxi in Mississippi, relatively speaking, had been just as devastated as New Orleans. My preference was to help Mississippi and an old friend, George Phillips, commissioner of the Mississippi Department of Public Safety. Phillips was formerly the U.S. attorney for Mississippi, then director of the Mississippi Bureau of Narcotics, and an old bird-hunting buddy of mine. He is a true gentleman, well respected across Mississippi, and a fun guy in good times. I knew he would treat my people like his own.

I tried unsuccessfully to reach George by telephone and also via fax and e-mail. Phone calls to and from Mississippi in those early days went from impossible to extremely difficult. As it turned out, George was trying to reach me while I was attempting to reach him. The commissioner finally got through to me by phone, on Friday, September 2, 2005. There was so much exhaustion in his voice that, at first, I did not recognize my friend's voice. A day later, in another telephone conversation, it was clear he was actually losing his voice and was not in the best of health, despite his hoarse protests to the contrary. George explained that he was asking for KBI assistance specifically because of our friendship and because he needed experienced, veteran criminal investigators to assist and/or relieve his own weary agents. They were needed, he pointed out, to assist in house-to-house searches, with security patrols, with searches for missing persons, with the identification of bodies, and in the fraud cases that were already becoming quite evident. I pledged our support to Commissioner Phillips and Mississippi and then respectfully declined the request from Louisiana. I am certain our people would have received equally professional treatment in Louisiana, but I felt more comfortable entrusting our agents to a personal friend, who had been a guest in my home, and with whom I had shared fine meals and conversations and enjoyable pheasant and quail hunting experiences.

Associate Director Dale Finger issued a call for volunteers. More than forty of our sixty-two special agents quickly responded. The others were attempting, mostly unsuccessfully, to change court dates, subpoenas, other commitments, and resolve other schedule conflicts. There was no shortage of eager volunteers.

The KBI has a history of following investigative leads wherever they lead. We have sent an agent or two or three at different times to every state in the union, and to several foreign countries on various investigative errands. But this commitment was a historical first for us. We had never before deployed such a large contingent of agents to assist law enforcement in another state for an extended period. Our agents were willing to participate in the unusual assignment, even though it meant vaccinations (tetanus, diphtheria, and hepatitis B) for everyone we would send. They were also aware the assignment would mean absence from their families, personal inconvenience, discomfort, hardship, and maybe danger, based on some of the first reports from Louisiana.

KBI Assistant Directors Kirk Thompson and Bob Blecha coordinated the selection of agents, logistics, and transportation at my request. Special Agent in Charge Rod Page of our Wichita office was selected to command the unit, and he was assigned Senior Special Agents Tony Weingartner, Doug Younger, Frank Papish, Bill Roland, Chris Bumgarner, Mike Metzler, and Duane Robért, and Special Agents Marc Perez, Glen Virden, and Greg Skelton for the mission.

Although we were involved in the early phases of hiring new KBI special agents, nineteen of our eighty-one special agent positions were then vacant. On paper, it didn't make much sense to send eleven KBI agents to Mississippi. I could have been criticized for such a deployment of precious KBI manpower outside the state, but, led by Attorney General Kline, we received only support and encouragement from citizens, legislators, and fellow law enforcement administrators.

I officially named the project "KBI Operation Katrina." The volunteer group of KBI special agents, however, dubbed themselves "Mississippi Mud." Preparations for the squad's departure progressed rapidly under the direction of Associate Director Dale Finger, Assistant Directors Kirk Thompson and Bob Blecha, and Special Agent in Charge Rick Sabel, as equipment, materials, supplies, and vehicles were assembled.

Their Mississippi counterparts, with whom they were communicating almost daily, had suggested to our people that our KBI military Humvee and our tactical crime scene vehicle (twelve rear seats) would both be helpful to our delegation while on assignment in Mississippi. They also indicated to us that we would have to be self-sufficient (water, food, bedding, etc.) for at least the first three days. Self-sufficiency was not a major problem, but getting the Humvee and tactical truck to Mississippi was a problem at first. Rick Sabel contacted Kansas Department of Transportation (KDOT) Supervisors Kenneth McKenzie and Mick Holz, and those gentlemen made it happen. KDOT drivers Tim Baker, Chuck Kincaid, and Jake Baush transported the two KBI vehicles to and from Mississippi for us on a flatbed tractor-trailer.

Our eleven agents traveled in two Ford Explorers, a Chevrolet Suburban, and two pickup trucks.

The Mississippi Mud team, soon to be known as Mississippi Mud I, departed from KBI headquarters in Topeka on a rainy Thursday morning, September 15. They arrived the next day in Gulfport, Mississippi. Pursuant to our agreement with Mississippi, they would remain there twenty-one days.

The KBI agents were immediately divided into two groups. One group was assigned to work closely with Mississippi Bureau of Investigation (MBI) agents. The other group was paired with Mississippi Highway Patrol (MHP) troopers on a SWAT Team. The first two days the MHP-SWAT KBI agents were involved in roving security patrols designed to prevent looting and checking on the welfare of survivors camping out on their own property (sans homes), and in the distribution of food, water, and other supplies. They also responded to bomb threats and civil disturbances. On September 20, they provided security for President Bush, Vice President Cheney, and other visiting federal and state officials.

The MBI-KBI team also pulled security patrol duty, assisted overworked local police and sheriffs' units in three counties, distributed water, food, and supplies, and were involved in many search and recovery operations. In addition, they helped with the recovery of bodies on the beaches of the Gulfport area.

The first few days working with the MHP and MBI units permitted the KBI agents the opportunity to learn the geography and to develop strong liaison with local police and sheriffs' departments. Thereafter, our agents started working independently, in pairs, receiving assignments from Commissioner Phillips and from MBI and MHP officials. After the first few days our agents stayed together in a large air-conditioned tent. Commissioner Phillips grilled venison burgers for our agents at the end of one long day.

In one typical assignment Doug Younger, Bill Roland, Marc Perez, Tony Weingartner, Frank Papish, and Rod Page were asked by the Red Cross to look for a disabled veteran who had not been seen since the storm. Street signs were missing, as were entire houses or parts of houses reflecting house numbers. The agents conducted a door-to-door search, often without doors, in a particular neighborhood of the Gulfport beach area. The gentleman was located, after several hours, in a storm-damaged house two blocks from the beach. He was evacuated by ambulance. Two days later the disabled veteran's wife tracked down Page and personally thanked the KBI for saving her lost husband's life.

During one of their routine anti-looting and bodies-seeking patrols, Greg Skelton and Glen Virden came upon the scene of a one-vehicle accident, with the injured driver trapped in the car. They administered first aid until the ambulance arrived and then assisted in freeing the woman from the wreck. It is not known whether she survived.

Incredibly, during all the chaos that followed Katrina's departure, bomb threats were a significant problem. The KBI's Mike Metzler and an MBI agent were assigned a couple of bomb-threat incidents, and they were able to arrest the individual responsible in the act of making another such call. He was placed in custody on federal charges.

The recovery of bodies and the identification of those bodies continued as major priorities throughout the deployment. Most days involved house-to-house or, more accurately, debris-to-debris searches, often working with cadaver dogs. The last two weeks the agents spent considerable time on a missing-children task force with federal agents and Mississippi state agents. Our agents handled more than 100 missing-children cases, clearing almost 97 percent of their assignments—most joyfully, some sadly.

With another task force that targeted adults, KBI agents handled 42 percent of the more than 700 cases pursued by the large seventy-person, multiagency task force. They accounted for fifty-nine missing persons in one record day, October 1, 2005, twenty-five the day before, and twenty-one more the day after. Again, most cases were cleared with happy results, but some were not.

Mississippi Mud I was scheduled to return to Kansas on October 7. Several days before that, Commissioner Phillips called me again. He highly praised the efforts of the KBI deployment and requested that I send a second team to continue the great work being done by KBI agents in Mississippi. He quoted one of his top assistants: "Those KBI agents came down here to work, not just to sightsee, and boy, did they work!" I, of course, agreed to send another team. Again, Attorney General Kline and my assistants all agreed with my opinion. I did emphasize that Mississippi Mud II would have to be our final Katrina deployment.

Associate Director Finger issued a second call for volunteers. To command Mississippi Mud II we selected Special Agent in Charge Jeff Brandau and assigned to him Senior Special Agents Bruce Adams, Bill Halvorsen, Troy Rhodes, John Gauntt, Jim Carmack, Dave Hutchings, and Mark Kendrick and Specials Agents Tim Leakey and Keith Lumry. Following immunizations and appropriate outfitting, Mississippi Mud II departed on October 8, the day following the return of Mississippi Mud I. The Mississippi Mud II team would return on October 24.

Thus, a total of twenty-one KBI agents labored in Mississippi most of September and October 2005, putting in long days, seven days a week, without complaint. All were volunteers.

Mississippi Mud II, like its predecessor, was involved in house-to-house searches for missing persons, dead bodies, and the injured, but the emphasis of our second deployment related to the growing problem of missing sex offenders. At first, our agents participated in a joint effort with MBI agents and deputy U.S. marshals to attempt to locate 189 missing, noncompliant, registered sex offenders. After five intense days, more than 100 had been located across Mississippi and in twelve other states through the task force's efforts. The KBI team was then placed in charge of the operation. Within days, 175 of the original 189 missing sex offenders had been identified and located. Warrants were issued for the remaining fourteen missing offenders on the basis of affidavits provided by KBI agents. Four of those fugitives were arrested by the agents the day Mississippi Mud II departed. The KBI agents furnished the state of Mississippi a complete list of all sex offenders who had moved, been killed, or arrested, again earning high praise from state officials.

I think the feelings of our Katrina agents can be summarized by comments of their respective commanders. In a briefing memorandum to me on his return, Rod Page concluded, "In summary, KBI participation in Mississippi was greatly appreciated. Hundreds of persons said 'thank you.' . . . As agents we participated in an operation from which we came away knowing we touched individual lives and made a difference. Thanks for sending us." Later, on his return, Jeff Brandau, in his briefing memorandum to me, closed with, "Personally, this effort was one of the most rewarding in my career. The agents you sent could not have done better. Each one worked hard and was dedicated to being successful in locating the offenders assigned. . . . Thank you for the honor to lead these individuals and to represent the KBI and the state of Kansas in this effort."

Shirley and I saw both KBI contingents off when they departed for Mississippi in September and October. I felt immense pride in the two groups of KBI agents as they headed to the Gulf Coast with my thanks and best wishes. That pride was quickly validated by the complimentary reports from Commissioner Phillips and other Mississippi officials about our agents' performance.

By any standard, KBI Operation Katrina, or Mississippi Mud I and II, was a noble cause, a law enforcement success, a rewarding experience for the KBI and each agent involved, the right thing to do, and the only such out-of-state undertaking by the KBI in its proud history.

Following fingerprint identification, the next significant crime-solving development was the 1967 establishment of the FBI's National Crime Information Center (NCIC), the first national computerization of current criminal information available to the nation's law enforcement patrolmen and investigators. Prior to 1967, a KBI agent or any law enforcement officer who was suspicious of the status of a particular vehicle, or suspicious of the vehicle's driver or a passenger therein, had to resort to his or her own resourcefulness, guile, ingenuity, and interview skills, and, often, time-consuming telephone calls and/or teletype inquiries, to determine whether the vehicle was stolen or if the person in question was the subject of an outstanding arrest warrant somewhere. With NCIC, the officer can advise the dispatcher of the suspicious car's vehicle identification number, license plate registration number, and/or the individual's correct name and date of birth or social security number, and receive instant confirmation if the vehicle has been reported stolen somewhere or if the individual is a wanted fugitive.

DNA and CODIS, DNA's computerized database, and AFIS, the computerized database for fingerprints, followed NCIC in the parade of forensic science innovations. When I retired from the FBI in 1986, the FBI's Identification Division, central repository for the millions of fingerprint cards received from the nation's law enforcement agencies and correctional facilities, had only been authorized on one occasion to initiate a massive manual search of those fingerprint records. On that occasion, the unusual search was conducted by scores of fingerprint technicians, assisted by scores of fingerprint-trained special agents brought to Washington, D.C., from FBI offices at Baltimore, New York City, Philadelphia, and Richmond. That was, of course, prior to fingerprint computerization (AFIS), and the objective was to compare a single unidentified latent fingerprint impression by a tedious, painstaking, manual process involving only human hands, eyes, and expertise, with the FBI's millions of fingerprint cards, in a desperate attempt to identify a killer.

The lone case wherein such an unprecedented intensive effort was ordered was the murder of the Reverend Dr. Martin Luther King Jr., in April 1968, in Memphis. Dr. King had been shot from a rooming house located across the street from his motel as he stood on a balcony of that motel with several civil rights associates. An abandoned rifle, equipped with a telescope, and obviously recently fired, was soon recovered near the rooming house. The rifle was later identified, ballistically, as the murder weapon. A single latent fingerprint impression was found on the rifle and, following almost twenty hours of continuous effort by those scores of FBI fingerprint examiners manually examining thousands of fingerprint cards, that single latent print impression lifted off the rifle was identified as a fingerprint of James Earl Ray, a career criminal and recent escapee from a Missouri prison. Ray was subsequently apprehended and he eventually entered a plea of guilty to the murder charge. That massive fingerprint comparison project was the first and last time FBI Director J. Edgar Hoover requested a complete manual search of FBI fingerprint records.[4]

Today, thanks to AFIS, identification of the perpetrator, if his or her fingerprints are among the millions stored in the national computer database, would require only seconds and the time and expertise of just one KBI fingerprint technician.

Prior to the fingerprint automation of AFIS, an investigator submitting a latent fingerprint impression from a crime scene to the FBI or KBI for possible identification of an unknown suspect was required to also provide the name of a possible suspect for comparison purposes. The latent fingerprint impression would then be manually compared with any fingerprint records available for that particular suspect and only that suspect. If the investigator had no possible suspect with whom to compare the latent print, that print simply went into the case file, uncompared and unused, unless and until a suspect was developed.

AFIS technology was developed in the late 1980s. The KBI's AFIS system went into operation in 1990. By March 2006, our KBI AFIS system had produced 3,450 fingerprint matches, often identifying fugitives and perpetrators of crimes, solving criminal cases, and helping convict the guilty.

On March 21, 2006, at KBI headquarters, in the auditorium crowded with media representatives and Kansas law enforcement officials, Attorney General Phill Kline and I announced that the impressive KBI AFIS system was about to get even better, thanks to an approved $3.6 million upgrade, the most ambitious improvement since 1990. We had received funding for the first phase of the enhancement, a $752,000 Homeland Security grant. The rest of the funding was coming from our own agency budget and from additional federal grants. The central part of the AFIS upgrade program was new technology that not only permitted Kansas law enforcement officers to compare fingerprints through the national AFIS database but, incredibly, allowed them to do it from their patrol cars, instantly comparing a person's two index fingerprints with the ten million fingerprints in the KBI system, connecting as well to the FBI's central database.

As technicians demonstrated the state of the art technology, we explained that eighty of the new portable devices (seventy small black boxes and ten special laptop computers) were already being tested by officers around Kansas. Other tests were also scheduled in New York, Milwaukee, and Hawaii, in similar planned AFIS improvements. Again, the KBI was on the cutting edge of new technology. The attorney general and I also announced at that news conference that the AFIS system was being used to store palm prints, suspects' mug shots, and photographs of suspects' scars, marks, and tattoos, and, furthermore, that almost sixty Kansas law enforcement agencies were submitting fingerprints electronically to the KBI, forsaking the old, cumbersome ink-and-paper method of submission.

The importance of forensic technology, like AFIS, DNA, and CODIS, in the solution of crime cannot be exaggerated. Witnesses, victims, suspects, and defendants sometimes change their stories and human memory fades. AFIS, DNA, and CODIS, on the other hand, never change their stories and their memories never fade. Today's criminal investigators must appreciate and respect the wonders of such modern crime-solving forensic technology. Today's investigators, however, must also be cautioned to look beyond such technology. There is danger in overreliance on those powerful forensic weapons. Officers can become too complacent awaiting DNA and/or AFIS results to name a suspect to pursue, delaying traditional investigative tactics and strategies. Most crimes are solved by determined, intelligent, educated, trained, and experienced investigators asking the right questions, listening to the answers, making proper deductions, and drawing appropriate conclusions. Good listeners, shoe leather, and old-fashioned guile and police work solve more crimes than forensic science magic.

On January 23, 2007, the Central Registry of the Kansas Law Enforcement Training Center in Hutchinson, Kansas, the state repository for Kansas law enforcement data, reported that there were 7,334 full-time law enforcement officers in Kansas to serve and protect the more than 2.7 million citizens of the state. It also reported that 73 percent of all Kansas law enforcement agencies had ten or fewer full-time officers, and 52 percent of all Kansas law enforcement agencies had five or fewer full-time law enforcement officers.[5]

The dependence of the Kansas law enforcement community on the investigative and forensic services and resources of the KBI was never greater since the bureau's formation in 1939. Another historical constant was that the contributions of the KBI to the Kansas criminal justice system and the Kansas law enforcement community continued to be disproportionate to the size and resources of the KBI.

In July 1939, Kansas legislators budgeted $46,000 for the fledgling KBI—one director, nine agents, and a secretary—to "pay all salaries, buy all equipment, and support the criminal investigations."[6] On June 1, 2007, our budget was $30 million and our complement was just under 300 employees. We had added a field office in Pittsburg to the field offices in Topeka, Great Bend, Wichita, and Overland Park, and we had added forensic laboratories in Pittsburg and Kansas City to the original forensic laboratories in Topeka and Great Bend, achieving forensic accreditation for all four laboratories. Most important, we had significantly decentralized our complements of special agents and forensic scientists, placing more of them than ever before around the state and away from Topeka.

One of the most consistent accomplishments of the KBI since 1939 relates to the day in, day out, exceptional performance of our KBI special agents, almost always too few in number. Many of those exploits—Macksville to Hurricane Katrina—have been documented in this book.

Exceptional courage has often been a common virtue in those stories. No exception to that lofty standard was the valor demonstrated by the KBI High Risk Warrant Team (HRWT) during the evening of January 8, 2003, at a rural home in Elk County, Kansas, in support of Sheriff Janet Harrington and her small department in the execution of a search warrant and an arrest warrant. The suspect, a longtime user of methamphetamine with a history of violence, had severely beaten his wife and threatened to kill her if she reported his physical abuse to the sheriff. He also vowed to kill any officer who came to arrest him, after which he would commit suicide. He was known to be in possession of several firearms. The battered wife was able to escape with the couple's children after two days of abuse and immediately reported the situation to Sheriff Harrington, who requested KBI assistance in execution of the warrants. Accordingly, the KBI's HRWT led the entry into the rural Elk County home that cold January evening in 2003. The subject was encountered in his bed, armed with a semiautomatic pistol, with another pistol hanging in a holster on a bedpost. He ignored repeated commands to surrender and was fatally shot when he pointed his handgun toward KBI agents.

More than a year later, on March 12, 2004, at KBI headquarters, before more than 100 guests, Attorney General Kline, Associate Director Finger, and I presented KBI Medals of Valor to Special Agent in Charge Rod Page and Senior Special Agent Tony Weingartner for their professional response to the dangerous Elk County confrontation. Two months later, on May 21, 2004, at the concluding banquet of the Kansas Joint Law Enforcement Training Conference (Kansas Association of Chiefs of Police, Kansas Peace Officers' Association, and Kansas Sheriffs' Association) at the Hilton Hotel in Wichita, the KBI HRWT and individual KBI Agents Rod Page, Tony Weingartner, Doug Younger, and Frank Papish were among the sixty-eight recipients of awards presented to Kansas law enforcement agencies and officers for exceptional performance in 2003. The KBI HRWT received a special unit citation from the Kansas Association of Chiefs of Police for the team's efforts the year before during the Elk County adversarial situation, and Page, Weingartner, Younger, and Papish were each singled out for Gold Valor Awards for their courageous individual responses in that confrontation.

Perhaps a more stressful but less dangerous assignment for KBI agents occurred in October 2005, when Mikhail Gorbachev, the former Soviet president, visited Kansas State University in Manhattan to deliver the annual Governor Alf Landon Lecture and then spent the weekend in nearby Lindsborg. Both Kansas State University and the city of Lindsborg requested a KBI protective detail to assist with security for President Gorbachev and his traveling delegation during their Kansas visit. As Lindsborg Chief of Police Tim Berggren, a good friend, put it when he called me for assistance, "Larry, as you know, I have six full-time officers. I need your help." We assigned eighteen KBI agents to "The President Mikhail Gorbachev Protective Detail" under the direction of Special Agent in Charge Rick Sabel and Senior Special Agents Tony Weingartner and Doug Younger.

Since Lou Richter's days as director, the KBI has been called on by the U.S. Secret Service to help protect American presidents visiting Kansas. KBI agents have also responded to requests from our good friends, the Kansas Highway Patrol, to assist in the protection of Kansas governors on special occasions. We similarly honored requests from the chief justice of the Kansas Supreme Court to provide KBI protective details on special occasions for Kansas Supreme Court justices, the court itself on occasion, and for judicial conferences held across the state. And the primary responsibility for the security of Kansas attorneys general has always belonged to the KBI. I believe, however, that the events of October 28–30, 2005, in Manhattan and Lindsborg represent the first time KBI agents helped protect a former president of a foreign nation.

Several observers in both Manhattan and Lindsborg reported overhearing interpreters indicating that the former president and others in his traveling party mistakenly thought the KBI protective detail was actually a U.S. Secret Service detail and were very complimentary of the detail's performance at both sites. I referred to that reported confusion in my letter of commendation to all eighteen members of "The President Mikhail Gorbachev Protective Detail," dated November 9, 2005:

> I wish to join in the compliments recently directed to each of you by officials of Kansas State University and the city of Lindsborg, in connection with the KBI's participation in the protection of former President Gorbachev, October 28–30.
>
> Your professionalism and your dedication in that historical assignment have brought considerable acclaim to the KBI.
>
> I understand more than one observer confused you with special agents of the U.S. Secret Service. High praise, indeed, for the Secret Service.

As always, your efforts and your expertise are very much admired and appreciated. Thank you.

Sincerely,

Larry Welch, director

No individual protected by KBI special agents anywhere or at any time was ever harmed.

During 2005 and 2006, thirteen of our eighty-one authorized agent positions were usually vacant for budgetary reasons. Thus, we normally had sixty-eight special agents and senior special agents covering the entire state. Half were narcotic agents and half were field agents primarily investigating homicides, rapes, violent crimes, computer crimes, armed robberies, in-custody deaths of inmates, and officer-involved shootings. Those sixty-eight agents were assigned to eight special agents in charge, who also worked cases themselves.

The sixty-eight men and women, under the leadership of Special Agents in Charge Bill Delaney (Overland Park); Randy Ewy and Rod Page (Wichita); Bruce Mellor and Kelly Ralston (Great Bend); and Jeff Brandau, Tony Weingartner, and Rick Sabel (Topeka), recorded 676 felony arrests and 542 felony convictions during that two-year period. As impressive as those figures are, they place in perspective single-year arrest records for 2000 (795); 2002 (666); and 2003 (558); and single-year conviction records for 2002 (545); 2001 (444); and 2003 (404). We had ten agent positions vacant in 1996, fifteen in 2003, and seventeen in 2004.

Another consistency with KBI agents has been the strong liaison between the KBI and the Kansas Peace Officers' Association (KPOA), originally the Kansas State Peace Officers' Association, since the law enforcement association joined with Kansas bankers and ranchers in the 1930s to lobby the legislature for the creation of the KBI. Not only have many KBI agents been active KPOA members through the years, ten lawmen with KBI connections have served as president of the state's largest law enforcement association: Lou Richter, Logan Sanford, Harold Nye, Jack Williams, Fred Howard, George Schureman, Wiley Kerr, John Green, Bruce Mellor, and Larry Thomas.

Similarly, there has always been a close relationship between KBI agents and the FBI National Academy (FBINA) and that academy's alumni association, the FBI National Academy Associates (FBINAA). I was especially pleased and grateful that, in each year of my tenure as KBI director, I was invited by the FBI to nominate a candidate for attendance at the elite law enforcement leadership school in Quantico, Virginia. The FBI National

Academy provided vital leadership training for those whom Dale Finger, and later Kirk Thompson, and I selected—primarily special agents in charge or assistant directors—for attendance.

Much of the credit for the development of first-rate KBI leaders during my tenure must be given to the intensive executive leadership training many received at Quantico's FBI Academy. Not only did the FBI provide that excellent management training to us, but they also provided it free of charge. The FBINA attendance of our people cost the state of Kansas and the KBI nothing. Room, board, the actual training, and even the transportation to and from Quantico, Virginia, were furnished at FBI expense. All I had to do was continue the attendee's KBI salary during that training. Those nominated and selected for FBI National Academy attendance from 1994 to 2007 were Bill Delaney, Bob Blecha, John Green, Kirk Thompson, Larry Thomas, Jeff Brandau, Dave Sim, Rod Page, Kelly Ralston, Ray Lundin, Tony Weingartner, and Dave Hutchings.

The twelve graduates listed above do not represent the full extent of FBINA influence within KBI ranks after 1994. Dale Finger, Chuck Sexson, Bruce Mellor, Floyd Bradley, Lanny Grosland, George Schureman, Dave Wood, and Gary Pettijohn, all in place when I arrived in July 1994, were already FBINA graduates. Moreover, John Nachtman and Wiley Kerr, hired as KBI agents during my tenure, were FBINA graduates when they were hired. Nachtman attended the academy when he was undersheriff of Dickinson County, Kansas, and Kerr attended FBINA as the sheriff of Washington County, Kansas. Furthermore, there were former FBI agents on the KBI roster other than Terry Knowles and me during my tenure. Native Kansans Bill Mueller and Randy Ewy, two of the finest law enforcement officers I have known, each spent brief stints with the FBI as special agents, like Al Dewey before them, prior to returning to Kansas to accept positions as KBI agents. The close KBI-FBI ties developed under KBI Directors Lou Richter and Logan Sanford continued in 2007.

During my law enforcement career—twenty-five years in the FBI, eight years at KLETC, and nearly thirteen years as KBI director—I never attended a political rally, a political fund-raiser, or a postelection victory celebration or election concession event. Nor did I ever enter anyone's election campaign headquarters or participate in any manner in anyone's election campaign. Casting a ballot on election day was the extent of my political activity.

In my opinion, no director of the KBI should ever engage in any political activity. The KBI director, of course, must necessarily work in an environment surrounded by politicians and politics, but he or she must avoid any appearance of personal involvement in political activity. Granted, such avoidance is a difficult task and challenging responsibility, inasmuch as the KBI director holds that position as a result of an appointment by the state attorney general—a politician—subject to confirmation by the state senate—forty politicians—subject to subsequent oversight by the attorney general. It is imperative that directors of the KBI recognize that their primary responsibility is to protect the independence of this great agency. Administrative oversight by the attorney general is one thing. Political influence or manipulation is quite another. The KBI, pursuant to state law, is a division of the office of attorney general. It must not, however, ever be perceived as the political ally or security arm of the attorney general, or of the governor, who has no oversight responsibility other than the important one of budget, with the KBI. Directors Richter and Sanford established the principle of political independence within the KBI directorship during their respective tenures. Every director who followed Richter and Sanford and preceded me embraced that concept.

I endeavored to keep each attorney general briefed and up to date on major issues and developments within the Kansas law enforcement community and Kansas criminal justice system in general and within the KBI in particular. I always copied the attorney general on every report I submitted to the Kansas legislature and on all my statewide letters and reports to Kansas law enforcement administrators and prosecutors. It was a self-imposed priority to ensure that no attorney general was ever surprised or blindsided by news of a development of which they should have been aware.

Dolph Simons, editor of the *Lawrence Journal-World*, commented on January 13, 2007, when he wrote of my announced retirement and of the KBI directorship: "This is no place for political games to be played; the KBI office should never be used as a means of passing out a payback or IOU for some previous political or monetary favor."[7] Indeed.

The *esprit de corps* that developed within the first generation of KBI agents—Richter, Anderson, Bulla, Dyer, Fowkes, Griffith, Henderson, Huse, Maupin, and Neal—survives today. Since 1939, the succeeding generations of KBI employees have been faithful caretakers of that spirit and staunch guardians of the KBI tradition of "Dedication, Service, and Integrity" fostered by that spirit. It has been a great honor to have personally known so many of those men and women and, moreover, to have served with many of them. These have been ordinary men and women doing extraordinary work in the name of criminal justice, well aware of the legacy that must be honored and protected, and equally aware that any compromise of the KBI tradition and reputation could be more than detrimental and embarrassing. Such a compromise could be fatal to the KBI's well-being.

I was fond of pointing out to new KBI agents and forensic scientists that they must understand and appreciate that when they arrive at that first crime scene or first set foot in a sheriff's office or police station or take the witness stand in a court of law, they enjoy instant credibility because of those agents and forensic scientists who preceded them. As new KBI agents and scientists they have not yet done anything that would entitle them to immediate, unqualified respect from the sheriff, deputy, police chief, patrolman, detective, trooper, prosecutor, defense attorney, jury, or judge. Yet instant respect is theirs, because of the KBI reputation and tradition already established— reputation and tradition built case upon case, arrest after arrest, and conviction after conviction. It falls to each KBI employee to cherish that legacy of credibility and respect. Each inherits that legacy, and it is his or hers to protect and build upon, and not tarnish, diminish, or destroy.

Some things at KBI headquarters, 1620 S.W. Tyler, Topeka, Kansas, on June 1, 2007, remained much as they were in 1939 at the headquarters of the bureau—those small, cramped offices in the state capitol building. As in 1939, a relatively small group of ordinary men and women—ten men and one woman in 1939 and slightly fewer than 300 in 2007—were still doing extraordinary things in the service of the state, in pursuit of justice. Excellence was still commonplace. Kansas police chiefs, sheriffs, investigators, and prosecutors—the Kansas law enforcement community, small departments and large departments alike—were still seeking KBI assistance in the solution and prosecution of crimes challenging their respective communities. As in 1939, there were more requests for KBI services, expertise, and assistance than could be honored, given limited KBI resources and manpower. The positive impact the KBI had on the Kansas criminal justice system remained greatly disproportionate to the size of the agency, and the KBI was still the best bargain in state government in 2007, as in 1939. Another similarity linking the 1939 KBI and the 2007 KBI was the absence of scandal, disgrace, and dishonor. There was still no such blemish on the proud KBI tradition and reputation established by the KBI's founding generation.

Furthermore, the basic principles adopted by Lou Richter and Logan Sanford during the KBI's infancy continued to provide the foundation for the modern KBI's operations: Go only when and where summoned; assist, do not usurp; and upon success, let others issue the commendatory media release—credit will come, if deserved. Atop those three guiding principles sprinkle a healthy dose of "Dedication, Service, Integrity," and one has the formula for KBI success, 1939–2007.

As reflected in the early chapters of this book, the most serious challenges to Richter and that earliest KBI generation were bank robbery, cattle theft, and the violent crime associated with that era's gangs and gangsters. Among the most serious future challenges to the KBI of 2007 were the frustrating unpredictability of the fragile annual budget and the steady decline in the percentage of KBI operations covered by state funds. There is a strong correlation between inadequate funding and failure of mission.

Because there was never enough capital in the capitol, because most of the KBI's budget is encumbered for salaries and payroll, and because I promised my employees there would be no personnel layoffs, furloughs, or budget-imposed terminations during my directorship, we were compelled to address budget constraints and spending cuts through personnel attrition and with reactive reductions in operating expenses, supplies, materials, equipment, and maintenance.

Aside from budget issues, the most serious crime challenges to the modern KBI and today's Kansas law enforcement are computer crimes—especially child exploitation and pornography, fraud, and identity theft—and gangs and drugs—especially methamphetamine imported from Mexico, given the successful reduction of local meth labs in Kansas, the previous longtime KBI investigative and forensic priority. Kansas citizens can be assured that there is less to fear from the Taliban or al-Qaeda within our geographical boundaries. The foreign-born terrorists posing the greatest threats to Kansas citizens are Mexican methamphetamine, Mexican marijuana, and Mexican cocaine.

Retiring executives are fond of saying, at career's end, that they hope they are leaving their organization better than when they found it. I pray that, on June 1, 2007, when I stepped down as the bureau's tenth director, the KBI was as good as I found it on July 18, 1994, when Attorney General Bob Stephan administered the oath of office to me at KBI headquarters in Topeka.

It was an exceptional law enforcement agency, one of the finest in the nation, when I assumed the responsibility of its leadership. I trust that it was as well when I relinquished the privilege of KBI leadership almost thirteen years later as the second-longest-serving director, behind only the original director, Lou Richter, and just a step ahead of my mentor, Logan Sanford, the second director.

Any evaluation of the KBI over my tenure, 1994–2007, must come, as KBI evaluation always has since 1939, from Kansas sheriffs, police chiefs, law enforcement investigators, prosecutors, defense attorneys, legislators, judges, the media, attorneys general, and crime victims and their families. They know best.

Notes

Chapter 1: Macksville

1. *Topeka Daily Capital,* July 13, 1941.
2. *Stafford Courier,* September 25, 1941.
3. *Kansas City Star,* August 29, 1943, 1C.
4. *Wichita Beacon,* September 17, 1941.

Chapter 2: Genesis

1. "How to Solve the Crime Problem," Kansas State Peace Officers' Association (1931), 1.
2. Ibid.
3. Ibid., 2.
4. *Topeka Daily Capital,* June 24, 1939.
5. Chapter 310, Laws of Kansas for 1939 (House Bill No. 427).
6. *The Peace Officer,* official publication of the Kansas State Peace Officers' Association, 1926, 71.
7. Ibid.
8. *Marion Record,* October 30, 1941.
9. K.S.A. 75–712, April 8, 1939.
10. *Topeka Daily Capital,* January 10, 1954.
11. *Kansas City Times,* June 27, 1939.
12. "This Bureau requests that all Sheriffs, Police Officers, County Attorneys and other law enforcement officers who have knowledge of the growth of Marihuana in their districts notify the landowner or tenant the weed must be destroyed at once, and to notify the County Commissioners of any such growth, and urgently request the Commissioners to order their highway maintenance crews to destroy the weed along the roadsides, and to assist in its destruction on farms where infestation is widespread." Lou P. Richter, letter to Kansas law enforcement, July 27, 1939.
13. *Kansas City Star,* November 10, 1939.
14. "KBI Wins Its Spurs," *Kansas City Times,* November 7, 1939.
15. *Peabody Herald,* December 7, 1939.
16. "Plan a Service to Fight Crime," *Manhattan Mercury,* January 10, 1940.
17. "The Kansas Bureau of Investigation to Celebrate First Birthday Monday," *Leavenworth Times,* June 30, 1940.

Chapter 3: Transition

1. *Making Do and Doing Without: Kansas in the Great Depression,* Division of Continuing Education and KANU, University of Kansas, 1983, 3,5,19.

2. David M. Kennedy, *Freedom from Fear* (New York: Oxford University Press, 1999), 194–195.

3. *Making Do and Doing Without: Kansas in the Great Depression,* 73.

4. *Denver Post,* April 21, 1966.

5. *Kansas Banker,* official publication of the Kansas Bankers' Association, October 1938, 7.

6. Ibid.

7. Ibid.

8. *Kansas Banker,* April 1939, 9.

9. Jeff Guinn, *Go Down Together, Bonnie and Clyde* (New York: Simon and Schuster, 2009), 302, 353, and 356.

10. Kansas State Historical Society, Law Enforcement Memorial Statistics, Topeka, Kansas.

11. Tom Brokaw, *The Greatest Generation* (New York: Random House, 1998), 342.

12. *Wichita Eagle,* August 13, 1995, 1A, 10A, 11A.

13. *Topeka Capital-Journal,* September 13, 2006.

14. *Wichita Eagle,* August 13, 1995, 10A, 11A.

15. *Lawrence Journal-World,* August 21, 2005, 7D.

16. David Mold, ed., *The Kansas Immigrants,* "Prisoners of War Only a Memory Now," Division of Continuing Education, University of Kansas, 1980, 87–88.

17. Director Richter's letter to Commissioner Miller, January 13, 1943, included a breakdown of all KBI investigations conducted from July 1, 1939, through November 30, 1942—190 in all.

18. *State of Kansas v. Fred L. Brady,* Kansas Supreme Court, May 8, 1943, 156 Kansas 831, 833.

19. *Kansas City Star,* February 5, 1940.

20. *The Kansas Stockman,* official publication of the Kansas Livestock Association, December 15, 1943.

21. "KBI Chief Leads Fight on Crime," *Topeka Daily Capital,* January 10, 1954, 9A-10A.

22. Ibid., 9A.

23. "Pat on the Back," *Hutchinson News-Herald,* December 15, 1953.

24. *Smith County Pioneer,* August 28, 1947, 1.

25. *Topeka Daily Capital,* August 28, 1951.

26. *Topeka State Journal,* December 31, 1945.

27. Copy of an undated, unidentified newspaper article by reporter Jim Petterson, from the author's personal archives.

Chapter 4: Clutter

1. Dennis Domer and Barbara Watkins, eds., *Embattled Lawrence: Conflict and Community*, Division of Continuing Education, University of Kansas, 2001, 55–58.

Chapter 5: Sanford

1. *St. John News*, October 29, 1942; reprinted in *Kansas Sheriff,* official publication of the Kansas Sheriffs' Association, vol. 27, no. 1, (spring 2004).
2. *Denver Post*, bonus supplement, August 23, 1966, 1.
3. Ibid.
4. Ibid., 3.
5. Ibid.
6. Ibid.
7. Ibid.
8. Ibid.
9. Ibid.
10. Ibid., 6.
11. "Kansas State Investigators Fill Big Gap," *Albuquerque Journal*, January 27, 1968.
12. *Wichita Beacon*, January 30, 1960.
13. "Success of Police Bureau in Kansas Based on Best Men," *Denver Post*, December 23, 1963.
14. *Albuquerque Journal*, January 27, 1968.

Chapter 6: KBI Directors, 1969–1994

1. Personal conversation between former director Logan Sanford and the author at KBI headquarters, July 18, 1994.

Chapter 7: Samaritan

1. Letter of Judge Harry G. Miller, January 30, 1969.
2. Investigative report of Special Agent W. F. Cowan to Judge Miller, March 4, 1969, 5.
3. Ibid., 6.
4. Report of Special Agent W. F. Cowan to Judge Miller, February 18, 1969.
5. Investigative report of Special Agent W. F. Cowan to Judge Miller, March 4, 1969, 6.
6. Ibid.
7. Ibid., 8.

Chapter 8: Pyle

1. Story related by Sheriff Bill Hogan to KBI special agent Duane Bell and the author in Pratt, Kansas, May 1971.
2. *State of Kansas v. Michael Duane Pyle*, Kansas Supreme Court, 216 Kansas 423, 432, 433, March 1, 1975.

Chapter 9: Nemechek

1. KBI teletype issued to all law enforcement agencies nationwide, February 24, 1975.
2. *Salina Journal,* January 22, 1976.
3. *Hays Daily News,* October 13, 1976.

Chapter 10: Stephanie

1. Interview of Donald Ray Gideon by FBI Special Agent R. Todd Rowley, Ormond Beach, Florida, July 17, 1993.
2. *State of Kansas v. Donald Ray Gideon*, Kansas Supreme Court, 257 Kansas 591, 602, April 28, 1995.
3. Ibid.
4. Ibid, 610.
5. John Douglas and Mark Olshaker, *Obsession* (New York: Scribner, 1998), 366.
6. Letter from John Walsh to Gene, Peggy, and Jeni Schmidt, May 19, 1999; *Topeka Capital-Journal,* May 25, 1999.
7. Welcome address of Director Larry Welch at KBI headquarters, May 24, 1999; *Topeka Capital-Journal,* May 25, 1999; *Kansas Peace Officer,* September 1999, pp. 18, 19; *Kansas Sheriff,* Winter 1999–2000, pp. 12, 13.
8. *Johnson County Sun,* July 31, 2003.

Chapter 11: Carrie

1. Comments of tennis coach John Seal, *Kansas City Star,* April 1, 1996, 1B, 3B.
2. From a search warrant affidavit filed with the clerk of the Crawford County District Court, Pittsburg, Kansas, April 5, 1996, by KBI special agent Bruce Adams.
3. *Pittsburg Morning Sun,* July 17, 1997.
4. *State of Kansas v. Gary W. Kleypas*, Kansas Supreme Court, 272 Kansas 894, December 28, 2001; *Wichita Eagle,* July 31, 1997.
5. *Pittsburg Morning Sun,* July 18, 1997; investigative report of KBI special agent Tom Williams, April 2, 1996.
6. *Wichita Eagle,* July 16, 1997; investigative report of KBI special agent Bruce Adams, April 3, 1996.
7. *Pittsburg Morning Sun,* July 20, 1997.
8. *Topeka Capital-Journal,* July 7, 1997; *Wichita Eagle,* July 13, 1997.

Chapter 12: Shannon

1. One of several telephone conversations between Brad and/or Jeanette Stauffer and Mark Culliane of the U.S. Embassy in San José, Costa Rica, May 13, 2001.

2. *Kansas City Star*, June 15, 2001, 3B.

3. *Topeka Capital-Journal*, June 15, 2001, 1A.

4. Ibid., 12A.

5. *Lawrence Journal-World*, June 16, 1B, 3B.

6. *Topeka Capital-Journal*, Wednesday, June 27, 2001.

7. "KBI to Work Student Death," *Topeka Capital-Journal*, June 23, 2003, 1C.

8. Testimony of Jeanette C. Stauffer before the Senate Judiciary Committee of the Kansas State Senate, February 2, 2004.

9. *Lawrence Journal-World*, November 25, 2003, 1A, 6A.

10. *Lawrence Journal-World*, Public Forum page, November 14, 2004.

Chapter 13: Liz

1. Investigative report of Special Agent Raymond Lundin, August 7, 2002.

2. *Kansas City Star*, September 28, 2004, 1.

3. Ibid.

4. Letter of Prairie Village Police Chief Chuck Grover to the state legislators of Johnson County, Kansas, January 4, 2005.

Chapter 14: 9/11

1. Authority: FBI field office, Kansas City, Missouri.

2. Federal Bureau of Investigation: www.fbi.gov/priorities.htm.

3. George Will, "Mueller Right Man for FBI," *Lawrence Journal-World*, February 6, 2003, 7B.

4. Letter of U.S. Attorney General John Ashcroft to Kansas governor Bill Graves and all U.S. governors, September 19, 2001.

5. "Questioning: The Government Would Be Remiss in Not Interrogating Foreign Students about Terrorist Activities," *Lawrence Journal-World*, 10B, November 25, 2001.

6. Robert Tanner, "Interviews Divide Police Opinion," *Topeka Capital-Journal*, December 4, 2001.

7. Ibid.

8. Mark Morris, "Heartland Sentries Take a Low-Profile Approach," *Kansas City Star*, September 11, 2004, 1A.

9. Testimony of Kevin L. Stafford, Special Agent in Charge, Kansas City Field Office, Federal Bureau of Investigation, before the House Committee on Government Reform Subcommittee on Government Efficiency, Financial Management and Intergovernmental Relations, August 20, 2002, Washington, D.C.

10. Remarks of Director Robert Mueller, June 27, 2005, during opening session of conference of National Sheriffs Association, Louisville, Kentucky; quoted in the

official publication of the National Sheriffs Association, *Sheriff* (September-October 2005): 22.

11. Ibid.

Chapter 15: Meth

1. *New York Times,* editorial page, December 8, 2002.

2. *Lawrence Journal-World,* October 10, 1997, 1B.

3. "Clandestine Drug Labs," *FBI Law Enforcement Bulletin,* April 2000, 1.

4. *Lawrence Journal-World,* May 15, 2001, 1B; *Wichita Eagle,* May 15, 2001, 11A; *Topeka Capital-Journal,* May 15, 2001, 3C.

5. "Threat to Rural Communities from the Production, Trafficking, and Use of Methamphetamine," Report of the Subcommittee on Crime, House Judiciary Committee, August 8, 2000, Salina, Kansas, 1, 2.

6. Ibid., 2–4, 7.

Chapter 16: Matt

1. Interview of Tammy Samuels, Eureka, Kansas, January 25, 2005, by KBI Special Agent Robert K. Jacobs regarding letter from Brenda Freisner, January 23, 2005, given to Samuels by Lillian Cheever January 24, 2005.

2. *Wichita Eagle,* February 1, 2005, 1A.

3. *Lawrence Journal-World,* January 26, 2005, 1B, 3B.

4. *Wichita Eagle,* October 27, 2007, 1A, 5A.

Chapter 17: BTK

1. Thousands of tips were received through the years, but none led to the identification of BTK to earn the reward.

2. Roy Wenzl, Tim Potter, L. Kelly, and Hurst Laviana, *Bind, Torture, Kill: The Inside Story of the Serial Killer Next Door* (New York: HarperCollins, 2007), 27–29.

3. Ibid., 60–66.

4. "Another Poem by BTK Is Released," *Wichita Eagle,* August 27, 2004; "Wichita Police Identify 1979 Poem as BTK's Work," *Lawrence Journal-World,* August 27, 2004, 5B.

5. Ibid.

6. Hurst Laviana, "BTK Case Unsolved, 30 Years Later," *Wichita Eagle,* January 17, 2004, 1A, 4A.

7. "BTK Resurfaces after 25 Years," *Wichita Eagle,* March 25, 2004, 1A, 6A.

8. From page 3 of the seven-page letter, dated December 20, 2004, received by all 165 Kansas state legislators, as well as the governor, attorney general, Kansas newspapers, Kansas law enforcement administrators, members of the Kansas Supreme Court, and the Kansas Congressional Delegation.

9. The thirteen-page memorandum of understanding provided for everything from the number of personnel and vehicles to be furnished by the Wichita Police Department, FBI, and KBI, to investigative reports, informants, prosecution, media releases, seizures, and forfeitures.

10. "2 More Letters Are from BTK, FBI Says," *Wichita Eagle*, June 25, 2004, 1A, 3A.

11. Ibid.

12. "Search for BTK Touches Others," *Wichita Eagle*, August 15, 2004.

13. "DNA Dragnets Raise Troubling Issues" (editorial), *Wichita Eagle*, September 15, 2004.

14. "Search for BTK Touches Others," *Wichita Eagle*, August 15, 2004.

15. Final report of the BTK Task Force, 2005, 11.

16. "FBI Confirms Wichita Letters Are from BTK," *Lawrence Journal-World*, June 25, 2004.

17. "New Letter Might Be from BTK, Police Say," *Wichita Eagle*, October 27, 2004; final report of the BTK Task Force, 13.

18. "Poem, Prof Linked in BTK Killings," *Lawrence Journal-World*, August 21, 2004, 1A, 9A.

19. "BTK Likely Used UPS Drop," *Wichita Eagle*, October 28, 2004.

20. The first of the two media releases, issued December 2, 2004, was entitled "Police Appreciate Public's Help" and included the following statement: "The local media and the public have both played an important role in the [BTK] investigation." The second, issued December 7, 2004, was entitled "BTK May Change Regular Routine" and included this statement: "There may be observable changes in BTK's behavior."

21. "Park Parcel May Be from BTK," *Wichita Eagle*, December 15, 2004.

22. Ibid.

23. "Missing Jewelry May Be BTK Clue," *Wichita Eagle*, January 6, 2005, 1B, 3B.

24. Final report of the BTK Task Force, 19.

25. "Did the Police Use Ads to Talk to BTK?," *Wichita Eagle*, July 9, 2005; Norman D. Williams, Chief of Police, and Kenneth Landwehr, Lieutenant, Wichita Police Department, "Bind, Torture, Kill: The BTK Investigation," *The Police Chief*, International Association of Chiefs of Police, December 2006, 19.

26. "A New Message from BTK?," *Wichita Eagle*, January 26, 2005; "Wichita Police Find Missing Communication Linked to BTK," *Lawrence Journal-World*, January 28, 2005, 5B; "Police Confirm Finding 2nd Item," *Wichita Eagle*, January 28, 2005.

27. "Police Confirm Finding 2nd Item," *Wichita Eagle*, January 28, 2005.

28. Ibid.

29. The January 27, 2005, public media release was entitled "Police Submit Package Contents to FBI," and the February 3, 2005, release was entitled "Police Submit Another Letter to FBI." Both contained references to BTK.

30. "New Postcard May Be from BTK," *Wichita Eagle*, February 4, 2005.

31. "Station Gets Potential BTK Package," *Wichita Eagle*, February 17, 2005.

32. This final media release, the longest issued by Landwehr, was entitled, "FBI Confirms BTK Letters," and included statements such as: "I still contend that this is our most challenging case, but I am very pleased with the ongoing dialogue through these letters . . . and that BTK would be very interesting to talk with."

33. Note from the author's personal archives.

34. Ibid.

35. "Liked by Many, Loathed by Some," *Wichita Eagle*, February 27, 2005, 1A, 6A; *Lawrence Journal-World*, March 1, 2005, 1A, 4A; *Wichita Eagle*, March 16, 2005; *Lawrence Journal-World*, March 17, 2005, 5B; *Wichita Eagle*, April 8, 2005, 1A, 7A.

36. Wenzl et al., *Bind, Torture, Kill*, 266.

37. *Wichita Eagle*, June 28, 2005, 1A, 4A.

38. *Wichita Eagle*, February 27, 2005, 10A.

39. Ibid., 1A.

40. *Wichita Eagle*, August 20, 2005, 8A; *Lawrence Journal-World*, August 20, 2005, 1A, 6A; *Topeka Capital-Journal*, August 20, 2005, 1A.

Chapter 18: Expansion

1. "The Cold Case Concept," *FBI Law Enforcement Bulletin*, August 1997, 1–3.

2. The story "KBI Cold Case Squad Created" invited Kansas law enforcement to submit suggestions and observations to the KBI about operation of the new squad; *Kansas Sheriff*, summer 1998, 39.

3. Two years later District Attorney Tomasic was also a strong, unconditional supporter of the fourth KBI forensic laboratory when it opened in Wyandotte County.

4. This is another example of the media coming to the assistance of law enforcement. More often than not, media are allies of law enforcement, if properly approached. In this case, materials found in the archives of local newspapers and television stations were of great assistance to the prosecution.

Chapter 19: Forensics

1. Reprinted in *Kansas Peace Officer*, official publication of the Kansas Peace Officers' Association, December 2002, 28 and 29, with permission of the *Lawrence Journal-World*.

2. Similar stories appeared in the *Lawrence Journal-World*, "Jurors in Carr Trial Visit Crime Scenes," October 24, 2002; *Topeka Capital-Journal*, "DNA Links Carrs to Victims," October 25, 2002.

3. "Verdict in Rapes: Guilty," *Wichita Eagle*, May 26, 2000, 1A and 10A.

4. Memorandum of Dr. Keith Coonrod, March 20, 1998, following his preliminary inspection of the KBI Laboratory—on display KBIHQ.

5. Forensic accreditation is granted by the Laboratory Accreditation Board (LAB) of the American Society of Crime Laboratory Directors (ASCLD). Reaccreditation was achieved five years later in all four KBI forensic laboratories.

6. Berry interviewed grateful law enforcement administrators including Chief of Police Lee Bynum of Independence, who asserted that it would be a "tremendous benefit" in fighting the growing threat of methamphetamine to have a KBI forensic laboratory close, and Crawford County sheriff Sandy Horton, who stated, "Now we're going to be able to kick in a door and have a lab two blocks away to test the stuff."

7. Neighborhood News section, *Kansas City Star,* August 29, 2001, 1, 22.

8. *Rawlins County Square Deal,* September 9, 2004, 1, 12.

9. "Analysis of Red Phosphorus Using a Pyrolysis Gas Chromatograph-Mass Spectrometer," *Journal of Analytical and Applied Pyrolysis* 71, no. 1 (March 2004): 47–50.

Chapter 20: Reflections

1. "The state of Kansas is ranked first in the United States in Law Enforcement and Court technology in a recent survey conducted by the Center for Digital Government and Progress and Freedom Foundation. The annual survey, conducted among all 50 states, determines which states are using technology most effectively in the area of criminal justice. The 2002 survey results ranked Kansas tied for first place with Colorado and Wisconsin," Gordon Lansford, KCJIS Project Manager, Kansas Criminal Justice Coordinating Council, August 13, 2002.

2. Statewide media release, March 29, 2004, by Kyle Smith, director of public and governmental affairs, KBI.

3. T. H. Watkins, *The Hungry Years* (New York: Holt and Co., 1999), 433–435.

4. Hampton Sides, *Hellhound on His Trail* (New York: Doubleday, 2010), 319–321.

5. "Quick Facts," Kansas Law Enforcement Training Center, Hutchinson, Kansas, January 23, 2007.

6. Chapter 310, *Laws of Kansas for 1939* (House Bill 427).

7. *Lawrence Journal-World,* January 13, 2007, 1B.

Index